A HEALTH economics PRIMER

The Addison-Wesley Series in Economics

A HEALTH economics PRIMER

Shirley Johnson-Lans

Vassar College

PEARSON

Addison Wesley

Boston San Francisco New York
London Toronto Sydney Tokyo Singapore Madrid
Mexico City Munich Paris Cape Town Hong Kong Montreal

Editor-in-Chief: Denise Clinton
Acquisitions Editor: Roxanne Hoch
Editorial Assistants: Catherine Bernstock and Julia Boyles
Managing Editor: Jim Rigney
Sr. Production Supervisor: Nancy Fenton
Executive Marketing Manager: Stephen Frail
Sr. Design Manager: Gina Hagen Kolenda
Cover and Text Designer: Leslie Haimes
Cover painting by Randy Beckelheimer, represented by Triangle Gallery, San Francisco
Media Producer: Melissa Honig
Sr. Manufacturing Buyer: Hugh Crawford
Project Coordination, Electronic Paging, Art Studio: Nesbitt Graphics, Inc.

Grateful acknowledgment is made to the American Economic Association, Elsevier Press, the Organization for Economic Cooperation and Development, Southern Economic Association, and the International Bank for Reconstruction and Development/The World Bank for permission to reproduce material in this text. Specific source citations are noted on individual tables, charts, and figures.

Library of Congress Cataloging-in-Publication Data

Johnson-Lans, Shirley.
 A health economics primer / Shirley Johnson-Lans.
     p. cm.
 Includes bibliographical references and index.
 ISBN 0-321-13669-1
 1. Medical economics.
 [DNLM: 1. Economics, Medical. W 74.1 J67h 2005] I. Title.

RA410.J64 2005
338.4'33621—dc22
                              2004030285

1 2 3 4 5 6 7 8 9 10—DOH—09 08 07 06 05

To Erin Kathryn and Thomas Langdon

May you have long and healthy lives
and good and affordable health care

Contents

Preface

The economics of health care, like health care itself, is a dynamic and rapidly changing field. Health-care policies and programs shift as quickly as the world around us, coinciding with changes in population characteristics, government leaders, corporate environments, and global and social issues. In the United States, the 2004 presidential candidates put a spotlight on the national debates about the rising cost of prescription drugs; the impending retirement of the "baby boomers" and the impact on health programs for the elderly; and the importation of prescription drugs into the United States. At the global level, the HIV/AIDS pandemic and the rise of drug-resistant forms of other communicable diseases have made health care an issue that knows no national boundaries. Paralleling a rise in popular interest, health economics has become a pivotal area of research and policy.

I wrote *A Health Economics Primer* because when I teach health economics to undergraduate students, I like to incorporate the latest news and research findings. Students engage enthusiastically when they can apply the course content to the news stories that arise during the semester. In addition, professors frequently seek a textbook that provides a basic framework but leaves room to assign other headings. This shorter, succinct primer achieves this balance.

The blueprint for this book evolved over years of teaching the course. It allows faculty to adapt their syllabi to incorporate recent empirical and policy work. Chapters include both basic microeconomic analysis and a history of how particular institutions have evolved, whether the topic is health insurance, hospitals, physician office practices, the pharmaceutical industry, or health-care systems. The book takes a wide-angle view, looking at health care not only in the United States and other developed countries like Germany and Canada, but also in developing countries such as India. It focuses on the incentives of major players in health-care systems.

The text exposes students to a carefully prescribed dose of diagrams and theoretical models. Economic analysis is presented in the context of the institutions and market structures that characterize twenty-first century health care so as to foster an understanding of the evolution in the delivery of health care and the degree to which there is government involvement, even in the market-oriented health-care system of the United States.

Audience for *A Health Economics Primer*

With so much activity in this field, it is no wonder that students with diverse backgrounds and interests take a health economics course. This book is written for courses taught in a variety of departments—economics, public health, public policy, and business—and is appropriate for the mix of students who take those courses. It assumes only an understanding of introductory microeconomics, for which I provide a brief refresher in an appendix.

Within the economics department the health economics course is often an intermediate-level elective, and students who take the course represent a wider range of disciplines than those who elect most other economics courses. A high proportion of my own class is composed of science majors who are premedical students. Another subset consists of non-economics majors whose primary interest is the complex policy problems that health care involves. Many are contemplating graduate work in public health or policy programs. And, of course, there are the economics students who are rounding out their major by taking the course. Studying health economics provides a wonderful way for economics majors to integrate all the applied micro fields within the discipline, including labor economics, industrial organization, public finance, international trade, and the economics of risk and uncertainty.

For more advanced courses in health economics, professors often include outside readings on health economics research. In addition to the core content, this text includes abundant end-of-chapter references to the relevant scholarly literature. Chapters provide suggested readings for incorporating journal articles, recent NBER working papers, and relevant chapters in the comprehensive "bible" of the discipline, the two-volume *Handbook of Health Economics* (Elsevier). When used this way, the text is truly a primer for graduate students in economics and health-policy research. It is succinct and, at the same time, includes summaries of empirical research and current policy debates.

Content and Organization of the Text

The organization of the book proceeds as does my one-semester health economics course. After an introduction to the field in Chapter One, Part One continues with Chapter Two, which outlines a model of the demand for health, considered as a form of investment in human capital. This model provides a bridge between the demand for health and the demand for health care. Part Two examines health insurance, both public and private, in the United States. Chapter Three introduces the student to the insurance market and to decision making when there is risk and asymmetric information. This important theme is carried forward throughout the book. Chapter Four considers the evolution in the health insurance market to its present state, in which managed care plays an important role. Chapter Five documents the evolution of the main programs of social insurance in the United States, Medicare and Medicaid.

Part Three covers the markets for the providers of health care: physicians, nurses, and hospitals. Chapter Six considers physicians and nurses as inputs into the production of health care. The important role of the physician as the patient's agent is the subject of Chapter Seven. Chapter Eight analyzes the behavior of the complex institution, the modern hospital. Part Four introduces cost-benefit and cost-effectiveness analysis, discusses the role of technological change in health care, and presents the economics of the bio-pharmaceutical industry, viewed in a global context. The importance of innovation and the role of government regulation make the pharmaceutical industry an especially important one to study. Chapter Ten, which considers the importance of innovation, includes a brief discussion of the problems associated with constructing price indices for medical goods and services, given the rapid technological change in medical care.

Part Five turns to the important and difficult task of evaluating health-care systems. Chapter Twelve builds on the previous chapters in its examination of the health-care systems of Canada, Germany, and the United Kingdom, looking at the way in which these countries deal with the problem of providing high-tech medicine within systems of social insurance that necessarily impose some form of global budget. It also presents a case study of health care in a developing nation, India. Chapter Thirteen considers global public health problems as they affect both the high- and low-income nations and looks at the role of public health in controlling communicable diseases. Chapter Fourteen outlines the trade-offs involved in the main proposals for reform of the U.S. health-care system. The extent to which there is a trade-off between equity and efficiency is considered as is the argument that "need" not "demand" is the criterion that should be used in evaluating the success of a health-care delivery system. This final chapter returns to the fundamental question, "How do we value health and health care?"

Alternative Syllabi

A Health Economics Primer covers the critical concepts in a flexible format. Every chapter is self-contained and can be understood even if select chapters are skipped or the instructor rearranges the order in which chapters are assigned. Below I outline a few different ways to use the book in a variety of courses. For more detailed syllabi suggestions and Web links related to the discipline, visit the book's companion Web site at www.aw-bc.com/johnson-lans.

Economics and health policy focus. When teaching the course to economics students, I find that it is better to cover the chapters on insurance fairly early because it is hard to understand the behavior of health-care providers, and the evolution of the markets in which they function, without understanding the central role played by insurance. Depending on the desired emphasis, the instructor may wish to move the material on technological change and the pharmaceutical industry (Chapters Ten and Eleven) forward in the syllabus. Likewise, the comparative systems material in Chapter Twelve can be presented early, right after the introductory material in Chapter One, if the instructor teaches a more institutional course and wants to set the stage by considering alternatives to the U.S. system.

Business focus. An instructor teaching the health economics course to business students may wish to focus on markets for insurance, physicians and nurses, hospitals, and pharmaceuticals in the United States, and omit the comparative systems material (Chapter Twelve).

Medical focus. For a health economics course taught to medical students, the instructor may wish to introduce the material on cost-benefit and cost-effectiveness analysis (Chapter Nine) right after the introductory chapter.

Instructors teaching nursing majors or registered nurses may consider focusing on the chapters discussing markets for physicians and nurses, hospitals, and health policy reform.

Acknowledgments

I am very grateful to all the reviewers and others who helped in the shaping of this book. I especially want to thank Sherry Glied for her detailed and inciteful comments and David Gohmann, David Grabowski, Stephen Mennemeyer and Karen Travis for their excellent suggestions at several stages in the process. In addition, I am grateful for the comments of reviewers: William Custer, Robert Jantzen, Daver C. Kahvecioglu, Eugene Kroch, Catherine Lynde, Robert McComb, Kerry Redican, David Ridley, Edward Schumacher, Stuart Shapiro, and Amy Wolaver. Thank you to colleagues in the Vassar economics department: Geoff Jehle, William Lunt, Alan Marco, and Jon Rork for providing valuable critiques of sections of the book and for their friendship and support during the gestation period. Former student David Nash, MBA, MD, graciously took the time to read the manuscript and provide insightful comments from a medical perspective. Student research assistants Nii Tackie and Tsvetan Tsvetanov and Ford Summer Research Fellow Shweta Kamdar provided invaluable assistance and were a delight to work with. My thanks extend to all the help from my excellent editors at Addison Wesley: Victoria Warneck, Roxanne Hoch, and Catherine Bernstock. Of course, while the quality of this book has been enhanced by the input of all those mentioned, any remaining mistakes are the responsibility of the author.

—Shirley Johnson-Lans

PART ONE

Introduction

The Subject Matter of Health Economics

It has been said that "an economist is someone who knows the price of every-thing and the value of nothing" (Oscar Wilde) and "that doctors are people who know the price of nothing and think they know the value of everything."[1] This quip by a health economist who is also an M.D. points to the fundamental questions with which health economics wrestles. How do individuals and soci-eties establish the value of health? How do they make decisions about allocating resources to the production of health? And, on what basis should access to health care be made available?

1   Why Study Health Economics?

The discipline of economics is concerned with value, more specifically, with maximizing well-being in a world where choices must be made about the allocation of scarce resources. Prices are important, both as indicators of value or willingness to pay (on the demand side), and of the cost of production (on the supply side.) Physicians have been taught to select the best treatments for their patients without thinking about price, and this gives them a somewhat differ-ent perspective, but in reality, they also do consider the cost-effectiveness of dif-ferent treatments and use cost-benefit analysis in deciding such issues as whether to urge a patient to undergo a grueling regimen of chemotherapy. Moreover, in the matter of their own training and medical practice, physicians make countless other economic decisions. Among them are: whether to undertake additional years of training in order to become a board certified specialist; whether to work as a salaried employee, a member of a large group practice, or a solo practitioner; how many nurses and technicians to employ; how many hours to work; whether to join an insurance network; and whether to treat Medicaid patients.

If we view economics broadly and understand that costs are not simply monetary in nature, triage decisions made in hospital emergency rooms are economic decisions every bit as much as the decisions one makes on how to use a monthly paycheck.

It may seem that sick people and their families do not consider costs in the case of medically necessary treatments. Such may be true for certain emergency services, but studies have revealed that price does make a difference in how much medical care is utilized. Chapters Two and Three will show this to be true in the United States, and a review of literature in Chapter Thirteen illustrates that the demand for medical care is sensitive to price as well in a variety of other countries.

Does the benefit justify the cost? A hospital administrator in deciding whether to recommend to his board of directors that it create a burn center or a neonatal center for high-risk patients must contemplate this question. Are there other sources for these important but not heavily used services within a reasonable distance so that the community is not at risk? Will the addition of these facilities result in greater prestige for the hospital and increase its patient base enough to warrant adding services that are likely, on balance, to lose money over time?

The director of a research institute who must allocate a fixed research budget among several competing projects faces an economic decision. Within the National Cancer Institute there have been tugs of war between those wanting more breast cancer research and those preferring to expand research on prostate cancer. An analysis of cost-effectiveness in such situations moves the debate from political lobbying to reasonable decision making.

When public funds provide medical care, how should priorities be set about who receives treatment and how much? This is yet another real-world problem. The state of Oregon chose to cover all people below a certain income level, but to prioritize which treatments would be covered out of its fixed annual Medicaid budget. The recent Medicare prescription drug bill provides coverage only up to a certain level of expenditure, after which there is no coverage until a much higher threshold of spending on prescription drugs is reached. This is what is known as the "donut" in prescription drug coverage. Medicare hospital benefits provide very good "first dollar coverage," but no catastrophic coverage for those who require more than 210 days of hospitalization. Is there an economic justification for these patterns of coverage?

Public health officials in South Africa have had to decide whether to provide the newer anti-retroviral HIV drugs to some high-risk patients, such as pregnant women, or use the same money to provide more basic health care to a wider segment of the population.

In the early twenty-first century the rising price of health care is a serious concern. The cost of health care continues to increase much more rapidly than the costs of most other goods and services, if we measure the cost increase by the Consumer Price Index (CPI). Nonetheless, a fairly compelling case can be made that the costs of many medical treatments, such as treatments for heart attack, are in fact declining if the cost of treatment per extra year of life or extra "quality adjusted year of life" gained is what we measure. This is even more likely to be true if the savings in patients' recovery time resulting from less invasive surgery are included in our computations. This example demonstrates that one good reason to study health economics is to learn to think about familiar problems in new ways.

Health economists have joined with members of the medical and public health communities in conducting studies that have had important effects on policy. The reform of the Medicare system for reimbursing hospitals and the introduction of the Resource Based Relative Value Scale (RBRVS) system for reimbursing physicians resulted from such collaborations. The decision of Medicare and Medicaid to cover the Pap smear diagnostic test for cervical cancer resulted from a study of its cost-effectiveness, jointly conducted by an economist-physician team. Economic analysis led to the realization that the state certificate of need (CON) restrictions on proposed hospital expansion were often founded on incorrect notions about the natural monopoly characteristics of hospitals.

2   The Basic Economic Questions Which Every Society Faces

Given limited resources, all societies and individuals must face making trade-offs. At any point in time, a society can only spend more resources on health (or health care) if fewer resources are devoted to producing other goods. One way to visualize this condition of the world is to construct what is called a **production possibility frontier.**

The Production Possibility Frontier

Imagine a simplified economy in which only two goods are produced: health and housing. In the short run the endowment of resources is fixed. When the society's resources are fully utilized, it can only produce more health if it sacrifices some housing. The **opportunity cost** of producing more health is the amount of housing that must be sacrificed in order to do so. Opportunity cost is defined as *the cost of the foregone opportunity.* Figure 1.1 depicts the possible combinations of health and housing that a society with a certain endowment of resources can produce.

When all resources are fully employed, the society can produce any of the combinations of housing and health care that lie within or on the production possibility frontier, *PP*, in Figure 1.1. Points *B* and *C* lie on *PP*; they are both **Pareto optimal** in that moving from one to the other involves a trade-off. Pareto optimality has been achieved when we cannot produce more of one good without sacrificing something else. Thus, every point on *PP* is Pareto optimal. Point *A* lies inside *PP* and is there-

Figure 1.1

Production Possibility
Frontier

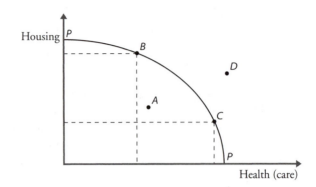

fore not optimal in that the society can, through better use of its resources, have both more health care and more housing. Point *D* lies outside the frontier and is unattainable with the society's current resource endowment and technology. Growth in the economy or opening up the economy to international trade may make *D* attainable.

The Positive Versus the Normative Approach to Economics

Another question facing every society is how the goods and services it produces should be distributed among its members. This is a normative question, and models of economy efficiency cannot answer normative questions.

The approach taken in this text is generally called **positive economics** (as contrasted with *normative economics*). Positive economics focuses on discovering what outcomes will result from particular paths of action or choices. Normative questions address what *ought to be* and thus are dependent on value judgments. An example of a statement that is phrased in normative terms is, "People should exercise more!" An alternative statement, "Evidence suggests that exercise lowers the risk of cardiovascular disease," expresses a relationship between a course of action and a consequence that can be investigated.

A normative question of perennial concern in the United States is whether health insurance coverage should be provided to all, regardless of whether they can afford to pay for it. Most people in American society agree that the lack of access to affordable health care on the part of some citizens and residents is a social problem, but no general consensus exists on how to accomplish this.* Many economists, like other members of our society, have strong opinions about the matter, and some have even entered the field of economics because of an interest in these kinds of normative questions. But when engaging in research, one needs

---

*Some do not even think it an important social problem. See for instance, Epstein, R. A., *Mortal Peril: Our Inalienable Right to Healthcare?* (Reading, MA: Addison Wesley, 1997.)

to ask the following sort of question: *If* universal health insurance coverage is the goal, what alternative ways of providing it are possible, and what are the relative costs and benefits of those alternatives to society and individual groups?

3   Research in Economics

In the social sciences, controlled laboratory conditions can rarely be created. Instead, statistical techniques are used to simulate a laboratory environment in which particular factors or "variables" can be isolated. Statistical techniques enable us to treat factors that, in fact, vary over the study as if they remained constant. Suppose we want to investigate how the demand for vaccinations will change if inoculations become cheaper. To isolate the effect of price, incomes of the subjects studied must be held constant even though both price and income and a variety of other relevant factors tend to vary over time. We "remove" the other effects through multivariate techniques such as correlation and regression analysis.

Economists have also occasionally conducted experiments in which a large number of subjects are randomly assigned to different groups. This kind of experiment is fairly rare in the social sciences because it is so expensive. An excellent example of a randomized study is the RAND Health Insurance Experiment. The data collected provided the basis for a large number of highly regarded research studies.

The RAND Health Insurance Experiment

The RAND Health Insurance Experiment (HIE) provides the gold standard for estimates of the effect of different levels of insurance coverage on the utilization of medical care and the resulting effect of increased medical care on health outcomes. The study group was a sample of approximately 2000 non elderly families (approximately 6000 individuals) from six regions of the United States who were randomly assigned to several different insurance plans that offered different levels of benefits. The study followed participants for either three years or five years. An additional group was assigned to a Health Maintenance Organization (HMO) that provided comprehensive care in exchange for a fixed capitation fee per year.

The importance of randomly assigning people to insurance plans is that it removes the selection bias which is always a problem when people self-select themselves into the plans. The findings based on this study are still widely used, although the data were collected from 1974 to 1982, when the delivery of health care and the insurance market were quite different from today. Several sources provide excellent detailed descriptions of the exemplary study design of the RAND HIE and the findings based on it.[2]

In some cases, the environment provides so-called natural experiments. For example, Tennessee's decision to raise its rate of Medicaid remuneration to physicians when a neighboring state, Maryland, did not do so provided researchers with an opportunity to examine the effect of fees on physicians' willingness to treat Medicaid patients. Chapter Five will examine the research emanating from this natural experiment.[3]

4   What Is Special About Health-Care Economics?

Several characteristics of health-care markets are particularly important.

1. *Uncertainty* and *imperfect information* are more important in the health-care sector than in almost any other part of the economy. Individuals face uncertainty about their health, what kind of medical care to seek when ill, and the cost of that medical care. This makes the ability to transfer risk to a third party, that is, an insurance company, very important. There is also vast asymmetry (inequality) in knowledge between physicians and patients. This lack of knowledge on the part of patients leads to institutional arrangements such as training and licensing requirements for physicians.[4] Physicians as well face uncertainty about diagnoses and what treatments to prescribe. They also face the risk of lawsuits from patients who have experienced poor outcomes from treatment. They can insure themselves against this kind of risk by buying malpractice insurance. The role of insurance is uniquely important in understanding health-care markets.

2. *Externalities* are very important in the health-care sector. An **externality** is a spill-over effect; it can be either positive or negative. An obvious example of a negative externality is the spread of a contagious disease by a sick person who rides a public bus. Another negative externality would be that imposed by someone who drives while intoxicated and injures others. A positive externality is that provided to a neighborhood when a nearby community drains a mosquito-infested swamp.

3. The health-care sector is subject to much more government intervention than most other sectors of the economy. Health care continues to be highly regulated at a time when deregulation has occurred in banking, air travel, telephone services, and other public utilities. Health care and health insurance are also highly subsidized. Government intervention is, in part, a response to the degree of uncertainty and imperfect information, and the amount of externality that characterize the health-care sector. It is also a response to the non-competitive market structure of the industries providing health care. Firms producing health care are sometimes monopolies, but more often large oligopolies or monopolistically competitive firms. One has only to think of hospitals, managed-care insurers, pharmaceutical companies, or even specialist group physician practices in all but the largest metropolitan areas.

5   Medical Care Versus Health Care

Until the mid-twentieth century, major increases in longevity were more strongly associated with improvements in nutrition and sanitation than with advances in medical care, even in the United States.* This is still true in developing nations, although medical intervention is extremely important in controlling diseases such as malaria, tuberculosis, and HIV/AIDS.

The role of public health agencies in health education and preventing the spread of infectious diseases is extremely important throughout the world and often involves very little high-tech medical intervention. From its inception, public health policy in the United States addressed much more than just medical care for the sick. Today, it continues to include such actions as the inspection of restaurant kitchens and community water supplies and the control of disease-carrying pests, as well as the collection of health statistics and the monitoring of the incidence of disease (epidemiology).

For individuals, health care also includes much more than medical care. Diet, exercise, social support systems, and the quality of the environment are important.

This text, like others in the field of health economics, centers on the medical-care component of health care. Medical care is unique in that it generally provides no utility or satisfaction in and of itself, unlike nutritious food and other goods that promote health. In fact, it may involve considerable pain and discomfort. A large part of medical care is conditional on illness. The need for it is therefore unpredictable. Moreover, the level of cost associated with some treatments can be catastrophic.

Medical care includes physician visits, care in hospitals and clinics, laboratory tests, the use of pharmaceuticals, and long-term nursing care at home or in an institution. It includes the treatment of both mental and physical illness, and more broadly construed, it includes alternative non-Western forms of healing as well.

The Effect of Medical Care on Health

A focus on medical care is justifiable, at least when studying health and health care in a high-income, technically advanced country at the start of the twenty-first century. But even in this context, the question of the impact of medical care on health remains. Let us briefly review the results of some studies that have attempted to answer the question of the efficacy of medical care in improving health.

---

*A recent study has revisited this subject and found that the process of chlorination and filtration required to provide clean water to American cities accounted for half the reduction in total mortality, three-quarters of the reduction in infant mortality, and two-thirds of the reduction in child mortality when it was introduced in the United States. See Cutler, David M. and Grant Miller, *The Role of Public Health Improvements in Health Advances in the 20th Century U.S.*, NBER Working Paper No. 10511 (Cambridge, MA: National Bureau of Economic Research, May 2004).

Studies conducted in the 1960s found at best only modest improvements in health that could be directly attributed to increases in medical care. For instance, one study found that the age-adjusted death rate decreased about 1 percent for every 10 percent increase in medical services in the United States.[5] Several studies of the same era found no appreciable decline in the age-adjusted death rate from 1955 to 1965 despite an increase in medical services per capita and an improvement in medical technology over that decade.[6] Subsequent studies in the 1980s yielded slightly more positive results, particularly when the effect on the death rate of increases in medical care for the elderly resulting from Medicare was examined. One found that a 10 percent increase in medical care was associated with a 2 to 10 percent reduction in the age-adjusted death rate of Medicare recipients.[7]

The question of whether extending medical care improves the health of communities has continued to be studied by a number of researchers. Studies evaluating the effect of making medical care more available to the community by expanding social insurance programs or by reducing its price through the mechanism of more generous insurance benefits have shown very modest results.[8] These results are particularly hard to discount when the body of evidence includes findings based on the RAND HIE data. In the RAND study group, people who were assigned to insurance programs with more generous benefits and who utilized significantly more medical services (up to 40% more) had no better average health status, with the exception of those who had both low income and health problems at the time they entered the study. Moreover, even for this subgroup, health improvements were limited to a few health conditions: high blood pressure, correctable vision problems, and dental health.[9] Nor did greater use of medical services appear to lead to an overall improvement in child health.[10]

It is important to distinguish between the effect of providing additional medical care to those who already have health insurance and reasonably good medical care, and the effect of providing access to families who have previously had no health insurance. The majority of studies have examined the effects on health of extra medical care resulting from more generous insurance benefits. The results of these studies undoubtedly underestimate the effects of medical care on health.

Moreover, expanding the amount of medical care utilized increases both appropriate and inappropriate care.[11] Inappropriate care may have little or no marginal benefit; in some cases, it may also have negative effects on a patient's health. Since the Institute of Medicine study, *To Err Is Human*, the risk of negative effects of medical intervention has been widely recognized.[12] This risk increases with more extensive medical intervention.

All the studies summarized here examined average outcomes for large populations. Averages mask marginal changes to particular groups. When studies of patients treated for specific diseases are undertaken, the *marginal effects* of newer technologies, such as those developed for the treatment of heart attack or gallbladder disease, are often associated with significant improvements in longevity and also in the quality of life-years remaining.[13] The newer technologies are often not only more effective in treating the medical condition, but also more cost-effective, yielding more life-years or quality-adjusted life-years per dollar spent on medical care.[14]

We will continue to address the question of the efficacy of medical care throughout this book. It is a particularly important question in a country that spends such a high proportion of its national income on health care with, at best, only comparable (average) health outcomes to those in countries that spend less. Considerable evidence exists that at least with respect to certain types of medical care, our society is near the "flat of the curve," with additional medical care yielding minimal improvements in health.* It is, however, very important to distinguish the marginal effects of particular aspects of medical care from broad averages.

6   International Comparisons: Some Stylized Facts About Health Care

Although we will return to a comparative approach to health-care systems in Part Five, it is a good idea to have some international comparative health data in mind when embarking on an examination of health-care markets in the United States. Here are a few basic facts.

■ The United States leads the world in the proportion of GDP spent on health care.

The Organization for Economic Cooperation and Development (OECD), whose members include all the major industrialized nations in the world, compiles important statistics on a number of economic indicators. *OECD Health Data*, an annual series, is a critical source of information for health economists.[†]

The gross domestic product (GDP) is a widely used measure of national income. It is the value of all the goods and services produced in an economy during a year.

As the United States entered the twenty-first century, with its economy in a remarkably robust state, health-care spending temporarily stabilized at around 13 percent of the GDP. By 2004 this proportion was again increasing, health-care spending comprised approximately 14 percent of the U.S. GDP. Many other nations impose global budgets on the proportion of GDP that can be allocated to health-care expenditures. Even with this constraint, most nations have experienced an increase in the proportion of their resources devoted to health care over the past quarter-century (Table 1.1).

---

*Think of a graph in which improvements in health are measured along the vertical axis and the amount of medical care is measured along the horizontal axis. As we reach diminishing returns to additional expenditure on medical care, the curve becomes flatter.

†The OECD can be reached at http://www.oecd.org.

Table 1.1   OECD Member Nations' Expenditure on Health as Percentage of GDP

Country	1980	1990	1995	2000
Australia	7.0	7.8	8.2	8.9
Austria	7.6	7.1	8.6	8.0
Belgium	6.4	7.4	8.7	8.7
Canada	7.2	9.0	9.2	9.2
Czech Republic	—	5.0	7.3	7.1
Denmark	9.1	8.5	8.2	8.3
Finland	6.4	7.8	7.5	6.7
France	—	8.6	9.5	9.3
Germany	8.7	8.5	10.6	10.6
Greece	6.6	7.4	9.6	9.4
Hungary	—	7.1	7.5	6.7
Iceland	6.2	8.0	8.4	9.1
Ireland	8.4	6.1	6.8	6.4
Italy	—	8.0	7.4	8.2
Japan	6.4	5.9	6.8	7.6
Korea	6.4	4.8	4.7	5.9
Luxembourg	5.9	6.1	6.4	5.6
Mexico	—	4.5	5.7	5.6
Netherlands	7.5	8.0	8.4	8.6
New Zealand	5.9	6.9	7.2	8.0
Norway	6.9	7.7	7.9	7.7
Poland	—	5.3	6.0	6.2 (1999)
Portugal	5.6	6.2	8.3	9.0
Spain	5.4	6.7	7.6	7.5
Sweden	8.8	8.2	8.1	8.4
Switzerland	7.6	8.5	10.0	10.7
Turkey	3.3	3.6	3.4	
United Kingdom	5.6	6.0	7.0	7.3
United States	8.7	13.3	13.3	13.1

Source: *OECD Health Data 2003* (Paris: Organization for Economic Cooperation and Development, 2003). The Slovak Republic was omitted for lack of data.

■ There is a very high correlation between national per capita income and national per capita medical spending, yet there is virtually no correlation between changes in life expectancy and changes in the proportion of GDP spent on health, and little correlation between per capita income and life expectancy.[15]

Table 1.2   Life Expectancy at Birth of Females and Males in Selected OECD Countries, 1999

Country	Females	Males
Australia	81.8	76.2
Canada	81.7	76.3
France	82.5	75.0
Germany	80.7	74.7
Italy	82.3	75.6
Japan	84.0	77.1
Spain	82.1	75.1
Sweden	81.9	77.1
Switzerland	82.5	76.8
United Kingdom	79.8	75.0
United States	79.4	73.9

Source: *OECD Health Data 2003* (Paris: Organization for Economic Cooperation and Development, 2003).

A comparison of the United States and other industrialized nations reveals that summary measures of health status are not, on the whole, better in the United States than in other modern nations, despite the more extensive resources allocated to health care in the United States. Table 1.2 provides comparative life-expectancy data at birth for males and females in 11 industrialized nations. The most recent year for which these data are available for all 11 countries is 1999. In 1999, 22 of the OECD countries outranked the United States in life expectancy at birth for both males and females.

Table 1.3 shows the years of healthy life expectancy for males and females who have reached the age of 60 in select OECD countries with whom the United

Table 1.3   Years of Healthy Life Expectancy at Age 60, 2001

Country	Males	Females
Canada	15.3	17.9
France	16.1	19.1
Germany	15.0	17.7
Italy	15.5	18.2
Japan	17.1	20.7
Spain	15.2	18.2
Sweden	16.5	18.5
Switzerland	16.9	19.4
United Kingdom	15.0	16.9
United States	14.9	16.6

Source: *OECD Health Data 2003* (Paris: Organization for Economic Cooperation and Development, 2003).

States is often compared. This measure of the quality of life expectancy is important because the effect of medical intervention on the health and longevity of older people is likely to be particularly great.

Infant mortality rates are another important indicator of the health status of a population. The correlation between average per capita income in a country and infant mortality is generally higher than it is for life expectancy, except for the United States, which is an "outlier" if we display the results on a graph.[16] United States comparative rates of infant mortality are particularly discouraging. Compared with the other OECD countries, in 1960 the United States ranked eleventh highest in infant mortality rates among the 20 countries who were then members of the OECD. By 1995 the United States had the second highest rate of infant mortality among OECD countries, with only Greece exceeding the U.S. rate of 8.0 infant deaths per 1,000 live births. In a 13-country comparison made in 2000, the United States ranked highest (worst) in percentage of low birth-weight babies, neonatal mortality, and overall infant mortality.

The comparative statistics presented in these tables are averages and do not reflect the fact that greater variance exists in insurance coverage and health outcomes between racial and socioeconomic groups in the United States than in many other OECD countries.[17] (See Table 1.5.)

■ Countries vary in the proportion of public/private expenditure on health.

Table 1.4 shows that the United States is the only country in North America or Western Europe, other than Mexico, in which less than half the total expenditure on health care is publicly funded. It is important to recognize that omitting the

Table 1.4   Select OECD Member Nations' Public Expenditure as Percentage of Total Expenditure on Health, 2001

Country	Public Health Expenditure (%)
Canada	70.8
France	76.0
Germany	74.9
Italy	76.0
Mexico	45.9
Netherlands	63.3
Spain	71.4
Sweden	85.2
United Kingdom	82.2
United States	44.4

Source: *OECD Health Data 2003* (Paris: Organization for Economic Cooperation and Development, 2003).

cost to society of subsidizing private health insurance leads to a serious underestimation of the public contribution to health care in the United States.

Using the market to achieve social goals with respect to the provision of health care is consistent with the dominant political-economic philosophy in the United States. The marketplace provides most goods and services, with the government intervening only when private markets are deemed to have failed. However, the government has, since the nineteenth century, engaged in a great deal of regulation and subsidization of health care, even in an era when deregulation is the order of the day.

■ Compared with Canada, Germany, and the United Kingdom, the United States perennially ranks first in the stock of medical technologies, such as magnetic resonance imaging, radiation therapy, laparoscopic surgery, organ transplantation, and cardiac catheterization.[18]

These findings, coupled with the figures on health outcomes, raise serious questions about the efficiency of the production and distribution of health care in the United States. In particular, one must consider the *marginal benefits* of the extra resources devoted to health care in this country, compared with other OECD countries.

Here, a cautionary note is in order. Making cross-country comparisons about the effect of medical care on health is a risky business. Many other factors are involved: genetics; environmental factors such as industrial pollution, crime rates, and stressful work environments; diet and life style. The difficulty of cross-country comparison has been illuminated by Jack Triplett, who noted that a society's level of health need be no more highly correlated with the level of medical interventions it supports than its expenditure on car repairs is correlated with how long cars last.[19]

■ The United States is the only major industrialized nation that does not have a system of universal health-care insurance.

Universal health insurance in the United States was originally proposed as part of the Social Security legislation enacted in the 1930s. Since then, proposals for mandated universal health insurance have been considered by a number of presidential administrations, including those of Harry Truman, Lyndon Johnson, Jimmy Carter, Ronald Reagan, and most recently, Bill Clinton. With the exception of the programs for the elderly and the poor, Medicare and Medicaid, which were enacted in the mid-1960s, none have received sufficient public support to be enacted, including the latest attempt in the early 1990s under Clinton. Recently, the chief preoccupation of the administration and Congress in terms of health care has been the passage of legislation adding a prescription drug benefit to Medicare. The possibility of a universal government-sponsored health insurance program is, however, a perennial part of political debate in this country. Pressure for change is again building, as employers scale back the amount of health insurance coverage they are willing to provide to their workers. In the fall of 2003,

Table 1.5   Individuals Under 65 Years of Age with No Health Insurance in the United States, 2000

By Poverty Status	%
Below poverty level income	34.2
100–149% of poverty level income	36.5
150–199% of poverty level income	27.3
200% + of poverty level income	8.7
By Race/Ethnicity	**%**
Black or African American (non-Hispanic)	20.0
American Indian or Alaskan	38.2
Hispanic or Latino	35.4
White (non-Hispanic or Latino)	15.2
By Age Group	**%**
Under 6	11.2
6–17	12.8
18–24	29.7
25–34	22.7
35–44	12.7
45–54	12.0
55–64	12.5

Source: *Health Interview Survey, 2000.* (Washington, DC: Centers for Disease Control and Prevention, National Center for Health Statistics, August 2002) p. 312, Table 129.

unionized workers in the large retail grocery chains of Southern California went on strike over the issue of employer contributions to employee health insurance coverage.

As of September 2004, nearly 45 million citizens and legal residents of the United States, about 16 percent of the population, did not have health insurance.[20] This represents an increase of about four million uninsured from 2001 to 2004. Many of these people are employed, but either are not offered health insurance at their jobs or find it too expensive to purchase.

The proportion of uninsured in the United States varies greatly by state, since a number of states have created their own initiatives to provide more extensive health insurance coverage.[21] It also varies widely by age, race or ethnicity, and poverty status. Table 1.5 provides some summary information.

Summary

The aim of this chapter has been to set the stage for the study of health-care economics. We began with a few examples of questions that health economics can illuminate and some examples of policy-oriented studies that have made a difference. The concepts of opportunity cost and Pareto optimality were introduced. We then identified some special features of the health-care sector that make health economics a particularly challenging subject. Of particular importance is the role of uncertainty and imperfect information. Since health economics centers on medical care, we considered the justification for this focus. The final section of this chapter provided cross-country comparative statistics on the health-care systems of OECD countries. Since the United States lacks universal health-care insurance, some summary information on the characteristics of the uninsured was supplied.

Key Concepts

Production possibility frontier

Opportunity cost

Pareto optimal

Positive economics

Externality

Marginal effects

Resources

[1] Meltzer, David, "The Shape of Health Care Research," in *Measuring the Price of Medical Treatments*, Triplett, Jack E., ed. (Washington, DC: Brookings, 1999), pp. 258–259.

[2] See, for example, Newhouse, Joseph P. and the Insurance Experiment Group, *Free for All: Lessons from the RAND Health Insurance Experiment* (Cambridge, MA: Harvard University, 1993) and C. N. Morris and J. L. Hill, "The Health Insurance Experiment Design Using the Finite Selection Model," in *Public Policy and Statistics: Case Studies from RAND*, S. Morton and J. Rolph, eds. (New York, Springer, 2000), Chap. 2.

[3] Gruber, Jonathan, et al., "Physician Fee Policy and Medicaid Program Costs," *The Journal of Human Resources*, 32 (1997): 611–634.

[4] Arrow, Kenneth, "Uncertainty and the Welfare Economics of Medical Care," *American Economic Review*, 53 (1963): 941–973. This classic article is an elegant statement of the way uncertainty affects health and health-care markets.

[5] Auster, Richard, et al., "The Production of Health, an Exploratory Study," *The Journal of Human Resources*, 4 (1969): 411–436.

[6] See Adelman, Irma, "An Econometric Analysis of Population Growth," *American Economic Review*, 52 (1963): 314–339.

[7] Hadley Jack, *More Medical Care, Better Health?* (Washington, DC: Urban Institute, 1982) and "Medicare Spending and the Mortality Rates of the Elderly," *Inquiry*, 25 (1988): 485–493.

[8] See, Newhouse, et al. (1993), op. cit.; Currie, Janet and Jonathan Gruber, "Saving Babies: The Efficacy and Cost of Recent Changes in the Medicaid Eligibility of Pregnant Women," *The Journal of Political Economy*, 104 (1996): 1263–1296; Dubay, Lisa, et al., "Medical Malpractice Liability and Its Effect on Prenatal Care Utilization and Infant Health," *Journal of Health Economics*, 20 (2001): 591—611; and Kaestner, et al., *Does Publicly Provided Health Insurance Improve the Health of Low-Income Children in the*

United States, NBER Working Paper No. 6887, (Cambridge, MA: National Bureau of Economic Research, 1999).

[9] Newhouse et al. (1993), op. cit., Chap. 6 and 7.

[10] Ibid. The exception was that children from low-income families who were at high risk of having anemia were slightly less likely to be anemic at the end of the three- to five-year study period.

[11] Newhouse, op. cit., Chap. 9.

[12] Kohn, L. T., et al., *To Err Is Human: Building a Safer Health System* (Washington DC: National Academies Press, 2000).

[13] See, for instance, Cutler, David and Mark McClellan, "Is Technological Change in Medical Care Worth It?" *Health Affairs,* 20 (2001): 11–29.

[14] Cutler, David, et al., "Are Medical Prices Declining? Evidence from Heart Attack Treatments," *Quarterly Journal of Economics,* 113 (1998): 991–1024.

[15] Jones, Charles I., "Why Have Health Care Expenditures as a Share of GDP Risen So Much?" NBER Working Paper No. 9325 (Cambridge, MA: National Bureau of Economic Research, 2002), p. 30.

[16] A very good summary of this, using perinatal mortality rates (stillborns plus infant mortality relative to live births plus stillborns), is given in Phelps, Charles E., *Health Economics,* 3rd ed. (Boston: Addison Wesley, 2003), pp. 575–576.

[17] Stanfield, Barbara, "Is U.S. Health Care Really the Best in the World?" *Journal of the American Medical Association,* 284 (July 20, 2000): 483–485. The countries used for comparison are Japan, Sweden, Canada, France, Australia, Spain, Finland, the Netherlands, Denmark, Belgium, Germany, and the U.K.

[18] See, for instance, Rublee, Dale A., "Medical Technology in Canada, Germany, and the United States: An Update," *Health Affairs,* 13 (1994): Exhibit 1.

[19] Triplett, Jack E., "What's Different about Health? Human Repair and Car Repair in National Accounts and in National Health Accounts?" in *Medical Care Output and Productivity,* Cutler, David M. and Ernst R. Berndt, eds. (Chicago University of Chicago Press, 2001), pp. 15–94.

[20] Wolk, Martin, "Eye on the Economy," MSNBC Aug. 26, 2004, http://www.msnbc.msn.com/id/5829707/.

[21] Five states in particular, Hawaii, Massachusetts, Minnesota, Oregon, and Tennessee created programs during the 1980s and 90s. Massachusetts has subsequently abandoned its program. See Oliver T. R. and Pamela A. Paul-Shaheen, "Translating Ideas into Action: Entrepreneurial Leadership in State Health Care Reforms," *Journal of Health Politics, Policy, and Law,* 22 (1997): 721–788; Paul-Shaheen, Pamela A., "The States and Health Care Reform: The Road Traveled and Lessons Learned From Seven that Took the Lead," *Journal of Health Politics, Policy, and Law,* 23 (1998): 319–361; Brown, L. D. and M. S. Sparer, "Window Shopping: State Health Care Reform Politics in the 1990s," *Health Affairs,* 20 (2001): 50–67.

PART TWO

The Demand for Health, Health Care, and the Insurance Market

CHAPTER TWO

The Demand for Health and the Demand for Health Care

"To your health!" "¡A su salud!"
"A votre santé!" "Zum Wohlsein!"
"Un brindisi alla vostra salute!"
"Za vashe zdorovie!"
"Que Dieu vous donne santé et prospérité!"
"May you be healthy, wealthy, and wise!"

1 Introduction

In every language there are greetings and toasts to health. It is perhaps no accident that greetings which mention health and wealth always seem to list health first. Most of us probably find it obvious that everyone desires good health both for the sake of continued quality of life and because it contributes to our remaining productive and earning income. Yet a great deal of study has gone into determining what factors affect the demand for health, and a formal model of investment in health is widely used by economists in structuring their research. But what exactly is health? We will view health as a stock of capital that yields a stream of healthy days, just as wealth is a stock of financial capital that yields a stream of income.

A person might decide to consult an allergist and take medication in order to experience fewer miserable days in the spring and fall. Another person might decide to have heart surgery in order to resume an active life and to increase the probability of living longer. In each case, medical care is undertaken to gain more healthy days; it may therefore be interpreted as an investment in the stock of health. Anything that contributes to producing better health such as nutritious food, clean air, exercise, much needed time away from one's job, or medical care should be considered as health care, even though this text and any related course you are taking focus on medical care.

This chapter presents a model of the demand for health, and then, treating medical care as an input into the production of health, examines the demand for medical care, which, within the context of the investment model, is understood to be conditional on the demand for health itself. This chapter also takes account of the fact that there can be "negative inputs" into the production of health.

This degree of formality may seem excessive to those of you whose main interest is the markets for physician services, hospitals, and pharmaceuticals, or healthcare policy issues. However, formulating an investment model of health provides a basis for understanding the demand for health care. It also provides insights that may affect public policy decisions. For instance, one might believe that it is a beneficial thing for society to devote a higher proportion of its resources to producing health, or education, or other investment goods. However, if expenditure on medical care is viewed as just another consumption choice, with medical care treated as a consumer good rather than a productive input, we may reach the conclusion that it is bad to spend a higher proportion on medical care since this reduces the amount of current income available to purchase other consumer goods.

2   Investment in Health as a Form of Human Capital

A model of the demand for health, developed in the 1970s by Michael Grossman, treats investment in health as a form of investment in human capital.[1] The general model of human capital was originally developed by Gary Becker in the context of investment in education, and it was logical to extend this to health.[2] The demand for health care is thus treated as conditional on the demand for health, because health care is an *input* into the production of a stock of health, which is the end product or *output*.

Consider what is involved in investing in any capital good. The analogy between medical care and car repair has often been made, so think about investing in a car.[3] A person might buy a car in order to earn income as a cab or livery driver. In that case, the car is clearly a capital good. Or, one might buy a car to drive to work and to use for pleasure trips. In that case, the car is also a capital good in that it provides a stream of services over time (travel) that has both a monetary value, getting to work, and a value in consumption (utility), such as the joy of driving through the countryside on a beautiful autumn day. If one only uses the car for recreation, it is still a capital good because it provides a stream of services over time.

In order to preserve the investment in a car, some preventive maintenance is necessary, including regular oil changes, new brake pads, an occasional tune-up, and so on. The car may nonetheless break down and require expensive and un-expected repairs. Maintaining a car is not unlike the maintenance of health, which involves both routine care and unexpected repairs in the case of illness or accident. The amount of repairs needed by the car will depend on how it is treated. A car used for drag racing will need its brakes replaced more often. If the oil is not changed every 3,000 to 5,000 miles, the car will probably require more repairs and not last as long. The routine maintenance and repairs on the car are performed to offset its depreciation. This is part of the *gross investment* in the car over its lifetime. Gross investment includes both the cost of purchasing the car and its upkeep.

Grossman's Investment Model of Health

The investment model of health views the demand for health as being condi-tional on both the cost of health capital and the rate of depreciation of the health stock. As in the investment in a car, or in any capital good that eventually wears out, the difference between *gross (total)* and *net* investment depends on the rate at which the capital good wears out or depreciates.

The **marginal efficiency of capital** (MEC) is a measure of how much extra output can be produced with an extra unit of input. Figure 2.1. depicts the sched-ule of the marginal efficiency of health capital. It shows how much extra expen-diture is required to produce an additional unit of health (stock). One measures the quantity of health stock along the horizontal axis and its cost along the verti-cal axis. The MEC curve slopes downward because additional units of investment are assumed to provide smaller marginal improvements in health; in other words, assume that the production of health is subject to diminishing returns. H_i and H_{i+1} are two levels of health stock chosen by an individual at different levels of cost of producing health. The total cost of producing any stock of health capital includes the cost of offsetting its depreciation. The model distinguishes between the cost of offsetting depreciation δ and the cost of producing incremental units of the health stock C.

One can think of the MEC schedule as the demand curve for health. It can also be seen as a "production function for health" since it relates the "inputs" and the "output," the stock of health. Once we know the MEC schedule, it is possible to determine the level of health stock that an individual will choose to produce. A rational person will invest additional resources in the production of health to the point where the value of an additional degree of healthiness is just equal to the marginal cost of producing it.

The MEC schedule is specific to an individual. The location of the MEC sched-ule depends on a person's initial stock of health at the beginning of the time

Figure 2.1

The Marginal Efficiency
of Health Capital
Source: Grossman, Michael,
"On the Concept of Health
Capital and the Demand for
Health," *Journal of Political
Economy,* 80 (1972): p. 237.

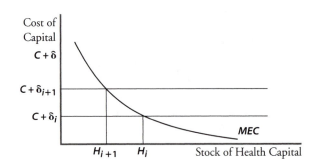

period under consideration. An individual who begins life with a lower endowment of health will require more inputs to achieve the same health stock, than will an initially healthier person. In that case, the MEC schedule will be located to the left of one that describes someone who begins life in a healthier state. The model does not assume that a given increase in inputs into the health production function will generate the same marginal improvement in different individuals.

This scenario has important implications when we contemplate the meaning of equity in access to health care. Should more resources be devoted to sicker people? More specifically, should an organ transplant be given to the most seriously ill person who is likely to die the soonest without it, or to a less sick person who is likely to be restored to a healthier state and live for a longer time as a result of receiving a new kidney? Constructing an MEC schedule certainly does not provide an answer to this difficult normative question, but it enables us to better understand the question.

The Wage Effect

We treat a change in the wage rate as a shift in the MEC schedule, since it changes the return from the stock of health. It does so because the wage rate measures an individual's market efficiency, the rate at which healthy days are converted into monetary earnings, and also the opportunity cost of nonmarket time, valued by the earnings foregone per hour or day. A stock of health is a better investment for a high-wage earner, since that individual's healthy working hours yield more income and the opportunity cost of his or her healthy nonmarket time is also greater.

The Consumption Model

For some purposes, it makes sense to shift to a model that focuses on the allocation of the budget (income) between investment in health and expenditure on consumer goods at a given time. In Figure 2.2, $B^1 B^1$ is a budget line. It shows the different combinations of health + consumption goods that one can purchase

Figure 2.2

The tradeoff between the investment good, health, and the consumption good.

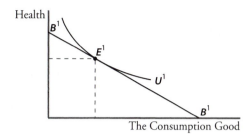

with a particular level of income (a given budget.) The quantity of goods that may be purchased from a budget depends on the prices of the goods. The slope of the budget line is determined by the relative prices of the two goods: here "the consumer good" and "health."

U^1 is an individual's indifference curve. Each indifference curve shows the various combinations of health and consumption goods that provide an individual with an equal amount of satisfaction or utility. A higher indifference curve represents a higher level of total utility. The standard assumption is that both the consumption good and health are subject to diminishing marginal utility; therefore, one can draw the indifference curves in the usual way, convex to the origin.*

E^1 shows the point where the consumer's utility is maximized when the budget constraint is B^1B^1. The individual has chosen the combination of consumer goods and health investment that puts him or her on the highest indifference curve attainable with that budget B^1.†

Additional Factors That Affect the Investment in Health

Age

As one ages, it takes more resources to obtain or maintain a given stock of health. In contrast, older people are generally not charged higher prices for most consumer goods. In fact, some goods, such as airplane travel and restaurant meals, may even be subject to senior citizen discounts. Therefore, the relative price of producing health versus purchasing consumer goods tends to increase with age. The substitution effect (relative price effect) would encourage the sub-

---

*Since one's productivity in the workplace is likely to be affected by one's health, investment in health could increase earnings to the extent that one might spend money on health care without reducing the consumption of other goods. Then there would be no trade-off between the two. This diagram assumes that the effects of investment on health do not occur instantaneously. This diagram is meant to be a snapshot of a moment in time. Appendix 1 provides a brief overview of indifference curves.

†This framework of analysis is also explained in Appendix 1.

Figure 2.3

Shift in Relative Prices

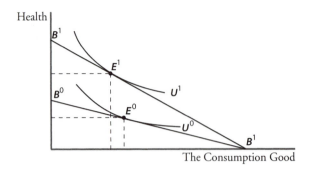

stitution of other consumer goods for investment in health as one ages. In Figure 2.3, an increase in the relative price of health investment is shown by a decrease in the slope of the budget line (from B^1B^1 to B^0B^1). This results in a new optimal combination of the consumer good and health E^0. An empirical study that investigated the relationship between age and the demand for health using both Grossman's investment model and the consumption model found that the demand for health declined with age in both models.[4] The models can illuminate the process of "dis-investing" in health. A person with a very serious and incurable illness may decide it is not worth investing in the minimal health stock necessary to stay alive.

Education

We can use both the investment and consumption models to analyze the effects of education on the demand for health. Considerable evidence exists that more highly educated people are more efficient in the production of health. In the investment model, education shifts the MEC schedule out to the right by raising the productivity of the inputs into the production of health.

This effect seems to be true not only in the United States and similarly developed countries, but also in countries that have much lower levels of per capita income and education, and less advanced technologies. In addition, increasing the educational level of parents, particularly mothers, seems to increase the productivity of inputs into children's health.[5] An alternative hypothesis is that education is correlated with a lower rate of depreciation in the stock of health.[6] This could be shown as a move downward along the MEC schedule associated with a reduction in the cost of producing the health stock. In either interpretation, we expect education to increase the demand for health.

Education may not only make investment in health less costly, it may also be associated with different "time preferences." Time preference is a term that refers to the extent to which people discount the future. The proverbial person who "lives from hand to mouth" is preoccupied with the present and ignores the future, that is, discounts it very heavily. Such a person is not likely to save or invest much in either education or health.[7] Even if investment in education is correlated with investment in health, the effect of education on expenditure for health *care* is still an open question if greater efficiency in the production of health enable the use of fewer inputs to attain any given level of health.* We will return to this question in the second section of this chapter.

Negative Inputs into the Health Production Function

Lifestyle Effects of Wealth In his early work on the demand for health, in 1972, Grossman found a negative relationship between income level and health.[8] This was surprising. Is health an inferior good, one that individuals invest in less when their income or wealth increases? The negative effect of income on health was found only when the wage rate was held constant; thus, it was associated only with the nonwage component of income. One explanation for this phenomenon is that higher income (more wealth) may be associated with a lifestyle detrimental to health. The MEC schedule may tend to shift to the left as people become wealthier. Eating rich foods, using the car for short trips instead of walking, participating in dangerous sports, consuming recreational drugs—we can view all of these as negative inputs into the production of health. Research has, in fact, shown an inverse relationship between upturns in the business cycles and level of healthiness of communities.[9] One might expect to find very different business cycle effects, at least for the poor, in countries with much lower per capita incomes. In low-income countries, periods of greater prosperity would be expected to reduce malnutrition and lead to better health outcomes.

Chemical Dependency We can regard addictive drugs as another example of negative inputs into the production function for health. In the case of addictive drugs, additional insight may be gained by utilizing both the investment and consumption models of health. Addiction might be viewed as shifting the marginal efficiency of health capital schedule to the left; one could also view it as causing a change in taste that would result in the substitution of the addictive good for an expenditure on health. For instance, one might skimp on dental care or preventive medical care in order to buy more heroin.[†] A common view of drug addiction associates it with a very short time horizon in decision making, which is consistent with a diversion of resources away from investing in health to purchasing "utility-producing" addictive goods.

---

*One's state of health probably also affects one's efficiency in acquiring or absorbing the other major form of human capital investment, education. The interdependency between health and the ability to absorb education can lead to problems in the construction of econometric models used in studies of health and education.

†In the context of Figure 2.2, this would be shown as a shift to a new indifference curve system. (U^1, U^2, . . . would change their shapes.)

Following this line of reasoning, anything that increases the value of a stock of health should tend to reduce chemical dependency. In the case of addiction, some more direct form of intervention would probably also be necessary. However, one might expect that better opportunities in the labor market, which increase the value of healthy days, would tend to discourage chemical dependency or at least provide an incentive for seeking help.

3   Research Studies Employing the Grossman Model

A large number of studies have been mounted using the Grossman framework of analysis to investigate the effects of age, schooling, and wealth on the demand for health.[10] Researchers have constructed dynamic models to study how investment in health changes over the life cycle[11] and have introduced uncertainty into the investment model. For instance, if we define illness as a state in which the stock of health capital falls below a certain critical level, the value of investing in a larger health stock is that it reduces the probability of falling into the illness state.[12] Accordingly, health status is a process in which the individual can only influence the probability of transitions from one health state to another.[13]

One recent study of the demand for health has used the quality-adjusted life-year, (QALY) as a measure of the health capital stock.[14] (This measure is commonly employed in evaluating the cost-effectiveness of expenditure on health. We will discuss it at length in Chapter Nine). In this study, the demand for health is modeled as a function of the price of medical care, income, education, and a set of variables affecting the rate of depreciation of the health stock, including patterns of exercise, smoking habits, and weight. The demand for quality-adjusted life-years was found to decrease with increases in the price of medical care and age and to increase with income and education. The lifestyle variables used as indirect measures of depreciation were also found to be significant predictors of the demand for health. Such findings are consistent with those obtained using Grossman's model of investment in health.

Critiques of the Model

Critics of the Grossman model have argued that viewing decisions about health care as part of a rational strategy for investing in health is belied by the facts. One argument is that expenditure on medical care is, in fact, correlated with ill health. Higher expenditure on health is simply the result of responses to negative shocks to the state of health. Others have posited that the great amount of uncertainty associated with the onset of illness makes it impossible to develop a rational plan for investing in health. Although it is undeniable that exogenous (external) shocks do alter the stock of health during the lifetime of an individual, dynamic modeling should be able to take this into account. After all, investment decisions of all kinds are made in a world where there is uncertainty and a lack of complete information.

4   The Demand for Medical Care

Having established that we can construct a production function for health, let us now consider the demand for medical care, one of the inputs in the production function. Medical care is different from the other inputs into health in several ways. It generally has no utility apart from promoting health, unlike food, housing, exercise, and so on. Unlike the other inputs, at least part of the demand for medical care is unpredictable in that it is conditional on illness, and the level of expenditure on medical care may be "catastrophic" when measured relative to household income and wealth.

Anything that increases the demand for health should increase the demand for medical care, other things being equal. For instance, higher wages, which make healthy days more valuable, should increase the demand for both health and medical care. The exception would be a situation in which the cost of an individual's time spent in obtaining medical care is perceived to be greater than the expected value of the medical care.[15]

The demand for medical care also depends on the particular production function for health. Production functions are always constructed assuming a particular technology. Technological improvements in medical care have increased the use of medical inputs into the production of health. They have also brought about rising expectations about attainable levels of health and, as a consequence, have increased the demand for health itself.[16] This, in turn, increases the demand for medical care.

The effect of education on the demand for medical care is not predictable. If education makes a person more efficient in producing health, for instance, increasing awareness of the value of good nutrition and early detection of disease or by improving the ability to select appropriate medical care providers, it will reduce the quantity of medical care required to produce a given stock of health. Education may also increase the demand for health itself. The more highly educated will demand more health but less medical care if the effect of education on the productivity of inputs into health outweighs the shift in the demand for health.* Empirical research provides evidence of the ambiguous effect of education on the demand for medical care.†

The effect of age on the demand for medical care has been found to vary by type of medical service. The demand for ambulatory care, particularly when measured as probability of seeing a physician at all during a given year, decreases sig-

---

*"If the elasticity of the MEC schedule were less than unity, the more educated would demand more health but less medical care. Put differently, they would have an incentive to offset *part* of the increase in health caused by an increase in education by reducing their purchases of medical services." Grossman (1972), op. cit., p. 246.

†Education has been found to reduce the demand for medical care when Grossman's investment model, but not the consumption version of the same model, is used. Wagstaff, A., "The Demand for Health: Some New Empirical Evidence," *Journal of Health Economics,* 5 (1986): 195–237.

nificantly with age, whereas the demand for in-hospital care increases with age, as does the demand for pharmaceuticals.[17] If we add health status as an explanatory variable, the relationship between age and demand for medical services is no longer significant. It appears to be the deterioration in health that accompanies age rather than age itself that increases the demand for medical care.[18]

The effect of insurance on the demand for medical care is very important and will be addressed in Chapters Three through Five. However, insurance primarily impacts the price of medical care. Therefore, for our present purposes insurance may be viewed as influencing the quantity demanded of medical care, but not shifting the demand.

A sizable literature exists on the principal-agent relationship between patients and physicians. The role of the physician in determining the patient's demand for medical care is the subject of Chapter Seven. For now, let us abstract from the principal-agent problem, bearing in mind, however, that it is important.

Estimates of Price Elasticity of Demand for Medical Care

We measure the responsiveness of consumers to changes in the price of a good by the price elasticity of demand:*

$$\frac{\text{Percent change in the quantity of medical care demanded}}{\text{Percent change in price of medical care}}$$

In general, goods for which there are close substitutes have higher price elasticities. The demand elasticity for a good that constitutes a higher proportion of the budget is also generally higher, since an increase in the price of such goods requires curtailing more consumption expenditure on other goods. Following on this logic, some extremely high-cost medical procedures might be expected to have relatively high price elasticities of demand. For instance, a patient might not elect to have a bone marrow transplant if his or her insurance will not pay for it

A large number of researchers have estimated the elasticity of demand for the various components of medical care services.[19] Many studies use the insurance copayment level as the price variable. A summary of estimates of price elasticity of demand for various medical services is presented in Table 2.1.[†]

Examining Table 2.1, we see that the highest price-elasticity estimates are those obtained for hospital outpatient services and for nursing home services.

---

*When measuring the degree of elasticity, we consider the absolute value of the elasticity coefficient. Thus, a coefficient of -3 is considered to be a higher degree of price elasticity than a coefficient of -0.5 because a coefficient of -3 reflects a 300 percent decrease in quantity demanded associated with a 100 percent increase in price whereas a coefficient of -0.5 reflects only a 50 percent decrease in quantity associated with a 100 percent increase in price.

†Chapter Thirteen reviews the findings of studies on elasticity of demand for medical care in a number of developing nations, including an experimental study of rural China that replicates the research design of the RAND HIE study for the United States discussed in Chapter One.

Table 2.1   Price Elasticities for Different Medical Services

Outpatient hospital	−1.00
Hospital admissions	−0.14 to −0.46
Hospital length of stay	−0.06 to −0.29
Nursing home services	−0.73 to −2.40
Physician office visits (all)	−0.08 to −0.35
Physician office visits (pediatric)	−0.03 to −0.06
Total spending on medical care	−0.22 to −0.79
Spending on preventive care	−0.43

Sources: Compilations of data by author from various sources. See notes at end of the Chapter.[20]

Why would you expect these services to have higher price elasticities? Here is a hint. Nursing home services have substitutes, home care provided by families or paid caregivers. Moreover, for the elderly who are not covered by Medicaid, the cost of inpatient nursing home care often represents a very high proportion of the budget, another standard reason why demand elasticities are higher.

Price elasticities of demand for medical services have also been estimated, conditional on health status. Several studies have concurred that health status affects the elasticity of demand only for initial decisions to seek health care, not for subsequent incremental health care. As would be expected, ill health increased the demand for medical care, but decreased its price elasticity, when other factors such as income and education were held constant.*

Researchers have also obtained price-elasticity estimates based on sensitivity to variations in prices among individual physician and hospital services. A range of estimates are displayed in Table 2.2. These are called "firm-specific" demand elas-

Table 2.2   Price Elasticity of Demand for Services (Firm-Specific)

Physician visits	−1.75 to −5.07
Hospital services	−0.02 to −1.12

Sources: *Physicians:* Lee, R. L., and J. Hadley, "Physicians' Fees and Public Medical Care Programs," *Health Services Research*, 16 (1981): 185-203; McLean, R. A., "The Structure of the Market for Physicians' Services," *Health Services Research,* 15 (1980): 271-280. *Hospital services:* Feldman, R., and B. Dowd., "Is There a Competitive Market for Hospital Services?" *Journal of Health Economics,* 5, (1986): 277–292.

*Newhouse, Joseph P. and the Insurance Experiment Group, *Free for All: Lessons from the RAND Health Insurance Experiment* (Cambridge, MA: Harvard University, 1993); Wedig, Gerard J., "Health Status and the Demand for Health," *Journal of Health Economics,* 7 (1988), p. 159. Using three measures of poor health: patient's perception, number of disability days, and activity limitations, Wedig obtained demand elasticity estimates for physician visits versus no visits for those in poor health in the range of −0.17 to −0.22, and for those in good health in the range of −0.245 to −0.33.

ticities. Since one can substitute between physicians or hospitals, we would expect the price elasticity of demand for a particular physician or hospital to be higher than the demand for the service of all physicians or all hospitals.

Table 2.2 shows the firm-specific elasticity coefficients to be higher for physician services than for hospitals. This is not surprising since in many communities, only one or two hospitals may exist. It is also the case that many people choose a physician, not the hospital. Once a physician has been selected, this also limits the choice of hospitals to those at which the physician has privileges to practice.

Demand for Unhealthy Goods: Cigarettes, Alcohol, and Illicit Drugs

Earlier in this chapter, you were introduced to the notion of negative inputs into the production function for health. Epidemiological studies have established the negative effect of cigarette-smoking on health. Alcohol, if used in excess, is also generally considered a negative input into the production of health (although some studies have found the moderate consumption of red wine to be associated with positive effects on cholesterol level). And society has almost always regarded addictive drugs such as heroin as "bads." Whereas cigarette smoking is regarded as bad enough to warrant high rates of sales taxes imposed on cigarettes, heroin is regarded as so bad that its sale is illegal.* Table 2.3 provides some estimates that have been found for price-elasticities of demand for various "bads."

Table 2.3   Price Elasticity of Demand for Alcohol, Illicit Drugs, and Cigarettes

Alcohol	
Beer	−0.35
Wine	−0.68
Spirits	−0.98
Cocaine	−0.28 to −1.43
Heroin	−0.94
Cigarettes	−0.27 to −1.31 (most estimates −0.45 to −0.47)[a]

[a]Price-elasticity estimates are higher for youthful users (cigarettes and cocaine), particularly when the demand is not conditional on respondents being confirmed users. The high-end estimate for cocaine is a short-run estimate based on individuals' one-month consumption and includes first-time experimenters.

Sources: Compilations of data by author from various sources. See notes at the end of the chapter.[21]

*The effect of marijuana is more controversial, especially in its use as a painkiller for patients with advanced stages of cancer, but it is often included in such a list of bads. Research on marijuana use has focused on the effects of decriminalization. It is estimated that decriminalization would increase the probability of marijuana use by 8 percent. Saffer, H. and F. Chaloupka, "The Demand for Illicit Drugs," *Economic Inquiry*, 37 (1999): 401–411.

Economists have developed a "rational addiction" model that takes into account the interdependency between past, current, and future consumption. This model is used to compare short- and long-run demands for such goods as cigarettes. The short-run price-elasticities of demand for addictive goods tend to be uniformly higher than long-run elasticities, since short-run elasticities include people who are making choices about becoming first-time users.[22]

Time Costs and Time-Price Elasticities

The time cost is the value of time used in a given activity. Estimates of the price elasticity of demand for any good or service that requires time will tend to be biased if one does not take account of the time as well as money costs. The time involved in consuming a medical service includes travel time and the time spent waiting for and receiving the service. The total cost of services that require time will be higher for patients with higher wage rates, since the wage rate is a measure of the opportunity cost of time. Any factor that increases the value of time will increase its opportunity cost. A mother of young children may not be employed for pay, but might nonetheless decide that the time costs of a doctor's appointment are too high since the opportunity cost of her time is also likely to be higher than for similar people who do not have young children.

If an individual pays less than full market price for a service, as when insurance covers part of the cost, the time component of the cost becomes a relatively larger component of the total cost. Insurance coverage has been shown to make time a more important consideration in the decision about how much medical care to seek and which providers to use.[23]

We illustrate the effect of the cost of time on the total cost of a physician visit in the following example, which compares the hypothetical costs of clinic treatments (with an average waiting time of $2\frac{1}{2}$ hours) and private office visits (with an average waiting time of 30 minutes) for workers with different wage rates. The higher-priced office visit is less expensive for the worker who earns $50 per hour.

Prices of Clinic and Physician Office Visits Including Time Cost

	At wage rate of $10/hour	At wage rate of $50/hour
Clinic visit	$10	$10
Waiting time	$2\frac{1}{2}$ hours	$2\frac{1}{2}$ hours
Total cost =	$35	$135
Office visit to physician	$50	$50
Waiting time	$\frac{1}{2}$ hour	$\frac{1}{2}$ hour
Total cost =	$55	$75

Studies have found that time costs are sometimes more important than money costs in decisions about which medical services to use. A study of the demand of women for physician care found that a 10 percent increase in the relative time price of a public provider (clinic) compared with a private office visit was associated with a 5 percent decrease in the probability of a woman's choosing the public provider, whereas a 10 percent increase in the monetary price of the public provider was associated with only a 2 percent reduction in the probability of using the public option.[24]

Is Medical Care a Normal or a Superior Good?

The answer to this often posed question differs, depending on whether we look at studies based on individual responses or those utilizing aggregated data, for instance, country averages.

A **normal good** is a good for which income elasticity is positive but less than 1. This means that if income increases by a given percentage, the quantity of the good consumed increases but by a lower percentage than the associated income increase. If the percentage increase in the quantity consumed is greater than the associated percentage increase in income, the good is called a **superior good**.

A number of studies in the 1960s through the 1980s provided estimates of income elasticities for medical services based on survey data derived from individual responses. A review of these studies reveals the consensus that most medical services have coefficients of income elasticity that are positive and in the range of 0 to <1; they can therefore be classified as normal goods. The exceptions to this are pediatric physician visits, including well-baby care, and nursing home care for which home care is a substitute. Estimates of incomes elasticities for long-run demand for medical spending also tend to be higher. A probable reason is that long-run demand includes elective procedures that can be scheduled during periods of higher income. Table 2.4 summarizes the findings on income elasticities for medical expenditures.

By contrast, studies using macroeconomic data, both time-series and cross-country comparisons of medical expenditure, tend to yield considerably higher income elasticity coefficients for medical care. A wide range of studies have generally found medical care to be a superior good. This is true both among industrialized nations and in comparisons between industrialized and developing nations.[26]

Summary

Economists view the demand for health as an investment decision. Using this model, health care is not a consumer good but rather an input into the produc-

Table 2.4   Income Elasticity Estimates for Individuals and Families

Household medical spending	0.25 to 0.45
Per capita medical spending	0.80 to 1.57
Short-run per capita spending	0.31 to 0.86
Long-run per capita spending	1.12 to 3.22
Physician services	0.57 to 0.85
Physician office visits (all)	0.06 to 0.07
Physician office visits (pediatric)	1.32
Nursing home care	0.55 to 2.27
Hospital care	0.04

Source: Compilations of data by author from various sources. See notes at the end of the Chapter.[25]

tion of the capital good, the stock of health. Understanding this analytical framework will be useful when we later examine the various components of the health-care market. The first section of this chapter also presented the widely-used model of demand for health developed by Michael Grossman.

In the second section, we directed our attention to the general characteristics of the demand for medical care. It proved to be conditional on age, education, income, and state of health. The demand for medical care appears to be generally sensitive to the usual economic variables, price and income, although for most components of medical care, price elasticities have values ranging between 0 and −1. Since patients can substitute among physicians, the demand for firm-specific physician services was found to be price-elastic. Medical services for which substitutes exist, such as nursing home care, tend to have higher demand elasticities than, for instance, hospitalization in an acute-care facility. The price elasticities for addictive goods, here viewed as negative inputs into the production of health, cover a wide range, but are also found to be more price-elastic than might be originally imagined, given the characteristics of addiction.

The association between income and the amount of medical care utilized shows medical care to be a normal good when such studies are based on responses from individuals. On the other hand, macro-economic data that compare country-wide aggregates in income and medical spending show medical care to be a superior good. This is true both among industrialized nations and in comparisons between them and developing nations.

Analogies are often drawn between the two main forms of investment in human capital: health and education. We have seen that education seems to make people more efficient in their investment in health. It is also correlated with the demand for health. However, the demand for medical care is much more unpredictable than the demand for schooling, since it is conditional on illness and injury. For this reason, people seek to avoid the risk of very large and unplanned expenditures on medical care. This leads to a demand for health insurance, which is the subject of our next chapter.

Key Concepts

Marginal efficiency of capital

Investment in human capital

Price elasticity of demand

Normal good

Superior good

Suggested Readings

1. Grossman, Michael, "The Human Capital Model," *Handbook of Health Economics,* Vol. 1A, A. Culyer and J. Newhouse, eds. (Amsterdam: Elsevier, 2000), Chap. 7.

2. Becker, G. S. and K. M. Murphy, "A Theory of Rational Addiction," *Journal of Political Economy*, 96 (1988): 675–700.

Questions for Discussion and Review

1. What factors tend to make people more efficient in the production of their stocks of health capital?

2. Draw a diagram showing the change in the demand for health when the wage rate increases.

3. What are the differences between the investment and consumption models of investment in health?

4. How does aging affect the cost of acquiring a stock of health?

5. How would you expect the price elasticity of demand for medical care to vary with health status?

6. Can you predict whether the demand for medical care will increase or decrease with an increase in the average educational attainment in the community? Explain.

7. Compute the time-price elasticity of demand if people reduce their physician visits by 20 percent when the traveling time to get to the nearest physician increases from 15 to 45 minutes.

Resources

[1] Grossman, Michael, "On the Concept of Health Capital and the Demand for Health," *Journal of Political Economy,* 80 (1972): 223–255 and "The Human Capital Model," in

Handbook of Health Economics, Vol. 1A, A. Culyer and J. Newhouse, eds. (Amsterdam: Elsevier, 2000).

[2] Becker, Gary S., *Human Capital* (New York: National Bureau of Economics Research, 1975).

[3] See, for instance, Triplett, Jack. E., "What's Different about Health? Human Repair and Car Repair in National Accounts and National Health Accounts," in *Medical Care Output and Productivity (2001),* NBER Studies in Income and Wealth, Vol. 62 (Chicago: University of Chicago Press, 2001), pp. 15–94.

[4] Wagstaff, A., "The Demand for Health: Some New Empirical Evidence," *Journal of Health Economics,* 5 (1986): 195–233.

[5] Gregson, Simon, et al., "School Education and HIV Control in Sub-Saharan Africa," *Journal of International Development,* 13 (2001): 487–511; Gopal, K. Rani, "Health Status and Female Literacy," *Indian Economic Journal,* 38 (1991): 117–119; Lin, Shin-Jong and Mei Lin, "Estimating the Infant Health Production Function in Taiwan," *Taiwan Economic Review,* 30 (2002): 77–111; and Pal, Sharmistha, "An Analysis of Childhood Malnutrition in Rural India: Role of Gender, Income, and Other Household Characteristics," *World Development,* 27 (1999): 1151–1171.

[6] Muurinen, J., "Demand for Health: A Generalized Grossman Model," *Journal of Health Economics,* 1 (1982): 5–28.

[7] See, for instance, Fuchs, Victor, "Time Preference and Health: An Exploratory Study," in *Economics of Health* (Chicago: University of Chicago, 1982), pp. 93–120. Fuchs hypothesized that those who take the future more into account, that is, assign it a lower discount rate, will tend to invest more in both education and health. However, despite a large amount of research on this subject, little empirical support exists. See Berger, Mark C. and J. Paul Leigh, "Schooling, Self-Selection and Health," *Journal of Human Resources,* 24 (1989): 433–455; Becker, G. S. and C. B. Mulligan, "The Endogenous Determination of Time Preference," *Quarterly Journal of Economics,* 112, (1997): 729–758; and Grossman, M. and R. Kaestner, "Effects of Education on Health," in *The Social Benefits of Education,* J. R. Behrman and N. Stacey, eds. (Ann Arbor: University of Michigan Press, 1997), pp. 69–123.

[8] Grossman (1972), op. cit., p. 249.

[9] See Ruhm, Christopher J., "Are Recessions Good for Your Health?" *Quarterly Journal of Economics,* 115 (2000): 617–650. However, with respect to binge drinking, the opposite has been found. People appear to do more binge drinking when incomes fall and unemployment increases. See Dee, Thomas, S., "Alcohol Abuses and Economic Conditions: Findings from Repeated Cross-Sections of Individual Level Data," *Health Economics,* 10 (2001): 257–270.

[10] Muurinen, J., "Demand for Health: A Generalized Grossman Model," *Journal of Health Economics,* 1 (1982): 5–28.

[11] Wagstaff, A., "The Demand for Health: An Empirical Reformation of the Grossman Model," *Health Economics,* 2 (1993): 189–198; van Doorslaer, E. K. A., *Health, Knowledge, and the Demand for Medical Care* (Maastricht: The Netherlands, Assen, 1987).

[12] See, for instance, Cropper, M. L., "Health, Investment in Health, and Occupational Choice," *Journal of Political Economy,* 85 (1977): 273–294. For a good summary of empirical studies employing the Grossman model, see Grossman, M., op. cit. (2000), Chap. 7, pp. 347–408.

[13] For treatment of this approach, see Zweifel, Peter and Friedrich Breyer, *Health Economics,* (New York: Oxford University Press, 1997), pp. 62–89.

[14] Gerdtham, U.-G., et al., "The Demand for Health: Results from New Measures of Health Capital," *European Journal of Political Economy,* 15 (1999): 501–521. These re-

searchers employed alternative methods of questioning respondents to get information on their state of health. They ran regression equations for the three specifications of the health status variable. The three methods were as follows: (1) asking people to rank their health from 0–1, where 0 is death, or a death equivalent, and 1 is full health, (2) asking people how many years in their current health state they would trade for a year in perfect health, and (3) asking people to supply a categorical measure ("excellent," "good," "fair," etc.).

[15] In studying the effect of employment of college graduate women on the demand for preventive medical care, researches uncovered a negative association between full-time employment and the probability of such women having an annual physical and a mammogram. The time costs of having these tests were considered to be too high (Johnson-Lans, S., "Life Style Effects on the Demand of College Educated Women for Preventive Health Care," Vassar College Working Paper Series, 2001–2002).

[16] See the material on technology, Chapter Ten.

[17] Newhouse, Joseph P. and Charles E. Phelps, "New Estimates of Price and Income Elasticities of Medical Care Services," in *The Role of Health Insurance in the Health Services Sector*, R. N. Rosett, ed. (New York: National Bureau of Economic Research, 1974), pp. 261–312, and Zweifel, P., "The Effect of Aging on the Demand and Utilization of Medical Care," in *Systems Science in Health and Social Services for the Elderly and Disabled*, C. Tilquin, ed. (Toronto: Pergamon Press, 1985), pp. 313–318.

[18] Zweifel and Breyer, op. cit., p. 121.

[19] See, for instance, Manning, Willard G., et al.,"Health Insurance and the Demand for Medical Care: Evidence from a Randomized Experiment," *American Economic Review*, 77 (1987): 251–277; Feldstein, Martin S., "Hospital Cost Inflation: A Study of Nonprofit Price Dynamics," *American Economic Review*, 61 (1971): 853–872; and Eichner, Matthew J., "The Changing Market for Health Insurance: What People Pay Does Matter," *American Economic Review*, 88 (1998): 117–121.

[20] *For hospital admissions:*
Manning, et al., op. cit.; Feldstein, Martin S., "Quality Change and the Demand for Hospital Care," *Econometrica,* 45 (1977): 1681–1702; and Newhouse, Joseph P., and Charles E. Phelps, "New Estimates of Price and Income Elasticities of Medical Care Services," in R. N., Rosett, ed., *The Role of Health Insurance in the Health Services Sector* (New York: National Bureau of Economic Research, 1974): 261–312.

For physician visits:
Manning, et al., op. cit.; Newhouse, Joseph P., et al., "On Having Your Cake and Eating It Too: Econometric Problems in Estimating Demand for Health Services," *Journal of Econometrics*, 13 (1980): 365–390; Goldman, F. and M. Grossman, "The Demand for Pediatric Care: An Hedonic Approach," *Journal of Political Economy*, 86 (1978): 259–280; and Wedig, G. J., "Health Status and the Demand for Health: Results on Price Elasticities," *Journal of Health Economics*, 7 (1988): 151–163.

For Nursing home services:
Lamberton, C. E., W. D. Ellington, and K. R. Spear, "Factors Determining the Demand for Nursing Home Services," *Quarterly Review of Economics and Business,* 26 (1986): 74–90: and Chiswick, Barry R., "The Demand for Nursing Home Care: An Analysis of the Substitution between Institutional and Noninstitutional Care," *Journal of Human Resources*, 11 (1976): 295–316.

[21] Chaloupka, F. J. and K. E. Warner, "The Economics of Smoking," Chap. 29, *Handbook of Health Economics*, Vol. 1B, ed. Anthony J. Culyer and Joseph P. Newhouse (Amsterdam: Elsevier, 2000): 1539–1567; Chaloupka, F. J., et al., eds., *The Economic Analysis of Substance Use and Abuse* (Chicago: University of Chicago Press, 1999), pp. 133–155; Clements, K. W. et al., "Is Utility Addictive? The Case of Alcohol," *Applied Economics*, 29 (1997): 1163–1167; Cook, Philip J. and Michael J. Moore, "Alcohol,"

Chap. 30, *Handbook of Health Economics*, Vol. 1B, op. cit.; 1628–1673; Desimone, Jeffrey and Matthew C. Farrelly, "Price and Enforcement Effects on Cocaine and Marijuana Demand," *Economic Inquiry*, 41 (2003): 98–115; Grossman, Michael, et. al., "Demand for Cocaine by Young Adults: A. Rational Addition Approach," *Journal of Health Economics*, 17 (1998): 427–474; Gruber, J. et al., *Estimating Price Elasticities When There is Smuggling: the Sensitivity of Smoking to Price*, NBER Working Paper No. 8962 (Cambridge, MA.: National Bureau of Economic Research, 2002).

[22] Sloan, F. A., et al., "Information, Addiction, and 'Bad Choices': Lessons from a Century of Cigarettes," *Economic Letters*, 77 (2002): 147–155; Gruber, Jonathan and Botond Koszegi, "Is Addiction 'Rational'? Theory and Evidence," NBER Working Paper No. 7507 (Cambridge, MA: National Bureau of Economic Research, 2000).

[23] Acton, Jan Paul, *Demand for Health When Time Prices Vary More Than Money: R-1189-OEO/NYC* (Santa Monica, CA: Rand Corporation, 1973).

[24] Coffey, Rosanna M., "The Effect of Time Price on the Demand for Medical-Care Services," *The Journal of Human Resources*, XVIII (1983): 422.

[25] Chiswick, Barry R., "The Demand for Nursing Home Care: An Analysis of the Substitution between Institutional and Noninstitutional Care," *Journal of Human Resources,* 11 (1976): 295–316; Fuchs, V. and M. Kramer, *Determinants of Expenditure for Physicians Services in the United State, 1948-1968*, Occasional Paper No.117 (New York: National Bureau of Economic Research, 1973); Moore, William J., Robert J. Newman, and Mohammad Fheili, "Measuring the Relationship Between Income and NHEs," *Health Care Financing Review*, 14 (1992): 133–139; Goldman, F. and M. Grossman, "The demand for Pediatric Care: An Hedonic Approach," *Journal of Political Economy*, 86 (1978): 259–280; Lamberton, C. E., W. D. Ellington, and K. R. Spear, "Factors Determining the Demand for Nursing Home Services," *Quarterly Review of Economic and Business*, 26 (1986): 74–90; Newhouse, Joseph P., and Charles E. Phelps, "New Estimates of Price and Income Elasticities of Medical Care Services," in R. N., Rosett, ed., *The Role of Health Insurance in the Health Services Sector* (New York: National Bureau of Economic Research, 1974): 261–312; Rosett, Richard N. and Lien-fu Huang, "The Effect of Health Insurance on the Demand for Medical Care," *Journal of Political Economy,* 81 (1973): 281–305; Scanlon, W. J., "A Theory of the Nursing Home Market," *Inquiry*, 17 (1980): 25–41; and Silver, Morris, "An Economic Analysis of Variations in Medical Expenses and Work-Loss Rates," in *Empirical Studies in Health Economics*, H. Klarman, ed. (Baltimore: Johns Hopkins, 1970).

[26] See, for instance, Newhouse, Joseph P., "Medical-Care Expenditures: A Cross-National Survey," *Journal of Human Resources,* 12 (1977): 115–125; Schieber, G. J., "Health Care Expenditure in Major Industrialized Countries, 1960–1987," *Health Care Financing Review*, 11 (1990): 159–167, Gerdtham, Ulf G., et al., "An Econometric Analysis of Health Care Expenditures: A Cross-Section Study of the OECD Countries," *Journal of Health Economics,* 11 (1992): 63–84.

CHAPTER THREE

The Nature of Health Insurance Markets

Illness is usually unexpected and often costly. Health insurance is a contingent claims contract that moves funds from the usual state of the world, when one is healthy, to the unexpected and costly state, when one is ill. In this sense, it is a market success: an institutional response to a natural feature of the demand for health care. Without such an institution, there would be no market to transfer funds between health states. In its operation, however, health insurance introduces its own set of market failures. The key features of the health insurance institutions we observe now are, in turn, responses to the existence of these market failures. *

1   Introduction

Why do people buy insurance? The simple answer is that they are risk-averse. Buying insurance allows a person to pay a certain known amount in order to transfer the risk of a much larger expenditure (in the case of an adverse event) to an insurer, known as a third-party payer. Why do firms sell insurance? Because they are paid to assume a risk that can be managed by spreading it over a large pool of the insured. Insurance markets exist where consumers are

---

*Glied, Sherry A., "Health Insurance and Market Failure Since Arrow," *Journal of Health Economics*, 26 (2001): 957. This short and very accessible article is highly recommended as supplementary reading for this chapter.

willing to pay enough to transfer risk to induce insurance companies to assume the risk. This chapter examines the characteristics of insurance markets and, together with Chapter Four, considers the unique aspects of the evolving health insurance market. An extensive body of literature addresses the question of whether Americans have too much or too little health insurance, from the standpoint of what is socially optimal. We will briefly examine the main arguments on both sides of this question in the course of this chapter.

Why Do People Buy Health Insurance?

There are a number of types of risk associated with health. There is the risk to one's health and life associated with illness or disease. There is the additional risk that if one undertakes treatment, it may not cure or alleviate symptoms of the disease but may even make one's state of health worse, either through unavoidable risks associated with treatment or through the provider's lack of skill or even negligence. There is also the risk of incurring the costs associated with the treatment of illness or disease. One can take certain actions to reduce the risk of illness, such as having inoculations, avoiding environments in which there is a high risk of contracting communicable diseases, leading a healthy lifestyle, and so on, but considerable risk of illness still remains and is largely uninsurable.[1] One can also not generally insure against bad health outcomes.* On the other hand, individuals can insure themselves, at least in part, against the financial losses associated with the treatment of illness by buying health insurance policies.

Why don't people self-insure themselves by saving money when they are well to use in times of illness?[†] There are a number of reasons, including the fact that many people could never save or borrow enough money to pay for potential catastrophic levels of medical expenditure. However, even people who have extensive wealth usually buy insurance. The reason is that most people want to avoid risk, that is, they are "risk-averse."

Economists define risk aversion as a characteristic of people's utility functions. Consumers' attitudes toward risk depend on the marginal utility of an extra dollar (lost or gained) that may be different in different ranges of wealth. If the marginal utility of an extra dollar is decreasing as wealth increases, a small probability of a large reduction in wealth entails a larger loss of utility than the certain loss of a smaller amount of wealth when the probability-weighted, or expected, value of the two alternatives is equal. This is what is meant by being risk-averse. A person is risk-prone if he or she gambles, when gambling involves an unfair bet. Betting on the horses or buying a lottery ticket will be rational behavior in a range of wealth where the marginal utility of an extra dollar is increasing. In general, it is

---

*There are a few exceptions. Lloyds of London has been known to insure the hands of a famous concert pianist against damage. Whether this would cover a gradual stiffening of the fingers due to progressive arthritis is not clear. One can also buy disability insurance.

[†]Medical Savings Accounts are a mechanism for self-insuring. They have been tried on a limited and experimental basis, but have not been widely accepted to date in the United States.

believed that people are more likely to buy insurance to cover low-probability events involving large losses than high-probability events that are associated with small losses, and to buy lottery tickets when there is a low probability of winning a large amount.*

Consider the following example:

Meredith has a stock of wealth (savings) of $15,000. In this hypothetical world there is only one kind of illness. The medical treatment cost for this illness is known to be $10,000. If the probability of illness is .01, *the expected wealth*, if we take account of the risk of illness, is

(Probability of remaining well) × (wealth if well) +
(probability of illness) × (wealth if illness occurs),
.99 × 15,000 + .01 × $5,000 = $14,900

An expected value is the probability-weighted risky outcome. Since probabilities are found by computing the relative frequencies of outcomes for a large number of repeated experiments (such as the tossing of a coin), probabilities are not reliable predictors of outcomes in single events. In this case, Meredith's health in any time period is a single event.

What Meredith faces is probably better described as *uncertainty* rather than *risk*. Uncertainty is the term used for contingencies to which one cannot even assign probabilities.[2] She calculates her expected wealth because it is the only way she has of evaluating the risk. (If she is completely risk-averse, she will consider only the disutility of the worst possible outcome, which in this case is losing $10,000.)

Meredith can buy an insurance policy for $200, which will completely pay for the medical treatment she may need. She chooses to reduce her wealth by $200 in order to avoid the risk of losing $10,000 even though this is not a fair bet since the cost of the insurance policy is greater than the expected loss: $200 > (.01 × $10,000 = $100).

Figure 3.1 shows Meredith's expected level of utility when she bears the risk of incurring a $10,000 medical bill and the level of utility when she has a riskless but lower level of wealth. Meredith is at *A* after purchasing the insurance. Her resulting wealth is $14,800. Her utility level is *U*. If she had not purchased the insurance, she would be at *B*, with an expected value of wealth of $14,900 and a utility level of *E(U)*. The utility of a certain $14,800 is greater than the utility associated with an expected (risky) level of wealth of $14,900.

---

*For a fuller explanation, see any standard intermediate micro-economics text or Friedman, Milton and L. J. Savage, "The Utility Analysis of Choices Involving Risk," *The Journal of Political Economy*, LVI (1948): 279–304.

Figure 3.1

Risk Aversion
Illustrated

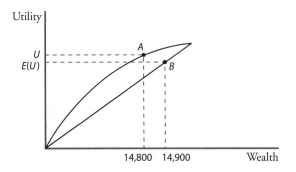

Table 3.1 Medical Expenses and U.S. Household Incomes, 1963 and 1996 (Statistics given are in constant 1996 U.S. $)

Average Medical Expenditure per Capita by Individuals in Top Percentile of Medical Care Costs	Average Annual Household Income
1963: $12,960	1963: $9,886
1996: $61,500	1996: $21,385

Source: See Glied, Sherry A., *Chronic Condition* (Cambridge, MA: Harvard University Press, 1997).

The medical costs that one *may* incur over one's lifetime have risen and are also greater relative to incomes than formerly, since so much more can now be done to lengthen life and improve its quality. As shown in Table 3.1 in 1963 the expenditure per capita by the top percentile of medical spenders in the United States was about 130 percent of average household income. By 1996 it had risen to about 300 percent of average household income for that year. This change in the financial risk associated with illness has increased the demand for health insurance.

How Are Insurance Premiums Set?

Insurance is a mechanism for assigning risk to a third party. It is also a mechanism for pooling risk over large groups. The price that an insurance company charges for an insurance policy, known as a *premium*, is based on the expected payout (the actuarial average payout for a large group of insured) plus administrative costs, reserve funds, and profits or surpluses to the insurance company.*

*Formerly, most health insurance companies were non-profit, as was the case with the various regional Blue-Cross and Blue-Shield companies. Today, most insurance companies are organized on a for-profit basis.

As a result, premiums charged generally exceed the fair value of the risk that the insurance company has assumed, where the fair value is the expected payout.

In a simplified case, where only one type of illness i can occur in the pool of insured, where i requires a specific treatment with a known cost C, where p, the probability of illness, is known, and where the illness and costs are incurred in only one time period, the expected payout on the part of the insurance company is

$$E_i = p_i \times C_i$$

Those of you who have had an introduction to statistics will recognize that this is an oversimplification in that it is a point estimate. Think of it as a mean or average. For any finite-sized sample (pool of insured), the insurance company will have to take account of the variance around this mean. The larger the pool of insured, the more reliable this point estimate will be. Insurance premiums reflect the insurer's need to allow for a margin of error around this point estimate. A premium that takes account of the variance will still be regarded as being based on the fair value of the bet the insurance company is making.

The part of the insurance premium that exceeds the fair value is called the **load** or **loading fee.** It is theoretically correct to think of the load, not the premium, as the price of insurance. The price of insurance is the cost of transferring risk. Particularly when comparing different insurance policies, it is convenient to express the loading fee as a percentage based on the ratio of premium to expected payout:

$$L = 100 \times \left(\frac{\text{Premium}}{E} - 1 \right)$$

Suppliers of insurance will be more willing to enter market situations where they can make reasonable estimates of what their payouts will be, that is, where they can assess the degree of risk they are assuming. They will be more willing to insure large groups for any given type of loss. They will also be more willing to insure risky events about which the probability of occurrence is better known. For this reason, so far there is not a functioning market in antiterrorist attack insurance.

Experience Versus Community Rating

One common method of pricing insurance is **experience rating**. This occurs when insurance companies base premiums on past levels of payouts, which is often done in the case of car insurance. Drivers who have been involved in an automobile accident will find their rates raised. In the case of individual health insurance policies, age and preexisting health problems may be fairly good predictors of future utilization of health-care services and may be used to determine premiums.

By contrast, **community rating** applies when each member of an insurance group pays the same premium per person or per family for the same coverage.

Although insuring against intertemporal differences between well and ill states is limited by the fact that people usually contract annually for insurance and therefore cannot make contracts about future health insurance premiums, interpersonal transfers between people in the same insurance group accomplish much the same end.*

Community rating is inefficient in the sense that the price of insurance to an individual subscriber does not reflect the marginal cost of that individual to the insurer. However, the trade-off between equity and efficiency is usually also considered. Not only do most societies support some intertemporal risk sharing, but also some sharing of risk between healthy (or low-risk) and ill (or high-risk) individuals.

2   Problems Facing Health Insurance Markets: Moral Hazard and Adverse Selection

Moral Hazard

Moral hazard refers to the phenomenon of a person's *behavior* being affected by his or her insurance coverage. Moral hazard is known to exist in all types of insurance markets. For example, people may be more careless with property that is insured. Although people may also be more careless about their health if they have health insurance, the main way in which moral hazard operates in the health insurance market is through the tendency for insurance to increase the quantity of medical care utilized.

Moral Hazard and the Structure of Health Insurance Contracts

The reason for the somewhat different manifestation of moral hazard in health insurance markets is that health insurance contracts differ from most other forms of insurance. Instead of paying a sum of money to the insured in case of an adverse event, they reduce the price of medical care associated with the adverse event (illness). True indemnity contracts, which pay the insured a fixed amount per adverse event, are rare in the contemporary health insurance market because they inadequately reduce the financial risk borne by subscribers, given the uncertainty about type and extent of treatments needed to alleviate symptoms or cure illnesses. They do not cover the risk that a treatment will be unsuccessful and further treatments will be needed. More typical are service benefit contracts that reimburse the subscriber on the basis of the fees charged. Service benefit contracts are still usually called indemnity policies (especially when they are distinguished

---

*Long-term care policies are an exception to this. In purchasing insurance for long-term care, one generally contracts at some age to pay a constant rate for the duration of the coverage. These contracts are more similar to term life insurance than other health insurance policies.

Figure 3.2

Effects of Insurance
on Consumption of
Medical Care

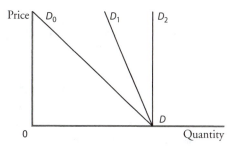

from membership in a health maintenance organization that integrates insurance with the provision of health care). The term **indemnity policy** will be used to refer to service benefit contracts throughout this book.

Moral hazard, in the context of the health insurance market, is illustrated in Figure 3.2. An individual's demand for a medical service when he or she has no insurance is represented by D_0D. If insurance pays 100 percent of the medical bill, the demand curve will shift to D_2D since the individual treats the service as free. D_1D depicts a situation in which insurance covers only part of the price charged for the service, for instance 50 percent. The price axis in this diagram is the full market price, not the proportion of the price paid out-of-pocket by the consumer. Thus, the insured has not had a shift in demand for medical care per se but is responding to the de-facto decline in price that results from the insurance company paying all or part of the medical bill.

Some degree of moral hazard will exist whenever the price elasticity of demand for covered health-care services is greater than zero. In theory, the problem of moral hazard should be greater in the case of policies covering a broader range of services including more "elective" ones, because the price elasticity of demand for these services is believed to be higher.*

The degree of moral hazard may also be increased if physicians take account of the patient's insurance status in making decisions about how much treatment to prescribe. The possibility of health-care providers engaging in "supplier-induced demand" will be addressed in Chapter Seven.

Major medical service benefit contracts also differ from most other types of insurance in that they generally cover more than unlikely catastrophic events, also fulfilling a function analogous to that of a service contract on an appliance or automobile. For instance, they often include reimbursement for annual physical ex-

---

*However, studies of the change in quantity of different medical services used when generosity of insurance varies indicate that people cut back on both highly and less highly valued services when they have less complete insurance coverage. See Newhouse, Joseph P. and the Insurance Experiment Group, *Free for All? Lessons from the RAND Health Insurance Experiment* (Cambridge, MA: Harvard University Press, 1993), Chap. 5.

aminations, well-baby pediatric visits, inoculations against influenza, treatment for chronic conditions such as arthritis or allergies, and various types of routine diagnostic tests. The demand for these services is neither unpredictable, nor does it usually entail catastrophic levels of cost.*

Income Effect of Insurance: Transfers from the Well to the Ill

The analysis in Figure 3.2 does not take account of any income effect on the utilization of medical care that may result from insurance coverage. If the income elasticity for medical care is greater than zero, part of the increase in quantity of medical care associated with being insured will be the result of the increase in income that the insurance provides. The increase in medical care resulting from the positive income effect should not be included in moral hazard. The size of the income effect may be trivial in the case of a flu shot, but extremely important in the case of an expensive medical intervention such as coronary artery bypass surgery. Consider the following example given by John Nyman:[3]

Actuarially fair insurance policies are purchased for a premium of $2,000 by each of a group of 10 people who have individual disposable incomes of $40,000. Each person then has a net disposable income of $38,000 after purchasing the insurance. If he or she becomes ill, an individual would spend $10,000 for medical care if uninsured. With insurance, the individual, when ill, will consume $20,000 worth of medical care, all of which is paid for by insurance. This is possible because there is a de facto $18,000 transfer in income from the other nine people. Nyman correctly argues that only the part of the increase in medical care that results from the price reduction should be counted as moral hazard.

Using this example, let us suppose that the income elasticity for medical care is +0.1. The increase in income of $18,000 will then account for $1,800 of the additional $10,000 of medical care consumed.

Offsetting Moral Hazard: Cost Sharing with Consumers

Deductibles One way to offset the problem of moral hazard is to structure an insurance policy so that it has a *deductible*, a level of expenditure that must be incurred before any benefits are paid out. Automobile and most other forms of property insurance policies usually have deductibles, with very heavy loads charged for no- or low-deductible policies. They typically have a deductible per

*The development of the health maintenance organization (HMO) that provides comprehensive health care in return for an annual fee per person or per family and that combines the function of insurer and provider of care has further widened the gap between health insurance and other forms of insurance. The analysis of HMO contracts will be deferred until Chapter Four. This chapter will focus on traditional indemnity-type health insurance contracts.

damage event. The difficulty of deciding what is a separate event in the case of health problems makes this kind of deductible impractical. Health insurance policies are much more likely to have an annual deductible, which is less effective in removing moral hazard, at least for those among the insured who tend to have annual medical expenses close to or exceeding the deductible level. As is typical of all kinds of insurance, the load factor tends to be higher on health insurance policies that have low deductibles since administrative costs constitute a higher proportion of the total cost of the policy to the insurer.

Coinsurance Another feature of health insurance that tends to reduce the extent of moral hazard is coinsurance, usually in the form of a **co-payment**, the part of the price of a given medical service paid by the insured. Co-payments help to reduce the moral hazard factor for the insured who have spent more than their deductible since medical treatments are not free to them.

Use of Customary or Usual Fees to Limit Payments It has become common practice for insurance policies that reimburse on the basis of fee-for-service to limit payment for covered services to a "customary" or "usual" fee within given geographical markets. If providers charge higher than customary fees, the insured is responsible for the balance of the fee as well as the co-payment on the covered portion. This increases the part of the risk that is borne by the consumer in traditional indemnity-type contracts. It also discourages consumer insensitivity to price, which may be another manifestation of moral hazard.

Managed Care Managed care is a bit of a catch-all phrase that describes a variety of different kinds of insurance instruments. The next chapter analyzes this complex market. It should be noted here, however, that managed care insurers have developed a set of strategies in addition to cost sharing with consumers to deal with moral hazard. Care is actually "managed" or rationed using such mechanisms as requiring that gatekeeping primary care physicians make all referrals to specialists, limiting coverage to service from providers with whom the insurance company has a contractual arrangement, and requiring permission (precertification) from the insurance company before certain services are rendered. Discipline is imposed on the supply side as well through the use of risk-sharing arrangements with providers of health care. Chapter Four will examine techniques of disciplining providers.

Stop-Loss Provisions Many policies also have annual limits on out-of-pocket expenditures (per person or per family) that must be borne by the insured. This is called a *stop-loss provision*. After the insured has paid out an amount equal to the stop-loss threshold, the insurance company pays 100 percent of additional covered medical expenses during the year. Note that stop-loss provisions *increase* the degree of moral hazard for those whose annual level of expenditure exceeds the stop-loss limit.

Imperfect (Asymmetric) Information: The Problem of Adverse Selection

If those who are more prone to buy health insurance or more extensive coverage differ from the average person in health-related personal characteristics, **adverse selection** exists. We would expect to find people with worse than average health purchasing more insurance at a given price, if we hold constant income, cost of medical care, and other factors affecting "tastes" for medical care, such as age, education, and gender.* People know more about their own health than insurance companies do. This inequality (asymmetry) in information is the basis for risk to insurers associated with adverse selection.

A familiar context in which adverse selection operates is the market for used cars. Akerlof's classic article on the effect of "lemons" in the used car market may be familiar to many of you.[4] In this market, the buyers do not know as much about the quality of cars for sale as do the sellers. Once a price is established for used cars of a given type, sellers who have cars worth more than the going market price will withdraw their cars from this market, reducing the average quality. Over time, the price of used cars in the market will fall, only cars that are lemons will remain in the market, and the market will shrink. This dynamic process is known as a *death spiral*. The market will only be stabilized if institutions are developed, such as warranties or lemon laws, that allow consumers to return defective cars.

In the health insurance market, the lemons would be people with more severe than average health problems. The lemons will be overrepresented in insurance pools, particularly in pools of the more inclusive policies. This will drive up the price, discouraging healthier people from buying insurance. Selection problems, both *adverse selection* and *positive selection*, are important phenomena in the fragmented health insurance market in the United States. The existence of adverse selection in fragmented insurance markets has been used as an argument to support a single-payer mandatory universal health insurance system. There can be no adverse selection problem if everyone is in the same insurance pool.

Insurers' Responses to Selection Problems

Insurance companies structure coverage to both avoid adverse selection and also attract lower-than-average-risk subscribers, in other words, they engage in strategies of "positive selection." Gym facilities or aerobic classes are sometimes provided by insurance companies to encourage younger, more fit individuals to become subscribers. Extremely expensive treatments for advanced cancer patients might be excluded (although this has become legally difficult to do). Marketing efforts may be concentrated in communities known to have younger and health-

---

*Feldman and co-authors found women choosing more inclusive employee health insurance packages than comparable male employees who were given the same set of options. Feldman, R. M., et al., "The Demand for Employment-Based Coverage in Health Insurance Plans," *The Journal of Human Resources*, 24 (1989): 115–142.

ier populations. In some cases, insurance companies either do not enter or withdraw from submarkets that are particularly prone to adverse selection. Since insuring groups has the effect of offsetting adverse selection, insurers often avoid the individual health insurance market.

The disappearance of insurance options due to the death spiral associated with adverse selection has been alleged to be a serious problem in the market for individual policies in regions that require community rating. However, New York State's move in 1993 to require community rating for all insurance companies selling policies to individuals or small groups does not appear to have had much effect. A study found no difference in the percentage change in individuals or small groups covered by health insurance in New York State before and after this reform, when compared with Connecticut and Pennsylvania that did not impose community rating in the small group and individual market.[5]

Can Adverse Selection Be Offset?

Some economists have questioned whether health insurance markets can reach equilibrium, given the important role of adverse selection and the potential for the death spiral phenomenon. Where there is little correlation between actual and anticipated future medical expenditures, adverse selection seems not to prevent equilibrium in the health insurance market.[6] This is because consumers no longer have much of an informational advantage in choosing the best package of insurance to cover their future expenditures.

The condition necessary for insurance markets to function even with the problems of adverse selection was well summed up 25 years ago, before many of the modern innovations in insurance plans had taken place. It is still relevant today:

Example of Adverse Selection Effects on a Community-Rating Insurer

Historically, the Blue-Cross/Blue-Shield companies were granted non-profit status partly because they agreed to use the principle of community rating within large geographic regions. Once the experience-rating commercial for-profit insurance companies became significant players in the insurance market, their costs declined over time relative to the Blues', in spite of the advantage of tax-free status to the latter. The Blues claimed that they suffered from adverse selection after the for-profit insurance companies who were allowed to use experience rating entered the market. In many states, the Blues have now been allowed to move to experience rating in their group policies in order to compete more effectively. In some locations they have chosen to do this, even when it required them to give up their tax-free non-profit status.

Source: Thomasson, Melissa A., *Did Blue Cross and Blue Shield Suffer from Adverse Selection?*, NBER Working Paper No. W9167 (Cambridge, MA: National Bureau of Economic Research, September 2002).

Neither insurance firms nor their customers have to be perfectly informed about the differences in risk properties that exist among individuals: What is required is that individuals with different risk properties differ in some characteristic that can be linked with the purchase of insurance and that somehow, insurance firms can discover this link.[7]

3   Employment-Based Group Insurance

Advantages of Employment-Based Group Insurance

The majority of nonretired Americans who have private health insurance are covered by group policies that are part of their employment contracts. Employment-based group insurance has dominated the private health insurance market since the 1950s, when price controls on wages made fringe benefits an important strategy for increasing worker compensation. Group insurance is an important mechanism for offsetting adverse selection. This is one of the reasons for its success. Community rating applies within the employment group. Thus, employment-based group health insurance results in some degree of risk sharing. Economies of scale in administrative costs and superior ability to estimate expected levels of payout also make group rates lower than those for individual policies.

Insurance companies may still use experience rating to charge higher prices to higher-risk groups. The success of this strategy depends on both the stability within the group of insured and the duration of the group's insurance coverage with the same carrier. Federal law now prohibits employment-based insurance from excluding coverage for preexisting health conditions even when workers change jobs. It does not, however, regulate what premiums can be charged to groups, although state insurance regulatory agencies may impose restrictions. Over time, as menus of choice among insurance plans have come to be offered within firms to employee groups, adverse selection has emerged as a problem not limited to the individual and small group market.

Downside to Employment-Based Insurance

When health insurance coverage is tied to employment, job loss involves the risk of losing access to affordable health insurance. The Consolidated Omnibus Budget Reconciliation Act of 1985 (COBRA) requires employers to offer former employees the option of purchasing their former group health insurance coverage for up to 18 months after termination of employment. This provides only a temporary solution and may in any event be unaffordable since the employee must pay the entire premium plus a 2 percent fee.

The tying of health insurance to employment reduces labor mobility and results in what is often called *job lock*. A body of research leads to the conclusion that employer-provided insurance has reduced labor mobility by about 25 to 30 percent.[8] The Health Insurance Portability and Accountability Act (HIPAA) of

1996 addresses part of the problem by making it illegal for insurers to exclude any employee from a group plan on the basis of health-related factors or past claims history. However, it may not be possible to find a new job that includes health benefits and, for an individual who has left employment because of ill health, it may not be possible to be employed at all. In addition, employers may be unwilling to hire a worker whose preexisting health conditions may drive up the group health insurance rates.

Tax Treatment of Employment-Based Group Health Insurance

Under federal and state income tax law, health insurance premiums paid by employers as part of the workers' compensation package have been tax-free income to employees and tax-deductible labor costs for firms since 1954. Over time this has solidified the tie between employment and group health insurance. It has led to worker preferences for higher proportions of their compensation packages in the form of health insurance, since firms can offer workers compensation that represents more after-tax (average) benefits than a cash wage package costing the firm an equal amount. There is a further saving to firms and workers in the form of payroll tax (FICA) exclusions on the portion of compensation paid in health insurance premiums rather than wages.

The income-tax-free status of employment-based health insurance has income distribution effects. Since the federal income tax is progressive, workers with higher wages and salaries who pay a higher marginal tax rate receive a larger subsidy. Consider this example:

> An employer contributes an insurance policy with an annual premium of $3,600 to every worker's compensation package. For a worker in a 40 percent marginal tax bracket, this is equivalent to $6,000 in taxable income. For a worker in a 21 percent marginal tax bracket, this is worth only $4,557 in taxable income.

4   Elasticity of Demand for Health Insurance

Do Choice Theoretic Models Apply?

Demand analysis is based on the assumption that individual consumers make choices about how much to consume. Because most health insurance in the United States is employment-based and tied to workers' compensation packages that are not usually individually negotiated, one needs to exercise caution in assuming that a model of demand based on the notion of individual choice is appropriate. Even where workers pay part of the cost of their own or their dependents' insurance directly, insurance plans may be chosen by employee compensation committees, union representatives, or employers rather than individual workers. Nonetheless, rational choice models can be applied to group decisions on the assumption that workers' representatives act as agents attempting to maximize worker utility. If that is the case, choices will tend to maximize utility for the average or typical worker.

Moreover, it has become increasingly common for a basic level of coverage to be included in compensation packages, with workers offered the option of paying the extra cost of more expensive insurance packages. This practice has provided researchers with "natural experiments" for studying the determinants of worker's demand for health insurance.

Why Should One Be Interested in Demand Elasticity for Health Insurance?

It is important to obtain information about how people respond to changes in the price of health insurance for several reasons. Widespread access to health insurance coverage is considered an important social goal. Estimates of the effects of increases in the price of health insurance can be used to make projections about the proportion of the population who are likely to be uninsured. There is also an on-going policy debate about the effect of the favorable tax treatment of workers' health insurance. Price-elasticity estimates can be used to estimate the effects on worker health insurance coverage of removing this subsidy to employment-based health insurance.

How Is the Price Elasticity of Demand for Health Insurance Measured?*

Theoretically, the price of insurance should be the load factor rather than the whole premium, since that is the cost of transferring the risk to someone else. But determining how much of the premium is the load is often virtually impossible for the researcher who does not have access to insurance companies' firm level data. The premium is therefore widely used as the price of insurance.

A change in the "quantity of insurance purchased" may take a number of forms. It may involve changing to a different level of deductible and/or coinsurance, or choosing a plan that is cheaper because it covers fewer services. At the macro-economic level, a reduction in the quantity of insurance may be manifested in a lower proportion of the population being covered by any health insurance, by the same number of people having less extensive coverage, or by a combination of the two.

A number of indirect measures of the price of health insurance have been employed by researchers:

1. The marginal income tax rate has been used as a proxy variable for the price of insurance.[9] The marginal tax rate is the rate that applies to the last dollar earned. The higher the marginal tax rate is, the lower the effective price of insurance. Using the marginal tax rate as a substitute for price suffers from the

---

*The concept of price elasticity of demand and the formula for measuring it are explained in Appendix 1, p. 325. Price elasticity of demand is also used throughout Chapter Two.

flaw that income is not held constant as it should be when we try to isolate the price effects on the demand for a good. This results in a distortion to the extent that the demand for health insurance is subject to an income effect.

2. Studies have sometimes used the size of an employee group as a proxy for the price of insurance, since insurance rates tend to be lower for larger buying groups due to economies of scale. A difficulty with this approach is that the demand for health insurance may be associated with the type of firm workers choose. For instance, people who are more risk-averse and therefore likely to purchase more insurance may also be more likely to work for larger firms.

3. Sometimes, the effects of price changes can be measured directly. Participants in the RAND Health Insurance Experiment who were assigned to insurance plans that covered less than 100 percent of their medical bills were offered several supplementary insurance options. Using these data, Marquis and Phelps obtained an estimate of −0.6 for the price elasticity of demand for health insurance.[10] More recently, natural experiments were provided when three large universities moved away from subsidizing all employee health insurance plans to covering only a basic level of health insurance for their employees. When the University of California changed from subsidizing plans that were more expensive than the base plan to paying only the premium on the least expensive option, an increase in monthly premiums of less than $10 was observed to lead to a 500 percent increase in switching between plans.[11] When Harvard University stopped subsidizing higher-priced plans and moved to a level dollar contribution scheme, the price elasticity estimate for out-of-pocket premium costs was found to be approximately −2.[12] In this case, a more inclusive plan had to be eliminated because adverse selection created a death spiral effect.[13] Even higher price elasticities of demand for insurance were found among Stanford University employees who were offered a menu of differently priced insurance options. The upper end of the range of estimates of price elasticities for insurance at Stanford was −3.[14] Studies of employee responses to different insurance options in a group of Twin Cities' (Minneapolis and St. Paul, Minnesota) firms yielded price-elasticity estimates in the range of −1.67 to −1.7.[15] The majority of studies support the notion that the amount of health insurance Americans will purchase is quite sensitive to price.

5   Optimal Insurance Contracts

Principles of Optimal Insurance Contracts

Specifying a formal model of optimization involves a presentation beyond the level of mathematical sophistication assumed in this book. However, we can gain some insights from considering what factors must be taken into account in specifying an optimal insurance contract. There are trade-offs between risk sharing and the problems of moral hazard and adverse selection. The costs and benefits have to be weighed. Optimality would be approached if patients paid out-of-pocket for their medical care up to the point where the marginal social cost of *less* risk sharing was just offset by the marginal social benefit from less "wasteful" use of medical care. Put another way, sharing the risk associated with costs of illness increases sick individuals' well-being (utility), but it tends to increase the consumption of medical care to a level where the marginal benefit is less than the marginal cost, since others are sharing in the cost.

A problem in constructing optimal insurance policies is associated with adverse selection. Where there is a menu of health insurance plans available, the less healthy will be more attracted to the more generous plans. A common form of partial risk sharing requires the more generous plan to charge only for the extra cost associated with the extra benefits. In this scheme, it is assumed that health-related characteristics of members of different plans are, on average, identical. This scheme is often used in the pricing of employment-based insurance. However, this degree of risk sharing still has the potential for leading into a death spiral effect in which the more generous plan attracts only the most high-risk individuals and therefore becomes prohibitively expensive.

A consideration of optimal insurance also needs to look at the degree of risk sharing between health-care providers and insurers. This form of risk sharing has become much more prevalent since the 1980s in both the private and public insurance markets. Optimality requires a balance such that providers neither provide more than the medically appropriate amount of care nor skimp on care.

Glied and Remler maintain that health insurance contracts that use the mechanism of reducing the price of medical care in the case of illness are always only second-best solutions to the contracting problem. If it were possible to construct a complete contingent contract that would specify the amount of income which would be transferred into each illness state, this would be preferable. They argue that it would provide better financial protection to the few individuals who encounter the need for extremely expensive medical treatment. Risk sharing with that subgroup is only very imperfectly handled by the existing kinds of contracts that rely heavily on cost sharing to deal with the problem of moral hazard.[16]

One problem in modeling the optimal insurance contract is that the degree of moral hazard may vary by type of illness or type of medical service. This may lead to very complicated insurance contracts with different degrees of co-payments for different services or treatments.

Empirical Work on Optimal Insurance Characteristics

Researchers who have attempted to construct optimal insurance contracts have come up with a wide variety of results. Estimates of the optimal coinsurance rates vary from 58 to 25 percent. Optimal stop-loss limits vary from $1,000 to >$25,000. Blomquist, using the RAND Health Insurance Experiment data, constructed an optimal policy that features coinsurance rates that vary by level of spending. In this plan, up to an expenditure of $1,000 out-of-pocket, one would pay a 27 percent coinsurance rate. Beyond that level, coinsurance rates would be gradually reduced. When out-of-pocket expenses rise above $30,000, the coinsurance rate declines to 5 percent.*

6   Effects of Health Insurance on the Consumption of Medical Care

Elasticity Estimates

We have seen that health insurance operates to increase the quantity demanded of medical care by lowering its effective price to consumers. The magnitude of the effect will depend on how much the policy reduces the out-of-pocket payment below market price and on the price elasticity of demand for medical care. A number of studies have used different levels of insurance coverage, that is, different levels of co-payments, to measure the price of medical services.† There is a potential problem in that the amount of insurance coverage people choose may not be independent of their demand for medical care. The RAND Health Insurance Experiment provided estimates that are free from this bias; and the study design allows estimation of the effects of marginal rates of insurance coverage on quantity of medical care consumed. As was noted in Chapter Two, the RAND study found a range of co-insurance elasticity estimates for medical care centering on −0.2.[17] This means that when the co-insurance rate changes by 10 percent, the quantity of medical care utilized changes by 2 percent. This estimate is still widely used in economic studies and by actuaries designing insurance policies[18]

Insurance Coverage Increases the Importance of Time Costs

When insurance coverage lowers the monetary cost of medical services to individuals, the time cost becomes a more important component of total cost. This will tend to increase the time-price elasticity of demand for medical care, with the result that consumers may shift to using medical services which have higher monetary costs but involve less waiting-room or travel time. Increases in a person's wage or salary will raise the opportunity cost of time, and this will lead to a tendency to substitute away from time-intensive medical care. To the extent that insurance coverage is positively correlated with earnings, the substitution from time-intensive medical services to more expensive services will be enhanced.

---

*A summary of utility and cost functions used to construct optimal insurance parameters and some of the empirical findings is given in Cutler, David M., and Richard J. Zeckhauser, "The Anatomy of Health Insurance," *Handbook of Health Economics*, Vol. 1A, Anthony J. Culyer and Joseph P. Newhouse, eds. (Amsterdam: Elsevier, 2000), pp. 586–588.

†An excellent summary of these studies is found in Cutler and Zeckhauser, ibid., pp. 580–584.

Effect of Insurance on the Substitution of Medical Care for Alternative Forms of Health Care

Insurance coverage, which lowers the *relative* price of medical care, may also cause individuals to substitute medical care for other inputs into health. A person might be more disposed to use psychotherapy rather than conversations with nonmedical counselors to alleviate the symptoms of anxiety or depression if insurance covers mental health care. In the following hypothetical example, insurance coverage results in a substitution of medical care (physical therapy) for exercise at a gym.

Physical Therapy Versus Gym Membership

Linda R. decides to undertake a regular program of supervised exercise to overcome her aches and pains. An hour per day, five days a week, at the gym averages out to a cost of $40 per hour. The membership and supplemental fees in a gymnasium or health club will not be covered by Linda's health insurance. The services of a physical therapy center that has the same equipment will be covered, if recommended by a physician. Linda knows an orthopedist who will write a prescription for physical therapy. His fee is $100 for an office visit. An hour-long appointment with the physical therapist costs $80. Linda has met the annual deductible on her insurance policy, so her co-payment rate for covered services is 20 percent.

The effective cost to Linda of the gymnasium sessions (for four weeks) is $800. The out-of-pocket cost of the physical therapist is $320 plus 20 percent of $100 for the physician visit = $340. The cost of physical therapy declines if one physician visit entitles Linda to more than a month of physical therapy.

If fitness is equally well promoted by gym or physiotherapy visits and there is no difference in the time required for the two alternative activities, which will Linda, a rational consumer, choose? In this case, the reduced price of physical therapy resulting from insurance coverage will cause her to substitute medical care for membership in a gym.

Now, figure which alternative Linda will choose if her co-payment rate is increased to 50 percent.

Effect of the Community's Insurance Coverage on the Market Price of Health Care

More extensive insurance coverage on the part of a community will tend to increase the quantity of health care that will be consumed at a given *market* price,

that is, there will be a *shift in demand*. Figure 3.3 illustrates a hypothetical increase in the community's demand for health care resulting from an increase in
insurance coverage.

The net change in the quantity of medical care consumed by the community
will depend on the change in its market price as well as the change in insurance
coverage. This, in turn, depends on the nature of the supply conditions in this
market. If the price of medical care rises as more is supplied, as is the case with a
typically upward sloping supply curve, *SS* in Figure 3.3, then the effect of the
community having more insurance coverage at least partly offsets the advantage
to any one person. Over time, out-of-pocket expenses for the same basket of
medical goods will rise with increases in the market price of medical care. Insurance companies will also experience higher payouts. They will respond by raising premiums charged for the same coverage, or by holding premiums constant
but reducing coverage.

What happens to the community's total expenditure on medical care as insurance coverage increases is a question of considerable interest to health policy an-
alysts. In Figure 3.3, the community's expenditure on medical care, net of insurance costs, is represented by the area $P_1 \times Q_1$ before the expansion of insurance
coverage and by $P_2 \times Q_2$ after demand shifts outward. Total expenditure on
health care will rise with an increase in insurance coverage even though total
out-of-pocket expenditure may not. Whether it will depends on the relative magnitude of the reduction in effective medical prices for the insured (resulting from,
for instance, lower co-payments) and of the price increases resulting from the
shift in demand. A full consideration of expenditure on health care should, of
course, also include the expenditure on insurance.

Research based on the RAND Health Insurance Experiment data estimated that
only approximately 10 percent of the increase in health-care expenditure in the
United States between the end of World War II and the mid-1980s was associated
with an increase in insurance coverage.[19]

Figure 3.3

The Community's
Insurance Coverage
and Demand for
Health Care

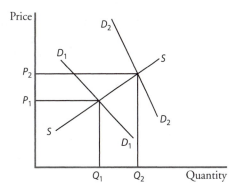

7   Is There a Welfare Loss Associated with "Excess" Insurance?

For several decades, there was agreement among the majority of economists that the favorable tax treatment afforded to health insurance created a **welfare loss** to society by inducing workers to have more extensive insurance coverage than is socially optimal.[20] The argument was that the tax-free status of employee health insurance leads individuals to be insured to the point where the marginal value of the insurance benefit is less than the marginal cost of the insurance in taxable dollars.[21]

In spite of the difficulty in specifying optimal insurance contracts, attempts were made to measure the welfare loss to society of "excess" health insurance. Martin Feldstein (1973) and Feldman and Dowd (1991), updating Feldstein's work, compared the monetary value of benefits to insured individuals with the costs to society of the extra amount of insurance coverage resulting from its tax-free status.[22] Feldstein measured the quantity of insurance coverage as the inverse of the average coinsurance rate of the community times the proportion of the community covered by health insurance. In his work, the price of health care is viewed as "expenditure risk." The group of insured consumers has a *gross gain in reduced expenditure risk*. However, the community as a whole has a *gross loss from the price distortion*, that is, the increase in price of health care induced by the subsidizing of health insurance. The net welfare effect is the difference between the two.

The cost to society of subsidizing health insurance was considered to be a function of the price elasticity of demand for medical care and the elasticity of supply for medical services. The social cost will be greater the lower the elasticity of supply is, since the effect of the increased demand for medical care will then cause a correspondingly greater increase in its price. (See Figure 3.3.) Feldstein argued that only in the very unlikely circumstances of both a highly inelastic demand for medical care and supply prices that are insensitive to level of insurance would the welfare gain from the subsidization of employment-based health insurance ever outweigh the welfare loss to society.[23]

A counter argument is that the favorable tax treatment of health insurance, which has stimulated the growth of employment-based group insurance, has increased access to group insurance on the part of those who otherwise may not have purchased individual health insurance policies. Thomasson argues that the social utility of wider access to insurance has to be considered as well as the disutility of excess amounts of insurance coverage for those who are covered.[24] John Nyman has argued that the estimates of negative effects of extra insurance that do not take account of the positive effects of income transfers from the well to the sick which insurance provides result in a serious overestimation of the negative welfare effects of extra insurance and exaggerate the amount of moral hazard. (See the discussion in Section 2 on page 48.) The income effect will be larger in the case of very expensive procedures, particularly those that would be unaffordable without insurance coverage.

Nyman maintains that the correct measure of the welfare loss due to moral hazard would calculate how much extra medical care a consumer would demand if he or she purchased an "actuarially fair contract" when ill.[25] Most empirical studies have examined the effects of increasing the extent of insurance coverage for those who already have some insurance coverage rather than studying the benefits of providing access to insurance for those previously not covered. A study by Nyman that did address the access issue found that removing the favorable tax treatment of employment-based health insurance would reduce medical spending by considerably less than has been predicted in most of the literature, and that more than half of the reduction in spending would result from a decline in the number of people having any coverage rather than from a reduction in generosity of benefits.[26]

Research by Ketsche and Custer further questions the extent of the negative welfare effects of the tax treatment of health insurance. They provide evidence that the tax subsidy helps to increase access to the health insurance market by increasing the probability that workers who are high-risk because of the health status of themselves or their family members will have insurance coverage and by disproportionately affecting the generosity of health insurance coverage for high-risk workers.[27]

8   Trends in Insurance Coverage

Over the past 20 years, there has been a noticeable trend in employers cutting back on the proportion of employees' health insurance premiums that they pay. Firms increasingly offer only a base-level health insurance plan and give employees the option of paying the differences if they choose more extensive coverage. (Examples of this practice at several major universities, including Harvard and Stanford, were presented earlier in this chapter in the section on price elasticity of demand for medical care.) Gruber and McKnight consider this cutback to be a more important change than the change in the proportion of employers offering any health insurance coverage to workers. By 1998, only 28 percent of workers with employer-provided insurance had their insurance costs completely paid by the employer in contrast with 44 percent in 1982.[28]

Several reasons have been given for this phenomenon in addition to the rise in health insurance premiums: the recession in the late 1980s and early 1990s; the extension of Medicaid coverage to more low-income worker families; and the growth in dual-earner families, which reduced the pressure on employers to cover dependents. The decline in unionization has been found to explain approximately a quarter of the reduction in the generosity of plans.[29] However, the rise in health insurance premiums is undoubtedly a major contributor. In 2002, during the annual November and December open enrollment period in health insurance plans, premiums quoted showed an average increase of 27 percent over the premiums offered the previous year.[30] Similar increases occurred between December 2002 and December 2003. Although the expected increase in health insurance premiums in December 2004 is only about 10 percent, this is still more than double the overall inflation rate in the United States.[31]

The rise in insurance premiums and the cutback in the proportion of premiums that employers are willing to pay have left many workers with insurance premiums that they find unaffordable. Health insurance coverage of workers has declined, in large part because workers have not exercised options to purchase it. Cutler found a significant drop in take-up rates on the part of employees offered insurance over the period 1988 to 2001.[32] The proportion of workers covered by employer-provided health insurance fell from 80 percent to 73 percent between 1982 and 1998.[33] There are important policy implications associated with the fact that a growing proportion of the 44 million uninsured Americans in 2004 were workers or families of those who were employed. This concern will be revisited in Chapter Fourteen.

Summary

The demand for health insurance exists because of the uncertainty associated with a person's state of health and the risk of very large expenditures in the case of illness. Health insurance provides risk sharing between the insured and insurer, pooling of risks among the insured, and sometimes risk sharing between the insurer and health-care provider. The latter will be discussed in the next chapter. Insurance is a mechanism both for transferring funds from the state when one is well to the "unexpected and costly" state of illness, and for transferring benefits in any given time period from those who are well to the ill. Since most private health insurance is purchased through the workplace in group plans, there is necessarily some degree of community rating involved in the pricing of insurance policies. Group insurance is an important mechanism for dealing with adverse selection.

Insurance increases the demand for medical care and also increases its market price. After decades of discussion and analysis, questions still remain about the social welfare effects of subsidizing employment-based group health insurance through the favorable tax treatment it receives. Recent literature suggests that there are positive welfare effects associated with increasing access to group insurance as well as the long-established negative effects associated with moral hazard. Moreover, increases in the price of insurance and cutbacks in the proportion of premium costs that employers are willing to include in workers' compensation packages have shifted the focus of policy concerns from whether employees have too lavish insurance coverage to whether too few have any insurance coverage at all.

Appendix: Government Regulation of the Private Health Insurance Market

1. Most aspects of insurance markets are regulated at the state level. Regulatory requirements vary widely throughout the United States. For instance, some states require all insurance companies to use community rating in small-group and individual insurance markets. Most require community rating for non-profit insurance companies. There is one notable exception to the

states' jurisdiction to regulate health insurance. The Employee Retirement and Income Security Act (ERISA) of 1974 gave the federal government the authority to regulate self-insured plans.

2. The Consolidated Omnibus Budget Reconciliation Act of 1985 (COBRA) requires employers to offer former employees the option to purchase their former group health insurance policy for up to 18 months after termination of employment. The employee must pay the entire premium plus a 2 percent fee.

3. An important piece of federal legislation that altered the ability of insurance companies to exclude individuals from coverage was the Health Insurance Portability and Accountability Act (HIPAA) of 1996 (the Kassebaum–Kennedy Act). HIPAA covers all health plans including ERISA plans. The main provisions of HIPAA are:

   a. Eligibility of any individual to enroll or continue to be enrolled in a group plan cannot be conditional on any health-related factors or claims experience.

   b. Insurance companies in the small group market (2–50 employees) may not exclude a group or an individual employee on the basis of health status.

   c. Individuals within a group cannot be charged a higher premium based on their health status.

   d. All group coverage and individual coverage must be renewed, except in cases of fraud, non-payment of premiums, or when the insurance company leaves the market.

   e. Insurance companies must provide at least two policy options. If these are less- and more-inclusive plans, there must be a risk-adjustment mechanism (to mitigate adverse selection problems).

   f. An insurer must provide coverage to an individual coming off of group insurance if the individual had coverage for 18 months, is not eligible for other group insurance, is not eligible for or has exhausted COBRA-type coverage, unless the individual was terminated from the group plan for nonpayment of premium.

Key Concepts

Load or loading fee

Experience rating

Community rating

Moral hazard

Indemnity policy

Co-payment

Adverse selection

Welfare loss

Suggested Readings

1. Cutler, David and R. K. Zeckhauser, "The Anatomy of Health Insurance," in *Handbook of Health Economics,* Vol. 1A, Anthony J. Culyer and Joseph P. Newhouse, eds. (Amsterdam: Elsevier, 2000), Chap. 11.

2. Arrow, Kenneth, "Uncertainty and the Welfare Economics of Medical Care," *American Economic Review,* 53, (1963): 941–973.

3. Glied, Sherry A., "Health Insurance and Market Failure Since Arrow," *Journal of Health Economics,* 26 (2001): 957–965.

Problems

1. The following information is available, based on market prices for physician services:

Price ($)	Average Quantity (office visits per year)
50	8
75	7
100	5
125	4
150	3

   Compute the price elasticity of demand for physician office visits for the group of people sampled when prices of office visits increase from $100 to $150. Use the preferred formula for elasticity: percentage change in quantity/percentage change in price, where $P = (P_1 + P_2)/2$ and $Q = (Q_1 + Q_2)/2$.

2. Now suppose that the same group of people acquire health insurance with no deductible and with a 50 percent co-payment shared between insurer and insured. Assuming that people now make decisions based on the out-of-pocket cost rather than the market price, what will be the price elasticity of demand for physician visits in the same (market) price range?

3. What would be the annual premium to a subscriber of the cooperative insurance plan described in the following?

   Imagine a situation in which it is reasonably certain that for groups of 1,000 people or larger, 1 out of 100 will have an illness resulting in medical costs of $15,000 each year. Given this information, a group of 1,000 associates joins together to pool their risks, each contributing an equal amount to a contingency fund. The money in the contingency fund is invested in such a way as to earn enough to cover the costs of running the fund, thus, there is no loading fee.

4. All workers have identical health insurance coverage. Their polices have no deductibles. From year 1 to year 2, the co-payment rate falls from 25 percent to 20 percent. This is accompanied by an increase in insurance premiums of

Suggested Readings

1. Cutler, David and R. K. Zeckhauser, "The Anatomy of Health Insurance," in *Handbook of Health Economics,* Vol. 1A, Anthony J. Culyer and Joseph P. Newhouse, eds. (Amsterdam: Elsevier, 2000), Chap. 11.

2. Arrow, Kenneth, "Uncertainty and the Welfare Economics of Medical Care," *American Economic Review,* 53, (1963): 941–973.

3. Glied, Sherry A., "Health Insurance and Market Failure Since Arrow," *Journal of Health Economics,* 26 (2001): 957–965.

Problems

1. The following information is available, based on market prices for physician services:

Price ($)	Average Quantity (office visits per year)
50	8
75	7
100	5
125	4
150	3

   Compute the price elasticity of demand for physician office visits for the group of people sampled when prices of office visits increase from $100 to $150. Use the preferred formula for elasticity: percentage change in quantity/percentage change in price, where $P = (P_1 + P_2)/2$ and $Q = (Q_1 + Q_2)/2$.

2. Now suppose that the same group of people acquire health insurance with no deductible and with a 50 percent co-payment shared between insurer and insured. Assuming that people now make decisions based on the out-of-pocket cost rather than the market price, what will be the price elasticity of demand for physician visits in the same (market) price range?

3. What would be the annual premium to a subscriber of the cooperative insurance plan described in the following?

   Imagine a situation in which it is reasonably certain that for groups of 1,000 people or larger, 1 out of 100 will have an illness resulting in medical costs of $15,000 each year. Given this information, a group of 1,000 associates joins together to pool their risks, each contributing an equal amount to a contingency fund. The money in the contingency fund is invested in such a way as to earn enough to cover the costs of running the fund, thus, there is no loading fee.

4. All workers have identical health insurance coverage. Their polices have no deductibles. From year 1 to year 2, the co-payment rate falls from 25 percent to 20 percent. This is accompanied by an increase in insurance premiums of

[3] Nyman, John A., "The Economics of Moral Hazard Revisited," *Journal of Health Economics*, 18 (1999): 811–824.

[4] See, for instance, Akerlof, George, "The Market for 'Lemons': Qualitative Uncertainty and the Market Mechanism," *Quarterly Journal of Economics*, 84 (1970): 488–500 and Arrow, Kenneth J., "Uncertainty and the Welfare Economics of Medical Care," op. cit.

[5] Buchmueller, Thomas and John DiNardo, *Did Community Rating Induce an Adverse Selection Death Spiral? Evidence from New York, Pennsylvania, and Connecticut*, NBER Working Paper No. 6872. (Cambridge, MA: National Bureau of Economic Research, 1999).

[6] See Rothschild, Michael and Joseph Stiglitz, "Equilibrium in Competitive Insurance Markets: An Essay on the Economics of Imperfect Information, *"Quarterly Journal of Economics,"* 90 (1976): 629–649; Cave, Jonathan, *Equilibrium in Insurance Markets with Asymmetric Information and Adverse Selection*, RAND Report R-3015-HHS (Santa Monica, CA: Rand Corporation, 1984); and Marquis, M. Susan and Charles E. Phelps, "Price Elasticity and Adverse Selection in the Demand for Supplementary Health Insurance," *Economic Inquiry*, 25 (1987): 299–313.

[7] Rothschild and Stiglitz (1976), op. cit., p. 640.

[8] See Gruber, Jonathan, "Health Insurance and the Labor Market," *Handbook of Health Economics*, Vol. 1A, Anthony J. Culyer and Joseph P. Newhouse, eds. (Amsterdam: Elsevier, 2000), p. 672.

[9] See, for instance, Taylor, Amy K. and Gail R. Wilensky, "Tax Expenditures and the Demand for Private Health Insurance," in *Market Oriented Reforms in Federal Health Policy*, J. Meyer, ed. (Washington, DC: American Enterprise Institute for Public Policy Research, 1983), pp. 163–184 and Holmer, Martin R., "Tax Policy and the Demand for Health Insurance," *Journal of Health Economics*, 3 (1984): 203–221.

[10] Marquis and Phelps, (1987), op cit., p. 307.

[11] Buchmueller, Thomas C. and Paul J. Feldstein, "The Effect of Price on Switching Among Health Plans," *Journal of Health Economics*, 16 (1997): 231–247.

[12] Cutler, David M. and Sarah J. Reber, "Paying for Health Insurance," *Quarterly Journal of Economics*, 113 (1998): 433–466.

[13] See Cutler, David M. and Richard J Zeckhauser, "The Anatomy of Health Insurance, *Handbook of Health Economics*, Vol. 1A, op. cit., p. 623.

[14] Royalty, Anne Beeson and Neil Solomon, "Health Plan Choice: Price Elasticities in a Managed Care Competition Setting," *The Journal of Human Resources*, 34 (1999): 33–34.

[15] Feldman, R. M., et al. "The Demand for Employment-Based Coverage in Health Insurance Plans," *Journal of Human Resources*, 24 (1989); Dowd, Bryan and R. M. Feldman, "Premium Elasticities of Health Plan Choice," *Inquiry*, 31 (Winter 1994–1995): 438–444.

[16] Glied, Sherry A. and Dahlia K. Remler, "What Every Public Finance Economist Needs to Know About Health Economics: Recent Advances and Unsolved Questions," *National Tax Journal*, 55 (2002): 771–789.

[17] Newhouse, Joseph P. and the Insurance Experiment Group (1993), op. cit. In this study co-insurance rate is used as a proxy variable for the price of medical care.

[18] A number of studies concur in this estimate. See particularly Newhouse and the Insurance Experiment Group (1993), op. cit., and Zweifel, Peter and Willard G. Manning, "Moral Hazard and Consumer Incentives in Health Care," in *Handbook of Health Economics*, Vol. 1A, op. cit., pp. 409–459.

[19] Newhouse, Joseph P. "Has the Erosion of the Medical Market Place Ended?" *Journal of Health Politics, Policy and Law*, 13 (1988): 263–277.

[20] See Arrow, Kenneth, "Welfare Analysis of Changes in Health Coinsurance Rates," in *The Role of Health Insurance in the Health Services Sector*, R. N. Rosett, ed., (New York:

NBER, Conference Series No. 27), pp. 2–27 and Ehrlich, Isaac, "Comment on Arrow," ibid., pp. 28-33 for a discussion of the effects of elasticity of supply of health services on the welfare implications of changes in health-care coinsurance rates.

[21] Feldstein, Martin S. and Bernard Friedman, "Tax Subsidies: The Rational Demand for Insurance and the Health Care Crisis," *Journal of Public Economics*, 7 (1977): 155–178; Gruber, Jonathan and James Poterba, "Tax Incentives and the Decision to Purchase Health Insurance: Evidence from the Self-Employed," *Quarterly Journal of Economics*, 109 (1994): 701–733; and for an excellent summary of the literature, see Pauly, Mark V., "Taxation, Health Insurance, and Market Failure in the Medical Economy," *Journal of Economic Literature*, 24 (1986): 629–675.

[22] Feldstein, Martin, "The Welfare Loss of Excess Health Insurance," *Journal of Political Economy*, 81 (1973): 251–280. The net welfare effects of reductions in health insurance were estimated using coinsurance rates to measure level of health insurance coverage. Increasing co-payment level was found to reduce private benefits much less than it reduced social costs.

See Feldman, Roger and Bryan Dowd, "A New Estimate of the Welfare Loss of Excess Health Insurance," *American Economic Review*, 81 (1991): 297–301. Using the RAND Health Insurance Experiment data for 1984, Feldman and Dowd estimated the net welfare loss to society of changing the co-payment level from 95 percent of the cost of medical care to 0. Using several different assumptions about price elasticity effects and risk aversion, they also derived estimates of welfare gains ranging between $33.4 billion and $109.3 billion a year (in 1969) from raising the coinsurance rate from 33 to 50 percent and a net gain of from $1.9 billion to $4.8 billion from further raising the coinsurance rate to 67 percent.

[23] Removing the tax-free status of employment-based health insurance was found to reduce insurance coverage by approximately 27 percent. One study estimated that this would translate into an increase in the average co-payment level of 20 to 25 percent. See Chernick, Howard, et al., "Tax Policy Toward Health Insurance and the Demand for Medical Services," *Journal of Health Economics*, 6 (1987): 1–25.

[24] Thomasson, Melissa A., *The Importance of Group Coverage: How Tax Policy Shaped U.S. Health Insurance*, NBER Working Paper No. 7543 (Cambridge, MA: National Bureau of Economic Research, 2000).

[25] Nyman (1999), op. cit., pp. 820–821.

[26] Nyman, John A., "The Income Transfer Effect, the Access Value of Insurance, and the RAND Health Insurance Experiment," *Journal of Health Economics*, 20 (2001): 295–298.

[27] Ketsche, P. G. and Custer, W. S., "The Effect of Marginal Tax Rate on the Probability of Employment-Based Insurance by Risk Group," *Health Services Research*, 35 (2000): 239–251; Ketsche, P. G., "An Analysis of the Effect of Tax Policy on Health Insurance Purchases by Risk Group," *Journal of Risk and Insurance*, 71 (2004): 91–113.

[28] Gruber, Jonathan and Robin McKnight, *Why Did Employee Health Insurance Contributions Rise?*, NBER Working Paper No. 8878 (Cambridge, MA: National Bureau of Economic Research, April 2002).

[29] Buchmueller, Thomas, et al., "Union Effects on Health Insurance Provision and Coverage in the United States," *Industrial and Labor Relations Review*, 55 (2002): 610–627.

[30] Geary, Leslie Haggin, "Choosing Your Health Plan," *CNN/Money.Com*, November 1, 2002.

[31] Freudenheim, Milt, "Increase in Health Care Premiums Are Slowing," *New York Times*, May 27, 2004, p. C1.

[32] Cutler, David M., *Employee Costs and the Decline in Health Insurance Coverage*, NBER Working Paper No. W9036 (Cambridge, MA: National Bureau of Economic Research, June 2002).

[33] Gruber and McKnight (2002), op. cit.

CHAPTER FOUR

The Evolution to Managed Care

The transition from Marcus Welby to managed care has been remarkable. In less than thirty years, the American health care system has evolved from one in which patients placed complete trust in their PCPs (primary care physicians) to one in which they delegate responsibility for life-and-death decisions to individuals and institutions they know little about and trust even less.*

1 Introduction

Although this quote is without doubt a bit of an exaggeration, the delivery of health care in the United States has evolved, most dramatically since the 1990s, to a system in which the majority of employees in the United States and a large part of the retired population are enrolled in some form of managed care insurance plan. The traditional solo-practitioner family doctor, who has no contractual arrangements with insurance companies, has also become a rarity. The main reason for the growth of managed care appears to be the inability of insurance companies to contain costs through the cost-sharing arrangements with consumers in traditional indemnity policies.

---

*Dranove, David, *The Economic Evolution of American Health Care* (Princeton, NJ: Princeton University Press, 2000): pp. 8–9. Marcus Welby was a fictional family doctor in a popular TV program of the 1970s. He was played by Robert Young, who was known throughout the United States for his portrayal of the father in the earlier traditional family TV series, "Father Knows Best."

This chapter will provide an overview of the evolution in private health insurance in the United States over the past half-century, outline the main types of managed care plans, compare managed care and traditional indemnity insurance, and consider whether managed care has been an effective deterrent to rising medical care costs.

What Is Managed Care?

The term *managed care* today includes a wide variety of contractual arrangements. Initially, the term referred to the integration of insurance and provision of health care embodied in the **health maintenance organization (HMO)**. The classic HMO supplied comprehensive care from a group of employee-providers in return for an annual prepaid fee, called a *capitation fee*. A number of other types of managed care contracts have since been developed. Managed care contracts have a few common characteristics. Insurance companies enter into contractual arrangements with providers of medical care. Subscribers are given financial incentives to use the in-network providers of care. This permits insurers to use cost-containment strategies both with respect to consumers of care and providers of care.

The Transition to Managed Care: A Brief History

For most of the twentieth century, the American Medical Association (AMA) strongly and effectively opposed insurance plans that entered into contracts with physicians to provide prepaid comprehensive care to subscribers. The resistance to such plans was based on opposition to any limitations on fee-for-service contracts. Legislation severely limited prepaid plans, and physicians were disciplined by their local medical societies if they participated in them.

There have been regional differences in the insurance market since the 1920s. California and the Pacific Northwest had a much earlier exposure to HMOs, and market penetration of HMOs was earlier and more extensive there. Examples of early HMOs were the Ross Loos, organized in Los Angeles in 1929, and Kaiser-Permanente, set up in Northern California in the 1920s to provide health care to the employees of the Kaiser company. Over time, Kaiser-Permanente broadened its enrollment beyond Kaiser employees and subsequently spread to other parts of the country. It is still the largest non-profit HMO in the United States, with a dominant presence in California and Hawaii.

An exception on the East Coast was the Group Health Association, an HMO established in the 1930s in the District of Columbia. It was such a success that when the federal government established the Federal Employees Health Benefits Program (FEHBP) in 1960, employees demanded to have the popular Group Health Association included as an option.

The Health Maintenance Organization Act, passed in 1973 as part of President Richard Nixon's plan to curb inflation, provided government subsidies for the establishment of non-profit prepaid insurance plans. HMOs received further governmental support in 1979, when the amendment of Public Law 93-641 restricted the ability of state regulatory agencies to prevent HMOs from constructing facilities or opening offices in a given area.* In spite of this legislation, the medical establishment continued to oppose HMOs, and enrollment in anything other than traditional indemnity plans involved only a small proportion of American workers until well into the 1980s. Except for California and the Pacific Northwest, the insurance market continued to be dominated by indemnity plans for another decade.

The health insurance market changed dramatically in the 1990s. By 1993, 70 percent of Americans who had any health insurance (including Medicare and Medicaid recipients) were enrolled in some form of managed care plan.[1] Between 1993 and 1995, a growth spurt in managed care increased the proportion of workers covered by such plans from about one-half to three-quarters.[2] Whereas in 1980, over 90 percent of privately insured Americans were enrolled in indemnity plans, by 1996, only 3 percent were.[3] Blue-Cross Blue-Shield plans still dominated the individual (as opposed to group) health insurance market in the late 1990s, but by then they had incorporated many aspects of managed care into their policies.[4]

Originally, the growth of managed care was limited by many legal requirements. As managed care has achieved prominence in the U.S. health insurance market in the 1990s, there has been a new wave of legislation imposing restrictions on managed care contracts. For instance, a number of states have enacted laws requiring managed care plans to include in their networks "any willing providers." This prevents selective contracting.

Main Types of Managed Care Contracts

Health Maintenance Organization (HMO)

The original form of HMO was the closed-panel or staff HMO. This type of HMO is a vertically integrated provider of health care, employing physicians directly and owning or controlling hospitals and laboratories. Several other types of HMOs now exist. An HMO may contract with a physician group practice or with a network of providers for the medical services it offers to its members. The **Independent Practice Association (IPA)** is a form of HMO that contracts with individual providers, who maintain their private practices and retain the options of treating other patients on a fee-for-service basis and of contracting with other managed care organizations. The ability of an IPA-type HMO to pay participating physicians on a capitation (per patient) basis, or to negotiate discounted fees if they are paid on a fee-for-service basis, depends on the market power of the

---

*This was accomplished by the ruling that state Certificate of Need (CON) laws, which limit hospital expansion unless need for new facilities can be demonstrated, did not apply to HMOs. The effect of CON laws on the hospital market will be discussed in Chapter Eight.

HMO in a region relative to the market power of the physician practice. The IPA is now the dominant form of HMO in the United States.

Insurance coverage for HMO subscribers is limited to services provided by employees of the HMO or those who have a contractual arrangement with it. An essential part of the structure is the requirement that primary care physicians, acting as gatekeepers, control referrals for patients by selecting laboratories and specialists from among those who participate in the HMO. In most HMO settings, consumers have some choice of primary care physician.

Most HMOs today charge a small co-payment for at least some services, but care is managed less by cost sharing with consumers than is the case in indemnity policies. Co-payments tend to be lower and are usually a fixed fee, typically $5 to $20 per visit, rather than a percentage of the fee, as in indemnity policies. Most HMOs still provide some services free of charge, such as diagnostic screening (mammograms), annual physical checkups, or routine pediatric visits. Utilization of these services that "maintain health" may reduce the long-run costs of the HMO if the health of subscribers is improved and a substantial part of the subscriber pool remains with the same plan over a number of years.

Preferred Provider Organization (PPO)

Preferred provider organization (PPO) plans emerged in the 1980s. They generally charge subscribers small co-payments, but have no deductibles when providers use providers who are contractual members of the network. Certain other goods and services such as laboratory tests and durable medical equipment are often completely free if one uses within-network providers. In this way, PPO plans resemble IPA HMOs. A PPO plan does not require the use of a primary care physician as a gatekeeper. The PPO also offers its insured the option of going outside the network for many services, although deductibles and higher co-payments then apply. In this way, the PPO has some of the characteristics of the traditional indemnity policy. Reimbursement for surgical procedures and certain other treatments and diagnostic tests typically requires the patient to obtain precertification (also called preauthorization) approval from the insurer before using the service.

PPOs generally pay providers on a discounted fee-for-service basis. By the beginning of the twenty-first century, the PPO had emerged as the dominant form of managed care contract in employment-based group insurance.

Point-of-Service (POS) Plan

Like the PPO, the **Point-of-Service (POS) plan** is a hybrid, incorporating features of both HMO and traditional fee-for-service indemnity plans. The POS plan gives subscribers the option to choose between an HMO, PPO, or managed indemnity type of plan at the time of service. Like the PPO plan, deductibles and higher co-payments are charged for out-of-network services. Unlike the PPO, the POS plan requires that the subscriber use a primary care physician as gatekeeper in the same way that an HMO does.

The movement away from closed panel or staff HMOs to IPA-type HMOs, PPOs, and POS plans is a modification of managed care in the direction of making it more like indemnity fee-for-service plans. The structure of these hybrid plans does address some of the problems of the original HMO plans. From the point of view of the insurance company, co-payments reduce the degree of moral hazard. From the point of view of consumers, there is the advantage that they are not limited to in-network providers.

2   Incentive and Strategy Differences Between Indemnity and Managed Care Insurers

Two extreme views of the relative merits of indemnity and managed care insurance have been widely espoused in the United States. Advocates of managed care have made a virtue of its incentive to be efficient in the provision of appropriate care to its subscribers. Fee-for-service-based insurance provided by indemnity policies is viewed by them as allowing patients and their physicians to "consume" as much care as desired, including inappropriate and wasteful care. The opposite view is that managed care has an incentive to skimp on care, whereas indemnity contracts allow patients to have the quality care that their physicians can only provide if care is not rationed and the physician has no contractual arrangement with the third-party payer. Where the truth lies can only be determined by examining the evidence. We will do this in the next section of this chapter. First let us characterize managed care. Here is a short list of some important aspects of it:

■ The staff HMO has an incentive to organize the production of integrated care on an efficient basis.

Efficiency with Respect to Inputs

Business firms that aim to be efficient need to assess the relative productivity of different inputs, compared to their cost. Productive efficiency is achieved when a firm substitutes between inputs until the ratio of the marginal product to the price of the factor (in this case a wage or salary) is equal across all inputs. For instance, a staff HMO will want to substitute general practitioners for specialist physicians and nurse-practitioners or physicians' assistants for MDs where it is more cost-efficient to do so. The HMO is being efficient if

$$MP_a/W_a = MP_n/W_n = MP_{pa}/W_{pa} = MP_{md}/W_{md}$$

where MP is marginal product, W is wage, a is aide, n is registered nurse, pa is physicians' assistant, and md is physician.

Legal restrictions on what tasks can be performed by non-MDs and by aides who are not registered nurses somewhat limits the ability of HMOs to substitute between different inputs. However, even when input substitution is limited, it is likely that integrated delivery of health-care services will still facilitate the efficient use of inputs. There is evidence that closed-panel HMOs use more nonphysician aides than is true of the average medical practice in the United States.[5] HMOs should be able to take advantage of both economics of scale and of scope.

■ Managed care may save money by paying providers less for the same services.

Managed care insurers may discount fees they pay to physicians and hospitals in exchange for including them in their networks. The ability to do this depends on the relative market power of the provider and the insurer. A dominant managed care firm may be able to name its own terms if there are many competing providers. If the managed care organization reimburses on a discounted fee-for-service basis, it will be able to save money compared with an indemnity insurer that reimburses the full list price for the service.

The downside, from the point of view of quality of service, is that physicians and hospitals may refuse to join the network. The network may therefore not include the highest-quality providers. If salaries or capitation payments in staff HMOs are set too low, the staff HMO will also have the same problem.

■ Managed care may save money by rationing services.

Service to consumers may be rationed directly by contract limits on what will be covered. This does not, however, distinguish managed care from indemnity contracts, since the latter may also set limits on services covered. Managed care may, however, also enlist providers in its rationing of care. In HMOs, gatekeeper primary care physicians may be given protocols on what kinds and how many referrals they may make. If the providers share financial risks with the insurance company, they will have an incentive to limit service.

An incentive system of bonuses, withholding of part of remuneration ("withholds") or even threat of termination of contract if physicians fail to cooperate with the cost-containment strategies of the insurer, will tend to affect the intensity of service provided to patients.*

Utilization review is usually employed by HMOs and other forms of managed care. Utilization review monitors the quantity of service provided by a primary care physician and also the number of referrals. Utilization review can be used either to limit service or to enforce quality control.

---

*If primary care physicians are required to pay for their patients' referrals out of their capitation fees, the degree of risk sharing is increased, as is the incentive to ration care. This is not the usual arrangement in the United States, but it is a strategy that has been introduced into the British National Health Service. The effects of this will be discussed in Chapter Twelve.

■ Managed care may consciously engage in strategies of positive selection.

Managed care, particularly when it provides integrated care, can be much more pro-active in designing a package of services that will attract desirable subscribers. For example, low cost and extensive coverage of pediatric services may be included to attract young families. One study even found an HMO that covered tattoo removal in order to attract a very young clientele.[6]

Factors Affecting Behavior of Managed Care Firms

The behavior of managed care insurance companies may differ widely in different markets and also depending on the type of company. Brand names are important in the managed care market, which includes many regional or even nationwide firms.[7] Kaiser-Permanente, which has maintained its reputation for providing high-quality care at a reasonable cost, is a prime example of a firm whose market power has been enhanced by its quality name. A reputation for quality may also be important in attracting superior physicians and acquiring connections with prestigious teaching and research hospitals. Competition among insurers may provide some degree of quality control as well as price competition. It will require the insurer to compete for contracts with both providers and subscribers.

Type of ownership may also be important. In general, non-profit firms are thought to be more likely to emphasize quality since they do not distribute surpluses (profits) to owners and therefore only have to cover costs. Kaiser-Permanente was founded as a non-profit organization, and this may also have contributed to its reputation for high-quality service. By contrast, a for-profit managed care firm will have an incentive to maximize profits even at the expense of quality, particularly in situations where patients cannot judge the quality of the care they are receiving. However, there is little or no evidence of any systematic variation in the quality of care between non-profit and for-profit HMOs.

Government regulations and laws protecting consumers who suffer damage when their HMOs fail to deliver appropriate care (patients' bill of rights legislation) also impose some limits on the ability of plans to skimp on care.*

3   Studies Comparing HMOs with Indemnity Plans

Treatment Intensity and Patient Outcomes

The sharp distinctions between types of insurance plans have been blurred by the proliferation of different types of managed care plans and by the cost-containment

---

*Regulation at the state level is however limited by the Employee Retirement Income Security Act of 1974 (ERISA) that supercedes state law in the regulation of certain employee benefits. The courts have interpreted this legislation to include federal jurisdiction over insurance provided through employment groups, particularly in large firms that self-insure their employees. In so far as local regulation may be more effective, ERISA regulations can result in less effective regulation of insurers.

strategies imposed even in traditional indemnity plans. This complicates the evaluation of the different types of plans. Many studies have compared only traditional HMOs and traditional indemnity contracts. Even here there are likely to be many unobserved factors that cannot be fully taken into account. This is particularly true when attempts are made to measure quality of treatment and health outcomes. With respect to quality of treatment, physician visits vary greatly, not only in length and in how much testing is done, but also in how attentive the physician is to the patient's medical history or even how good a listener he or she is. Subtle differences in the health status of a patient before and after treatment and between patients are also extremely hard to measure and compare.

Selection Bias

Measuring and adjusting for **selection bias** are major tasks facing researchers who do comparative studies of managed care and indemnity-type insurance plans. Study results that do not standardize for health-related differences between insurance pools will be unreliable. A number of studies have been directed to determining the extent to which selection bias is a problem. Although evidence is mixed, there does appear to be a good deal of positive selection into HMO pools.[8] A number of studies, dating from the 1980s, have found HMO populations to be younger and healthier.[9] Recent econometric studies provide further support for the existence of positive selection of enrollees into HMOs.[10] Favorable selection has been observed in the Medicare HMO population as well. There is also evidence that positive selection applies to other forms of managed care, including PPOs and HMOs of the IPA type, when compared with traditional indemnity insurance.[11] On the other hand, there is evidence of negative selection into HMOs among pregnant women and young children in the Medicaid population.[12] An excellent summary of findings on selection bias is provided in the chapter on managed care by Sherry Glied in the *Handbook of Health Economics*.[13] On balance, HMO subscribers seem to be somewhat healthier and, among the non-Medicare population, somewhat younger than those who choose indemnity-type insurance policies.

Intensity of Treatment

The evidence is mixed on whether HMO subscribers receive more or less treatment for the same conditions compared with patients who have indemnity insurance. Some studies have found that members of HMOs receive just as much diagnostic screening, on average, as do other insured persons. For instance, the rate of mammography for women, standardized by age, appears to be no different for HMO subscribers than for other insured women.[14] On the other hand, with respect to surgery, a study of coronary artery bypass surgery found significantly less intensity of treatment for patients of HMOs compared with those in indemnity plans.[15] A study comparing treatment for eight conditions that usually require medical treatment (heart attack; cancer of the breast, cervix, colon, and prostate;

diabetes I and II, and live births) found that with the exception of Cesarean section births, intensity of treatment did not vary between HMO enrollees and those enrolled in fee-for-service plans.[16] Since questions have been raised about possible inappropriate overuse of Cesarean section in obstetrics, this finding does not provide evidence of inappropriate skimping on care.

A recent study found greater intensity of treatment provided to patients in HMOs., even when selection bias was accounted for. Since HMOs are known for their attention to preventive care, this difference could not be explained by an assumption that HMO enrollees have more severe or advanced cases of the same illnesses.[17]

A wide range of studies support the view that HMO patients have both substantially lower rates of admission and shorter stays in hospitals when compared with those in fee-for-service plans, at least until the mid-1990s.[18] Results based on the RAND study concur. Forty percent lower admission rates and significantly shorter hospital stays were found for people randomly assigned to an HMO when comparisons were made between HMO members and people assigned to free (zero co-payment) fee-for-service plans.[19] A review of the literature on hospital admissions and length of patients stays for the period 1997 through 2001 shows shorter stays on the part of HMO patients, but no significant differences in rates of hospital admission.[20] This is probably because in-hospital procedures have been reduced a great deal across the boards by changes in technology and hospital policy. Consequently, in-patient services are largely limited to situations where out-patient alternatives are not viable. For instance, out-patient coronary artery bypass graft surgeries are not a medically acceptable option.

The evidence on the quantity of physician office visits is also mixed. The RAND study showed HMO members having more preventive care visits to physicians than did those who were assigned to the indemnity plans with free care.[21] Most contemporary studies show either slightly higher overall use of physicians or no difference on the part of HMO enrollees compared with those in traditional indemnity plans. There is considerable evidence, however, that patients in HMOs have fewer mental health visits than do those in indemnity plans.[22] This will be discussed below in connection with carve-outs of mental health care.

Patient Outcomes

A large number of studies have also addressed the question of treatment outcomes of HMO patients compared with those who have indemnity contracts.[23] Studies encompassing a variety of measures of patient outcomes show little evidence of difference, with the possible exception of outcomes for the most vulnerable groups. Miller and Luft note that the preponderance of studies with significant negative results for HMOs are those that studied patients who need the most ongoing care, including low-income and frail elderly. Even this result seems to be less pronounced in more recent studies.[24]

Patient Satisfaction

A survey of studies about patient satisfaction with insurance plans has found satisfaction to be, on average, lower among HMO subscribers, with the exception of their responses to questions about their satisfaction with preventive care. Travel distance to hospitals was one of the negative indicators, as was satisfaction with communication between patients and physicians.[25] Since HMOs deal with moral hazard more by direct rationing of services than by using price mechanisms to discourage overuse, it is not entirely surprising that consumer satisfaction is lower in these plans. Patients continue to value personal communication with a physician whom they know and trust.

Difference in Cost of Health-Care Services in HMO Versus Indemnity Plans

Does managed care reduce the cost of medical care? The problem of selection bias again complicates the answer to this question. If those who have better health are more concentrated in HMOs, then costs in conventional fee-for-service plans will suffer from the "cream skimming" provided by the competition from HMOs.

There is a confounding factor that may work in the opposite direction to reduce the observed differentials in costs. It is the spillover effect. Over time, fee-for-service insurers have come to act more like managed care plans. Utilization review establishes new norms for appropriate treatment, and the practice styles of all physicians and hospitals tend to reflect these standards. Productive efficiencies that were pioneered by staff HMO organizations are also adopted by providers in private practice. Economies of scale in HMOs may force solo and small partnership physician practices, which compete for patients, to form larger group practices.

Looking at costs per insured, the RAND study found significantly lower costs per subscriber for those randomly assigned to HMOs. The cost differences were attributed primarily to differences in rates of hospitalization and amount of testing.[26] Recent work by Altman and co-authors which standardizes for both enrollee health characteristics and treatment intensity, found HMO costs to be roughly 40 percent lower per patient. About half the difference was found to be due to different characteristics of the enrollee groups (lower incidence of disease in the HMO subscriber pool). The other half was attributed to HMOs paying lower prices for the same services. This study supports the view that the ability of HMOs to negotiate lower provider fees is one of the main reasons why they have been able to deliver comparable services at lower cost.[27] Dor and co-authors also found HMOs able to negotiate price discounts per unit of service in the range of 18 to 4 percent.[28] HMOs appear to have achieved some cost savings through their influence on the behavior of hospitals. Hospitals in markets with significant managed care penetration now appear to engage in price competition, a phenomenon that was largely absent until the 1990s. (See the discussion in Chapter Eight.)

4   Comparisons Between Different Types of Managed Care Plans

Results of studies comparing different varieties of managed care plans are hard to interpret, given the great variation among plans.[29] Characteristics of the plans that are studied are rarely explained in detail. Most of the comparative studies also suffer from the small numbers of plans surveyed. Nonetheless, a brief look at the results of several studies may be instructive. One study that compared HMO and POS plans sharing the same provider network found no evidence of higher expenditures per subscriber in the POS plan. When the level of co-payment was held constant, expenditures were higher in the HMO plan.[30] Another study found costs per subscriber to be lower in PPO plans than in either HMO or indemnity plans offered to workers in the same firms. The savings appeared to result from lower utilization levels of all services, particularly mental health services.[31]

If any conclusion can be drawn from this limited number of studies, it is a very tentative one: Costs, on average, are not significantly higher in PPO and POS plans than in traditional HMOs, despite the option of using out-of-network providers. It may be that the hybrid plans deal more effectively with moral hazard by charging consumers somewhat higher co-payments. HMOs can limit referrals to specialists and the amount of testing, but they can do little to ration use of the primary care physician. Requiring a primary care physician's referral for other services may sometimes lead to an inefficient overuse of physician services. If physician payments in an HMO incorporate any degree of fee-for-service payment, primary care physicians may also have an economic incentive to limit the number of referrals made on any one visit and to promote more follow-up visits.

5   Carve-Outs: The Case of Behavioral Health Care

It has become increasingly common for employers to provide mental health and chemical dependency (behavioral health-care) benefits to their workers through contracts with separate managed care entities known as managed behavioral health-care organizations (MBHOs). Government programs (principally Medicaid) have also begun to use MBHOs.

Health insurers have a history of rationing access to behavioral health care. This differential treatment of mental health care predates the dominance of managed care and was a typical feature of indemnity policies as well. Under pressure from mental health advocates to provide parity between behavioral health care and other services, managed care insurers have been particularly likely to "carve out" behavioral health care since they are at higher risk of cost increases from extending these benefits due to relatively low co-payments for services.[32] Spurred on by the behavior of HMOs, all types of insurers began to carve out behavioral health care. By the mid 1990s, MBHOs were handling more mental health-care cases than fee-for-service-based policies and HMOs combined.

Carving out these services does not necessarily promote parity in treatment between behavioral and other health-care services. Significant downward trends in the cost of behavioral health care for employers have been observed after their adoption of an MBHO.[33] Whether this results from greater efficiency due to specialization or whether it is the result of lower-quality care is an ongoing concern of mental health advocates. The AMA, in its 2001 resolution supporting parity for mental health care, encouraged the elimination of all mental health and chemical dependency carve-outs.[34]

Frank and McGuire have suggested that since managed care insurers can use such a complex variety of cost-containment measures, requiring parity between behavioral and other health-care services may simply lead to alterations in MBHOs' strategy.[35] For instance, access to care up to a certain level might be relatively easily available, but techniques may be developed for avoiding the most costly cases.

MBHOs have gone farther than other managed care insurers in shifting decision making away from clinicians to nonmedical managers. They often use networks of local clinicians, but are constituted as regional or even national for-profit firms. Two common risk arrangements between employers and MBHOs are (1) purely administrative contracts, where the MBHO passes the costs of claims through to employers and (2) contracts in which the MBHO actually is the third-party payer. A study of Massachusetts state employee benefits found even modest risk sharing with MBHOs to result in substantial reductions in costs, compared with contracts in which employers paid for mental health care that was merely managed by the MBHO.[36] This suggests that savings may be the result of reductions in quality of care rather than more efficient management.

Several studies have attempted to measure directly whether MBHOs skimp on quality. A study of substance abuse treatment found mixed results in its examination of the effects of carve-outs on quality of treatment. There appeared to be an improvement in access to care, brought about by free-standing 24-hour clinics replacing hospital admissions. Continuity of care also appeared to be improved, but the rate of rapid readmissions of those discharged from treatment centers increased.[37] The latter is usually regarded as a negative indicator. Another study of costs and quality trends in 52 MBHO plans found no evidence of reduction in quality of care accompanying the cost declines that occurred over time in these network plans. This study attributed cost savings to an organizational learning curve resulting from sophisticated information systems, case management procedures, patient education, and utilization review by clinical care managers.[38]

It seems that the jury is still out when it comes to deciding whether MBHOs provide inferior care. There is, however, no question but that carve-outs for behavioral health care lower costs.

6   Managed Care Versus Managed Competition: What Is the Difference?

The model of **managed competition** developed by Alain Enthoven is one in which competition plays an important role in an insurance market dominated by managed care.[39] Countervailing power is achieved by large insurers competing for contracts from large consumer buying groups (alliances). The large health insurance buying alliances are created from employee, union, or community groups. The alliances employ a sponsor or agent to bargain for them. In the model, cost sharing between providers and insurers and between consumers and insurers provide incentives for efficiency.

Experiments with managed competition have been tried to a limited extent in the private insurance market in the United States. In 1993 American Express formed coalitions with other big companies in local areas throughout the United States to negotiate insurance premiums on a competitive bidding basis. Standardizing for quality, HMO premiums at American Express fell by 18 percent in 1994 and by an additional 7 percent in 1995.[40]

In the summer of 2004, 50 of the largest employers in the United States formed a buyers' group to bargain directly with drug makers to get better prices on the 50 drugs on which its 5 million employees (both active and retired) and their families spend the most money.[41] The outcome of this arrangement is not yet known, but concern over prescription drug prices may spur the development of more consumer buying groups and stimulate competition among managed care insurers handling Medicare drug benefits. (See Chapter Five.)

To date, large health insurance buying alliances that would create consumer countervailing power have not developed on a wide-scale basis in the United States. One reason is that forming buyer groups which are not employment- or union-based is difficult. Another reason is that competition among insurers is limited in many geographic areas with lower population density and in other markets that insurance companies find less profitable. Most proponents of the managed competition model support its feasibility with studies based on data from California, a state in which managed care was introduced early and in which there is competition between several well-established, high-quality HMOs.

Although managed competition has not become a significant phenomenon in the U.S. health insurance market, the development of forms of managed care other than closed-panel HMOs has led to some degree of competition among insurers for contracts with providers of health care. In regions where there are competing insurance companies, providers have a choice of which networks to join. This affords some protection for individual consumers if providers, acting as agents for their patients, are able to impose requirements about quality of care. The designers of the managed competition model envisioned selective contracting on the part of both insurers and providers. The recent enactment in many states of "all willing provider" legislation, which prohibits selective contracting on the part of insurance companies, removes this form of quality control on the part of insurers. It may, however, also reduce the ability of insurance companies to pressure physicians to ration service, since physicians and other providers can join any other managed care networks in the region.

7   Dynamic Effects of Managed Care

Rate of Technology Diffusion

It is often alleged that managed care, with its emphasis on cost containment, slows the rate of medical technology diffusion. A review of a number of studies provides evidence of a reduction in the rate of adoption of at least some new medical technologies in markets dominated by managed care.[42] Baker and Spetz, using an index of technology available in hospitals, examined the association between degree of HMO market share and technology growth.[43] The index of technology gave higher weights to technologies that are "new, expensive, or difficult to implement" and lower weights to common technologies such as standard operating rooms.[44] They found an association between HMO market share and a slowing in the rate of growth of available technology in hospitals in the mid-1980s, but no evidence of this by the early 1990s. Lawrence Baker found increased managed care market share to be associated with lower rates of diffusion of MRI equipment in hospitals over the period 1983 to 1993 and less availability of MRI equipment both within and outside of hospitals from 1993 to 1999.[45]

On the other hand, Baker and Phibbs found higher HMO market share associated with equally good diffusion of the most advanced high-level neonatal facilities, but less diffusion of mid-level facilities.[46] With respect to surgery, the extent of use of laparoscopic surgical procedures in hospitals was found not to vary with the degree of HMO penetration into the hospital marketplace. A study of mammography by Robinson and co-authors found the number of patients per mammography machine to be higher in HMOs.[47] This may simply be a reflection of economies of scale associated with larger group practices or more integrated delivery of health care.

The evidence is mixed. On balance, growth in managed care does seem to slightly reduce the diffusion of high-tech equipment, particularly diagnostic equipment such as MRI machines. There is also some evidence that the growth in managed care is associated with a slowing in the rate at which medical procedures involving new technologies are adopted.[48]

Growth Rates in Costs of Medical Care

Although costs of providing health care seem to be lower, on average, for HMOs than for indemnity-type policies, *growth rates* in medical costs are only slightly lower (about 1%) in managed care than in traditional insurance plans.[49] For a brief period in the early 1990s, managed care plans showed somewhat lower rates of cost increase, but by the end of the 1990s this difference was no longer significant.[50] This suggests that a one-time reduction in costs due to HMO penetration into insurance markets will have little effect on long-term trends in the cost of health care in the United States. The coexistence of managed care may raise the cost of medical care delivered in indemnity-type fee-for-service insurance contracts, given the ability of managed care to take advantage of positive selection or "cream skimming."

Summary

Managed care has come to dominate the U.S. insurance market at least in part because of the inability of indemnity-type insurance to control the rise in the cost of medical care through cost sharing with consumers.

Managed care employs a variety of additional cost controls including risk sharing with providers and several forms of nonprice rationing of care, limiting referrals to specialists, requiring precertification before receiving surgery or other procedures, utilization review (applied to providers), and direct limits on the quantity of services covered.

Complex forms of managed care have evolved and the distinction between them has become somewhat blurred. Pure capitation plans, with no co-payments, have been largely replaced by some cost sharing between the insurer and insured. Even in HMOs, subscribers often pay a co-payment per unit of service. Traditional fee-for-service insurance contracts now also usually embody some of the cost-containment features of managed care. Hybrid plans, which combine higher degrees of coverage for services supplied by in-network providers with some coverage for nonnetwork services, have become increasingly popular with consumers and are now the dominant form of employment-based insurance.

A large number of studies have attempted to compare managed care with traditional indemnity-type insurance coverage. Selection bias makes evaluation difficult. The RAND Health Insurance Experiment, a large randomized study that avoids this problem, is one of the best sources of reliable estimates even though it is now about 20 years since the study was concluded. Estimates obtained from these experimental data are still widely used as a benchmark for comparisons of HMO and indemnity insurance on such indicators as cost/patient, utilization of medical services, and patient outcomes.

When managed care is compared with service provided to patients on a traditional fee-for-service basis through indemnity-type insurance contracts, there is no evidence that either quality of care or patient outcome is less good for the general population. This may not be true for mental health care or for certain subpopulations. The quality of care received when behavioral health care is carved out from major medical insurance and provided by separate managed care entities is also controversial.

There is fairly strong evidence that cost/patient is lower under managed care arrangements. Studies agree that one major reason for lower costs is the ability of managed care insurers to tailor their insurance contracts so as to take advantage of positive selection. There is also evidence that they benefit from lower use of in-patient hospital services or shorter stays on the part of their patients, even when selection bias has been removed. Another important source of lower costs seems to be the superior ability of managed care insurers to negotiate lower fees from providers. Tighter controls on the diffusion of technology may also help to contain costs. Nonetheless, by the late 1990s, the promise of managed care as a cost-containment vehicle proved somewhat disappointing. Although there was a one-time decrease in costs accompanying the dramatic shift to managed care, the rate of increase in health-care costs has again resumed its long-term upward trend. More research is needed to provide a full understanding of the dynamics of managed care.

Key Concepts

Health maintenance organization (HMO)

Independent Practice Association (IPA)

Preferred provider organization (PPO)

Point-of-service (POS) plan

Utilization review

Selection bias

Managed competition

Suggested Readings

1. Glied, Sherry A., "Managed Care," in *Handbook of Health Economics* Vol. 1A, Anthony J. Culyer and Joseph P. Newhouse, eds. (Amsterdam: Elsevier, 2000), Chap. 13.

2. Pauly, Mark, "Insurance Reimbursement," in *Handbook of Health Economics,* Vol. 1A, op. cit., Chap. 10.

Questions for Discussion and Review

1. In a couple of sentences, characterize each of the following types of managed care: staff HMO, PPO, and POS.

2. What is selection bias? How does it complicate research?

3. Compare managed care with "unmanaged" indemnity contracts with respect to:

   a. Coverage of preventive care.
   b. Access to choice of providers

    c. Quality of care

    d. Access to high-tech equipment (MRIs, mammography machines, etc.)

4. How do HMOs and insurance that reimburses on a fee-for-service basis differ in the methods they employ to control costs?

5. What are the main explanations of the fact that expenditure per insured tends to be lower in HMOs than in indemnity policies?

6. What are "carve-outs" in insurance coverage? Give an example.

Resources

[1] Glied, Sherry A, "Managed Care" *Handbook of Health Economics*, Vol. 1A, Anthony J. Culyer and Joseph P. Newhouse, eds. (Amsterdam: Elsevier, 2000), Chap. 13, p. 709.

[2] Jensen, Gail A., et al. "The New Dominance of Managed Care: Insurance Care in the 1990s," *Health Affairs*, 16 (January–February 1997): 125–136.

[3] Cutler, D. M. and R. J. Zeckhauser, "The Anatomy of Health Insurance," Vol. 1A, *Handbook of Health Economics,* op. cit., Chap. 11, p. 591.

[4] Chollet, D. J., et al., *Mapping State Health Insurance Markets: Structure and Change in the States' Group and Individual Health Insurance Markets*, 1995–1997 (Washington, DC: Academy for Health Services Research and Health Policy, 2000).

[5] Hart, L. G., et al., "Physician Staffing Ratios in Staff-Model HMOs: A Cautionary Tale," *Health Affairs*, 16 (1997): 55–70 and Brown, Douglas M., "Do Physicians Underutilize Aides?" *Journal of Human Resources*, 23 (1988): 342–355.

[6] Frick, Kevin D. and Neil R. Power, "HMO Coverage of Cosmetic Procedures: Responses to Market Competition," *International Advances in Economic Research*, 4 (1998): 398–410.

[7] Glied, Sherry A. (2000), op. cit.

[8] Wilensky and Rossiter's summary of patient self-selection studies showed mixed results. See Wilensky, F. D. and L. R. Rossiter, "Patient Selection in HMOs, *Health Affairs*, 5 (1986): 66–80. Good summaries of research on this subject are given in Luft, Harold S. and Robert H. Miller, "Patient Selection in a Competitive Health System," *Health Affairs*, 7 (1988): 97–119 and Glied (2000), op. cit.

[9] Two studies helped to establish this: Berki, S. E. and Ashcraft, Marie L. F. "HMO Enrollment: Who Joins What and Why," *Millbank Memorial Fund Quarterly*, 58 (1980): 607, surveyed the literature and found that when employee groups were offered choices, single people and older people tended to select traditional plans, whereas families with children preferred HMOs. Dowd and Feldman also found evidence of favorable selection bias in HMO patient groups: Dowd, R. and R. Feldman, "Biased Selection in Twin Cities Health Plans," in *Advances in Health Economics and Health Services Research*, R. M. Schleffer and L. F. Rossiter, eds., (Greenwich, CT: JAI Press, 1985).

[10] See, for instance, Altman, Daniel, et al., *Enrollee Mix, Treatment Intensity, and Cost in Competing Indemnity and HMO Plans,* NBER Working Paper No. 7832 (Cambridge, MA: National Bureau of Economic Research, August 2000).

[11] Hellinger, Fred J., "Selection Bias in HMOs and PPOs: A Review of the Evidence," *Inquiry*, 32 (1995): 135–143.

[12] See, for instance, Robinson, J. C. and L. B. Gardiner, "Adverse Selection Among Multiple Competing Health Maintenance Organizations," *Medical Care*, 32 (1995): 1161–1175 and Goldman, Dana P., et al., "Cost-Containment and Adverse Selection in Medicaid HMOs," *Journal of the American Statistical Association*, 93 (1998): 54–62.

[13] Glied (2000), op. cit. See particularly her two-page table, Table 2, on pp. 729–730.

[14] Baker, L. C. and M. L. Brown, *The Effect of Managed Care on Health Care Providers*, NBER, Working Paper No. 5987 (Cambridge, MA: National Bureau of Economic Research, 1997).

[15] Dor, Avi, et al., *Transaction Prices and Managed Care Discounting for Selected Medical Technologies: A Bargaining Approach,* NBER Working Paper No. 10377 (Cambridge, MA: National Bureau of Economic Research, 2004).

[16] A widely publicized study of the rate of Cesarean section deliveries also found a reduced rate of use of this procedure in geographical areas dominated by managed care. See Tussing, A. D. and M. A. Wojtowycz, "Health Maintenance Organizations, Independent Practice Associations, and Cesarean Section Rates," *Health Services Research*, 2 (1994): 75–93.

[17] Altman, et al. (2000), op. cit., pp 28–34.

[18] Miller, R. H. and H. S. Luft, "Managed Care Performance Since 1980: A Literature Analysis," *Journal of the American Medical Association*, 271 (May 18, 1994): 1512–1519; Miller, R. H. and H. S. Luft, "Does Managed Care Lead to Better or Worse Quality of Care?" *Health Affairs*, 16 (1997): 7–25.

[19] Newhouse, Joseph P., et al. *Free for All? Lessons from the RAND Health Insurance Experiment* (Cambridge, MA: Harvard University Press, 1993), p. 272.

[20] Miller, R. H. and H.S. Luft, "HMO Plan Performance Update: An Analysis of the Literature, 1997-2001," *Health Affairs*, 21 (2002): 63-86.

[21] Newhouse (1993), op. cit. p. 273.

[22] Miller and Luft (1994, 1997, 2002), op. cit. See particularly Miller and Luft (1994), p. 1514.

[23] Ibid.

[24] Miller and Luft (1997, 2002), op. cit.

[25] Miller and Luft (2002), op. cit.

[26] Manning, Willard G, et al, "A Controlled Trial of the Effect of a Prepaid Group Practice on use of Services," *New England Journal of Medicine*, 310 (1984): 1505–1510.

[27] Altman, et al. (2000), op. cit., pp. 28–36.

[28] Dor, et. al. (2004), op. cit.

[29] An excellent review of the literature is provided in Glied (2000), op. cit.

[30] Escarce, Jose J. et al., "Medical Care Expenses Under Gatekeeper and Point-of-Service Arrangements," *Health Services Research*, 36 (2001): 1037–1057.

[31] Hosek, Susan, et al., *The Study of Preferred Provider Organizations: Executive Summary,* RAND Report R-3798-HHS/NIMH (Santa Monica, CA: Rand Corporation, 1990). However, another study, coauthored by the same researcher, found PPO plans to have higher costs per subscriber than conventional indemnity plans. See Hosek, S. D., M. S. Marquis, and K. B. Wells, *Health Care Utilization in Employer Plans with Preferred Provider Organization Options*, RAND Report/R-3800-HHS/NIMH (Santa Monica, CA: Rand Corporation, 1990).

[32] Frank, R.G., and T. G. McGuire, "Parity for Mental Health and Substance Abuse Care Under Managed Care," *Journal of Mental Health Policy and Economics*, 1 (1998): 153–159.

[33] Ma, C.A., and T. G. McGuire, "Cost and Incentives in a Mental Health Carve-Out," *Health Affairs*, 17 (1998): 53–69 and Goldman, David P. et al., "Costs and Use of Mental Health Service Before and After Managed Care," *Health Affairs*, 17 (1998): 40–52.

[34] Herman, Barry, M.D., *Coalition Report: The National Coalition of Mental Health Professionals and Consumers* (Washington, DC: The National Coalition of Mental Health Professionals and Consumers, March 2001), p. 1.

[35] Frank and McGuire (1998), op. cit., p. 158.

[36] Ma and McGuire, (1997) op. cit.

[37] Shepard, Donald S., et al., "Managed Care and the Quality of Substance Abuse Treatment," *Journal of Mental Health Policy and Economics*, 5 (2002): 163–174.

[38] Sturm, Roland, "Managed Care Risk Contracts and Substance Abuse Treatment," *Inquiry*, 37 (2000): 219–225 and "Cost and Quality Trends under Managed Care: Is There a Learning Curve in Behavioral Health Carve-Out Plans?" *Journal of Health Economics*, 18 (1999): 593–604.

[39] Concise descriptions of managed competition are given in Enthoven, Alain C., "The History and Principles of Managed Competition," *Health Affairs*, 10 (1993): 24–48 and Ellwood, Paul M., Alain Enthoven, and Lynn Etheredge, "The Jackson Hole Initiatives for a Twenty-First Century Health Care System," *Health Economics*, 1 (1992): 149–168. The Jackson Hole Group was a name adopted by a pro-managed competition think tank after a meeting at Jackson Hole, Wyoming, in 1990.

[40] Maxwell, James and Peter Temin, "Managed Competition Versus Industrial Purchasing of Health Care Among the Fortune 500," *Journal of Health Politics, Policy, and Law,* 27 (February 2002): 5–30.

[41] Freudenheim, Milt, *The New York Times*, June 12, 2004, http://www.nytimes.com/2004/06/12/business/12drug.html.

[42] Chernew, Michael E. et al., "Managed Care, Medical Technology, and Health Care Cost Growth: A Review of the Evidence," *Medical Care Research and Review*, 55 (1998): 259–288.

[43] Baker, L. C. and J. Spetz, *Managed Care and Medical Technology Growth,* NBER Working Paper No. 6894 (Cambridge, MA: National Bureau of Economic Research, 1999).

[44] Ibid., p. 5.

[45] Baker, L. C., *Managed Care and Technology Adoption in Health Care: Evidence from Magnetic Resonance Imaging*, NBER Working Paper No. 8020 (Cambridge, MA: National Bureau of Economic Research, 2000).

[46] Baker, L. C. and C. S. Phibbs, "Managed Care, Technology Adoption, and Health Care: The Adoption of Neonatal Intensive Care," *RAND Journal of Economics*, 33 (Autumn 2002): 524–548.

[47] Cutler, David M., and Louise Sheiner, "Managed Care and the Growth of Medical Expenditures," in *Frontiers in Health Policy Research*, Vol. 1, ed. Alan M. Garber (Cambridge, MA: MIT Press for National Bureau of Economic Research, 1998): 77–116.

[48] Miller and Luft (1997), op. cit.

[49] Miller and Luft (2002), op. cit.

[50] For a good summary, see Newhouse, Joseph, "Reimbursing Health Plans and Health Providers: Efficiency in Production Versus Selection," *Journal of Economic Literature*, XXXIV (1996): 1236–1263.

CHAPTER FIVE

Social Insurance in the United States: Medicare and Medicaid

I am proposing that every person over sixty-five years of age be spared the darkness of sickness without hope. I am asking that every person under Social Security during his working lifetime contribute a modest amount, so that his basic health services can be financed. It will help meet the costs of hospital bills without in any way interfering with the freedom to choose their doctor or to choose their hospital.*

No longer will older Americans be denied the healing miracles of modern medicine.†

1   Introduction

Principles of social insurance are quite different from those that pertain to the private market. Social insurance programs are generally funded by mandatory contributions through some form of taxation. They usually have goals in addition to the pooling of risk, which include transfers of benefits between groups, for instance, from the more affluent to the poor, from younger adults to senior citizens, from adults to children, or from the able-bodied to the disabled. Consequently, much

---

*Speech of President Lyndon B. Johnson before the 89th Congress of the United States in which he asked them to enact the Medicare bill, January 7, 1965.

†Statement of President Johnson at the signing of the Medicare bill in Independence, Missouri, in the presence of former President Harry S Truman, who had originally proposed a similar bill, July 30, 1965.

less attempt, if any, is made to equate marginal costs and benefits for the individual. Rather, the goal is to equate marginal *social costs* and marginal *social benefits*.

Social insurance for health care in the United States is limited to certain categories of citizens and residents: Senior citizens, a segment of the poor, and people with qualified disabilities are covered by Medicare or Medicaid. A few other special groups are also covered by public insurance programs, including Native Americans on reservations, veterans of the armed forces, members of Congress, and children from low-income families. Some states have also moved in the direction of expanding social insurance to larger numbers of children and other low-income people who are not eligible for the federal programs.

In this chapter we will explain the structure of the Medicare and Medicaid programs instituted in 1965 and how they have changed since then. Two questions to keep in mind while reading this chapter are:

1. How well do these programs meet their goal of providing appropriate coverage to the groups for which they are designed?
2. What are the problems created by the ways in which they are financed?

2   Social Health Insurance Coverage for the Elderly: Medicare

Description of the Program Instituted in 1965

Medicare is a federal program of subsidized medical insurance for senior citizens, certain qualified permanently disabled persons, and individuals with end-stage renal (kidney) failure. Medicare was enacted in 1965 as Title XVIII of the Social Security program. The program for senior citizens was up and running by July 1966. Treatment for end-stage renal patients was added in 1972; medical care for the qualified disabled was added in 1973. All U.S. citizens and legal residents 65 years of age and older who have an employment record (or are married to someone with an employment record) that entitles them to Social Security benefits are eligible for Medicare. Over 95 percent of the elderly are eligible for this subsidized health insurance program.*

The program was designed to give seniors health insurance coverage that closely resembled the insurance plans which they had during their working years. Hospital coverage was modeled on Blue-Cross fee-for-service indemnity insurance. The model for other services was the typical major medical fee-for-service indemnity policy of the 1960s. This made the legislation more acceptable to the Medical establishment as well. The Medicare legislation also provided funding for hospital construction, since it was recognized that the demand for hospitalization would increase.

---

*For people who have reached the age of 65 and are still employed in firms that provide health insurance and employ more than 20 persons, Medicare A is the secondary insurer. Medicare only pays if its coverage exceeds the private insurance benefit.

Medicare Part A

Medicare Part A is a universal mandatory program. It covers hospitalization. Benefits include acute care hospital services (up to 150 days) and some posthospital services: 100 days in a skilled nursing facility when preceded by hospitalization, 4-day a week home health care with no time limit, 210 days of hospice care when life expectancy is less than 6 months, 190 days in-patient psychiatric care per lifetime, but no long-term care. Patients have a deductible of approximately $800 (in 2002), and after that has been met, there is no co-payment for the first 60 in-patient hospital days, after which there are increasing co-insurance rates for additional days up to 150. Each Medicare recipient also has 60 additional lifetime reserve days available, which can be used when the 150-day limit has been exceeded.

Medicare Part A is thus structured in an unusual way for a social program: It has, after the initial deduction, very good "first dollar" coverage but very poor catastrophic coverage. It has been described as being "upside down" with respect to the usual risk-management principles of insurance, for after a total of 210 consecutive days of hospitalization, there is no additional hospital coverage. This makes it a very expensive program, but one that leaves seniors bearing the full risk of medical care costs if they require extensive hospitalization.* Hospitals are generally required to treat Medicare patients and accept the Medicare rate of reimbursement for service provided.

Medicare Part B

Medicare Part B is a major medical plan that covers medical expenses other than hospital bills. It is a highly subsidized program to which senior citizens can subscribe. Even though the subsidy has been reduced over time, the premiums paid by subscribers still cover only about 25 percent of the cost of Part B benefits. All physician benefits, including physician services that take place in hospitals (such as anesthesiologist, pathologist, and radiologist services), are paid out of Medicare Part B. There is an annual $100 deductible, after which Medicare B pays 80 percent of the prescribed reimbursement rate for covered services. The government has allowed seniors to assign their Medicare Part B to participating private insurance companies since 1982. This alternative is only available in some geographical areas, since participation on the part of private insurers is voluntary. The options have changed over time and will be discussed below when we consider reforms in Medicare.

Payments to Providers

Medicare originally reimbursed hospitals on a fee-for-service basis. This was changed and will be discussed on pages 92 and 93. Physicians are reimbursed on a fee-for-service basis. They have the option of accepting the Medicare reimbursement (called *accepting assignment*) in return for being paid directly by

---

*For a period of one year, the Medicare Catastrophic Coverage Act, passed in 1988, was in effect. It was repealed in 1989. There was broadly based criticism from seniors since they were the primary group taxed to pay for this program.

Medicare for services provided to recipients. Physicians who do not accept assignment but who treat Medicare patients are allowed to charge more than the Medicare reimbursable amount (called *balance billing*). Reimbursement to physicians has also undergone some changes since 1965. (See pages 93 and 94.) Physicians are not required by law to treat Medicare patients.

Financing of Medicare

Medicare Part A is financed, as is the Social Security retirement benefit, from payroll taxes. Unlike the FICA contribution to the retirement benefit, Medicare FICA is an uncapped proportional tax on wages and salaries. The current tax is a payroll deduction of 2.9 percent of earnings, paid on a 50/50 basis by employers and employees. Self-employed persons pay the full 2.9 percent. Contributions go into the Medicare Trust Fund. Like the Social Security retirement benefit, Medicare is a pay-as-you-go program. Current benefits to recipients are paid out of current amounts paid in by workers and their employers plus any surpluses that may have accumulated. Since in any given year Medicare may collect more than it pays out or, conversely, may pay out more than it collects, the solvency of the program is, like the Social Security retirement benefit, vulnerable to demographic shifts. The Medicare program is at even greater risk, since the costs of medical care are increasing more rapidly than the overall cost of living, to which the retirement benefit is tied.

This program of social insurance, which is not means-tested, transfers income from younger to older citizens regardless of wealth levels. Medicare is regarded as an entitlement. The justification is that people now receiving benefits have paid into the system for most of their working lives, since the program has been in existence for 40 years.

If real incomes, the Medicare FICA contribution rate, the age at which one can collect Medicare benefits, life expectancy, the size of the population, and the cost of medical care were all constant over time, there would be no intergenerational transfer, once beneficiaries were from an age cohort that had paid into the program throughout their working lives. There would be only transfers from higher- to lower-income workers since the program is financed by a proportional tax on earnings. In reality, none of these conditions holds. Your generation will be subsidizing the Medicare benefits of the baby boomer generation unless Medicare financing is radically reformed.

Medicare Cost-Containment Measures: Reforms in Payments to Providers

Prospective Payment to Hospitals: The DRG System

In 1968, Medicare reduced its payments to hospitals to 92 percent of the average per diem billed; this was further reduced to 80 percent by 1977.[1] In 1983, in response to rapidly increasing hospital costs, Medicare replaced cost-based reimbursements to hospitals with the Diagnostic Related Group payment system. This was a dramatic change. Patients were placed into **diagnosis-related groups** (commonly known as **DRGs**) categorized by their principle diagnosis. The basis for payment was changed to a per case basis rather than an item-of-expenditure basis. It was hoped that this would provide hospitals with an incentive to be efficient in their use of resources. However, the way in which the system was structured when the prospective payment system was newly instituted encouraged strategic behavior on the part of hospitals. It encouraged them to report diagnoses that would lead to the highest possible reimbursement. It penalized hospitals for treating the most seriously ill patients and rewarded them for "cherry picking" the less difficult cases.

The refining of the DRG system is one area in which economists have had an important input into public policy. Payments are now risk-adjusted. In addition to adjustments for age, sex, low-income status, and county of residence of patient and for teaching hospitals and hospitals that have a disproportionate number of charity cases, the Balanced Budget Act of 1997 mandated that the prospective payment system be reformed to include diagnostic-based risk adjustments. The reforms have led to the introduction of sophisticated systems to identify and standardize for the underlying health status of patients and relate diagnostic information to probable cost and duration of treatment.[2]

Effects of the Prospective Payment System   Hospital admission rates, which had increased dramatically with the advent of Medicare, dropped in the first several years after the DRG system was instituted, but rates of out-patient services increased dramatically during the same period.[3] Some research, undertaken shortly after the new system was implemented, found evidence of poor outcomes for patients associated with the prospective payment system. For instance, hip fracture patients who were discharged sooner were more likely to be in nursing homes six months to one year later. Other studies found higher mortality rates among patients shortly after surgery but no differences in survival rates among those who survived for a year or longer. As more studies have provided additional evidence, it now appears that, on balance, the prospective payment DRG system has no significant negative impact on patient health outcomes.[4]

Reform in Physician Reimbursements: The Resource-Based Relative Value Scale
Medicare Part B also faced rapidly accelerating costs for services. In 1989, the Omnibus Budget Reconciliation Act established the Agency for Health Policy Research to monitor health outcomes and establish policy guidelines. A principal research area of this agency, which employs a staff of economists, is the study of the cost-effectiveness of different providers and programs. The agency implemented the **Resource-Based Relative Value Scale (RBRVS)** system. This is a system for determining rates of reimbursement to physicians, factoring in the amount of input resources (effort) used to produce a given service and the costs of providing the service. The cost of maintaining a physician practice (including

malpractice insurance) is also included in the computation of cost of service. The RBRVS has resulted in changes in relative reimbursement rates for different physician specialties. Rates of reimbursement to primary care physicians have been raised relative to those for surgeons.

The RBRVS was instituted after economic studies showed the ineffectiveness of simply lowering physician fees as a cost-containment measure. Physicians, like hospitals, behaved strategically. In an experimental situation in Colorado, when fees were lowered in some locales but not in others, physicians were found to adjust their behavior by increasing the quantity of care provided when fees were lowered.*

Another change in Medicare physician reimbursements imposes limits on the practice of balance billing, which formerly allowed providers considerable freedom in charging more than the Medicare rate of reimbursement if they chose not to accept assignment. Under the new system, the Medicare base rate of reimbursement is lower for physicians who do not accept assignment. In addition, a balance-billing limit of 125 percent of the Medicare rate was imposed in 1991. This has been subsequently reduced to 115 percent. The effective balance-billing premium is, in fact, less than 115 percent if one factors in the lower base rate of Medicare reimbursement to nonparticipating physicians.

Caps on Rates of Increase in Medicare Expenditures

The **Medical Volume Performance Standard** was also introduced in 1989. It set allowable rates of increase in total Medicare expenditures, weighing the increase by factors such as volume of recipients and types of care given. If the expenditure limit is exceeded in a given year, the reimbursement rates for the following year can be adjusted downward. The Balanced Budget Act of 1997 altered the Medical Volume Performance Standard by tying it to performance in the aggregate economy in an attempt to develop a sustainable rate of growth in Medicare expenditure. This resembled the kinds of caps that are commonly used to control social insurance program costs in countries such as Canada and Great Britain. About half the saving was to be accomplished by reducing reimbursements to hospitals.[5] After studies indicated that 70 percent of U.S. hospitals would have costs exceeding revenues by the end of 2002, the Balanced Budget Refinement Act was passed in 1999, which modified the original level of cuts but still maintained the commitment to contain increases in Medicare reimbursements.

Medicare Managed Care

In 1982, the Medicare Tax Equality and Fiscal Act (TEFRA) made the federal government the manager of a system of competing health plans offered by private insurers. Private managed care companies competed with Medicare Part B by of-

---

*Results of studies of physicians showing the relationship between Medicare fee schedules and demand inducement, that is, proscribing more care when fees are reduced, are presented in Chapter Seven in the section on physician induced demand.

fering more comprehensive benefits. Seniors were allowed to assign their Medicare Part B to a private insurer, in some cases with no additional premium payment. There was virtually no limit on how often one could switch between plans, which could be done at any time during the year.

The Balanced Budget Act of 1997 increased the types of private insurance plans that can be chosen by Medicare beneficiaries to cover their nonhospital insurance needs. It introduced the Medicare + Choice program (renamed Medicare Advantage in 2003) that changed the contractual arrangements between Medicare and the private supplementary insurers. HMOs, PPOs, fee-for-service plans, and medical savings account plans can all participate by accepting assignment of Medicare Part B, and participating plans no longer have to have a 50/50 split between non-Medicare and Medicare subscribers. To offset the problem of adverse selection, the Balanced Budget Act of 1997 introduced limits on how often Medicare recipients can change plans. Switching is now limited to an annual open enrollment period.

In 1997, Medicare HMOs were reimbursed at the rate of 95 percent of the expected payout to a similar pool of beneficiaries enrolled in traditional Medicare Part B. Because the cost per subscriber in the late 1990s was so much lower in Medicare managed care than in traditional Part B, capitation payments to participating HMO plans were risk-adjusted by Medicare beginning in 2000. Reimbursement adjustments were subsequently computed on the basis of actual average costs incurred by HMOs. This resulted in less generous reimbursement of the plans by Medicare. It also resulted in many HMOs withdrawing from the Medicare market, leaving seniors with no alternative to traditional Medicare Part B in many geographical areas.

Selection Bias in Medicare HMOs

Medicare recipients who choose HMO plans tend to be healthier than those who choose traditional fee-for-service coverage. In fact, studies of Medicare recipients have yielded some of the strongest evidence of selection bias favoring HMOs.[6] Allowing the Medicare population to switch between plans every month (until 1997) facilitated studies of enrollment and dis-enrollment patterns. A study of the differences in mortality between Medicare HMO enrollees, dis-enrollees (who switched to fee-for-service plans), and fee-for-service enrollees found that Medicare HMO enrollees were healthier (had lower risks of mortality) than comparable fee-for-service beneficiaries, but that HMO dis-enrollees had higher odds of mortality than either HMO enrollees or FFS beneficiaries.[7] This finding reinforces the evidence on negative selection into fee-for-service Medicare and supports the view that for populations with special needs, particularly those with very serious illnesses, HMOs may provide less good care.[8]

One interesting phenomenon is worth noting. Although Medicare recipients seem prone to shift between plans on the basis of their health status, retirees appear to be less sensitive to price differentials between HMOs and fee-for-service plans than are nonelderly individuals.[9]

Evaluation of Medicare + Choice (renamed Medicare Advantage in 2003)

There was initially a great deal of enthusiasm for Medicare + Choice on the part of both seniors and policy makers, who saw it as embodying the virtues of managed competition. Medicare + Choice plans tended to include some prescription drug coverage and more preventive care, including annual physical exams, both of which had been excluded from coverage in traditional Medicare Part B. In the first few years of the program, many programs provided more benefits than traditional Medicare B at no additional cost. In 1999, 55 percent of the Medicare + Choice plans had no additional premium over the Medicare B contribution. However, by 2002 only 13 percent of the plans had no additional premiums and some had supplemental premiums of $50 or more per month.[10] There has also been a widespread reduction in the generosity of benefits. The prescription drug benefits were reduced, particularly with respect to coverage of drugs not on the plan's approved list. There are often high out-of-pocket costs for other treatments of major illnesses as well.

Between 1998 and 2002, many Medicare + Choice enrollees were faced with their managed care plans leaving the program. By 2002, approximately 536,000 Medicare + Choice enrollees no longer had a plan in which to be enrolled. There are now major geographical disparities in the availability of the Medicare + Choice plans. New York City and Los Angeles have experienced slower declines in the number of participating plans than have many other cities; in those cities there are still a variety of options to choose from. However, by 2002 there was even some evidence of trouble looming in the New York City Medicare + Choice market as the number of plans serving that city's seniors began to decline.[11] The viability of the **Medicare Advantage program** is likely to be increased with the introduction of the new prescription drug program in 2006, which provides new incentives for private managed care companies to reenter the Medicare market.

The Medicare Prescription Drug, Improvement, and Modernization Act of 2003: Medicare Part D

This act, which created Medicare Part D, is complex in that many different options are provided to Medicare-eligible citizens, depending on whether they are enrolled in Medicare Part B or one of the Medicare Advantage (MA) plans.

Medicare Part D goes into effect in January 2006. Medicare Prescription Drug Discount Cards are available for purchase by Medicare-eligible seniors in the interim. Subsidies to low-income beneficiaries are available during this period under the Transitional Assistance Program. In 2006, seniors who are enrolled in traditional fee-for-service Medicare Part B may enroll in the Medicare Prescription Drug Plan (PDP). Enrollees in MA plans will receive drug benefits through their plans. People enrolled in MA fee-for-service plans that do not include a drug benefit are also eligible for the PDP. Eligible Medicare beneficiaries who do not enroll in PDP plans during the open enrollment periods will pay a penalty when they do enroll.

Standard Prescription Benefit Package

The premium for Part D drug coverage in 2006 is estimated by the Congressional Budget Office to be $35 per month. Medicare Part D-eligible individuals who are also Medicaid-eligible or Supplemental Security Income (SSI) recipients are eligible for a full premium subsidy. The annual deductible will be $250 and will be indexed to the annual growth in average per capita Medicare D expenditure on drugs. Once the deductible has been met, participants in the plan will pay a coinsurance rate of 25 percent, up to a coverage limit of $2,250 in 2006. (There are also adjustments in coinsurance rates for Part D enrollees with incomes below 135% of the poverty level.) When the coverage limit is reached, the enrollee will pay 100 percent of the plan's negotiated drug prices until the out-of-pocket limit of $3,600 is reached. This is sometimes referred to as a **"donut"** structure of reimbursement since there is a hole in the coverage in the middle range of spending. Once the out-of-pocket limit has been reached, the enrollee will pay the greater of the following: either $2 for a generic drug and $5 for a brand name drug, or a 5 percent co-payment rate for all covered drugs.

Alternative Drug Plans

MA drug plans may offer the standard benefit package or an equivalent package, with a deductible level that is not higher than the standard deductible. Drug plans available to seniors through their MA plans may have different levels of coinsurance as long as they are equivalent to an average cost sharing of 25 percent. The alternate plans will be subject to the same out-of-pocket limit that applies to the standard prescription benefit package, and they are subject to government approval. Enhanced packages may be offered by private companies, but only if they also offer the standard package as an option to seniors in the same area. In all plans, reimbursement for drugs treated as nonformulary (not on the approved list) do not count toward the out-of-pocket limit.

An interesting aspect of the prescription drug act is that the government may not negotiate prices with pharmaceutical companies, but plan sponsors from the private sector are allowed to negotiate discounts from both manufacturers and suppliers of covered drugs. This gives the MA plans a competitive advantage over Medicare Part D and is the basis for predictions that the prescription drug benefit will attract more managed care companies back into the Medicare market. It is likely to result in virtual privatization of the prescription drug program for seniors, since the government will probably not be able to successfully compete with the private third-party payers.

Private Supplementary Insurance for the Elderly

Medicare recipients often purchase additional private **Medigap insurance** policies or use retirement insurance benefits provided by their former employers to supplement their Medicare coverage. These private insurance options need to be clearly distinguished from the various components of Medicare's social insurance plan. The wide use of private supplementary insurance is, in part, a response to the lack of catastrophic health-care coverage included in Medicare Part A. In the past, these supplementary policies have often included a prescription drug benefit. Private insurance contracts for senior citizens will undoubtedly be altered as a result of the Medicare prescription drug benefit to provide coverage for the "donut hole" in the Medicare coverage.

3   Social Health Insurance for the Poor and the Disabled: Medicaid

Description of the Program

The other large social health insurance program in the United States is Medicaid, set up to provide health care to certain low-income families and individuals. Medicaid was enacted in 1965 as an amendment to the Social Security Act, Title XIX.

Who Are Medicaid Recipients?

Although the single largest group of people covered by Medicaid is children, in terms of total payments, the largest amount of expenditure is for the disabled, with the second largest expenditure going to the elderly poor. One main reason for this distribution of benefits is that Medicaid covers nursing home and home health care for low-income seniors.

Most poor families do not qualify for Medicaid. There is a means test that limits personal property owned to $1,000. Low-income single males below the age of 65 are also rarely eligible for Medicaid. Although the distribution of Medicaid funds varies by state, comparing enrollment and expenditures in New York State's Medicaid program in 2001 is illustrative. (See Table 5.1.)

The Medicaid program has evolved over time along with changes in the welfare system; however, certain aspects of the program have remained the same. States are required to cover in-patient and out-patient hospital services, physician services, and vaccines for eligible infants and children. In addition, prenatal care must be covered for Medicaid-qualifying pregnant women.

Financing of Medicaid

Medicaid is funded through cost sharing between the federal and state governments, with states given a good deal of freedom in the way in which eligibility is determined.* The federal portion of the funding for the program comes from general income tax revenues. The federal contribution to states varies from about 50 percent to about 80 percent, depending on state average per capita income. The federal government also contributes funds to states to use for payments to hospitals that care for an unusually high proportion of low-income patients; however, the amount available through this provision has been reduced over time. States

---

*Oregon, for instance, has an unusual Medicaid system that covers all people below a certain income level, but rations what medical treatments are covered. See the boxed example in Chapter Nine.

Table 5.1 Medicaid Enrollment and Spending by Categories, New York State, 2001

Category	Percentage of Enrollment (%)	Percentage of Spending (%)
Elderly	11	26
Disabled	19	46
Adults	23	11
Children	47	10

Source: *Health Insurance: The New York Agenda* (New York: United Hospital Fund, 2004).

have been able to get more money from the federal government by shifting their mental health facilities and facilities for the developmentally challenged into the Medicaid program.

Medicaid outlays vary with the state of the economy since Medicaid is **means-tested,** and more people qualify and apply for Medicaid benefits in periods of economic recession The cyclical variability of outlays is somewhat reduced by the fact that the majority of the funds go to the disabled and the low-income elderly, not, as is commonly believed, to low-income mothers and children.

If a state cannot meet its required portion of funding for Medicaid in any year, the federal contribution to Medicaid is cut back. Since tax cuts at the federal level have reduced federal support for other state programs, including education, many states have found it harder to meet their Medicaid budgets and have had to abandon plans to expand medical coverage for the poor or even reduce coverage.

Changes in Legislation, 1984 to 1990

The eligibility requirements for Medicaid were changed a number of times before the major welfare reform of 1996. From 1984 to 1990, there were a number of expansions in eligibility, particularly for pregnant women, infants, and children. Table 5.2 summarizes the main changes.

Impact of Welfare Reform on Medicaid

Under Aid to Families with Dependent Children (AFDC), Medicaid coverage was closely tied to eligibility for that program and to those eligible for Supplemental Security Income (SSI). The passage of the 1996 **Personal Responsibility and Work Opportunity Reconciliation Act** replaced AFDC with Temporary Assistance to Needy Families (TANF). Medicaid coverage is no longer guaranteed to welfare recipients, and some people who are not in the TANF program are eligible. The legislation also gives the states more discretion in their use of federal Medicaid contributions, since they now receive bloc grants rather than a payment per eligible recipient.

The decoupling of welfare and Medicaid has been accompanied by an extension of Medicaid coverage to some additional two-parent, low-income families.

Table 5.2   Legislation Expanding Medicaid, 1984 to 1990

The Deficit Reduction Act of 1984

Eligibility: all children born after September 30, 1983, in families eligible for Aid to Families with Dependent Children(AFCD), up to their 5th birthday. Women pregnant for the first time or pregnant in an unemployed two-parent family eligible for AFDC. Coverage for one year of all infants born to Medicaid-eligible women.

Consolidated Omnibus Budget Reconciliation Act of 1985 (COBRA)

Coverage for children up to age 5 in AFDC-eligible families and for pregnant women in two-parent AFDC-eligible families.

Omnibus Budget Reconciliation Act of 1986

Means-tested eligibility for some children in AFDC families up to age 8. Optional expansion to pregnant women and infants in families with incomes up to 185 percent of the Federal Poverty Level (FPL) and for children up to age 8 in families earning no more than 100 percent of the FPL.

Family Support Act of 1988

Optional expansion to pregnant women and children above the levels of income required by previous legislation.

Omnibus Reconciliation Act of 1989

Eligibility: all pregnant women and children under age 6 in families earning up to 133 percent of the FPL.

Omnibus Budget Reconciliation Act of 1990

Eligibility: all children 6 to 8 years of age in families earning up to 100 percent of the FPL.

Source: Institute of Medicine, *Insuring America's Health: Principles and Recommendations* (Washington, DC: The National Academies Press, 2004), Box 3.3, p. 84.

Coverage has also been extended to more pregnant women and children. All children born after 1983 whose family incomes are below the poverty level are now covered by Medicaid, whether or not their families qualify for public assistance.[12]

Results of Studies Assessing Effects of Welfare Reform

A study using firm-level data rather the more typical household data found some evidence of Medicaid expansion "crowding out" private insurance. Crowding out refers to the substitution of Medicaid for private insurance coverage. Employers of low-income workers appear to have cut back on the generosity of private insurance when workers and their families are covered by Medicaid. Medicaid take-ups on the part of eligible workers were found to be associated with firms requiring employees to contribute financially to their own or their dependents' health insurance coverage.[13]

Studies of the effect of greater coverage of pregnant women have revealed some interesting results. A 30 percent increase in the proportion of women eligible for Medicaid in the event of pregnancy has been found to decrease the infant mortality rate by 8.5 percent. However, closer examination by Currie and Gruber revealed that merely expanding Medicaid eligibility to all low-income pregnant women had little, if any, effect on birth outcomes, because changing the eligibility did not translate into actual increases in Medicaid coverage among the intended group. (It did result in more payments to hospitals for in-hospital treatments.) Targeting high-risk clients was found to be more effective in improving health outcomes than was expanding broad coverage for prenatal care.[14] When state-level public relations programs advertising the program were combined with increased eligibility, improvements in health outcomes were also much greater. A review of the research on the subject indicates that the health of infants and children in low-income families has been improved by Medicaid, but not necessarily through the most efficient use of resources.[15]

Medicaid Managed Care

Since individual states administer Medicaid, which is paid for on a cost-sharing basis with the federal government, there is a great deal of variation in how health care is provided among the different states. Over time more states have mandated managed care for at least part of the Medicaid-eligible population. Some states have mandated Medicaid HMOs on a county-by-county basis. Others have done so on a statewide basis. An example of the latter is Michigan, which quickly adopted and fully implemented a mandatory statewide program during 1997 and 1998.[16]

By 1998, 49 of 50 states had some form of Medicaid managed care program; by 2003, 59 percent of all Medicaid clients were covered by managed care.[17] The tendency for states to move in this direction was accelerated by the Balanced Budget Act of 1997. This act allowed states to require managed care (primarily care in HMOs) for all Medicaid clients except children with special needs and people with dual Medicare/Medicaid eligibility. In most states, managed care has not been extended to the portion of the Medicaid population who are disabled. This is probably advisable since there is some fairly substantial evidence that patient outcomes in low-income populations with disabilities seem to be less good when they receive care from HMOs.[18]

Evaluation of Medicaid Managed Care: Costs and Patient Outcomes

Medicaid managed care has been supported by a number of state governments because it is believed to be an effective cost-containment policy and to deliver a higher quality of on-going care, particularly to low-income families with dependent children and to pregnant women. That HMOs provide savings is well demonstrated by a study of the treatment costs of children of over a thousand Medicaid-eligible AFDC families. Some families in the sample were randomly assigned to either HMOs or fee-for-service based care. Others self-selected themselves. Savings of 13.8 percent were found in the randomized sample, but no savings were found in the self-selected group. This supports the view that there is negative selection into HMOs in the population of Medicaid recipients, unlike most other groups.[19]

An advantage of Medicaid managed care is that it may tend to reduce the inefficient use of the hospital emergency room as a substitute for physician office visits by assigning patients to a primary care physician.

Tennessee Medicaid Program

Tennessee raised the reimbursement rate for physicians treating Medicaid patients in an attempt to accomplish two goals: increasing the supply of physicians willing to treat Medicaid patients and reducing the use of emergency rooms by Medicaid recipients who had no primary care physician. Raising fees increased physician participation in the Medicaid program and increased the cost of the state's Medicaid program, compared with nearby Georgia, but did not reduce the use of emergency rooms by Medicaid patients, nor did it appear to reduce avoidable hospitalizations of Medicaid recipients. As a result, Tennessee instituted a mandatory managed care Medicaid program, Tenncare, in 1994.[20] This did reduce emergency room use for nonemergency treatment.

Despite fears that HMOs would provide less good prenatal care for pregnant women and infants, studies of the effect of Medicaid managed care on infant health have found no adverse affects associated with it.[21] States also find it helpful to their clients to contract with physicians who agree to take on Medicaid clients in exchange for a capitation fee, since independent providers paid on a fee-for-service basis may be unwilling to treat Medicaid patients, given lower rates of reimbursement compared with either private insurance or Medicare.[22] The effects of Medicaid reimbursement rates on the willingness of physicians to treat Medicaid patients will be discussed at greater length in Chapter Seven.

4   Other Social Insurance Programs

State Children's Health Insurance Program (SCHIP)

The **State Children's Health Insurance Program (SCHIP)**, set up under the Balanced Budget Act of 1997, established a ten-year program of federal matching grants to cover low-income uninsured children. An important difference between the two programs is that Medicaid creates an entitlement for those who qualify for eligibility. This is not true for SCHIP recipients, and states can either reduce or eliminate SCHIP programs or reduce enrollments at will. Children in families with incomes up to 200 percent of the Federal Poverty Level (FPL) can be eligible. Some states have increased eligibility beyond this level. Unused funds can in some cases be made available to low-income parents as well. SCHIP recipients must have been without private insurance coverage for a specified period that varies by state. There are more safeguards in the structure of this program than in Medicaid to avoid substitution of SCHIP on the part of families who otherwise would have private insurance.[23]

SCHIP is often treated as a revision to the Medicaid program, but as states have discretion whether to administer the program as part of Medicaid or set it up under a separate program, it is not an integral part of Medicaid. As of February 2003, 21 states have built SCHIP programs on an expansion of Medicaid, 16 states have combined their separate SCHIP programs with their existing Medicaid programs, and 19 states have kept their SCHIP programs completely separate from Medicaid.[24]

Effects of Economic Cycles on SCHIP and Medicaid

Both programs are perennially vulnerable to economic cycles. In economic downturns more people qualify, but states are also more economically strapped and find it harder to pay their portions of the Medicaid and SCHIP programs. States, unlike the federal government, are required to have balanced budgets, although they get around this requirement in various ways by issuing bonds for particular purposes. As noted above, if states cannot meet their portion of the matching funds grants from the federal government, the federal portion of the funding is reduced. This applies to SCHIP as well as Medicaid.

Programs of the Veterans Administration (VA) and Civilian Health and Medical Program for the Uniformed Services (CHAMPUS)

The Veterans Administration (VA) was set up in 1930 to coordinate veterans services. At that time a number of hospitals established by the U.S. Public Health Service in the 1920s to provide care for veterans with service-related illnesses were transferred to the VA. Veterans may also be treated for non-service-related medical problems if facilities are available and they can satisfy a means test. The VA still maintains a large number of hospitals, although it has faced deficits and resulting hospital closures in recent years. Retired members of the military and their dependents may also be eligible for care through the Civilian Health and Medical Program for the Uniformed Services (CHAMPUS). This is a smaller program than the VA and is largely limited to on-base facilities.

Summary

Social health insurance programs in the United States have covered the elderly, certain qualified disabled persons, and a portion of the poor since 1965. Medicare greatly expanded the accessibility of health care for seniors. It still provides a major subsidy of approximately 75 percent of covered expenses. However, it does not provide very good catastrophic coverage for those who need extensive hospitalization. The forthcoming Medicare prescription drug benefit also has big gaps in its coverage.

Although Medicaid is commonly regarded as a program for poor female-headed families with children, in fact, more than half of Medicaid expenditures are directed to health care for the disabled and the elderly poor. Many of the very poor nonelderly do not qualify for Medicaid. It is thus a very imperfect safety net when evaluated as a method of providing universal health-care insurance to the poor.

Like the private insurance market, Medicare and Medicaid have come to make greater use of managed care in recent years. There is a good deal of empirical support for positive selection into Medicare managed care programs, compared with traditional Medicare B. Standardizing for differences in characteristics of sub-scribers, costs are generally lower under managed care than under traditional fee-for-service indemnity insurance contracts. Since the federal government has used risk adjustment to reduce reimbursement rates to the participating private managed care insurers, many insurance companies have withdrawn from the program. The new prescription drug program is expected to attract back more private third-party payers into the system, where they will compete with Medicare Part D by negotiating lower drug prices from pharmaceutical companies.

Private HMO participation in the Medicaid program has, by contrast, increased. The findings on selection bias in the Medicaid population are mixed, but there is some evidence of negative selection into HMOs in that group. Many states now require Medicaid recipients to enroll in Medicaid HMOs, which, for the most part, appears not to have had negative effects on health outcomes, and which eliminates the adverse selection problem in the Medicaid managed care population.[25]

The role of economic analysis in reforming the Medicare reimbursement systems for both hospitals and physicians is important. When Medicare instituted its initial prospective payment system based on DRG classification, hospitals behaved strategically, which distorted the objectives of the system. There were similar problems with the reforms in reimbursement of physicians. Payment schemes incorporating risk-adjusted criteria have been introduced to offset this problem.

Medicaid has also been through a number of reforms since it was set up in 1965. Welfare reform in 1996 decoupled eligibility for Medicaid from eligibility for public income assistance and through the bloc grant system gave individual states much more discretion in the handling of Medicaid funds. Social insurance now covers some children's health care even when their parents are not eligible for Medicaid. The SCHIP program, jointly funded by states and the federal government, has been the foundation for this in a number of states. SCHIP may be piggy-backed onto Medicaid or administered as a separate program.

Both Medicare and Medicaid (and the related SCHIP program) are financially vulnerable. Medicare is endangered by rising medical costs and by changes in demographic patterns, which lead to a much higher proportion of retired to employed Americans. Since Medicare is funded on a pay-as-you-go basis out of payroll taxes, either benefits have to be cut or payroll taxes have to be raised when benefits for a larger group have to be supported by a smaller one. Medicaid and the SCHIPS program are vulnerable to economic cycles. Since both of these programs are means-tested, more people qualify in recessions when lower tax receipts make it harder for governments to fund the programs. Medicaid and SCHIPS are doubly vulnerable at such times since states lose federal funding if they cannot meet their matching funds requirement.

Key Concepts

Diagnostic-related groups (DRGs)

Resource-Based Relative Value Scale (RBRVS)

Medical Volume Performance Standard

Medicare Advantage program

Medicare trust fund

"Donut"

Medigap insurance

Personal Responsibility and Work Opportunity Reconciliation Act

Means-tested

Medicaid managed care

State Children's Health Insurance Program (SCHIP)

Suggested Readings

1. Van de Ven, W. P. M. M. and Randall P. Ellis, "Risk Adjustment in Competitive Health Care Plans," *Handbook of Health Economics,* Vol. 1A, Anthony J. Culyer and Joseph P. Newhouse, eds. (Amsterdam: Elsevier, 2000), Chap. 11.

2. Institute of Medicine, *Insuring America's Health: Principles and Recommendations* (Washington, DC: The National Academies Press, 2004).

3. Sisk, Jane, et al., "Evaluation of Medicaid Managed Care," *Journal of the American Medical Association,* 276, 1996: 50–55.

4. For an excellent discussion of state initiatives with respect to broadening health insurance coverage, see Holahan, John and Mary Pohl, "Leaders and Laggards in State Coverage and Expansion," in *Federalism and Health Policy,* Holahan J., et al., eds. (Washington, DC: Urban Institute, 2003), pp. 179–214.

Questions for Discussion and Review

1. What are the main differences in principle between social and private insurance?

2. Explain how the Medicare prospective payment system to hospitals has been modified over time. Why was this done?

3. It is sometimes said that the structure of Medicare coverage is "upside down" with respect to the usual insurance principles. Explain, using the concepts of "first dollar coverage" and coverage of catastrophic events.

4. How has Medicare reimbursement to physicians been altered over time? What problems have been addressed by the changes?

5. Explain how Medicare is financed and why its solvency is linked to demographic changes.

6. Evaluate the argument that the financing of Medicare involves regressive taxation.

7. How is the passage of the recent prescription drug bill related to the probable changes in the supply of private insurers in the senior citizen insurance market?

8. How did the reform of welfare in 1996 alter Medicaid?

9. Many states now place Medicaid recipients into HMOs. What are the advantages and disadvantages of HMO membership for this population?

Resources

[1] Drake, D. F., "The Cost of Hospital Regulation," in *Regulating Health Care: The Struggle for Control*, Arthur Levin, ed., (New York: Academy of Political Science, 1980).

[2] The main systems that have been employed to interpret these complex data are the Principle Inpatient-Diagnostic Cost Groups or PIP-DCG, the Hierarchical Co-existing Conditions system (HCC), the Disability Payment System (DPS), and the Clinical Diagnostic Groups (CDGs). A good analysis of these risk adjustment systems is given in Newhouse, Joseph P., "Risk Adjustment, Market Equilibrium, and Carveouts: Pulling a Rabbit out of the Hat?" *Pricing the Priceless* (Cambridge, MA: MIT Press, 2002), Chap. 6.

[3] Feinglass, J., and J. J. Holloway, "The Initial Impact of the Medicare Prospective Payment System on U.S. Health Care: A Review of the Literature," *Medical Care Review*, 48 (1991): 91–115.

[4] For a summary of this research see Cutler, David M. and Richard J. Zeckhauser, "The Anatomy of Health Insurance," *Handbook of Health Economics*, Vol. 1A., Anthony J. Culyer, and Joseph P Newhouse, eds. (Amsterdam: Elsevier, 2000), p. 630.

[5] Medicare Payment Advisory Commission, *Report to the Congress: Medicare Payment Policy*, Vols. I-II (Washington, DC: March 1998).

[6] See Glied, Sherry, "Managed Care" in *Handbook of Health Economics*, Vol. 1A., op. cit., Chapter 13, for a good summary of 24 studies of selection bias.

[7] Maciejewski, Matthew L. et al., "Comparing Mortality and Time Until Death for Medicare HMO and FFS Beneficiaries," *Health Services Research*, 35 (2001): 1245–1265.

[8] Holahan, John, "Medicaid Managed Care in Thirteen States," *Health Affairs*, 17 (1998): 43–63. For a summary of findings on Medicare patients with chronic illnesses, see also Miller and Luft (1997) op. cit. pp. 14–15.

[9] Buchmueller, Thomas C., "The Health Plan Choices of Retirees Under Managed Competition," *Health Services Research*, 35 (2000): 949–976.

[10] Achman, Lori and Marsha Gold, *Trends in Medicare + Choice Benefits and Premiums, 1999–2002* (New York: Commonwealth Fund, November 2002).

[11] Stuber, Jennifer, et al., *Medicare + Choice in New York City: So Far, So Good?* (New York: Commonwealth Fund, September 2002).

[12] See Yelowitz, Aaron S., "Will Extending Medicaid to Two-Parent Families Encourage Marriage?" *Journal of Human Resources*, 33 (1998): 833–865.

[13] Shore-Sheppard, Lara, et al., "Medicaid and Crowding Out of Private Insurance: A Re-examination Using Firm Level Data," *Journal of Health Economics*, 19 (2000): 61–91.

[14] Currie, Janet and Jonathan Gruber, "Saving Babies: The Efficacy and Cost of Recent Changes in the Medicaid Eligibility of Pregnant Women," *The Journal of Political Economy*, 104 (1996): 1263–1296.

[15] For a good summary of this, see Currie, Janet, "Child Health in Developed Countries," in *Handbook of Health Economics*, Vol. 1B, Anthony J. Culyer, and Joseph P. Newhouse, eds. (Amsterdam: Elsevier, 2000), Chap. 19, pp. 1055–1090.

[16] See Weissert, Carol S. and Goggin, Malcolm L., "Nonincremental Policy Change: Lessons from Michigan's Medicaid Managed Care Initiative," *Public Administration Review*, 62 (2002): 206–216.

[17] Centers for Medicare and Medicaid Services data, 2004. Available at http://www.ems.hhs.gov/medicaid/managedcare.

[18] Holahan (1998), et al., op. cit.

[19] Goldman, Dana P., et al., "Cost-Containment and Adverse Selection in Medicaid HMOs," *Journal of the American Statistical Association,* 93 (1998): 54–62.

[20] See, Gruber, Jonathan, et al., "Physician Fee Policy and Medicaid Program Costs," *The Journal of Human Resources*, 32 (1997): 611–634.

[21] Kaestner, Robert, et al., *Medicaid Managed Care and Infant Health: A National Evaluation,* NBER Working Paper No. 8936 (Cambridge, MA: National Bureau of Economic Research, May 2002).

[22] Travis, Karen, "Physician Payment and the Supply Side Effect on Access to Prenatal Care for Heterogenous Medical Patients," *Economic Inquiry,* 37 (1999): 86–102.

[23] Institute of Medicine (2004), op. cit., pp. 85–88.

[24] Centers for Medicare and Medicaid Services (CMS), *State Children's Health Insurance Program Plan Activity Map,* 2003, http://www.cms.gov/schip/chip-map.asp.

[25] Goldman, et al. (1998), op. cit.

PART THREE

The Providers of Health Care: Physicians, Nurses, and Hospitals

CHAPTER SIX

Physicians and Nurses as Inputs into the Production of Health Care

As a senior medical student about to move on to residency, the overwhelming emotion I have at this time is one of disillusionment. At the heart of the Hippocratic Oath, both classical and modern, is the vow to avoid doing harm and to help when appropriate and necessary. Yet medical education, both undergraduate and graduate, brutalizes its students . . . . Sleep deprivation is the norm—I have seen residents working up to 120 hours a week. With such inhuman work hours for so many years, alienation from one's family, health, and peace of mind is often the result. *

1 Introduction

Two differing points of view have characterized American attitudes toward medical professionals in the United States. One focuses on the high monetary and psychic costs of the lengthy training period and the long hours and great responsibility that being a practicing physician entails and concludes that the economic returns to practicing medicine are not excessive. The other asserts that physicians and other health-care providers have been able to extract "economic rents" by charging fees that are higher than those which would prevail in a reasonably competitive market.[1] Whether this is true in the age of managed care and administered prices will be investigated in the next two chapters.

*Nova Online, "Survivor M.D., The Hippocratic Oath," Doctors' Responses Set 2, March 30, 2001, http://www.pbs.org/wgbh/nova/doctors/oath_modern.html.

Two chapters of this book are devoted to physicians because they are such an important part of the health-care system in any country. Physicians' decisions are crucial in determining the course of medical treatment and hence the demand for most other medical services, even though physician fees represent only about a quarter of the total spending for medical care in the United States.* Thomas McGuire describes physician behavior as "the central issue in health economics."[2]

This chapter will focus on the supply of physicians and nurses and, in particular, on their decisions to undertake training and enter the field of medicine. Health planners define the adequacy of the supply of doctors and nurses in relation to the community's health needs. Economists use supply and demand to analyze markets. This analysis is applied to understanding why shortages and surpluses may exist.

Physicians

2   Understanding The Physicians' Market

The supply of physicians depends upon a combination of individual career decisions and public policy. Since the middle of the nineteenth century, medical associations have interacted with federal and state governments to regulate the practice of medicine. Medical schools and hospitals with residency programs also make decisions that affect the opportunities for training As a result, individuals' ability to enter the profession and their financial returns from doing so are not left to the unfettered interaction of supply and demand in the private market.

The Requirements for Becoming a Physician

The professionalization of medical training and the practice of medicine date from the mid-nineteenth century, when under the urging of the American Medical Association (AMA), state licensing boards were established to set examinations for doctors of medicine (MDs). Licensing limited the scope of activity of other medical practitioners: homeopaths, osteopaths, chiropractors, midwives, and so on. In the twentieth century, the AMA also began to oversee the quality of medical education. In 1910, it commissioned a study that came to be known as the Flexner Report. This highly critical review of medical education led to many U.S. medical schools being closed and the addition of a second requirement for becoming a licensed physician, graduation from an accredited medical school.[†]

---

*In 1998, total personal consumption expenditures on physicians were approximately 22 percent of personal consumpton expenditures on all medical care in the United States. (Computed from U.S. Department of Commerce, Survey of Current Business, August 1998, Table 2.4.)

†The number of medical schools in the United States was reduced from 162 in 1906 to 85 by 1920 and 69 by 1944. Kessel, Reuben A., "Price Discrimination in Medicine," *Journal of Law and Economics*, 1 (1958): 20–53.

The M.D. degree requires four years of medical school, plus a year of practical training in hospitals, the internship. Physicians must pass examinations in a particular state in order to be licensed to practice medicine in that state. Most physicians in the United States also undertake additional postgraduate training in the form of a hospital residency in some specialty. This is now often combined with the internship. In addition, many become board-certified specialists. A board-certified specialist must complete one or more residencies and also pass an examination in one of 24 specialist fields. A physician can practice in a specialist field such as cardiology without being board-certified, but the certification carries with it prestige and the likelihood of higher earnings. Some specialties, such as neurosurgery, require very long residencies. A physician's training often requires a commitment of more than a decade. In 2001, approximately 67 percent of the total actively practicing physicians in the United States were board-certified specialists.[3]

3   Post-World War II Shortage of Physicians

Health Planners' Evaluation of the Physician Supply

By the late 1950s, the quantity rather than the quality of physicians had become the main policy focus in the United States. Health planners evaluate the supply of physicians by looking at the theoretical number of physicians required to perform the medical procedures "needed" by a community, estimating need by reference to statistics on incidence of disease in a population of a given size.* Using this definition, it was determined that there was a **physician shortage**, particularly in certain regions, given the uneven geographical distribution of practicing physicians.[4]

Economic Analysis of the "Physician Shortage"

Economists define a shortage as a situation in which quantity supplied is less than quantity demanded *at a given market price*. Shortages are not easy to measure in a profession where a high proportion of the members are self-employed. Except for young physicians in training employed by hospitals, there are few data on vacancy rates. Researchers studying markets for professionals therefore study relative earnings or relative returns to training.

Comparisons of the earnings of physicians with those of dentists, lawyers, and other professionals found them to be higher in the 1950s and early 1960s.[5] However, higher earnings in one professional field do not necessarily indicate barriers

---

*Within the health planner/medical professional approach, there are two slightly different ways of defining shortages. In one, the number of professionals needed to handle the projected illness rate in the population is defined, based on the judgment of a medical professional. The other approach looks at existing physician/population or nurse/population ratios and compares shifts in these. If the ratio declines, this is regarded as a shortage. The two approaches become virtually equivalent if an ideal health professional/population ratio is defined, based on need, rather than just derived from what exists at some historical point in time.

to entry into that field. Earnings differences may simply reflect "compensating differentials" for differences in length and cost of training. Therefore, the return to training is a much better instrument to use. The return to training is also a useful measure for analyzing individual decisions to enter medical training and choices about which field within medicine to pursue.[6] Incorporating the human capital model into the analysis of the supply of physicians led to an approach that focused on returns over the lifetime to investment in training rather than current earnings.

A medical degree can be thought of as a stock of human capital that yields a stream of returns over time. A convenient way to evaluate the return on any form of investment is to find its discounted present value (PV).* Using the concept of **internal rate of return**, defined as the discount rate that will equate the (discounted) present value of the returns streams with the (discounted) present value of the training costs, internal rates of return in different professions would be expected to converge over time in competitive markets with freedom of entry. Higher rates of return may be indications of what are called dynamic shortages. These occur when there are lags in adjustment between supply and demand. In a field where training may take a decade or more, the lags can be lengthy and there can be miscalculations about the economic return on the part of those entering the field, since supply and demand conditions may shift during the training period. However, since people are attracted to fields with higher returns, persistent differentials in internal rates of return provide indirect evidence of market imperfections.

In the 1950s and 1960s, physicians were found to receive higher internal rates of return on their training compared with the other learned professions.[7] Therefore, economists and health planners concurred that there was a shortage of physicians.

Barriers to Entry

In analyzing the reason for the higher returns to medical training, one hypothesis was that it was the result of barriers to entry to practicing medicine. The limited number of places in U.S. medical schools and the licensing requirements that, coupled with immigration policy, greatly restricted the entry of foreign-trained physicians, could explain the higher than equilibrium returns to medical training. Some economists linked the high returns to strategic (profit-maximizing) behavior on the part of the AMA.[8] The AMA was viewed as a guild that imposes strict apprenticeship requirements and limits entry to the profession. If demand remains constant, imposing restrictions on the number of physicians will increase the price of their services, even if the reason for the restriction is quality control.

*PV $= \Sigma[R_t + R_{t+1}/(1 + r) + \ldots + R_{t+n}/(1 + r)^{t+n-1})]$, where R is the extra amount that would be earned in a given time period as a result of the investment, t the initial time period, n the number of time periods, and r the interest rate.

Figure 6.1

Pricing of Physicians'
Services

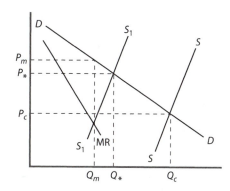

Moreover, if entry restrictions are coupled with rules prohibiting price competition, monopoly level prices could result, even when there are many suppliers of the same service.[9] County medical associations had the power to impose sanctions on physicians if they did not cooperate (loss of hospital privileges, exclusion from the medical association, etc.) so the lack of price competition was not an unreasonable assumption.

In a competitive market with freedom of entry, the equilibrium price (fee for a service) would be P_c and the equilibrium quantity would be Q_c. Restrictions on supply are shown in Figure 6.1 as a movement from SS to S_1S_1, with a resulting competitive price of P_*. If physicians' associations set prices collusively within local areas, the profit-maximizing price will approach P_m, as in Figure 6.1. (A model of monopoly is provided in Appendix 1.)

Policy Responses to the Shortage

Public policy in the 1960s had the goal of relieving the doctor shortage. The Immigration Act of 1965 (greatly modified in the 1970s) made it easier for internationally trained physicians to practice medicine in the United States. The Health Professions Education Act, also passed in 1965, increased federal assistance to medical schools, but required them to increase enrollments in order to qualify.* These measures led to an approximate doubling in the size of physician training programs and a significant increase in the number of physicians between 1965 and 1980.[10] Table 6.1 shows the increase in the physician population ratio between 1960 and the end of the century.

---

*This was spearheaded by hospitals that needed more staff as a result of the increased demand for services and the expansion of subsidized residency programs that resulted from the passage of the Medicare and Medicaid bills. The increase in the size of residency programs in teaching hospitals was only partly related to patient care. Training and research were also expanded greatly in the post-Medicare period.

Table 6.1   Physicians per 100,000 Persons in the United States, 1950 to 2001

Year	Physicians per 100,000 Population	Physician/Population (excludes internationally trained physicians)[a]	Internationally Trained Physicians as Percentage of Active Physicians[a]
1950	139	—	—
1960	139	130	6.1
1970	154	127	17.5
1980	207	164	21.1
1990	273	213	21.9
2001	294	224	24.4

[a]The category "internationally trained" does not include physicians trained in U.S. territories or Canada.
Source: Derived from *OECD Health Data 2003* (Paris: Organization for Economic Cooperation and Development, 2003) and Pasko, Thomas and Derek R. Smart, *Physician Characteristics and Distribution in the US 2003–2004* (Chicago: AMA 2003), Table 5.16.

By 1970, returns to physicians' training, adjusted for hours worked, had become approximately equal to the returns to lawyers and dentists, but were still higher than the returns in some other professions requiring graduate degrees.[11] By 1991, internal rates of return to physicians were comparable to, and in the case of primary care physicians lower than, the returns to training in business or law.

Table 6.2 shows hours-adjusted internal rates of return (IRR) and net discounted present values (PV), discounted at 5 percent for several professions. It is necessary to adjust for average hours worked per year in different professions because they differ significantly.

Table 6.2   Rates of Return in Selected Professions, 1991

Profession	Hours Adjusted IRR	Hours Adjusted PV
Business	23.26	4.47
Law	23.93	8.31
Dentistry	19.69	5.93
Procedure-based medicine[a]	20.23	9.44
Primary care medicine	15.28	3.97

[a]Procedure-based medicine includes surgical specialties, anesthesiology, and radiology. Primary care includes internal medicine, family practice, and pediatrics.
Source: Weeks, W. B., M.D., et al., "A Comparison of the Educational Costs and Incomes of Physicians and Other Professionals," *New England Journal of Medicine*, 330 (1994), Table 3.

4   Choice of Field of Specialization

Physicians, even limiting the definition to licensed MDs, are not a homogeneous group. Very few physicians in the United States today have only the basic M.D. degree. Primary care physicians have usually completed residencies in fields such as internal medicine or family medicine.*

Some additional facts, not revealed in Table 6.3, are instructive. The proportion of graduates of U.S. medical schools undertaking residencies in internal medicine declined by over 30 percent between 1986 and 1994. This means that an ever higher proportion of physicians in primary care fields had their training outside the United States. There was a decline of 45 percent over the same time period in office-based primary care physicians in poor urban settings.[12] Higher earnings, greater prestige, and also more regular hours attracted physicians to other specialties.[13] However, as Table 6.3 shows, between 1996 and 2001 the proportion of physicians in the practice of primary care was stabilized and remained roughly constant.

Using Economic Incentives to Alter the Distribution of Physicians

Subsidies for medical training in the form of below market (and deferred) interest-bearing loans to students and subsidies to medical schools and teaching hospitals for residency training programs result in private costs of training that are much lower than the total costs to society (social costs). Individuals' decisions about how much training to undertake are based on private costs and returns. Individuals will undertake additional training until the private marginal return on an additional unit of training is just equal to the private marginal cost. This may result in a balance of physicians trained in specialties that is not ideal from society's

Table 6.3   Percentage Distribution of GPs and Primary Care Physicians in the United States, 1970 to 2001

	1970	1980	1990	1996	2001
Primary care	40.2%	36.5%	34.7%	34.0%	33.9%
General practice (GP)	17.3%	7.0%	3.7%	2.3%	1.7%

Sources: Rich, Eugene C., *Physician Characteristics and Distribution in the US, 1997–1998 Edition* (Chicago: AMA, 1997), Table A3, and Pasko, Thomas and Derek R. Smart, *Physician Characteristics and Distribution in the US, 2003–2004 Edition* (Chicago: AMA, 2003), Table 1.

*As will be discussed in Chapter Twelve, the ratio of other specialists to primary care physicians in the United States is the inverse of that which pertains in Canada and the United Kingdom, both of which have about two-thirds of their physicians providing primary care.

point of view. Figure 6.2 illustrates this. It uses number of years of training to approximate different specialty fields.

Optimality, from the point of view of the society, is achieved when the marginal social benefit is just equal to the marginal social cost of the last unit of a good or service produced. If there is a divergence between society's goals and the incentives provided by the private market, society's goals are not likely to be achieved unless the incentive structure is changed.

Public Policy to Change Incentives

The U.S. government has a policy of forgiving a limited number of student loans for physicians who agree to practice medicine in underserved geographical areas under the National Health Service Corps.* Changes in the fee structure of Medicare to favor primary care physicians can also be viewed as a public policy designed to alter the supply of physicians in different specialties.

Incentives Provided by the Private Insurance Market

The enhanced use of the primary care physician in HMOs increases the opportunities for primary care physicians. Increased market penetration by managed care insurers over the period 1985 to 1993 was found to be associated with a narrowing of the difference between earnings of primary care physicians and specialists such as radiologists, anesthesiologists, and pathologists.† Metropolitan areas with greater HMO penetration experienced slower rates of growth in specialists and in total number of physicians, but no change in the rate of growth in general practitioners, over the period 1987 to 1997.[14]

Has Changing the Incentives Made a Difference?

Fields Chosen by Younger Physicians

The distribution of physicians by specialty shows a different pattern if we take account of age. As is shown in Table 6.4, by 2001, over half of the female and over 40 percent of the male physicians under 35 years of age were practicing in the fields of internal medicine, family practice, and pediatrics. (The first two fields of practice are often classified as primary care.) By 2001, female physicians comprised about 25 percent of the total number of practicing physicians in the United

---

*However, the rate of retention of these physicians in the underserved areas has been very low. See Cullen, T. J., et al., *The National Health Service Corps: Rural Physician Service and Retention* (Seattle, WA: WAMI Rural Health Research Center, 1994).

†Simon, Carol J., et al., "The Effect of Managed Care on the Incomes of Primary Care and Specialty Physicians," *Health Services Research*, 33 (1998): 549–569. Physicians also appear to have responded to downward pressures on independent private practice income by moving into salaried positions as the differential in earnings between self-employed private practice and salaried positions declined. There is evidence that HMO penetration reduces the probability that both specialists and generalists will be self-employed.

Figure 6.2

Diverging
Private and
Social Optima

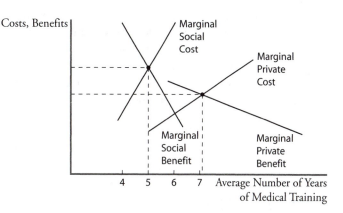

States.* The proportion of females is much higher in younger physician cohorts. By 1990, first-year medical school student classes were approximately 40 percent female. This proportion rose over the next decade and now approaches 50 percent.[15]

Table 6.4   Distribution of Physicians <35 years of age by Sex and Field (includes fields comprising 2% or more, 2001[a]

Female Physicians		Male Physicians	
Internal medicine	23.3%	Internal medicine	23.7%
Pediatrics	18.3%	Family practice	10.2%
Family practice	13.6%	General surgery	8.1%
Obstetrics/gynecology	8.5%	Pediatrics	7.3%
General surgery	3.5%	Emergency medicine	4.9%
Psychiatry	3.3%	Orthopedic surgery	4.2%
Emergency medicine	2.8%	Anesthesiology	3.6%
Anesthesiology	2.0%	Obstetrics/gynecology	2.6%

[a]Includes internationally trained physicians as well. Their decisions about training will have been made in different institutional settings and often before the decision to immigrate to the United States.
Source: Center for Health Policy Research, American Medical Association, *Physician Marketplace Characteristics, 1997–1998* (Chicago: AMA, 1998) Table 1.14.

*The distribution of racial and ethnic minorities in fields of specialization shows some distinct patterns. However, this has very little effect on the overall distribution since in 2001 blacks comprised only 2.5 percent of active physicians and Hispanics comprised only 3.4 percent. Asians, the largest minority group of physicians, comprised only 8.8 percent of the total. See Pasko and Smart (2003), op. cit., p. 6.

Physicians under the age of 35 in 2001 who were trained in the United States would have been making decisions about fields beginning in approximately 1991, when the Medicare payment reforms were already in place and managed care was beginning to make serious inroads into national markets. However, decisions must have been based on factors other than the earnings in different specialist fields, given the distribution of earnings in different specialties at that time. (See Appendix in this chapter, Table 6.7). A recent study of factors influencing medical students' choice of specialty found that expected earnings were important, but guaranteed annual vacations, more certain work schedules, and shorter periods of residency training were more important determinants of choice.[16]

5   Supply of Physician Services

The supply of *physicians' services* depends on not only the number of licensed MDs, but also physicians' decisions about how many hours to work and about how many nonphysicians to employ in office practices. The latter decision is made by both physicians in independent private practice and by HMOs.

Utility Functions and Production Functions

To illustrate how physicians in private practice decide on hours and practice styles, we can use *production functions* and *utility functions.* Let us begin by assuming that physicians want to maximize "utility" and that utility is a function of income and leisure. This can be formally expressed in the following specification, called a utility function:

$$U = U(I, N, L)$$

where U is utility, I physician's income from the practice of medicine, N nonlabor income, and L leisure. In labor economics, the word "leisure" is used as a shorthand for all time spent in activities related to life in the household, for example, as a consumer. This includes time for recreation and time in "household production," which includes such activities as parenting, cooking, cleaning, doing yard work, handling personal finances, and so on.[17] Leisure is assumed to provide utility directly. Time spent working (in the labor force) provides utility as a result of earning income. Of course, it may also provide some utility directly if work is enjoyable. People will tend to substitute labor for leisure when the wage or salary level increases. This is the *substitution effect* or relative price effect. At a higher wage, leisure is more expensive because the opportunity cost of time is higher, since one is sacrificing more income per hour of leisure. However, as income increases, people are also observed to substitute leisure for labor. This is known as the *income effect.*

Income from a fee-for-service-based private physician practice is a function of the number of hours devoted to the practice of medicine, how productive the practice is (how many office visits are "produced" per day or week), and the price charged per unit of service. A generalized production function for physician services can be represented as

$$\theta = F(X_1, \ldots, X_n)^{18}$$

where θ is the output (number of office visits per week) and the X_i's are the inputs, including physician hours, nurse hours, receptionist hours, hours of equipment use, and so on. The various inputs may be either substitutes or complements for each other. If p is the price of an office visit, then

$$I = F(\theta, p)$$

Physician income can be altered by adjusting hours worked, purchasing different amounts of help from others, or changing the price of a unit of service. Empirical studies show that physicians worked fewer hours, employed fewer registered nurses, but used more administrative aides in 2000 than in the 1970s.[19]

A Backward-Bending Labor Supply Curve for Physicians?

This framework of analysis allows us to see that production and consumption decisions of physicians are, in fact, interdependent. Martin Feldstein developed a model incorporating this interdependency in 1970.[20] Studies using this approach have shown that increases in physician fees lead them to reduce their own hours devoted to the practice of medicine, but to increase the size of their practices by hiring enough nonphysician aides to more than offset the reduction in their own hours of work.[21] When greater HMO penetration into markets changed the relative earnings in favor of primary care physicians, they were also observed to reduce the number of hours they worked relative to other specialists.[22] Thus, the income effect dominated the substitution effect. The supply of physician *hours* appears to be subject to what is called a **backward bending labor supply curve**.

In Figure 6.3 when the imputed wage rises above A, hours worked decline. (The term *imputed wage* is used because physicians are not usually paid by the hour. We impute a wage by taking annual income from the practice of medicine and dividing it by the number of hours worked per year.) Up to point A, a rise in the imputed wage is associated with an increase in hours worked. At A, the inflection point in the labor supply curve, the income effect begins to dominate the substitution effect. At higher imputed wages, more leisure time is traded for additional income. This phenomenon does not appear to be true for physicians in training. Studies of residents have shown an increase in wages to be associated with an increase in hours worked in hospitals.[23] The explanation is that residents' wages are below the inflection point A on the supply curve in Figure 6.3.

If physicians' ability to substitute nonphysician aides results in the same number or more office visits per week when physician incomes rise, the supply curve of physician services will not be subject to the backward-bending supply curve phenomenon. One reason why physicians may have cut back on time spent in

Figure 6.3

A Backward-Bending
Physicians' Supply
Curve

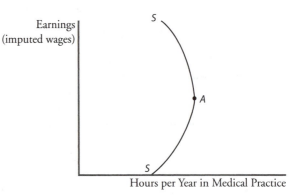

office practices is that fewer physicians are now engaged in solo practices and the average size of a group practice has increased.[24] Research has shown that physicians are more able to use aides efficiently when they are in group practices.[25]

6   Projections About the Supply and Demand of Physicians: Views of Economists and Health Planners

By the late 1970s, it was widely believed that there had been a "policy overshoot" and an oversupply of physicians would soon develop. Congress, concerned whether Medicare should continue to provide several billion dollars a year in support for residency programs, established the Council on Graduate Medical Education. This council concluded that by the year 2000 the overall physician/population ratio would be more than adequate. It also predicted that the supply of specialists would be 60 percent higher than needed. It recommended that subsidies to hospital residency programs be scaled back and more medical students be directed into the field of primary care medicine.[26] The number of places in U.S. medical schools was stabilized and has remained roughly constant.

The physician surplus projected in 1980 has not occurred. It was based on a wrong assumption that traditional staff-type HMOs would dominate the market for the delivery of health care. This led to predictions that physicians would be seeing a larger volume of patients per week and that gatekeeper primary care physicians would ration referrals to specialists. Instead, the popularity of hybrid forms of insurance policies, such as PPOs, has left Americans with a good deal of choice in their use of physicians. That plus unforeseen improvements in medical technology have resulted in a higher demand for physician services than was predicted 20 years ago.

At the present time, predictions about the adequacy of the future supply of physicians vary.* Some see a shortage looming ahead, but this view is not universally accepted. A roundtable discussion in the journal *Medical Crossfire* in August 2001, provided a representative sample of views.[27] Uwe Reinhardt predicts a likely shortage of physicians and other health-care workers when the baby boomers reach senior citizen age.[28] He would, however, leave it to the market to make the adjustment. The CEO of a major teaching hospital predicts that there will continue to be an inadequate number of American graduates of U.S. medical schools to fill hospital residencies.[29] He would reorganize medical school and residency programs to make them more attractive to students, such as the one quoted at the beginning of this chapter. Jonathan Weiner does not foresee a global shortage of physicians in the United States, but he predicts that present shortages in some specialties and geographic areas will continue.[30] Weiner's confidence in the adequacy of the overall physician supply is based on his belief that there will be a substitution of more nonphysician health-care workers for MDs in the delivery of medical care. His approach is one that, unlike the early health planners' evaluations, takes account of shifting production functions for health care.[31] The director of a training program in family medicine believes that present shortages in rural areas which have large Medicare and Medicaid populations will increase. He would not leave the adjustment of this geographical imbalance to the market, but would use some planning device to alter the number of openings in medical schools and residency programs. His approach is that of the health policy planner favoring a needs-based allocation of resources to achieve social goals.

Two questions come to mind: Would not rationing openings for what are now popular specialist fields depress the demand for medical education in the United States? And, given American preferences, will Weiner's plan to offer a new style of medical care with more nurse practitioners, physicians' assistants, and fewer MDs be acceptable to the "consumers" of medical care? The difference between the economist's and the medical/health planner's perspective is revealed in this representative sample of expert opinions.

Supply and Demand of Nurses

7   Understanding the Nurses' Market

The term *nurse* will be used throughout this chapter to mean a registered nurse (RN). There are three different paths to achieving an R.N. degree. Two-year associate programs in community colleges and three-year diploma programs in hospitals coexist with B.A. programs in four-year colleges. Graduate programs in nursing, leading to an M.A. or even a Ph.D., are also available. Registered nurses, like

---

*A perusal of the *Journal of the American Medical Association* will confirm this. Or, log onto google.com and you will find thousands of references if you search on "doctor shortage."

physicians, can undertake additional training in specialist areas.* As the production function for health care changes, the demand for nurses is affected.

The main employer of registered nurses has traditionally been the hospital, even though by the end of the 1990s the proportion of nurses employed in hospitals had fallen to about 60 percent.[32] The greater intensity of care within acute-care hospitals increases the desired nurse/patient ratio and the demand for hospital nurses, whereas a reduction in the use of in-patient hospital services tends to reduce nurse employment in hospitals. To the extent that HMOs and other integrated health-care delivery systems are able to substitute nurses for physicians in ambulatory settings, this tends to increase the demand for nurses in nonhospital settings.

The supply of nurses depends on the decisions of young men and women to undertake nurses training and to work in the profession once training is completed. Public policy is just as important in determining the training opportunities for nurses as it is for physicians. The relative rate of return to this occupation compared with other occupations that require comparable training undoubtedly affects the supply. As nursing is an occupation that is predominantly female, it is usually compared with other female-dominated occupations. As opportunities in occupations that were formerly closed to women or difficult for them to enter become more available, the supply of women who choose to enter any of the traditional female occupations will tend to decline. Opportunities for women to become physicians undoubtedly provides an alternative for those who might otherwise enter the nursing profession. As the proportion of male RNs has remained small, under 5 percent, we cannot assume that a substitution of male for female nurses will do much to offset the increase in other professional opportunities for women.

8   Has There Been a Chronic Shortage of Nurses?

There have been perennial allegations of a **nurse shortage**, using both the health-care planners' and the economists' definitions of shortage. The American Hospital Association complained of nurse shortages in the 1950s and 1960s and supported these claims by noting the high vacancy rates in registered nurse positions and the substitution of less highly trained licensed practical nurses for RNs. The demand for nurses was greater than the supply *at the going wage rate*. From the 1940s to the early 1960s, vacancy rates for hospital nurses never fell below 13 percent and reached a level of 23 percent in 1962.[33]

Congress responded by passing the Nurse Training Act (NTA) in 1964, which began a tradition of government subsidization of nurses' training. Using vacancy rates in hospitals as an indicator, the legislation that supported nurses' training

---

*A number of medical schools now offer two-year graduate training leading to the certification as a physician's assistant (PA). This is not a graduate R.N. degree, but a substitute form of training.

appears to have mitigated the shortage. Vacancy rates fell to below 10 percent by 1971.*

Between 1971 and the present, there appear to have been a number of periods of adjustment in which high vacancy rates were followed by policy to expand nurses' training, followed by reductions in shortages. Wages have responded, for the most part, to shortages. Since the training period is so much shorter, responses to imbalances in supply and demand are more rapid than in the case of physicians' training.

Historical Overview: 1980 to the Present

Cyclical Shortages and Policy Responses

Nurses' decisions about whether to enter the labor force and how many hours to work are also very cyclical. The reason for this is that a very high proportion of nurses are married and therefore are part of two-earner families. They go in and out of the labor force as employment opportunities and real wages change, but also in response to the employment situation of their spouses. Vacancy rates in nursing are typically much lower in periods of economic recession.

A recession in the early 1980s increased the labor force participation rate of trained nurses and reduced the vacancy rate to a record low of under 5 percent, but by the end of the 1980s it exceeded 12 percent A decline in the participation rate of nurses when the economy improved, an increase in the demand for hospital nurses, and a decline in entrants into nurses' training in the early 1980s all contributed to the reemergence of a shortage.[34] This led to the passage of the Nurse Shortage Reduction Act of 1988, which provided additional subsidies for nurses' training, and The Nurse Relief Act of 1989, which relaxed restrictions on the immigration of foreign-trained nurses. The result was a rapid increase in the supply of nurses. Vacancy rates declined again by the mid-1990s, due in part to the 1992 recession that was again accompanied by higher participation rates of nurses. However, since then vacancy rates have been rising again in many parts of the country.†

---

*Feldstein, Paul J., *Health Care Economics*, 5th ed. (Albany: Delmar, 1999), Chap. 15, argues that the NTA was not that effective. Two-year associate programs in nursing in community colleges increased dramatically during this period. Rates of return on these shorter degree programs were high, compared to alternative employment for women with certificates from other two-year college programs. Moreover, the increase in enrollments in the associate degree programs preceded the passage of the NTA.

†A representative sample shows them to vary considerably across the United States. The overall RN vacancy rate in California in 1997 was 8.5 percent. The hospital vacancy rate was 9.6 percent. In 2000, hospitals in the Dallas-Fort Worth area reported an RN vacancy rate of 9.3 percent in emergency room service and a rate of 16.9 percent in critical care units. Vermont reported nursing home RN vacancy rates of 15.9 percent. Scanlon, William, Director, Health Care Issues, GAO, *Nursing Workforce: Recruitment and Retention of Nurses and Nurses Aides Is a Growing Concern* (Washington, DC: U.S. Government Accounting Office, May 2001), p. 4.

Table 6.5   Number of RNs, Licensed MDs, and Nursing and Medical Students, United States

Active RNs	Total Physicians	First Year Enrollment: Nursing School	First Year Enrollment: Medical School	Date
1,273,000	487,000	105,952	17,204	1980
2,162,000	775,000	119,205	17,058	1996

Sources: *Statistical Abstract of the United States, 1998–1999;* (Washington, DC: U.S.G.P.O., 1999); U.S Department of Health and Human Services, *Health United States, 2000* (Washington, DC: DHHS, 1999); and Jonas, H. S. et. al., "Educational Programs in U.S. Medical Schools," *Journal of the American Medical Association,* 7 (1991), p. 916 and 9 (1996), p. 716.

Using the statistics in Table 6.5, we discover that although there were cycles in the supply of nurses, between 1980 and 1995 the ratio of nurses to U.S. population increased from 5.6/1,000 to 7.9/1,000. Comparison of changes in enrollments in nurses' training programs and in medical schools, 1980 to 1996, shows an increase of 12.5 percent in enrollments in nurses' training, during which time there was a virtual freeze on medical school enrollments.*

The number of practicing physicians, including foreign-trained physicians, increased by 59 percent over the same period compared with a 69 percent increase in active RNs.† Therefore, the nurse/physician ratio increased as well as the nurse/population ratio.

Despite public subsidies supporting nurses' training, after peaking in 1994 at 129,897, first-year enrollments in nursing programs began to fall.[35] Between 1993 and 1995, enrollment in associate degree programs declined by 11 percent and enrollment in diploma programs dropped by 42 percent. The decline in entrants to nurses' training programs has continued to decline.

Nurses Wages

From the late 1940s to the early 1960s, nurses' wages declined relative to other female professionals despite high vacancy rates. During that same period, nurses who were employed in nonhospital jobs experienced relative increases in wages compared with those employed in the hospital sector.[36]

The situation changed with the advent of Medicare. Hospital nurses' salaries increased relative to their nonhospital colleagues, and they achieved parity with earnings in other female occupations requiring the same level of education. Price controls in the 1970s restrained nurses' wages, but they rose again as soon as the controls were removed in 1974. Even during the 1979 and 1980 recession, nurses' real wages were observed to increase. Wage levels were maintained throughout the 1980s.[37] Nurses' real wages increased between 1983 and 1993, followed by a temporary decline from 1993 to 1997.[38] The increase in the supply of nurses re-

---

*If 1995 had been used instead of 1996, the increase in enrollments in nurses training from 1980 would have been approximately 20 percent.

†These figures have been computed from Table 6.5.

sulting from the Nurse Shortage Reduction Act of 1988 was probably a factor, since vacancy rates also declined during the same period. However, demand side pressures may also have contributed. Cost-containment policies of managed care insurers have frequently been alleged to result in hospitals skimping on nursing care.* However, HMO penetration of markets appears to have explained at most a very small proportion of the short-term real wage decline for nurses in the 1990s.[39] Since 1998, the wages of hospital nurses have increased both absolutely and relative to wages for other women with comparable education levels.[40]

Is the Market for Nurses a Monopsony?

Two dominant themes in the literature about nurses markets have been the alleged chronic shortage of registered nurses and the notion that nurses are "underpaid." The linking of shortages and low wages is puzzling. Since a shortage occurs when the quantity demanded is greater than the quantity supplied at a given wage, in a well functioning competitive market a shortage should be resolved by wages increasing until equilibrium has been restored. The model of monopsony has often been used to explain this puzzle. A monopsonist is a monopoly buyer (employer). The market for registered nurses has been used as a classic textbook example of monopsony. If there is only one hospital in a region, it has potential monopsony power over its nursing supply. Several hospitals might collude with respect to wages offered to nurses, in which case the effect would be the same.

For monopsony to affect market outcomes, the supply curve of workers must be upward-sloping, which means that in order to attract more workers, the employer has to raise wages. The supply curve is an average factor cost curve from the point of view of the employer, if we assume that all persons who do the same work are paid an equivalent wage.† If a firm is the only firm employing a given kind of worker, it is the wage setter. Therefore, it must look at the *marginal* cost of hiring additional workers. When the supply curve (average factor cost curve) is upward-sloping, the marginal factor cost curve rises more steeply than the average factor cost curve, as is shown in Figure 6.4. If the firm has to offer a higher wage to get additional workers, it must also raise the wages of the workers it already employs.

The demand schedule for any input into production is its marginal revenue product curve. The demand curve shows the maximum amount that an employer

*For instance, the California Nursing Association alleged that Kaiser-Permanente hospitals were reducing nursing staffs to dangerous levels during the last half of the 1990s. There has been political pressure in a number of states for legislation to mandate minimum levels of nursing staff requirements for hospitals. A thorough discussion of the effect of HMO penetration on utilization of registered nurses in California hospitals is given in Spetz, Joanne, "The Effects of Managed Care and Prospective Payment on the Demand for Hospital Nurses," *Health Services Research,* 34 (1999): 993–1010.

†This is consistent with people who have more seniority earning more per hour as long as the wage scale shifts up and down with changes in the number of workers employed.

Figure 6.4

Monopsony : An
Employer Who Has
Monopoly Buying
Power

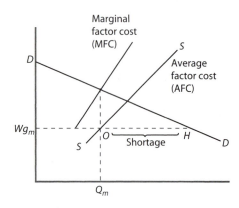

will pay for any given quantity of workers hired. A hospital will not pay more for an extra nurse (or extra hour of nursing service) than its *marginal* contribution to revenue. A firm will hire workers up to the quantity where the marginal factor cost (MFC) of the last worker (or hour of work) hired just equals the marginal revenue product (MRP) of that last worker (or hour). This satisfies the profit-maximizing criterion, MR = MC. In Figure 6.4, (Wg_m, Q_m) shows the quantity of nursing help that will be employed and the wage that will be paid by the monopsonist. At (Wg_m, Q_m), quantity demanded exceeds quantity supplied by OH. OH measures the amount of vacancy. The monopsony model can explain the coexistence of high vacancy rates and lower than competitive wages of nurses.

The period from the 1940s until the advent of Medicare in the mid-1960s appears to be one in which the monopsony model fits the facts reasonably well. This model is less useful in explaining the trends in employment and earnings of registered nurses in the post-Medicare period. After 1965, except for short periods of adjustment, real wages for nurses increased along with demand. The decline in nurses' wages from 1993 to 1997 can be explained without reference to monopsony as the result of a rapid increase in supply and some downward pressure in demand for hospital nurses.

However, economists have revisited the issue of monopsony in the market for nurses. Hospitals have been found to be wage setters and the short run supply of nurses to be extremely wage-inelastic.[41] Staiger and co-authors employ the model developed by Card and Krueger to explain the employment effects of minimum wages.[42] The model incorporates an assumption that workers have imperfect information. Lack of information about alternatives ties workers to a local employer even when that employer is not, strictly speaking, a monopoly buyer. Janet Currie and co-authors use the same model but apply it in a different way. They argue that monopsony may not even manifest itself in downward pressure on wages. Instead, nurses are made to exert more effort when employers have greater market power.[43] A study of the Australian nursing market makes a strong case for the existence of monopsony there. Australian nurses are paid roughly 20 percent less than other comparable workers in a period of high vacancy rates.[44]

On the other hand, Hirsch and Schumacher have found nurses' wages to be no lower in areas in which there was greater concentration in the hospital markets.[45] They reject the hypothesis of monopsony in the market for hospital nurses on either the classic or "new" interpretations of the monopsony model, since they find evidence of greater mobility of nurses to move between employers within local or regional markets than is true of other workers, both men and women. They argue that this is inconsistent with hospitals having effective monopsony power.[46] They do find some evidence of "short-run" monopsony.

Does the choice of the model used to analyze the nurses' market make a difference in the real world of health-care policy? Lane and Gohmann have shown that it does. Where monopsony exists, policies to eradicate shortages by increasing the supply of workers may actually increase shortages.[47]

In Figure 6.5 the increase in supply from S to S' increases the gap between demand and supply from $ND_1 - NS_1$ to $ND_2 - NS_2$. Under these circumstances, subsidizing nurses' training or importing more nurses from abroad will not be an effective policy. Alternative ways of reducing shortages would have to be employed. For instance, promoting unionization among nurses would provide them with countervailing power. Nursing has not been a highly unionized occupation. The rate of unionization peaked in the late 1970s, at which time it slightly exceeded 20 percent and has since declined.* The imposition of a minimum wage

Figure 6.5†

Effect of Increase in
Supply of Workers
Under Monopsony

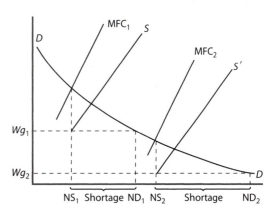

*Non-profit hospitals were exempt from the National Labor Relations Act until 1974. This meant that nurses had no protection of their rights to unionize. The majority of hospitals in the United States are non-profit institutions. (See Chapter Eight.)

†This figure is adapted from Lane, Julia and Stephan Gohmann, "Surplus or Shortage: Economic Approaches to the Analysis of Nursing Labor Markets," *Southern Economic Journal,* 61 (1995), p. 645. By permission of the *Southern Economic Journal.*

for nurses, which would have to be higher than the minimum wage that applies to unskilled labor, is another possibility. Another possible policy is direct wage subsidies to hospital nurses.*

Increasing the skill level of training might give nurses more power, especially if it were combined with changes in legal restrictions on what tasks they can perform. These have been aims of the American Nurses Association since the 1960s. However, studies over the past 20 years have found that employers pay only modest premiums for B.A. degrees.[48] Since 1990 there has been some increase in the number of nurses receiving baccalaureate degrees in four-year colleges, but the most prevalent form of degree is still the two-year associate degree.

An innovative way of dealing with hospital nurse shortages is the use of **contract labor**. "Temp agencies" supply nurses on a short-term basis. When nurses supply their services through these temp agencies they trade off fringe benefits and job security for higher hourly wages and more flexible hours.[49] In a profession dominated by married women, this trade-off may be optimal for both employer and employee. The use of RN temps is efficient for hospitals facing highly variable demand for nurses. Moreover, since salaried staff nurses' wages are not directly affected by the wages paid to temp nurses, employment of nurses might be expanded more than otherwise where hospitals have monopsony power.

9   Projections About Future Demand and Supply for Nurses' Services

Health planners are again expressing concern about a shortage of nurses. This is typified by a statement before the Committee on Health, Education, Labor and Pensions, in the U.S. Senate:

> Recruitment and retention of both nurses and nurses aides are major concerns for health care providers. Experts and providers are reporting a current shortage of nurses, partly as a result of patients' increasingly complex care needs. While comprehensive data are lacking on the nature and extent of the shortage, it is expected to become more serious in the future as the aging of the population substantially increases the demand for nurses. Moreover, several factors are combining to constrain the current and future supply of nurses. Like the general population, the nurse workforce is aging. . . . Enrollments in nursing programs have declined over the past 5 years.[50]

---

*Feldstein notes that the federal expenditure for nurses' training programs from 1965 to 1981 was about $1.57 billion. He estimates that the increase in employment of nurses over that period was only 24,000. This leads to the conclusion that a subsidy of $65,000 per employed nurse was given to nursing schools. He argues that direct subsidies to nurses would have been less expensive. Feldstein (1999) op. cit. p. 451.

Table 6.6   Projected Supply and Demand for RNs

Year (December 31st)	Full-Time Equivalent RN Supply	Demand for Full-Time-Equivalent RNs
1998	1,926,000	1,915,000
2000	1,957,000	1,943,000
2003	2.075,000	2,048,000
2010	2,214,000	2,232,000
2015	2,277,000	2,391,000
2020	2,284,000	2,575,000

Source: Levine, Linda, et al., "A Shortage of Registered Nurses: Is It on the Horizon or Already Here?" *Congressional Research Report for Congress,* May 18, 2001 (Washington, DC: Library of Congress, 2001), Table 6.

The American Nurses Association testimony to Congress on methods for reducing medical errors has noted the negative impact of the nurse shortage, which leads to excessive hours of work and rotations to services for which training and experience are inadequate.[51]

A U.S. government projection of the future supply and demand conditions for RNs shows quantity demanded exceeding quantity supplied by the year 2010. The figures in Table 6.6 assume that nurses' wages are maintained at a constant real level, that is, they are adjusted by expected increases in the price index.

Summary

Historically, the physician market was characterized by entry barriers leading to higher than competitive rates of return. In the past 15 years, average hours-adjusted rates of return have been no higher for physicians as a whole than for a variety of other professionals and lower for primary care physicians. Managed care and Medicare appear to have exerted downward pressure on physicians' earnings and also changed the relative returns to different specialties. This plus the large increase in the proportion of women physicians appears to be resulting in a trend toward more primary care physicians, but as their earnings have increased, they have cut back on the number of hours worked. This results in a relatively smaller increase in primary care physician services.

Over time, the pendulum has swung back and forth between perceived physician shortages and projected surpluses, but there has been a persistent geographical maldistribution of physicians.

Unlike the market for physicians, the historical nurses' market appears to have been one in which the employer had monopoly power. This is the usual explanation for the combination of low wages and high vacancy rates that prevailed from the 1940s to the mid-1960s. The present situation is more complicated. Vacancy rates are again rising, but so are wages. Projections are that the demand for nurses will outstrip the supply in the next two decades. Some researchers still find evidence of monopsony. If monopsony is important, increasing the supply of nurses will not be effective in eliminating shortages and may even lead to a larger gap between supply and demand. In that situation, unionization, a minimum nursing wage, or even direct wage subsidies to nurses might help alleviate shortages. Developing more highly differentiated services through specializing and upgrading of skills should make nursing more attractive and possibly also give nurses more market power. Productivity in the delivery of health care might also be improved by removing some of the legal barriers that limit the substitutability between nurses and physicians. This has been proposed by not only nurses associations but also other health-care professionals.

Appendix: Earnings Differences by Selected Specialties

The information given in Table 6.7 takes account of the costs of a medical practice, including malpractice insurance. It does not account for differences in length and cost of training. Moreover, if the average age of physicians differs by specialty, that will create a bias since physician earnings tend to rise with age. However, this information does indicate a wide difference in incomes between specialties, including those that have residencies of roughly the same length, for instance, neurology and orthopedic surgery.

Table 6.7   Mean Net Income After Expenses for Nonfederal Physicians ($1000's), 1996

Family practice	139.1
General internal medicine	161.9
General surgery	241.7
Orthopedic surgery	341.1
Obstetrics/gynecology	231.1
Diagnostic radiology	269.1
Psychiatry	133.7
Neurology	175.0
Anesthesiology	228.4
Dermatology	223.6

Source: Center for Health Policy Research, American Medical Association *Physician Marketplace Characteristics, 1997–1998* (Chicago: AMA, 1998), Table 75, p. 88.

Key Concepts

Physician shortage

Internal rate of return

Backward-bending labor supply curve

Nurse shortage

Monopsony

Contract labor

Suggested Readings

1. Scott, Anthony, "Economics of General Practice," in *Handbook of Health Economics,* Vol. 1B, Authony J. Culyer and Joseph P. Newhouse, eds. (Amsterdam Elsevier, 2000) Chap. 22.

2. Lane, Julia and Stephan Gohmann, "Shortage or Surplus: Economic and Noneconomic Approaches to the Analysis of Nursing Labor Markets," *Southern Economic Journal,* 61 (1995): 644–653.

Questions for Discussion and Review

1. The AMA has often been thought to behave like a trade union in restricting the supply of physicians (in order to keep earnings high). What evidence is there that the AMA has acted in this way?

2. Explain what is meant by the "return to an investment in human capital" and then summarize the findings on the relative returns to training of physicians versus other professionals.

3. What economic reasons are there for the high ratio of specialists to general practitioners in the United States compared with most other countries?

4. Draw a "backward-bending" supply curve for physicians. Then explain, using the notion of income and substitution effects, why this phenomenon may exist in the market for physicians.

5. Explain how there could be both a backward-bending supply curve for physicians and an increase in the supply of physician services associated with increases in physicians' incomes.

6. The quotation at the beginning of Chapter Four suggested that the independent private practitioner, offering services on a fee-for-service basis, has become nearly extinct. What do we know about the trends in solo versus group practice and physicians in private practice firms versus salaried physicians?

7. Is there a chronic shortage of nurses in the United States? Define what you mean by shortage. Differentiate between the economic and health planners' definition of shortage.

8. "The market for hospital nurses may still have some of the characteristics of monopsony." Outline the arguments on both sides of this statement.

Resources

[1]See, for instance, Reinhardt, Uwe E., "Resource Allocation in Health Care: The Allocation of Lifestyles to Providers," *The Millbank Quarterly*, 65 (1987): 153–176.

[2]McGuire, T. G., "Physician Agency," in *Handbook of Health Economics*, Vol. 1A, Anthony J. Culyer and Joseph P. Newhouse, eds. (Amsterdam: Elsevier, 2000), p. 463.

[3]Pasko, Thomas and Derek R. Smart, *Physician Characteristics and Distribution in the US, 2003–2004 Edition* (Chicago: AMA, 2003), p. vi.

[4]Rimlinger, G. V., and H. B. Steele, "An Economic Interpretation of the Spatial Distribution of Physicians in the U.S.," *Southern Economic Journal*, 30 (July 1963): 1–12 and Benham, Lee, et al., "Migration, Location, and Remuneration of Medical Personnel: Physicians and Dentists," *Review of Economics and Statistics,* 50 (1968): 332–347.

[5]See, for instance, Blank, David M. and George W. Stigler, *The Demand and Supply of Scientific Personnel* (New York: National Bureau of Economic Research, 1957).

[6]The general model of investment in human capital is set forth in Becker, Gary S., *Human Capital* (New York: National Bureau of Economic Research, 1963).

[7]Hanson, W. Lee, "Shortages and Investment in Health Manpower," in *The Economics of Health and Medical Care: Proceedings of the Conference on the Economics of Health and Medical Care, May 10–12, 1962* (Ann Arbor: University of Michigan, 1964).

[8]Friedman, Milton and Simon Kuznets, *Income from Independent Professional Practice* (New York: National Bureau of Economic Research, 1945).

[9]Kessel, Reuben A., "Price Discrimination in Medicine," *Journal of Law and Economics*, 1 (1958).

[10]Medical school enrollment in the United States was approximately 33,000 in the academic year of 1965/1966. By 1980, it had risen to approximately 65,000. See Jonas, H. S., et al., "Educational Programs in U.S. Medical Schools," *Journal of the American Medical Association*, 226 (1973): 910 and Barzansky, B., et al., "Education Programs in U.S. Medical Schools," *Journal of the American Medical Association,* 266 (1991): 916.

[11]Mennemeyer, Stephen T., "Really Great Returns to Medical Education?" *Journal of Human Resources,* 13 (1978): 75–90.

[12]Bindman, Andrew B., M.D., "Primary and Managed Care: Ingredients for Health Care Reform," *Western Journal of Medicine,* 161 (1994): 78–82.

[13]McKay, Niccie L., "The Economic Determinants of Specialty Choice by Medical Residents," *Journal of Health Care Economics*, 9 (1990): 335–357.

[14]Escarce, Jose E. et al., "HMO Growth and Geographical Redistribution of Generalist and Specialist Physicians," *Health Services Research*, 35 (2000): 825–848.

[15]Association of American Medical Colleges *AAMC Data Book/2002* (Washington, DC: AAMC, 2002).

[16]Thornton, James and Fred Esposto, "How Important Are Economic Factors in Choice of Medical Specialty?" *Health Economics*, 12 (2003): 67–73.

[17]Becker, Gary, "A Theory of the Allocation of Time," *Economic Journal*, 75 (1965): 493–517.

[18]Reinhardt, Uwe E., "A Production Function for Physician's Services," *Review of Economics and Statistics*, 54 (1972): 55–65 and Thurston, N. K. and A. M. Libby, "A Production Function for Physician Services Revisited," *Review of Economics and Statistics*, 84 (February 2002): 184–191.

[19]Thurston and Libby (2002), op. cit., p. 190.

[20]Feldstein, M., "The Rising Price of Physicians' Services," *Review of Economics and Statistics,* 52 (1970): 121–133.

[21]Brown, D. M. and H. E. Lapin, "The Rising Price of Physicians' Services: A Comment," *Review of Economics and Statistics*, 54 (1972): 101–105 and Thornton, James and B. Kelly Eakin, "The Utility Maximizing Self-Employed Physician," *Journal of Human Resources,* XXXII (1997): 98–128.

[22]Mitchell Jean M. and Jack Hadley, "Effects of Managed Care Market Penetration on Physicians' Labor Supply Decisions," *Quarterly Journal of Economics,* 39 (1999): 491–511.

[23]Culler, S. D. and G. I. Bazzoli, "Moonlighting Behavior Among Young Professionals," *Journal of Health Economics*, 4 (1985): 283–292.

[24]Center for Health Policy Research, American Medical Association, *Socioeconomic Characteristics of Medical Practice 1997–1998* (Chicago: AMA, 1998), Table 2, p. 21.

[25]Brown and Lapin (1972), op. cit. and Thornton and Eakin (1997), op. cit.

[26]Weiner, Jonathan P., "Perspective: A Shortage of Physicians or a Surplus of Assumptions?" http:// content.healthaffairs.org/cgi/reprint/21/1/160.

[27]"Help Wanted: Is a Physician Shortage Looming on the Horizon?" *Medical Crossfire*, 3 (August, 2001), http://www.medicalcrossfire.com/debate_archive/02001/Aug01/Shortage.htm.

[28]Reinhardt, Uwe, as quoted in *Medical Crossfire* (2001), op. cit.

[29]Herbert Pardes, M.D., President and CEO of New York Presbyterian Hospital, a large and prestigious New York City teaching hospital associated with the medical schools of Columbia and Cornell Universities, as quoted in *Medical Crossfire* (2001), op. cit.

[30]Weiner, op. cit.

[31]Jonathan Weiner, Professor of Health Policy and Management at Johns Hopkins University, as quoted in *Medical Crossfire,* (2001) op. cit.

[32]Feldstein, Paul J., *Health Care Economics*, 5th ed. (Albany: Delmar, 1999), Chap. 15.

[33]For a comprehensive analysis of the historical market conditions for nurses, see Yett, Donald E., *An Economic Analysis of the Nurse Shortage* (Lexington, MA: Heath, 1975).

[34]Feldstein (1999) op. cit. pp. 440–441.

[35]*Health United States, 2000: With Adolescent Chart Book* (Washington, DC: U.S. Department of Health and Human Services, 2000), Table 10.4.

[36]Feldstein (1999), op. cit., pp. 440–441.

[37]Schumacher, Edward J., "The Earnings and Employment of Nurses in an Era of Cost Containment," *Industrial and Labor Relations Review,* 55 (2001): 116–132.

[38]Schumacher, Edward J., "Technology, Skills, and Health Care Labor Markets," *Journal of Labor Research,* 23 (2002): 397–415.

[39]Schumacher (2001), op. cit.

[40]Hirsch, Barry T. and Edward. J. Schumacher, *Classic Monopsony or New Monopsony? Searching for Evidence in Nursing Labor Markets,* IZA Discussion Paper No. 1154 (Chicago: Institute for the Study of Labor, May 2004).

[41]See, for instance, Staiger, Douglas, et al., *Is There Monopsony in the Labor Market? Evidence from a Natural Experiment,* NBER Working Paper No. 7258 (Cambridge, MA: National Bureau of Economic Research, July 1999).

[42]Card, David A. and Alan B. Krueger, *Myth and Measurement: The New Economics of the Minimum Wage* (Princeton, NJ: Princeton University Press, 1995).

[43]Currie, Janet et. al., *Cut to the Bone? Hospital Takovers and Nurse Employment,* NBER Working Paper No. 9428 (Cambridge, MA: National Bureau of Economic Research, 2003).

[44]Howak, Margaret J. and Alison C. Preston, "Can Human Capital Theory Explain Why Nurses Are So Poorly Paid?" *Australian Economic Papers,* 40 (June 2001): 232–245.

[45]Hirsch, Barry T. and E. Schumacher, "Monopsony Power and Relative Wages in the Market for Nurses," *Journal of Health Economics,* 14 (1995): 443–476.

[46]Hirsch and Schumacher (2004), op. cit.

[47]Lane, Julia and Stephan Gohmann, "Surplus or Shortage: Economic Approaches to the Analysis of Nursing Labor Markets," *Southern Economic Journal,* 61 (1995): 644–653.

[48]See Mennemeyer, Stephen T. and Gary Gaumer, "Nursing Wages and the Value of Educational Credentials," *Journal of Human Resources,* 18 (1983): 32–48 and Spetz, Joanne, "The Value of Education in a Licensed Profession: The Choice of Associate or Baccalaureate Degrees in Nursing," *Economics of Education Review,* 21 (2002): 73–85.

[49]See Bellemore, Fred. A., "Temporary Employment Decisions of Registered Nurses," *Eastern Economic Journal,* 24 (1998): 265–279.

[50]Scanlon, William, *Nursing Workforce: Recruitment and Retention of Nurses and Nurses Aides Is a Growing Concern* (Washington, DC: U.S. Government Accounting Office, May, 2001), p. 2.

[51]Testimony of American Nurses Association to House Subcommittee for Reducing Medical Errors, 106th Congress, May 8, 2002.

CHAPTER SEVEN

Physicians as Providers of Health Care

It is clear from everyday observation that the behavior expected of sellers of medical care is different from that of business men in general. These expectations are relevant because medical care belongs to the category of commodities for which the product and the activity of production are identical. In all such cases, the customer cannot test the product before consuming it, and there is an element of trust in the relation. But the ethically understood restrictions of the activities of a physician are much more severe than those of, say, a barber. His behavior is supposed to be governed by a concern for the customer's welfare which would not be expected of a salesman. . . . Advice given by a physician as to further treatment by himself or others is supposed to be completely divorced from self-interest. *

1 Introduction

This chapter considers the behavior of physicians in their capacity to organize and direct the path of medical treatment. It will address the question of the physician/patient relationship when patients (the principals) delegate authority (agency) to physicians to make decisions about their health care. Since the institutional context, including the nature of physician firms, market structure,

*Arrow, Kenneth, "Uncertainty and the Welfare Economics of Medical Care," *American Economic Review*, 53 (1963): 949–950.

and method of reimbursement, affects physician incentives, we will examine physician incentives under different market conditions and different payment mechanisms. The practice of defensive medicine will also be considered.

Physician Agency

A patient-initiated physician visit is generally the first step in attaining medical treatment. Once an individual has decided to visit a physician, he or she generally delegates a good deal of authority to the physician to be his or her agent in diagnosing illness and recommending the appropriate path of treatment. This delegation of authority requires the patient's trust that the physician is behaving in the patient's best interest. The complexity of the physician patient relationship in a world with asymmetric information favoring the physician was well described in Kenneth Arrow's classic 1963 article "Uncertainty and the Welfare Economics of Medical Care" from which the quote at the beginning of this chapter is taken.

If we define perfect agency on the part of a physician as acting in the patient's best interest in determining the path of treatment, there are still questions that need to be answered. Does a perfect agent ignore costs and prescribe all treatments that have some positive marginal benefit, or should cost-effectiveness be taken into account? Does the agent take account of ability to pay and recommend a different path of treatment for a patient who is wealthier or has better insurance coverage? Agency is not imperfect as long as the physician uses his or her judgment to make a decision in the interest of the patient's welfare.

Physicians may also be imperfect agents. Imperfect agency manifests itself to a different extent and in different ways in different market situations and under different payment systems. The competitiveness of the market may be relevant. When there is less competition, an imperfect agent may be able to provide inappropriate treatment with less risk that the patients will leave and consult some other physician. It is, however, important to distinguish between imperfect physician agency and other types of behavior that result from market imperfections.

Physicians may be employees or entrepreneurs, owners or part owners of firms that produce and sell services. Physician practices are not expected to be non-profit firms. Nor are physicians expected to be saints. They may charge prices above competitive levels, receiving economic rents. They may locate their office practices in affluent neighborhoods where they can charge higher fees. They may not take on charity cases or even treat Medicaid patients. This is not imperfect agency. Imperfect agency is concerned with the relationship between a physician and a patient. If one accepts a patient for treatment and then provides inappropriate treatment because of self-interest, that is imperfect agency.

We will begin by introducing some fairly standard economic models that assume physician firms have discretion over both price and quantity of the services they produce and sell, and then turn to a newer model that focuses on physicians' ability to alter the quantity of service they provide.

2   Market for Physicians' Services

Monopolistic Competition

The contemporary markets for physician's services provide some examples of behavior that we associate with collusive oligopoly or cartels, organizations that set output quotas and sometimes directly set prices. This is illustrated by the current controversy over whether a large independent practice association, MedSouth, is exempt from antitrust law in jointly contracting with third-party payers.

MedSouth and the FTC

The Federal Trade Commission (FTC) has been involved in recent years with many cases involving independent practice associations (IPAs). One recent high-profile case is that of MedSouth Inc., a 400+ doctor group in Denver, Colorado, which was formed when two IPAs merged. After the merger, the new IPA ceased contracting with local HMOs on a capitation basis and became a group of separate fee-for-service physician practices. Antitrust law allows clinically integrated groups to jointly contract, but in this case the affiliation has the characteristic of a number of separate firms, joined together solely for the purposes of negotiating joint contracts. In ruling on such cases, the FTC has argued that even if physician networks are not financially integrated, they can receive special treatment under the Rule of Reason. MedSouth has attempted to make the case for special treatment under the Rule of Reason on the basis that its negotiations for this large group will improve efficiency in the physician marketplace. The AMA argues that allowing IPAs to bargain with powerful insurance companies and large HMOs provides a balance of power between providers and insurers that would otherwise be lacking.[1] The MedSouth case has received a qualified favorable ruling from the FTC but is being closely monitored.

Examples of vertically and horizontally integrated networks of physicians that have attained a virtual monopoly over local or even regional provision of physician services can also be found.[2]

Even though examples of monopolies or cartels can be found, the contemporary market for physician services is usually described as monopolistically competitive. The model of monopolistic competition provides a broad brush-stroke description of the interaction between an independent physician practice and patients who have traditional fee-for-service indemnity insurance contracts.

In the model, consumers have choice among firms, but firms (physician practices) are not perfect substitutes for one another. Each physician practice is faced with a downward-sloping demand curve; the firm can be assumed to operate in

Figure 7.1

A Monopolistically
Competitive
Physician Firm

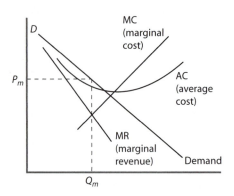

the downward-sloping section of its average cost curve.* The firm produces somewhat less and charges a higher price than would be the case if it were in a perfectly competitive market, faced with perfect substitutes for its services. The quantity of service that a profit-maximizing physician firm will provide is shown in Figure 7.1 as Q_m. The fee for the service is set at P_m.

Price Discrimination

Throughout the nineteenth and twentieth centuries, doctors have been observed to practice **price discrimination**. Price discrimination may be based on ability to pay. The country doctor accepting a chicken or whatever a farm family could pay for his services is a familiar story in our culture. Doctors may have altruistic motives that lead them to charge lower fees to poorer patients (or those with less complete insurance coverage), but the argument that price discrimination is a way of maximizing profits can also be made.

Medical care is a good that has the classic characteristics making price discrimination possible: Physicians can identify separate patients or groups of patients who differ in their price elasticities of demand for the physician's service, and personal medical care is not a good that can be resold in the marketplace. When price discrimination is possible, a firm maximizes profits by equating marginal revenue (MR) and marginal cost (MC) in each of the submarkets, differentiated by degree of price elasticity of demand.

Price and marginal revenue are related through the price elasticity of demand in the following way:

$$MR = P(1 - 1/\eta)$$

where MR is marginal revenue, P = price, and η = elasticity of demand. Profits are maximized by setting MC = MR_1 = MR_2, which is equivalent to

---

*A quick review of monopolistic competition can be found in Appendix 1.

Figure 7.2

Two Way Price
Discrimination

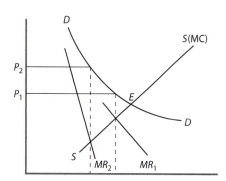

$$MC = P_1 \left(1 - 1/\eta_1\right) = P_2 \left(1 - 1/\eta_2\right)$$

Higher prices will therefore be charged in that segment of the market characterized by the lower price elasticity of demand. Price-discriminating physician firms will tend to charge higher prices to those with more complete insurance coverage, for, as we learned in Chapter Three, insurance coverage reduces the price elasticity of demand.

But how can firms that are not monopolies price-discriminate? One answer is that firms collude, or at least agree not to compete on the basis of price. Direct advertising to consumers was illegal until 1982 and even today physicians and hospitals do not generally engage in overt price competition. That there is an accepted level or range of fees in a local market is shown by the practice of insurance companies who reimburse on the basis of "usual and customary" fees in a locality. Price discrimination is also possible when firms are able to "differentiate their product" in the eyes of the consumers. Patients develop brand loyalty to the physicians whom they know and trust and do not shop around to get the best price for services. A well-known specialist often has a highly differentiated product, based on reputation.

Price discrimination has consequences for economic efficiency. Marginal revenue and marginal cost are equated for separate segments of the market. The quantity supplied is greater with price discrimination than without. This increases economic efficiency since the quantity produced and the price of the last unit sold are closer to the level that would pertain under perfect competition at E in Figure 7.2.* Whether equity is served by price discrimination is a separate issue.

---

*Perfect price discrimination consists of a firm charging exactly what the market will bear for each separate unit offered. If it were possible for firms to engage in perfect price discrimination, the quantity produced under imperfect market conditions would equal the quantity that would be produced and sold in a perfectly competitive market. The reason for this is that the demand curve becomes the marginal revenue curve under conditions of perfect price discrimination.

Cost Shifting: Myth or Reality?

Cost shifting occurs when firms charge higher prices to one group of consumers in order to offset lower payments from others. Price discrimination by itself does not therefore constitute evidence of cost shifting. Cost shifting is commonly believed to be a feature of the market for medical services. It is argued that a higher price will be charged to those who will pay, or whose insurance companies will pay, in order to offset losses incurred from taking charity cases or from receiving lower rates of remuneration from Medicare, Medicaid, or cost-conscious managed care firms.

Cost shifting makes sense only if firms do *not* initially set prices at the profit-maximizing level. Returns will only be increased by raising the price to one set of patients if the firm is initially charging them less than the profit-maximizing price, for instance, P^1 or P^2 in Figure 7.3. The firm can benefit from raising the price of its service from P^1 or P^2 to P^*. If it sets the price higher than P^*, profit declines. The argument against cost shifting can be stated this way: If a firm can increase its profits by raising prices to one group of patients, why does it not do so even in the absence of a reduction in the price that can be charged to another group?

A good deal of empirical work has been devoted to testing for evidence of cost shifting. Much of the research has focused on the behavior of physicians when faced with lower rates of reimbursement from Medicaid.[3] The majority of economists who have studied the issue believe that cost shifting on the part of physicians is not well substantiated.[4] Since the phenomenon of cost shifting is also believed to apply to the pricing of hospital services, this subject will be revisited in the next chapter.

Do Physicians Behave Altruistically?

Most people can probably provide anecdotes of what appear to be acts of altruism on the part of particular physicians. But can a significant pattern of altruistic behavior be observed in large groups of physicians? Fifty years ago, most people would probably have thought the answer was such an obvious "yes" that the question was hardly worth asking. In the ensuing years, physicians have gotten a "bad rap" as the model of profit-maximizing came to be widely accepted as explaining the behavior of physicians.

Broader models of physician behavior have been developed in which physicians are assumed to maximize utility, not just profits. This leaves room for the possibility that altruism can enter into physicians' utility functions. For instance, using a standard utility function in which the physician's utility is a function of income I and leisure L, we can simply add a term for altruism to the physician's utility function:

$$U = f(I, L, A)$$

Utility then becomes a function of income, leisure, and altruism A. A physician will sacrifice some income if the utility received from altruistic behavior, such as

Figure 7.3

Limits to Cost-Shifting

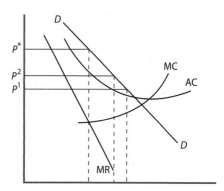

taking on charity cases (patients who cannot pay), more than offsets the loss of utility resulting from the sacrifice in income.

Researchers have attempted to provide empirical tests of altruistic behavior on the part of physicians. Cullen and Ohsfeldt use a model in which the amount of charity care provided is a function of the level of need in the community and the level of fees that can be charged to paying patients. They find the amount of charity care to be positively associated with the level of need in the community and negatively associated with fee level.[5] They explain the latter by introducing the concept of the opportunity cost of time. Physicians' time is less valuable when fees are lower. It is, of course, also possible to argue that physicians who are less materialistic may both charge lower fees and undertake more charity care. Or, it may be the case that fees are related to the level of need in the community. Fee levels are likely to be lower in poorer communities.

Older physicians were found to be more likely to take on charity care; therefore, accepting charity cases was not attributed to practice-enhancing behavior masquerading as charity. Psychiatrists were more likely than other physicians to accept charity patients. This finding supports the hypothesis that charity on the part of physicians is related to patient's need, since psychiatric care is generally less well covered by insurance than most other medical services. Emmons and Rizzo, using the same model, found no relationship between the imputed hourly net earnings of physicians and the amount of charity care provided, but they found specialists of all types, not just psychiatrists, were more disposed to take on charity cases than were primary care physicians.[6] If the costs of specialist treatments are less well covered by insurance, this behavior is consistent with the notion that physicians respond to level of need. Note that these studies provide no evidence of cost shifting, which would require that charity care be associated with higher prices being charged to paying patients.

Do Doctors Avoid Treating Medicaid Patients?

It is interesting to contrast physicians' behavior toward charity patients with their response to participation in the Medicaid program. Physician reimbursements from Medicaid are "below market" and even below Medicare levels in most cases. A number of studies show physicians more willing to treat Medicaid patients when Medicaid fees are raised and the differential between the Medicaid reimbursement and other fees is narrowed.[7] Board-certified specialists are also less likely to accept Medicaid patients. This suggests that the Medicaid program is not regarded by most physicians as an outlet for their altruistic or charitable sentiments. The investigation of the charitable behavior of physicians is a field that invites more research.

3   New Model of Physician Behavior: Physicians as Quantity Setters

Thomas McGuire has developed a model, consistent with the notion of a monopolistically competitive market for physician services, that focuses on the physician's ability to set *quantity* of services for the patient.[8] It is a useful model in an environment in which physicians do not have the ability to set prices. In this model, the demand curve is replaced by the patient's *marginal benefit function*.

The patient is assumed to receive all services of a particular kind from a given physician. However, since there are other physicians in the marketplace, the patient can switch between physicians. The total benefit a patient receives from a physician's services is $B(x)$, where x is the quantity of service. Net benefit is

$$NB(x) = B(x) - p(x)$$

where p is the price of a unit of service.

The model assumes that a given patient has a minimum net benefit level, NB^0, that must be received from a given physician or the patient will leave. In Figure 7.4, this occurs at a quantity x^0. For purposes of simplification, let us assume that the cost to the physician of providing a unit of service c is constant. Profit to the physician from providing a given number of units of service is then $p(x) - c(x)$. The physician is able to make more profit by providing more units of service than the patient would choose on his or her own if the price more than covers the cost of the service.

The lightly shaded triangle in Figure 7.4 is additional net benefit above the minimum required by the patient. For those who are familiar with the concept of consumer surplus, the lightly shaded area may be thought of as consumer surplus. At x^* the consumer surplus is exactly offset by an area of negative net benefits, shown by the darker triangle. The total net benefit at x^* is equal to that at x^0. If the physician tried to require the patient to purchase more than x^* amount of service, the patient's net benefit would fall below the minimally acceptable level and he or she would cease to be the physician's patient.

Figure 7.4

The McGuire Model

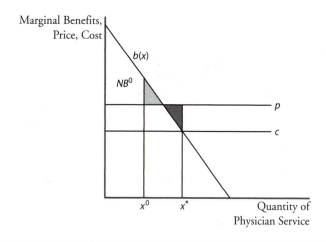

Source: Based on McGuire, T. G. "Physician Agency," Handbook of Health Economics, Vol. 1A, Culyer, A. K. and J. P. Newhouse, eds. (Amsterdam: Elsevier, 2000), Fig. 3, p. 480.

For instance, a patient might think that having a sonogram is adequate, but the radiologist might recommend an MRI as well. If the patient finds value in having this particular radiologist interpret the results (and regards that as providing more than the minimum level of net benefit), he or she will accept the extra test. But if the physician insists on repeat tests every three months, the patient may leave and discontinue treatment or choose another physician.

The model assumes that the physician is the patient's agent, but it is neutral with respect to whether the physician is a perfect or an imperfect agent. It can be used to illustrate the behavior of a doctor in a situation in which the patient does not perceive enough marginal benefit to "choose" the extra units of care $(x^* - x^0)$, but the doctor believes it is good medical practice and in the interest of the patient to prescribe it. The model can also be used to illustrate imperfect agency, since x^* amount of service may be in the physician's, not the patient's, best interest.

4   Hypothesis of Physician-Induced Demand

The Model

The observation that prices of physicians' services were not lower in areas where there were more physicians per population (greater physician density) and that physician density seemed to be positively correlated with intensity of treatment of patients led to the notion of **physician-induced demand (PID)** in the 1970s. PID exists when a physician influences a patient's demand for medical care in a way that is contrary to the physician's judgment of what is in the best interest of the patient.

Demand inducement could not take place in a competitive market where patients had complete knowledge about their own health and appropriate treatment. Even where there is great asymmetry of medical knowledge between patient and physician, the need to maintain the patient's trust imposes a limit on how much demand inducement the physician can undertake. Inducing demand for the purpose of enhancing one's income also runs counter to physicians' professional training and the ethic it imbues. Robert Evans has developed a model of demand inducement that assumes this behavior provides *disutility* to the physician.[9]

If we envision a world in which physicians maximize utility, and in which utility is a function of income *I* and hours of leisure *L*, we can add another term *D* to the utility function:

$$U = U(I, L, D)$$

D is the amount of inducement engaged in by the physician. *I* and *L* are expected to have positive coefficients, and *D* is expected to have a negative coefficient. In Evans's model, *D* is characterized by increasing marginal disutility. If *D* has a negative effect on utility, why would physicians engage in it? The answer is that it increases income, by effectively shifting demand to the right. With inducement, the patient will be willing to purchase more service at the same price. A physician will be willing to induce demand as long as the amount of utility provided by the extra income exceeds the disutility associated with inducing demand.

Referring back to the McGuire model, we see that the limit on how much inducement can be employed in the case of an individual patient is set by the patient's minimum net benefit level. In Figure 7.4, the limit to the amount of inducement that can take place is set at x^*. Physician-induced demand will only be an income-enhancing strategy if doctors are paid on a fee-for-service basis.

Target-Income Hypothesis

A version of the PID model, popular in the 1970s and 1980s, incorporated the notion that physicians do not aim to maximize profits but rather seek to maintain a target income T.[10] The idea was simple and appealing. When income falls below a certain benchmark level, the physician will either increase fees or induce more treatment. If fees cannot be raised, physicians will increase the intensity of treatment. The **target-income hypothesis**, although plausible and once popular, has fallen out of favor. Critics have found it less than theoretically sound and difficult to observe. It is hard to specify what target-income level would trigger PID behavior or how it would be specified in a physician's utility function.

Empirical Studies of PID

The 1970s provided several institutional contexts for testing the hypothesis of PID. Utilization of physicians' services was observed to increase during the price freeze imposed as part of President Nixon's Economic Stabilization Program.

When Medicare lowered relative rates of reimbursement to physicians practicing in urban areas in the state of Colorado, this was associated with an increase in intensity of physician services in cities versus nonurban areas throughout Colorado.[11] A slight tendency for physicians to increase quantity of treatment provided to Medicaid patients when fees declined was also observed in the 1970s.[12]

A study in the 1980s distinguished initial physician visits, assumed to be patient initiated, from follow-up visits. Rossiter and Wilensky found evidence consistent with the theory of inducement, but inducement was of quantitatively minor importance. Initial visits were unaffected by the number of physicians practicing in an area, but follow-up visits increased by about 10 percent when supply of physicians increased by 100 percent.[13] An ingenious study by Dranove and Webner (1994) questioned the validity of the PID theory by testing the absurd hypothesis that obstetricians "induce" the number of pregnancies and births. Using the methodology of some highly respected studies, they found empirical support for their hypothesis.[14] Their work was followed in 1996 by a study of obstetricians that, on the other hand, provided support for the PID hypothesis.[15] Gruber and Owings investigated the association between changes in fertility rates and the rate of cesarean deliveries. There had been a remarkable increase in the use of cesarean section in the delivery of babies in the United States that had raised the question whether financial incentives of physicians played a role. Since, presumably, physician behavior cannot affect fertility rates, despite the tongue-in-cheek findings of Dranove and Webner, fertility rates were used as a measure of an exogenous change in the demand for obstetrical services. A 10 percent decline in cross-state fertility rates was found to be associated with an approximately 1 percent increase in the use of cesarean section for deliveries.

The PID hypothesis has also been tested by looking at the behavior of physicians in cases where they have an economic interest in referrals of patients. If similar patients are more likely to receive prescriptions for auxiliary services when their physicians benefit, this provides indirect support for the PID theory. When physicians benefit from fee splitting, from income generated within their own multispecialty firm, or from earnings of a facility in which they have an ownership interest, we might expect to see more referrals than otherwise. Several studies have shown some evidence of inducement in this context. In one study, physicians who owned imaging machines were observed to order more than 400 percent more tests than those who referred patients to independent radiology labs.[16] Because of a concern over this, many states now prohibit physician ownership of tie-in services.

Since demand inducement requires patients to delegate authority to physicians, one would expect better information on the part of patients to reduce the amount of inducement. Studies of the behavior of physicians and their families as patients found them receiving more care than the average patient for the same medical condition, when extent of insurance coverage, reduced fees due to professional courtesy, and other economic and demographic factors were taken into account. This does not prove the absence of demand inducement, and medical families may indeed have a greater "taste" for medical care than others, but it does not provide any support for it.[17]

The jury remains out on the question of whether PID is an important phenomenon. Some studies show it to have a statistically significant but quantitatively small effect on demand for medical care. Criticism of the empirical work on PID has focused on the failure of researchers to completely control for all the other factors affecting demand. The econometric identification problem may apply to studies of PID. The identification problem exists when there is a problem identifying whether supply, demand, or both have shifted. There might be a shift in demand (independent of physician behavior) that has not been identified. For instance, demand may be greater in areas of greater physician density simply because travel and waiting time are reduced.

Another problem arises from the inability to distinguish between observable utilization rates and unobservable demand. There may be effective rationing of services in communities where physicians are relatively scarce. In that case, utilization of physician services will not accurately reflect demand.

Physicians may also locate their practices in areas of high demand. So, there may be demand-induced supply as well. The issue of supplier-induced demand continues to absorb economists' attention although no definitive answer has been reached about whether it is an important problem.[18] According to a survery conducted by health economist Victor Fuchs, the majority of economists, health economists, and physicians believe that physicians have this power and that "their propensity to induce utilization varies inversely with the level of demand."[19]

5   Physician Behavior in the Age of Managed Care

Almost all physicians now have at least part of their practice income derived from contractual arrangements with third-party payers. By 1997, 92 percent of all physicians in the United States participated in some kind of managed care contracts, with approximately 50 percent of their practice revenues being derived from this source. Fifty-eight percent of all physicians participated in Medicare contracts, 57 percent participated in Medicaid contracts, and 28 percent of physician practice revenue for participating physicians came from these two sources. Ninety percent of physicians participated in private managed care contracts, with 32 percent of their revenues coming from this source.[20]

An environment in which prices for physician services are set by private or governmental third-party payers is well depicted by the McGuire model, since it treats quantity (and quality) as the variable(s) over which physicians have control. In Figure 7.4, p may be an administered price set by the insurer. As long as the price is above the cost of a unit of service, there is an incentive to induce extra treatment, if the physician is an imperfect agent.

Effects of Alternative Reimbursement Methods: Capitation, Salary, or Revenue Sharing

Capitation-Based Pay

Managed care may not only impose limits on what fees physicians charge but also change the form of reimbursement, for instance, from fee-for-service to capitation. The McGuire model is applicable to this situation as well. With a capitation fee, it will be in the interest of a profit-conscious physician to provide the minimum level of service that will satisfy the patient's minimum net benefit requirement, since returns are based on the number of patients one has on one's roster, but costs are a function of quantity of service provided. Skimping on service probably provides disutility to a conscientious doctor just as inducement does, so it will also fit into the physician's utility function as a negative term. If physicians are rewarded for skimping, if, for instance, they receive a bonus from an HMO for economizing on service, this will reduce the negative effect of skimping. Skimping is likely to involve more disutility to the physician than inducing a little unnecessary treatment, since failing to provide an appropriate level of treatment is probably more dangerous to the patient's health. It also may subject the physician to risk of malpractice charges. Studies have compared the amount of treatment provided under capitation versus fee-for-service payment arrangements. At least for surgical procedures, several studies found the amount of treatment per patient to be significantly lower when reimbursement is by capitation.[21] Whether the reduction in service is associated with eliminating unnecessary service (induced demand) or involves skimping is not easy to discover from such studies.

Salaries and Revenue Sharing

Most physicians in the United States who work for staff HMOs are employed on a salaried rather than a capitation basis. There is no incentive either to skimp on care or to induce demand when physicians are paid by salary. However, a salaried position involves the possibility of shirking. Physicians who are in salaried positions or in revenue-sharing partnerships have an incentive to shirk by seeing fewer patients or doing less support work in the office.* This need not involve imperfect agency. It will only do so if shirking is accomplished by skimping on service, such as performing fewer tests or cutting the length of office visits.

---

*Some insight into the way economic incentives affect physician behavior is provided by a study of large group physician practices, where earnings are a function of the productivity of the entire group. In a large group practice, the effect of any one physician's behavior is spread over the whole group. In this setting, it was found that moving from fee-for-service to revenue sharing involved significant costs to large group practices as a result of reduced effort on the part of physicians within the group. Gaynor, Martin and Paul Gertler, "Moral Hazard and Risk Spreading in Partnerships," *RAND Journal of Economics*, 26 (1995): 591–613.

6   Medical Malpractice and the Practice of Defensive Medicine

Reducing medical mistakes, known as iatrogenic mistakes, is the main motivation behind medical malpractice law. The IOM report, *To Err Is Human,* defined a medical error as a "failure of a planned action to be completed as intended or the use of a wrong plan to achieve an aim."[22] However, medical errors are not necessarily the result of medical malpractice. A Harvard study, based on the medical records of over 31,000 patients in a random sample of 51 hospitals in New York State, found that roughly 3.7 percent of hospitalized patients suffered an injury but that only approximately 1 percent of hospitalized patients suffered an injury due to negligence.[23] Medical errors may be the result of system failure at a number of levels.

Even when there is malpractice, the assignment of the act of malpractice may be a complex matter. For instance, if a physician misreads an X-ray and makes a misdiagnosis because of the poor technical quality of the film, who is at fault? In one case, the court opined: "If the quality of the image is so poor that a reasonably responsible and prudent radiologist would not have interpreted it, then poor image quality alone may be a source of negligence."[24] Most physicians purchase malpractice insurance.

Medical malpractice cases in the United States involving physician conduct fall under civil tort law that varies by state. In all cases, liability depends on whether there has been (provable) negligence. A bad outcome from a medical treatment is not by itself grounds for medical malpractice. However, patients often initiate malpractice law suits when they have experienced a bad health outcome from medical treatment. Negligence is shown to be present in less than half the claims filed.[25] There is also evidence that a fairly small proportion of those suffering injury due to negligence actually bring malpractice suits.*

In the eyes of the general public and doctors as well, the medical malpractice system in the United States is one of the important contributors to the rising cost of medical care. Malpractice insurance is an important component of the cost of practicing medicine. The average proportion of self-employed physician office expenses attributed to malpractice insurance premiums in 1994 was more than the proportion spent on either medical equipment or supplies.[26] Particularly for some specialists such as obstetricians, malpractice insurance premiums represent a fairly high proportion of net incomes. Average 1996 net income was $231,000 for obstetrician/gynecologists.[27] Using the figures in Table 7.1, we see that mal-

---

*A study of hospital care in California in the 1970s found that less than 1/10 of patients injured due to negligent care filed a malpractice suite and only approximately 1 in 25 received any compensation. See Mills, D. H., et al., *Report on Medical Insurance Feasibility Study* (San Francisco: California Medical Association, 1977). The Harvard Study conducted in 1984 using data from New York hospitals also found a low rate of negligence claims among patients suffering injuries due to negligence. See Brennan, T. A., et al., "Incidence of Adverse Events and Negligence in Hospitalized Patients," *New England Journal of Medicine,* 324 (1991): 370–376.

Table 7.1   Average Annual Cost of Medical Liability Insurance by Type of Physician Practice, 1996.

All	$14,000
GP	8,400
Ob/gyn	35,700
General surgery	24,700
Cardiology	13,400

Source: American Medical Association's Physician Marketplace Statistics, 1997–1998 (Washington DC: Center for Health Policy Research, 1998, Table 59, p. 71.

practice insurance premiums constituted over 15 percent of net incomes earned in ob/gyn practices.

The rising cost of malpractice insurance has led to tort law reform in many states.[28] Some states have passed legislation setting limits on the amount that can be awarded for noneconomic damages. Some have required awards to be in the form of scheduled payments over the lifetime of the plaintiff rather than a lump sum payment. States have also set limits on attorneys' fees, often with respect to the proportion of the settlement that can go to attorneys. In some cases, state supreme courts have ruled that setting limits on awards is unconstitutional. However, other reforms are possible. One that is frequently proposed and has been enacted for certain types of injuries is no-fault insurance for iatrogenic injuries. Florida and Virginia have programs of no-fault compensation for serious iatrogenic neurological injuries that are birth-related.[29]

An argument against limiting malpractice settlements is that the risk of malpractice damage improves the quality of medical care. This is a hard question to investigate and, to date, there is little evidence to support this view. Kessler and McClellan investigated the effects of state tort reform on intensity of treatment and outcomes for heart attack patients. Treatment intensity was observed to fall but no significant differences in patient outcomes (measured by mortality and rehospitalization rates) were found.[30] Dr. Lucien Leape, a chair of the IOM commission that produced *To Err Is Human,* makes the argument that medical mistakes are often the result of exhaustion, or badly organized protocols in hospitals and clinics, in other words, system failures. He believes that making the individual doctor liable for mistakes is counterproductive since it provides incentives for hiding mistakes rather than promoting a spirit of openness that would lead to quality-enhancing reforms at treatment centers.[31]

The Practice of Defensive Medicine

Risk of malpractice suits may lead physicians to practice defensive medicine as well as to buy malpractice insurance. **Defensive medicine** is defined as "liability-induced changes in medical practice that entails costs [to patients] in excess of benefits and that would not have occurred in the absence of liability."[32]

Defensive medicine can be thought of as a form of physician-induced demand.[33] The maximum amount of medical testing and intervention that the patient will tolerate will be undertaken by a risk-averse physician if it is deemed to reduce the probability of being accused of negligence. The practice of defensive medicine may not only increase the cost of medical care but may also result in inappropriate care. An example of inappropriate care is the unnecessary implantation of pacemakers. One study found approximately 20 percent of the pacemakers installed in the Philadelphia area to be inappropriate.[34]

Health insurance coverage may increase patients' demand for medical services that yield relatively low marginal benefits. If so, it will be easier for physicians to practice defensive medicine when patients are well insured. It is very hard to distinguish empirically between liability-induced changes in medical practice and insurance-induced changes.[35]

Does not the purchase of malpractice insurance remove the need to practice defensive medicine? This would only be true if a physician (or the physician's reputation in the community) could be completely indemnified by insurance. Whether physicians do, in fact, practice defensive medicine in response to risk of liability has been studied by examining the relationship between rates of malpractice claims and regional differences in treatment intensity and by looking at the effects of state tort reforms on physician behavior. In a wide range of studies, treatment intensity in hospitals seems to be positively related to the probability of malpractice suits and the degree of financial risk that these potential suits impose.[36] Studies that looked at the relationship between risk of liability and behavior of physicians treating patients in ambulatory settings are much less conclusive. Weak evidence of a positive relationship between risk of liability and time spent per patient visit was found. However, the quantities of laboratory tests and procedures performed were negatively related to liability costs as was the total number of office visits per patient.[37]

Does Liability Insurance Affect Physicians' Likelihood of Negligence?

Patricia Danzon, a scholar who has done considerable research in this area, has concluded that the existing structure of malpractice insurance and the behavior of courts in the United States creates a situation in which all physicians have an incentive to buy insurance and in which it is cheaper for physicians "to practice with less than due care and to purchase liability insurance than to be non-negligent."[38] Her concluding remarks in her chapter in the *Handbook of Health Economics* provide a good summary of one expert's view of the state of medical malpractice law in the United States[39]:

The basic rationale for medical malpractice liability is to improve provider incentives for safety, assuming that asymmetric information leads to market failure in medical markets. The evidence of a significant rate of negligent injury, invalid claims and physicians' preference for insurance policies with minimal explicit co-payment or experience rating indicate that the efficiency of the malpractice system is severely constrained by imperfect information on the part of courts, doctors, patients, and liability insurers with respect to appropriate care and legal standards.

Summary

A potential principal/agent problem occurs whenever people delegate responsibility for their own welfare to others. The role of the physician in the process of providing health care is that of agent for the patient. The demand for physician services is a demand for expertise and guidance in the process of treatment. This chapter has examined the way in which agency is affected by physicians' utility functions (including their professional ethics and their desire for income) and by the characteristics of the markets in which they operate and the payment systems within those markets.

When there is imperfect agency, the results depend on the type of payment system. Under a fee-for-service system, too much care will be provided when physicians induce demand. Imperfect agency under a capitation system will lead to a reduction in quantity of service, which may reduce quality of care. Payment by salary provides little incentive to either skimp on care or inflate it, although it may encourage shirking. Risk of malpractice suits appears to promote the practice of defensive medicine, which is another example of imperfect agency. Professional standards and concern to maintain patients' trust are probably the best protection against imperfect agency today as well as when Arrow emphasized their importance 40 years ago.

Key Concepts

Physician agency

Price discrimination

Cost shifting

Physician-induced demand (PID)

Target-income hypothesis

Defensive medicine

Suggested Readings

1. McGuire, T. G., "Physician Agency," *Handbook of Health Economics,* Vol. 1A, Anthony J. Culyer and Joseph P. Newhouse, eds. (Amsterdam: Elsevier, 2000), Chap. 9.

2. Danzen, Patricia M., "Liability for Medical Malpractice," *Handbook of Health Economics,* Vol. 1B, op. cit, Chap. 26.

3. Michael A. Morrisey, *Cost Shifting in Health Care: Separating Evidence from Rhetoric* (Washington, DC: AEI Press, 1994), Chap. 1, Chap. 3, pp. 28–31, and Chap. 5, pp. 55–59.

Questions for Discussion and Review

1. What do we mean by physician agency?

2. What is physician-induced demand? Is the existence of higher fees in areas with a larger physician/patient ratio sufficient evidence to support the hypothesis of supplier-induced demand?

3. Give two alternative explanations of the phenomenon of price discrimination in the physician services market.

4. In a physician office practice, the marginal cost of an additional office visit is $300. The business manager is able to estimate the price elasticity of demand for two groups of patients. Group 1 has a price elasticity of demand of −0.5. Group 2 has a price-elasticity of demand of −0.2. The firm sets prices so as to maximize profits. Using the formula relating marginal revenue and price, compute the price that will be charged to group 1 for an office visit. What price will be charged to group 2?

5. What is the difference between price discrimination and cost shifting?

6. What factors are likely to affect the amount of charity care that a physician practice will undertake? Describe two hypotheses about physician behavior that will lead to opposite results in terms of the propensity to take charity cases.

7. Under what circumstances are physicians less likely to engage in defensive medicine?

Resources

[1] A good analysis of monopsony power on the part of insurers is provided by Herndon, J. B., "Health Insurer Monopsony Power: The All of None Model," *Journal of Health Economics,* 21 (2002): 197–206.

[2] See, for instance, Greenberg, Warren, "Marshfield Clinic, Physician Networks, and the Exercise of Monopoly Power," *Health Services Research,* 33, Part 2 (1998): 1461–1476.

[3] Showalter, Mark H., "Physician Cost-Shifting Behavior: Medicaid vs. Other Patients," *Contemporary Economic Policy,* XV (1997): 74–84.

[4] For a thorough treatment of the pros and cons of cost shifting, see Morrisey, Michael, *Cost Shifting in Health Care: Separating Evidence from Rhetoric* (Washington, DC: AEI Press, 1994). See especially Chap. 3 and Chap. 5.

[5] Culler, Steven D. and Robert L. Ohsfeldt, "The Determinants of the Provision of Charity Medical Care by Physicians," *Journal of Human Resources*, 21 (1986): 138–156.

[6] Emmons, David W. and John A. Rizzo, "Alms and MDs: A Reconsideration of the Determinants of Charity Medical Care by Physicians," *Journal of Human Resources*, 28 (1993): 412–428.

[7] Tucker, Jessie L. III, "Factors Influencing Physician Participation in Medicaid in the USA," *International Journal of Social Economics,* 29 (2002): 753–783 and Coburn, A. F., et al., "Effects of Changing Medicaid Fees on Physician Participation and Enrollee Access," *Inquiry*, 36 (1999): 265–280.

[8] McGuire, T. G., "Physician Agency," in A. K. Culyer and J. P. Newhouse, eds., *Handbook of Health Economics*, Vol. 1A, (Amsterdam: Elsevier, 2000), Chap. 9.

[9] See, for instance, Evans, Robert G., "Supplier-Induced Demand: Some Empirical Evidence and Implications," in *The Economics of Health and Medical Care*, M. Perlman, ed. (London: Macmillan, 1974).

[10] See, for instance, Fuchs, Victor R., "The Supply of Surgeons and the Demand for Operations," *Journal of Human Resources*, 13 (Supplement 1978): 35–56 and Rice, Thomas, "The Impact of Changing Medicare Reimbursement Rates on Physician-Induced Demand," *Medical Care*, 21 (1983): 803–815.

[11] Rice (1983), op. cit. A good survey of the literature is also provided in Rice, Thomas H. and Roberta J. Labelle, "Do Physicians Induce Demand for Medical Services?" *Journal of Health Politics, Policy, and Law*, 14 (1989): 587–600.

[12] Holahan, John, "Physician Availability, Medical Care Reimbursement, and the Delivery of Physician Services: Some Evidence from the Medicaid Program," *Journal of Human Resources*, 10 (1975): 378–402.

[13] Rossiter, Louis F. and Gail R. Wilensky, "Identification of Physician-Induced Demand," *Journal of Human Resources*, 19 (1984): 231–244. This study used the National Medical Care Expenditure Study of 1977.

[14] Dranove, D. and P. Webner, "Physician-Induced Demand for Childbirths," *Journal of Health Economics*, 13 (1994): 61–73.

[15] Gruber, Jonathan and Maria Owings, "Physician Financial Incentives and Cesarean Section Delivery," *RAND Journal of Economics*, 27 (1996): 99–123.

[16] Hillman, B. J., et al., "Frequency and Costs of Diagnostic Imaging in Office Practice: A Comparison of Self-Referring and Radiologist-Referring Physicians," *New England Journal of Medicine*, 323 (1990): 1604–1608.

[17] Hay, Joel W. and Michael J. Leahy, "Physician-Induced Demand: An Empirical Analysis of the Consumer Information Gap," *Journal of Health Economics*, 1 (1982): 231–244; Levy J. M., et al., "Impact of the Medicare Fee Schedule on Payment to Physicians," *Journal of the American Medical Association*, 264 (1990): 717–722; and Nguyen, N. X. and F. W. Derrick, "Physician Behavioral Response to a Medicare Price Reduction," *Health Services Research*, 32 (1997): 283–298.

[18] That this is not a dead issue is shown by two recent articles in the prestigious *Journal of Health Economics*: Carlsen, Fredrik and Jostein Grytten, "Consumer Satisfaction and Supplier Induced Demand," 19 (September 2000): 731–753, and DeJaegher, Kris and Marc Jegers, "A Model of Physician Behaviour with Demand Inducement," 19 (March 2000): 231–258.

[19] Fuchs, Victor R., "Economics, Values and Health Care Reform," *American Economic Review,* 86 (1996), p. 8.

[20] Center for Health Policy Research, *Socioeconomic Characteristics of Medical Practice 1997–1998* (Chicago: AMA, 1998).

[21] See, for instance, Fuchs, Victor R., "The Supply of Surgeons and the Demand for Operations," *Journal of Human Resources*, 13, (Supplement 1978): 35–56, and Pauly, M. V., *Doctors and Their Workshops: Economic Models of Physician Behavior* (Chicago: University of Chicago Press, 1980).

[22] Kohn, L. T., et al., eds., *To Err Is Human: Building a Safer Health System* (Washington, DC: National Academies Press, 1999). This report estimated that from 44,000 to 98,000 hospitalized Americans die each year as a result of medical errors.

[23] Weiler, P. C., et al., *A Measure of Malpractice: Medical Injury, Malpractice Litigation and Patient Compensation* (Cambridge, MA: Harvard University Press, 1993).

[24] Potchen, E. J. and M. A. Bisesi, "When Is It Malpractice to Miss Lung Cancer on Chest Radiographs?" *Radiology*, 175 (January 1990): 29–32.

[25] Farber, H. S. and M. J. White, "Medical Malpractice: An Empirical Examination of the Litigation Process," *RAND Journal of Economics*, 5 (1991): 199–217.

[26] McGuire (2000), op. cit., Table 2b, p. 470.

[27] American Medical Association, *Physician Marketplace Statistics, 1997–1998* (Washington, DC: Center for Health Policy Research, 1998), Table 75, p. 88.

[28] For an excellent discussion of medical malpractice law and its implications for the practice of medicine in the U.S. today, see Phelps, Charles E., *Health Economics*, 3rd ed. (Boston: Addison Wesley, 2003), Chap. 13.

[29] Danzon, Patricia M., "Liability for Medical Malpractice," *Handbook of Health Economics*, Vol 1B, Culyer, Anthony J. and Joseph P. Newhouse, eds. (Amsterdam: Elsevier, 2000), p. 1379.

[30] Kessler, D. and M. McClellan, "Do Doctors Practice Defensive Medicine?" *Quarterly Journal of Economics*, 111 (1996): 353–390.

[31] See, for instance, Leape E., "Error in Medicine," *Journal of the American Medical Association*, 272 (December 21, 1994): 1851–1873.

[32] Danzon, Patricia M., "Liability for Medical Malpractice," *Journal of Economic Perspectives*, 5 (1991): 51–69.

[33] This is the view of Danzon in "Liability for Medical Malpractice," in *Handbook of Health Economics*, Vol. 1B (Amsterdam: Elsevier, 2000), Chap. 26, p. 1368. She references the McGuire model in making this statement.

[34] See Greenspan, A. M., et al., "Incidence of Unwarranted Implantation of Permanent Cardiac Pacemakers in a Large Medical Population," *New England Journal of Medicine*, 318 (January 21, 1988): 158–163.

[35] Danzon (1991) op. cit., p. 54.

[36] See Kessler, D. and M. McClellan (1996) op. cit.; Dubay, Lisa, et al., "The Impact of Malpractice Fears on Cesarean Section Rates," *Journal of Health Economics*, 18 (1999): 491–522; and Kessler, Daniel and M. McClellan, "Malpractice Law and Health Care Reform: Optimal Liability Policy in an Era of Managed Care," *Journal of Public Economics*, 84 (2002): 175–197.

[37] See Danzon, Patricia M., *Medical Malpractice: Incidence and Incentive Effects* (Philadelphia: Wharton School, University of Pennsylvania Press, 1990) and Danzon, P. M., et al., "The Effects of Malpractice Litigation on Physicians' Fees and Incomes," *American Economic Review*, 80 (1990): 122–127.

[38] For a thorough discussion of this model and the logic leading to this conclusion, see Danzon (2000), op. cit., pp. 1399–1401.

[39] Ibid., p. 1395.

CHAPTER EIGHT

Hospitals

The modern hospital has its origins in European medieval religious institutions that cared for the dying, the indigent, and that also served as long-term custodial institutions for the mentally ill and orphans. A hospital was a hospice, a place of last resort that provided succor and prayers, not cures. The complex institution into which the modern hospital has evolved is largely the result of the dramatic technological advances in medicine in the second half of the twentieth century. In the United States and most other Western industrial nations, acute-care treatment centers are now generally separate from long-term care institutions, rehabilitation centers, and hospices, although they may be affiliated.

1   Introduction

In this chapter we will study the effects of type of ownership, market structure, government regulation, and cost-containment policies on the prices and quality of hospital services. We will look at several models of behavior of hospital managers and examine what has happened to hospital charity care in the age of cost containment. Government support for hospital construction, beginning in the late 1940s, and the promotion of indemnity-type hospitalization insurance, which dates from the Depression of the 1930s, encouraged the development of an extensive hospital system in the United States and assured the demand for its services. Demand for hospital services was boosted in the mid-1960s by Medicare, which made hospital care more affordable for the elderly and which provided subsidies to hospitals for expansion of facilities and, in the case of teaching hospitals, for the training of residents.

Throughout much of the twentieth century, in-patient care was favored by the medical profession that benefited from having a support system to aid in the treatment of its patients. Physicians acting as agents for their patients found it good medical procedure to have patients admitted for testing the day before surgery and to have them remain during periods of convalescence. It was also financially advantageous for patients to have their doctors proscribing hospitalization rather than ambulatory procedures from 1930 to 1960 when private health insurance typically covered only in-hospital procedures. There is some historical evidence that hospital admission rates and length of stay were positively correlated with hospital capacity. This phenomenon, known as Roemer's Law, has been characterized as "A built bed is a filled bed."[1] This was a world in which the contemporary worry about "drive-through deliveries of babies" or "drive-through mastectomies" was not a problem.

The 21st century hospital is no longer even in part a custodial institution. In-patient procedures have become more physical- and human-capital intensive. A high proportion of in-hospital procedures have been replaced by out-patient services; and average length of stay in U.S. hospitals has become shorter. This is the result of both improvements in medical technology and cost-containment measures imposed by Medicare and private insurers. Patient stays in acute care hospitals in the United States are generally limited to 30 days. The average length of stay in the United States, in spite of hospitalization now being limited to more serious illnesses, has declined from 7.6 days in 1960 to 5.8 days in 2001.[2]

2   Hospital Ownership: Does It Make a Difference?

Facts About Hospital Ownership

Hospitals may be either public or private. Private hospitals may be organized as either for-profit or non-profit firms. Although both non-profit and for-profit hospitals may make profits, that is, surpluses of revenue over costs, only in for-profit firms are the owners the residual claimants of profits. Non-profit institutions, by contrast, may not distribute surpluses to owners. While raising capital in the marketplace is generally easier in the case of for-profit firms, non-profit firms have the advantages that they can raise capital through tax-deductible charitable donations and can issue tax-exempt bonds. In addition, their property and earnings are not subject to tax.

In the United States the most common form of acute-care hospital is the private community-based nonprofit-hospital. This type of hospital cares for approximately 70 percent of all in-patient cases.[3] The growth in for-profit hospitals is a relatively new phenomenon, but even after a flurry of merger activity in the 1980s and 1990s created some large for-profit chains, the private non-profit hospital is still the dominant form of acute-care facility.* By contrast, for-profit hospitals represent only about 12 percent of all nonfederal acute-care hospitals.[4]

It is commonly believed that a non-profit firm is preferred by consumers in markets where they have imperfect information, since the non-profit ownership form promotes trust. In this connection, the nursing home field is interesting. The physician's role as agent for the patient is much more limited in long-term facilities. There is a widespread belief that for-profit long-term care facilities may skimp on quality.[5] Yet, in spite of this, the nursing home field is dominated by for-profit firms. Whether the asymmetry of information between patient and hospital is likely to be greater than in acute-care facilities is unclear. When patients have family overseeing their care, asymmetry of information is probably less great. However, the old and frail who have no one overseeing their care may have little ability to judge the care they are receiving, or in any event, little power to do anything to remedy low-quality care. Psychiatric hospitals, also thought to be settings in which asymmetric information plays an especially important role, are also more likely to be for-profit than are acute-care hospitals. This market is divided roughly equally between for-profit and non-profit institutions.[6]

Non-profit hospitals are an alternative source to governments for the provision of public goods.[7] Public goods include unprofitable community services such as health screening, immunization, hospices, and geriatric day care as well as charity (uncompensated) care. Non-profit hospitals have requirements to provide some public goods in exchange for their tax-free status. However, "public goods" are usually defined quite broadly.

Two contrasting views of non-profit firms result from the fact that they do not distribute profits to owners and therefore have no need to maximize profits. One view is that they are likely to provide a higher-quality product at the same price. The other view is that they have less incentive to be efficient and will therefore tend to have higher costs unaccompanied by any quality improvements. We will shortly examine some evidence comparing quality and efficiency of for-profit and non-profit hospitals.

Behavior of Hospital Decision Makers: Several Alternative Models

Modern hospitals tend to employ professional managers or CEOs who are separate from the owners or boards of directors. Thus, there is the separation between ownership and management that is typical of the modern corporation. Managers are concerned not only with the economic success of the firms they manage but also with their own pecuniary and nonpecuniary rewards: their salaries and bonuses, their job security and ability to advance. For managers of for-profit firms, the bottom line clearly counts. For managers of non-profit firms,

*Approximately a hundred years ago, for-profit hospitals were more common but declined as standards were raised. By the mid-twentieth century, they were a rarity.

other success indicators may be more important, including prestige of the institution, its service to the community, and ability to raise funds from donors.

Hospital managers have to make complex decisions since hospitals are multi-product firms. The decision about what mix of services to supply is an important part of the management function. Even a highly specialized cardiac center has to consider such things as whether or not to undertake transplant operations or whether to have a trauma center. Since demand for hospitals is affected by the range of services offered, both non-profit and for-profit hospitals may produce services that run at a loss. Moreover, the inventory problem, which faces all firms, is especially important in the case of hospitals. Since demand for hospital services is highly variable and unpredictable, some excess capacity is desirable.

The managerial function in American hospitals is further complicated by the fact that attending physicians are not, with the exceptions of some HMOs, employees of hospitals. The decision-making process in hospitals is thus one in which the goals of owners, professional managers, and physicians all interact. Let us consider three models of hospital management.

Utility Maximization of the Manager (CEO) in Non-Profit Hospitals

Let us start with the simplifying assumption that the hospital produces only one product which can differ in quality. A higher-quality product will cost more. Let us further assume that we can define quality by a single dimensional index. Then for a given budget, there will be a two-way quantity/quality trade-off. For any hypothetical quality level, it is then possible to estimate a cost function, tracing out average costs for different levels of output. Assume that consumers are willing to pay more (up to a point) for higher-quality services and that they are able to recognize quality differences. Then for each quality level, there will be a separate demand curve.

The non-profit hospital will charge a fee that just covers the average cost of its service (P = AC). For any quality level it is then possible to find the quantity at which demand intersects the average cost curve. Figure 8.1 shows two hypothetical quality levels of service and the corresponding cost and demand curves. A quality/quantity frontier made up of the points, where P = AC for each quality level, can then be constructed (Figure 8.2). The decision about what quantity/quality trade-off is optimal depends on the hospital manager's (CEO's) utility function, depicted in Figure 8.2 by the curve U. The curve made up of broken lines is a hypothetical utility function for a CEO of a for-profit firm.

In 1970, Joseph Newhouse proposed a theory of the non-profit hospital in which utility-maximizing behavior on the part of the hospital manager leads to a higher-quality product than would be provided by a for-profit firm with the same costs and demand curves.[8] This is consistent with theories of non-profit firms in general. Managers of non-profit hospitals may well have more discretionary authority since they do not have the profit-maximizing rule imposed on their decisions.

Figure 8.1

Costs and Demands
for Two Quality
Levels of Service

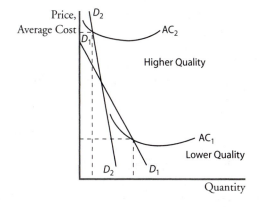

Model of Maximization of Physicians' Utility

An alternative model views the hospital surplus as controlled by its attending physicians. It is possible to simply interpret Figure 8.2 as reflecting the physicians' utility function, rather than that of the CEO. However, since physicians in the United States are generally not employed by hospitals and usually bill their patients separately, an alternative model has been developed.[9] Pauly and Redisch assume that physicians have the goal of maximizing the gains for their own constituency.

In this model, the patients' demand for the hospital's services is assumed to be a function of the total price of the hospitalization episode, including the physician's fee. If affiliated physicians can limit the number of physicians who are allowed to treat patients at the hospital, they will choose a physician-staff size that

Figure 8.2

A Quality/Quantity
Frontier

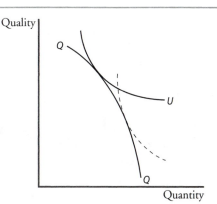

will yield the maximum net revenue per physician. Where it is possible to modify other inputs as well, physicians will opt for a production function and scale of operation that maximize (average) physician earnings.

The production function which the physicians favor will depend on whether patients pay out-of-pocket for nonphysician hospital services, or have hospital insurance that covers 100 percent of the nonphysician bill. If patients pay, physicians will want to economize on the cost of the nonphysician part of the hospital service so as to claim a greater share of the revenue. When insurance covers nonphysician costs, physicians will want the highest possible level of complementary inputs: equipment, operating room space, and number of nurses and interns per doctor. In this case, they regard these inputs as free.[10] In either case, physician control creates an incentive for a misallocation of hospital resources.

This model assumes that physicians behave as one group or cartel. In reality there may be fierce competition between different departments for allocation of resources within the hospital. The model can easily be modified to treat each department as maximizing for its own physicians.

Model of Competition for Control Between Doctors and Administrators

A third model views the hospital as an arena in which the physician staff and the nonmedical trustee-administrators vie for power.[11] Jeffrey Harris regards the hospital as a firm within a firm, or even two separate firms. The hospital is a firm that supplies inputs to the physician. An analogy has been made between this situation and an automobile repair shop in which the mechanics buy parts supplied by another firm. The mechanics will want to pay as little as possible for the parts. An equally apt analogy is that of a service department in an automobile dealership that has to requisition supplies provided by the parts department. It may be more efficient for the parts department to maintain only a small inventory. The mechanics in the service department will prefer excess capacity in order always to have the necessary inputs to meet peak demand. In Harris's model, physicians and administrators compete for power in determining the way in which hospital resources are allocated. He regards this as a kind of bilateral monopoly situation in which one strong (monopoly) buyer is pitted against one strong (monopoly) seller. The bilateral monopoly model (see Appendix 1) is most commonly used to analyze the interaction between a monopoly employer and a union. An implication of this model is that bilateral monopoly creates a balance of power, with hospital administrators and the physicians group being able to impose restraints on each other's actions. This may promote efficiency and quality control.

Findings of Studies Comparing For-Profit and Non-Profit Hospitals

Quality of Patient Care

The consensus of studies on hospital quality, using a variety of measures of patient outcomes, is that there is not much difference in average quality between *private* non-profit and for-profit nonteaching hospitals. Teaching hospitals, which are predominantly non-profit, appear to have a quality edge. Patient outcomes, at least for the elderly, have been found to be worse in public than in private hospitals, both for-profit and non-profit.[12] However, patients in the public institutions may be sicker on average. Public hospitals have a higher proportion of nonpaying (charity) patients whose lower socioeconomic status may be reflected in poorer overall health.

The effect of ownership appears to be somewhat different in the case of psychiatric hospitals and nursing homes. In both cases, non-profit firms appear to provide higher quality. There is evidence of fewer complaints from patients and fewer legal violations in non-profit psychiatric hospitals when they are compared with comparable for-profit institutions. Non-profit nursing homes also score better when quality is measured by level of complaints.[13] Moreover, competition appears to improve quality in the non-profit nursing home market but to have the opposite effect in the for-profit market.[14] There is also evidence of positive spillover effects from a non-profit presence in nursing home markets. When non-profit market share increases, an improvement in overall quality of care in all nursing homes is observed.[15] This effect may result in an underestimation of measured quality differences between non-profit and for-profit nursing homes.

Comparative Efficiency of For-Profit and Non-Profit Hospitals

Although economic theory suggests that non-profit institutions have less incentive to be efficient, the literature on hospitals provides mixed results in its assessment of the relative efficiency of non-profit and for-profit hospitals.[16] One study found non-profit hospitals to be less efficient in altering capacity in response to reductions in demand for hospital services.[17] Another study constructed an inefficiency index and found private non-profit hospitals to be more *inefficient* than either for-profit or public institutions.[18] A study of psychiatric hospitals found no significant difference in efficiency between for-profit and non-profit institutions.[19] A study of nonrural Medicare coronary patients found 2.4 percent lower average treatment costs, standardizing for patient outcomes, in markets where there were for-profit hospitals.[20] In summary, using a variety of measures of cost, and standardizing for patient outcomes, there seems to be somewhat more evidence supporting the view that non-profit hospitals are less efficient, but no consensus on their relative efficiency. Newhouse has argued that what appears to be inefficiency may be higher quality in the form of amenities valued by patients.[21] Frank Sloan's chapter in the *Handbook of Health Economics* provides an excellent review of this literature.[22]

Provision of Public Service

Frank, Salkever, and Mitchell have found "small but significant differences" favoring non-profit hospitals in the provision of public goods, defined very broadly to include departments or services that lose money, such as high-risk neonatal centers.[23] A broad survey of the literature leads to the conclusion that non-profit

firms do not, on average, charge lower prices for services than do for-profit institutions, nor do they appear to provide much more charity care, although the evidence on the latter is somewhat mixed.[24] One recent study finds that the non-
profit firms' need to issue tax-exempt bonds, which usually includes a
requirement about provision of charity care, has stimulated them to provide more
uncompensated care than do comparable for-profit institutions.[25]

3   Market Structure

Defining Hospital Markets

A firm's market is defined by both the product it produces and the geographic
area it serves. In the case of hospitals, it is often not easy to define the relevant
product or geographic market. The definitions of product and geographic markets are not independent. For example, people travel long distances to go to
well-known specialist medical centers such as the Mayo and Cleveland Clinics
and the Memorial Sloan Kettering Cancer Center. The geographic market is very
different from that of a community hospital. On the other hand, hospitals may be
branches of national or regional chains, but their relevant markets may be local.[26]

Hospitals Range from Monopolies to Monopolistically Competitive Firms

Hospitals range from having monopoly power in scarcely populated areas that
can support only one regional facility to operating in monopolistically competitive markets. We can therefore assume that individual hospitals have downward-
sloping demand curves and produce differentiated products. Feldstein has found
that 80 percent of the community hospitals in metropolitan statistical areas (cities
with populations of 50,000 or more) can be characterized as monopolistically
competitive; however hospital systems, if not individual hospitals, in metropolitan
regions tend to be oligopolies.[27] (Appendix 1, Section 5, outlines the models of
these types of markets.)

The notion that a hospital is a "natural monopoly," a firm that has average
costs falling as size increases, appears not to be substantiated. When survival and
growth rates of hospitals have been studied, modest economies of scale were
found for hospitals with a capacity of 200 to 370 beds; small hospitals with less
than 100 beds do not have good survival rates.[28] However, researchers studying
hospital cost functions in relation to numbers of beds have not found significant
evidence of economies of scale. Today, when hospitals provide such a wide mix
of in- and out-patient services, number of patient beds is a less useful capacity
measure, but it is still widely used.

Measuring Market Concentration

When it is possible to define the relevant market, measures of concentration such
as the **Herfindahl–Hirschman Index (HHI)** are often employed by economists
and by the antitrust division of the Department of Justice to measure the degree
of competitiveness of hospitals. The HHI is defined as the sum of the squares of

each firm's market share measured as a percentage. If a market consists of one monopoly firm, the value of the HHI is 10,000. If two firms share a market equally the value of the HHI is 5,000. As a general rule of thumb, when the value of the HHI exceeds 1,400, potential mergers are likely to be subject to antitrust scrutiny. HHIs are also sometimes presented as ranging between 0 and 1, where 1 represents a monopoly.

Has the Hospital Market Become More Concentrated?

The average degree of concentration within hospital markets has increased somewhat over time through mergers and the creation of multihospital systems. The latter may consist of agreements that are not full mergers. In the present climate of hospital consolidation, an increasingly important factor affecting the behavior of hospitals is the degree to which they are linked.[29] Each hospital site may retain a good deal of decision-making authority and a largely separate medical staff. However, the affiliation may still permit the hospital to take advantage of economies of scale in purchasing agreements and hiring contracts. It may also give it power in bargaining with employee unions and managed care insurance companies. These factors give the integrated hospital system advantages, permitting it to increase its market share in local markets over time.

The evidence is mixed on whether consolidation results in higher or lower prices to consumers. Some recent research shows that patients admitted to hospitals with more than 100 beds that were part of multihospital systems experienced lower prices even for higher-intensity services.[30] Particularly in the matter of purchasing inputs, consolidation may lead to lower costs regardless of individual hospital size.

Since hospitals are multiproduct firms, they may have considerable market power with respect to one specialty even when they are competitive with respect to their whole range of services. Facilities to treat conditions that occur with a low incidence in the population (burn centers, high-risk neonatal centers, etc.) are often located in one hospital per region, and this kind of monopoly is generally permitted by the government on the grounds that duplication of facilities is too expensive relative to the benefits to the community.

Effect of Competition on the Price of Hospital Services

Until the late 1980s, higher hospital costs were observed in hospital markets that were more competitive.[31] Costs, measured both per admission and per patient day, were substantially higher where there were more hospitals. The explanation was that hospitals did not compete on the basis of price, but on the basis of quality.

The "Medical Arms Race"

The notion of the medical arms race assumes that hospitals operate in imperfect markets, which are also characterized by imperfect information and that they do not collude. An analogy to the familiar "prisoner's dilemma" example may be in-structure.[32] The prisoner's dilemma results from the inability to collude. Collusion (or trust) between two partners in crime would lead to the best outcome for both when there is inadequate evidence to convict either without a confession from the other. However, each prisoner can reduce his penalty (if convicted) by cooperating with the authorities and implicating the other. If the prisoners are questioned separately, in the absence of trust each will act in his own self-interest and cooperate with the authorities by "ratting" on the other. Each prisoner is thus minimizing the damage to himself in the worst-case scenario.

Now, consider a hospital market in which there are two firms. The market is of fixed size. Each hospital can increase its clientele only by attracting patients away from the other hospital. A new type of MRI machine that allows a patient to stand up during the procedure is being widely advertised as providing more accurate results and more comfort for the patient. The two hospitals, like the two prisoners, cannot collude. Neither knows whether the other will invest in the new type of MRI machine. Information on the cost of this machine and the effects on the demand for each hospital's service if it does or does not add the machine (and if the other hospital does or does not do so) are summarized in the table below. The MRI machine costs $2,500,000. If both hospitals buy the MRI machine, neither gains any patients. If a hospital does not buy a machine, and its rival does, loss of revenue resulting from loss of patients will equal $5,000,000. Hospital 1's payoffs, for the two options are shown in the upper triangle of each cell in the table. Hospital 2's payoffs are shown in the lower triangle of each cell.

		Hospital 1	
		Add New MRI	Do Not Add
Hospital 2	Add New MRI	−$2,500,000 / −$2,500,000	−$5,000,000 / +$2,500,000
	Do Not Add	+$2,500,000 / −$5,000,000	0 / 0

If he does not know what the other hospital plans to do, each manager will invest in the new equipment. Each hospital will end up with a net loss of $2,500,000. In the language of game theory, this is the dominant strategy. This competition, leading to a duplication of facilities, is an example of what is known as the **medical arms race**.

The model is believed to describe fairly well the behavior of competing hospitals in the pre-DRG, pre-managed care period. It still has relevance in today's environment to the extent that hospitals can afford to compete on the basis of quality. It should be noted that competition based on quality rather than price can assume a number of forms, from acquiring the latest technology and hiring the most prestigious medical staff to having more nurses, better rooms, and other amenities that may be important indicators of hospital quality to consumers.[33] The literature on the medical arms race has focused on acquiring new technology.

Examples of quality competition are plentiful. Listeners to the New York City classical music station, WQXR, will find their listening experience interrupted by ads, often accompanied by soothing music, from such prestigious institutions as Memorial Sloan Kettering and the Johns Hopkins Medical Center, which explictly states that the trip from New York City is worth making in exchange for superior care. The example given above to illustrate the medical arms race was inspired by a local community hospital's ad about its new, more comfortable, more reliable, stand-up MRI machine.

Payer-Driven Competition in Hospital Markets

The effect of market competition on prices of hospital services appears to have changed in the last 15 years. What was true in a world where choices were made by patients and/or their physician agents does not seem to apply if the relevant consumers are cost-conscious "price shopping" third-party payers. Alain Enthoven, whom we have already encountered as a champion of managed competition, predicted that competition among managed care providers would bring about price competition.[34] The institution of the Medicare prospective payment system plus the increased penetration of managed care into hospital insurance markets appears to have accomplished this.

California was the leader in degree of market penetration of HMOs and PPOs. Studies of California hospitals in the 1980s anticipated what was to become a nationwide phenomenon. An examination of the relationship between prices and degree of concentration in local hospital markets in California over the period 1983 to 1988 reveals that profit margins, an indirect measure of prices, were lower in *less* concentrated markets.[35] In addition, increased HMO penetration appeared to increase the magnitude of the positive association between market concentration and prices of hospital services. A nationwide study of the effects of competitiveness of hospitals on treatment costs and patient outcomes for Medicare heart attack patients also found a change in hospital behavior from the 1980s to the 1990s: The cost of treating Medicare patients was found to vary inversely with the HMO enrollment rate in the area and with degree of competitiveness.[36] Studies focusing specifically on not-for-profit hospitals, which have been alleged not to compete on the basis of price, also found evidence of an association between price competition and the competitiveness of hospital markets. Recent research finds higher prices charged to Medicare (DRG prices) in merging and acquired hospitals, when compared with similar but nonmerging ones.[37] Significant price increases (not associated with any quality increases) were also observed when a merger reduced the number of competing hospitals from three to two in a relevant geographic market.[38] An examination of the effects of market concentration, mergers, and degree of managed care penetration on prices of services in a large number of U.S. hospitals from 1986 to 1994 provides corroborating evidence of a move away from nonprice toward price competition.[39]

In summary, cost-conscious third-party payers, both government (Medicare and Medicaid) and private managed care insurers, have altered the behavior of hospitals.[40] The countervailing power of buyers has promoted price competition. A change in the attitude toward mergers on the part of government antitrust policy reflects an awareness of this change.

Effects of Payer-Driven Competition on Quality of Care per Unit Cost

The increase in managed care from 1985 to 1994 also appears to have had an effect on the relationship between competition, cost of hospital care, and quality. Where HMO penetration was high, competition among hospitals appears to have resulted in both lower expenditure of resources per patient and better patient outcomes.[41] Thus, the combination of a dominant presence of managed care and a competitive market seems to generally result in unambiguous welfare improvements. There is, however, some evidence that inner-city hospitals in very large cities may provide an exception to this rule.[42]

4   Role of the Government

Government Support for Hospitals

1. Capital Assistance: The Hill-Burton Act of 1946 provided federal money for hospital modernization and expansion of physical capacity through 1978, with priorities given to hospitals in rural and poor areas. Over the years, billions of dollars of federal funds have been leveraged to encourage state and local governments to invest in hospitals. The subsidies carry the requirement that hospitals make services available to members of the community regardless of ability to pay.

2. Provision of Public Hospitals: Approximately 20 percent of the hospital beds in the United States are provided by state, county, and municipal hospitals. In addition, Veterans Administration (VA) hospitals have historically been the largest single public provider of hospital care.

3. Medicare and Medicaid: These programs (1965) made the federal and state governments major payers of hospital bills. These social insurance programs greatly increased demand and reduced the price elasticity of demand for hospital services. By 1997, government expenditure on hospital care was $228.4 billion out of a total of $371.1 billion.[43] In addition, Medicare allocates varying amounts of funds per year for hospital capital spending and for support of residency training programs. The aging of the population will tend to increase the proportion of hospital charges paid by Medicare. This will be offset to the extent that eligibility is altered and/or the rates of reim-

bursement from Medicare continue to decline relative to rates of reimbursement from private insurance.

Government Regulation of Hospitals

1. Certificate of Need (CON) Regulations: During the 1960s, states began to pass and/or enforce **certificate of need (CON) regulations** limiting growth in capital investment by hospitals. The first CON law was enacted in New York State in 1964. Other states followed suit in the 1970s. They were encouraged to do so by the passage of Section 1122 of the Social Security Act in 1972, which set up state-level review processes for proposed hospital investments. Reimbursement under Medicare and Medicaid for costs related to capital investment was conditional on approval by review boards.[44] Title XV of the Public Health Service Act, passed in 1974, made state-level CON programs an eligibility requirement for a variety of types of federal grants. This requirement was eliminated in 1986. Many states have subsequently abandoned the use of CON regulation.

Effects of CON Regulations

The economic effects of CON regulations are controversial. Most economists have not found that, on balance, they promote efficiency. There are several reasons for this:

(a) It is difficult to establish criteria of the community's "need."

(b) Even when a need level can be established, there remains the question of whether it is better to expand existing facilities or allow duplication. This requires regulators to have information about the size of a facility that would minimize average cost. They generally do not have this information.

(c) Economies of scale might justify a monopoly in the production of some service, but the monopoly power of a hospital might lead it to raise prices above the level that would pertain if there were more competition. Unless prices are also regulated, creating monopolies may therefore lead to higher prices even when the firm experiences economies of scale.

Effects of CON Regulation on Behavior of Nursing Homes: Excess Demand

State CON laws in most states have historically limited both the entry and expansion of nursing homes. A number of researchers have associated CON regulation with excess demand for nursing home beds, measured by waiting time for admission and high occupancy rates.[45] Nursing homes appear to have responded to excess demand by marking up prices, skimping on quality of care, and/or selecting patients so as to avoid those requiring heavy care, particularly when they are Medicaid patients.[46] Nyman found that excess demand in highly concentrated markets led to higher prices. This was more true in the case of for-profit nursing homes.[47]

A curious phenomenon, related to excess demand, is the finding of Gertler, (1989) and Nyman (1994) that increases in Medicaid reimbursement rates are associated with lower quality of nursing homes. The explanation is that firms have less incentive to raise quality in order to attract private patients when the differential in reimbursement between private and lower-paying Medicaid patients decreases. More recently, Grabowski has found a small but opposite effect. However, excess demand for nursing homes has declined considerably in the last few years, due in part to the relaxation of CON regulations.[48]

2. Price Controls:

(a) Nixon's 1971 Economic Stabilization Program (ESP) Phase I, imposed a three-month freeze on all wages and prices, including hospital prices. Phase II of this program (1972-1974) established a 6 percent cap on allowed revenue increases, adjusted for volume. This encouraged hospitals to expand both volume and costs so as to show less surplus per unit of service. This program had indirect effects on hospitals extending beyond the brief period of the ESA, since a freeze on wages encouraged unions to push for fringe benefits, including health insurance.

(b) During the 1970s, many states set up regulatory commissions to control hospital costs. However, once the Medicare Prospective Payment System (PPS) was in place, states tended to move away from any mandatory rate settings.

(c) The Medicare PPS adopted in 1983, which reimburses on the basis of a Diagnostic Related Group (DRG) classification, is the most important form of government regulation of hospital prices and practices.

Hospital Reactions to Medicare PPS

In the initial stages of the implementation of the Medicare PPS, hospitals were phased into the program. This provided a natural experiment for studying the effects of the PPS program. Initially, the market share of Medicare patients was observed to decrease in hospitals reimbursed by PPS and increase in others. Intensity of care was also found to be lower under PPS reimbursement.[49] Newhouse and Byrne found hospital stays of patients to be shorter under PPS as a result of patients being, on average, less severely ill.[50] In another study Newhouse found that patients with less profitable DRG classifications tended to be disproportionately placed in public hospitals of last resort.[51] Although the effects of PPS on hospital behavior are complex, on balance, research suggests that hospitals engaged in competition for less severely ill patients. This seems to have been particularly true with respect to psychiatric patients.[52]

As noted in Chapter Five, the DRG system has been greatly refined since it was first introduced and now employs risk adjustment using a number of dimensions in order to reduce hospital incentives to behave strategically.

3. Professional Standards Review Organizations: These local boards were set up in 1972 under federal law to review the appropriateness of hospital admissions and treatments. Both cost and intensity of treatment were reviewed at the time of preadmission, during treatment, or on a retrospective basis.[53] This legislation set the stage for major changes in the behavior of the private insurance industry and is associated with the move to more out-patient services and shorter stays.

4. Antitrust: A series of Supreme Court decisions, beginning in the 1970s, have interpreted antitrust law as applying to hospitals.[54] The belief that consolidation was associated with lower costs was maintained by the courts throughout the 1970s and early 1980s.[55] Since the late 1980s, the Justice Department has become highly critical of hospital mergers.[56] Government regulators have responded to the apparent change in the effects of concentration on hospital markets and now tend to see competition as beneficial. Difficulty in defining the relevant geographic markets in which hospitals operate has led to very limited success on the part of the government in blocking large hospital mergers to date, but government policy remains suspicious of increasing concentration in the hospital sector.*

5   Price Discrimination in the Contemporary Hospital Market

Forms of Price Discrimination

Price discrimination is known to exist in the hospital market. From its inception, hospitals gave discounted prices to Blue-Cross. Commercial insurers now negotiate various discounts from hospitals. HMOs and PPOs restrict insurance coverage to participating hospitals. This puts pressure on hospitals to lower prices in return for their inclusion in provider networks. Medicaid and Medicare negotiate prices on the basis of diagnosis. Moreover, hospitals have also always taken on patients who would not be able to reimburse them for service. Today, there is a wider range of prices for different categories of consumers than formerly.

---

*Since 1997, the Justice Department has continued to be largely unsuccessful in the courts in blocking the majority of hospital mergers that it has attempted to forestall. This is summarized succinctly in the McDermott, Will and Emery, *Health Law Update,* 16 (August 2, 1999): p. 3. Referring to a decision of the Eighth Circuit Court that a merger between the only two general, acute-care hospitals in Poplar Bluff, Missouri, would not be in violation of federal antitrust laws *(FTC v. Tenet Health Care Corp.),* they state:

> The Eighth Circuit's decision leaves the federal government "0 for 5" in recent hospital merger challenges. . . . Despite the recent losses, the government antitrust enforcers show no signs of abandoning their enforcement efforts.

Do Hospitals Engage in Cost Shifting?

In the last 20 years, it has often been alleged that prices for hospital services are as high as they are, and rising at the rate that they have been, because privately insured patients are subsidizing both the uninsured poor and Medicare and Medicaid patients. A model of cost shifting was presented in Chapter Seven with reference to physician behavior. The same model can be used here. Evidence of cost shifting requires that prices are raised for one group of consumers *in response to* lowered rates of remuneration for another group. Remember also that cost shifting will only be advantageous to firms if the higher-priced part of the market is not already being charged the profit-maximizing level price. It is therefore plausible that non-profit hospitals will be more likely to engage in cost shifting than will for-profit hospitals.

A number of researchers have studied the question of hospital cost shifting. Morrisey makes a good case that there is little evidence in support of this behavior, particularly in the post-DRG period.[57] He argues that hospitals would not reduce the amount of charity care that they provide if they could engage in cost shifting. Some evidence of cost shifting was provided when non-profit hospitals raised their fees for other patients in response to reductions in Medicaid payment rates in Illinois in the early 1980s.[58] A recent Institute of Medicine Study also documents a large amount of cost shifting to government on the part of hospitals. It estimates that 75 to 85 percent of the cost of uncompensated care that hospitals provide is paid for by the government, which means that there is cost shifting to tax payers.[59]

6   Role of Charity in the Modern Hospital

Charitable contributions are no longer the major source of funds for non-profit hospitals. Private donations for hospital construction peaked in the mid-1960s and then fell to approximately 5 percent by 1984. There appears to have been a change in attitude on the part of donors once the elderly and a certain proportion of the poor were covered by social insurance. The institution of Medicare and Medicaid is associated with a $1.9 billion drop in annual private donations to hospitals between 1965 and 1981.[60] This phenomenon is known as the "crowding out" of private philanthropy by government.

The aggregate amount of charity care provided by hospitals has not, however, declined appreciably, and during the 1980s, the cost of uncompensated care in the United States increased from approximately 5.3 percent to 6.3 percent of total hospital costs.[61] This proportion has remained roughly constant since then.

Model of Hospital Altruism

Frank and Salkever have developed a model that differentiates between **pure altruism** and **impure altruism** on the part of hospitals.[62] The level of charity care that each hospital chooses to supply is conditional on the amount supplied by other non-profit hospitals. Under pure altruism, altruism on the part of other hospitals will have a crowding-out effect, since hospitals respond to the level of need in the community. The authors find little evidence of a crowding-out effect. This leads them to the hypothesis of impure altruism that exists when hospitals compete for public good will by supplying charity care. In this case, more charity care is supplied when there are more hospitals competing for the community's stock of good will.[63]

Evidence About Hospital Altruism

A study of care supplied to the uninsured by California hospitals in 1984 to 1988 found that where cost cutting by insurers reduced hospital net incomes, hospitals responded by cutting back on the amount of uncompensated care offered.[64] However, uncompensated care as a fraction of *all* California hospital revenues rose because hospitals which were under less competitive pressure took on more charity cases. This appears to be an example of pure altruism. Support for this view is provided by evidence that the presence of public hospitals also reduces the amount of charity care provided by private hospitals in a market.[65]

Hospitals, even non-profit institutions, may also engage in "uncharitable" behavior toward the uninsured. In a world where health insurers are able to negotiate discounts, hospitals often charge the full list price to the uninsured. As a result, this group is frequently charged the highest prices for hospital care. On June 16, 2004, a group of lawyers filed a civil class-action suit against a number of non-profit hospitals across the country, alleging that the hospitals overcharged the uninsured and then hounded them for payment.[66]

We have noted that government contributions to hospital funding have tended to crowd out private donations. The question has been raised whether this also happens when governments contribute to charity care provided by private hospitals. Crowding out occurs when hospitals use the subsidy to make up for uncollected bills from patients who are not charity cases. Evidence that subsidies to hospitals increase the net provision of uncompensated care has been provided by studies of New York State's hospital revenue pool and New Jersey's Uncompensated Care Trust Fund.[67] State subsidies appear to have increased the net level of uncompensated care rather than just redistributed the burden of who paid, since no evidence was found of a change in behavior on the part of hospitals toward collecting debts.

Summary

Acute-care hospitals in the United States are predominantly non-profit and community-based. Average quality of care does not appear to differ between non-profit and for-profit nonteaching institutions, despite the widespread belief that non-profit hospitals provide higher-quality service.* This is less true for nursing homes and psychiatric hospitals, where a higher proportion of firms are for-profit and there is evidence of association between non-profit status and higher-quality care. The general view in economic theory is that non-profit firms lack incentives to be efficient. In the case of hospitals, where aspects of quality may be unmeasured, the evidence is less than conclusive. Non-profit hospitals are an alternative source, to governments, of public goods, providing services that are valuable to the community but which may involve financial losses to hospitals. However, even here the difference between non- and for-profit hospitals is not very great.

Government subsidies in the 1940s through the 1970s increased hospital capacity. The demand for hospital services was increased by the passage of the Medicare and Medicaid legislation in 1965. Since the 1980s, technological change and managed care have reduced demand for in-patient services. Hospitals have responded to excess capacity and shrinking revenues by consolidating, downsizing, closing, converting into forms other than acute-care centers, or cutting back on the provision of charity care.

Whereas competition was formerly thought to engage hospitals in a medical arms race and to raise costs, it now appears to be associated with lower costs. This has been brought about by the countervailing power of large third-party payers, including the government. The issue of cost shifting is a complex one in the case of hospitals. Evidence as to its importance is mixed. However, one type of cost shifting does occur. Government support for the provision of charity care in private hospitals involves cost shifting to taxpayers.

Key Concepts

Herfindahl–Hirschman Index (HHI)

Medical arms race

Payer-driven competition

Certificate of need (CON) regulations

Pure altruism

Impure altruism

---

*Teaching hospitals that run residency programs are generally non-profit, and they rate somewhat higher on most quality indexes.

Suggested Readings

1. Sloan, Frank, "Not-for-Profit Ownership and Hospital Behavior," in *Handbook of Health Economics,* Vol. 1B, Anthony J. Culyer and Joseph P. Newhouse, eds. (Amsterdam: Elsevier, 2000), Chap. 21.

2. Salkever, David S., "Regulation of Prices and Investment in Hospitals in the U.S.," in *Handbook of Health Economics,* Vol. 1B, op. cit., Chap. 28.

3. Norton, Edward C., "Long-Term Care," *Handbook of Health Economics,* Vol. 1B, op. cit., Chap. 17.

4. Morrisey, Michael A., "Movies and Myths: Hospital Cost Shifting," *Business Economics,* 30 (1995): 22–25. This is a very short and accessible article.

Questions for Discussion and Review

1. What are the main differences between a non-profit hospital and a for-profit hospital?

2. Referring back to Figure 8.2, and assuming a model in which hospital CEOs have authority to make decisions about the quantity/quality trade-off in services supplied, draw a diagram showing a likely difference between the utility-maximizing choices of a typical CEO of a for-profit hospital and a typical CEO of a non-profit hospital.

3. How would you measure quality of care in a hospital? Is there an overall difference in quality between for-profit and non-profit hospitals? Between government and private non-profit hospitals?

4. What is a natural monopoly? Do hospitals have the characteristics of natural monopolies?

5. Outline the main arguments that CON laws, on balance, do not improve the efficiency of hospital markets. Would you alter your answer if you were describing the nursing home market?

6. What is the "medical arms race"? Do you think it is still in effect in the twenty-first century?

7. How did hospitals react to the imposition of the Medicare PPS-DRG system? Was there a difference between the short-run and long-run effects of this legislation?

8. Faced with a reduction in Medicaid reimbursement rates, what are the possible actions a hospital can take?

9. What is the effect of level of Medicaid reimbursements on the quality of nursing home care? Explain.

10. Describe how competition in the U.S. hospital market has changed in the last 15 years.

11. What evidence would you use to determine whether a hospital is engaging in "pure" or "impure" altruism?

Resources

[1]Roemer, Milton I., "Bed Supply and Hospital Utilization: A Natural Experiment," *Hospitals, Journal of the American Hospital Association,* 35 (1961): 988–993.

[2]*OECD Health Data 2003* (Paris: Organization for Economic Cooperation and Development, 2003), Table 7.

[3]Frank, Richard G. and David S. Salkever, "Nonprofit Organizations in the Health Sector," *Journal of Economic Perspectives*" 8 (1994): 129–144.

[4]Sloan, F. A., "Not-for-Profit Ownership and Hospital Behavior," in *Handbook of Health Economics,* Vol. 1B, Culyer, Anthony J. and Joseph P. Newhouse, eds. (Amsterdam: Elsevier 2000), Chap. 2, p. 1144.

[5]See, for instance, Chou, Shin-Yi, "Asymmetric Information, Ownership and Quality of Care: An Empirical Analysis of Nursing Homes," *Journal of Health Economics,* 21 (2002): 293–311 and Hirth, Richard A., "Consumer Information and Competition Between Nonprofit and For-Profit Nursing Homes," *Journal of Health Economics*, 18 (1999): 219–240.

[6]Frank, R. G., D. Salkever, and J. Mitchell, "Market Forces and the Public Good: Competition Among Hospitals and the Provision of Indigent Care," in *Advances in Health Economics and Health Services Research*, R. Scheffler and L. Rossiter, eds. (Greenwich, CT: JAI Press, 1990), p. 129.

[7]Weisbrod, Burton A., *The Nonprofit Economy* (Cambridge, MA: Harvard University Press, 1988).

[8]Newhouse, Joseph P., "Toward a Theory of Nonprofit Institutions: An Economic Model of a Hospital," *The American Economic Review*, 60 (1970), 64–74.

[9]Pauly, Mark V. and Michael Redisch, "The Not-for-Profit Hospital as a Physicians' Cooperative," *American Economic Review,* 63 (1973): 87–100.

[10]Pauly and Redisch (1973), op. cit., p. 98.

[11]Harris, Jeffrey E., "The Internal Organization of Hospitals: Some Economic Implications," *Bell Journal of Economics*, 8 (1977): 467–482. In Harris's model, the tug of war between the two groups is structured as a noncooperative oligopoly game.

[12]Sloan (2000), op. cit., p. 1163.

[13]Weisbrod, B. A. and M. Schlesinger, "Ownership Form and Behavior in Regulated Markets with Asymmetric Information," in *The Economics of Nonprofit Institutions: Studies in Structure and Policy*, Rose-Ackerman, S., ed. (New York: Oxford University Press, 1986), pp. 133–151 and Mark, Tami L., "Psychiatric Hospital Ownership and Performance: Do Nonprofit Organizations Offer Advantages in Markets Characterized by Asymmetric Information?" *Journal of Human Resources*, 31 (1996): 631–649.

[14]Mark, (1996) op. cit., 643–647. However this study is based on a relatively small sample of 55 California hospitals.

[15]Grabowski, David C. and Richard A. Hirth, "Competitive Spillovers Across Non-Profit and For-Profit Nursing Homes," *Journal of Health Economics*, 22 (2003): 1–22.

[16]Pauly, Mark V., "Nonprofit Firms in Medical Markets," *American Economic Review, Papers and Proceedings,* 77 (1987): 257–262 and Sloan, F. A., et al., "Hospital Ownership and Cost and Quality of Care: Is There a Dime's Worth of Difference?" *Journal of Health Economics,* 20 (January 2001): 1–21.

[17]Hansman, Henry B., et al., *Ownership Form and Trapped Capital in the Hospital Industry*, NBER Working Paper No. W8989 (Cambridge, MA: National Bureau of Economic Research, June 2002).

[18]Zuckerman, Stephen, et al., "Measuring Hospital Inefficiency with Frontier Cost Functions," *Journal of Health Economics*, 13 (1994): 255–280, Table 5.

[19]Mark, (1996), op. cit.

[20]Kessler, Daniel P. and Mark B. McClellan, "The Effects of Hospital Ownership on Medical Productivity," *RAND Journal of Economics*, 33 (2002): 488-506.

[21]Newhouse, J. P., "Frontier Estimation: How Useful a Tool for Health Economics?" *Journal of Health Economics*, 13 (1994): 317–322.

[22]Sloan, (2000), op. cit., pp. 1141–1174.

[23]Frank, Salkever, and Mitchell (1990), op. cit., p. 139.

[24]Sloan, (2000), op. cit.

[25]See Hassan, Mahmud, et al., "Charity Care by Non-profit Hospitals: The Price of Tax-Exempt Debt," *International Journal of the Economics of Business*, 7 (2000): 47–62.

[26]A thoughtful treatment of the difficulties of defining geographic markets for hospitals is found in Whitesell, S. E. and W. E. Whitesell, "Hospital Mergers and Antitrust: Some Economic and Legal Issues," *American Journal of Economics and Sociology*, 54 (1995): 305–321.

[27]According to the calculations of Paul J. Feldstein, *Health Care Economics*, 5th edition (Albany, NY: Delmar, 1999), pp. 305–306.

[28]Frech, H. E. III and Lee R. Mobley, "Resolving the Impasse on Hospital Scale Economies: A New Approach," *Applied Economics*, 27 (1995): 286–296.

[29]Madison, Kristin, "Multiple System Membership and Patient Treatments, Expenditures, and Outcomes," Unpublished Ph.D. dissertation, Stanford University, 2002.

[30]Ibid., pp. 30–32.

[31]See, for instance, Robinson, James C. and Harold S. Luft, "Competition and the Cost of Hospital Care, 1972–1982," *Journal of the American Medical Association*, 257, No. 23 (June 19, 1987): 32–44.

[32]McKay, Marie L., "The Prisoner's Dilemma: An Obstacle to Cooperation in Health Care Markets," *Medical Care Review*, 51 (1994): 179–204.

[33]Gottlieb, Jerry B., "Understanding the Effects of Nurses, Patients' Hospital Rooms, and Patients' Perception of Control on the Perceived Quality of a Hospital," *Health Marketing Quarterly*, 18 (January–February, 2000): 1–14.

[34]See Enthoven, Alain E., "The History and Principles of Managed Competition," *Health Affairs*, (Supplement 1993): 24–48.

[35]Zwanziger, Jack and Glen A. Melnick, "The Effects of Hospital Competition and the Medicare PPS Program on Hospital Cost Behavior in California," *Journal of Health Economics*, 7 (1988): 301–320; Dranove, David, et al., "Price and Concentration in Hospital Markets: The Switch from Patient-Driven to Payer-Driven Competition," *Journal of Law and Economics*, XXXVI (April 1993): 179–203. See also Kessler, Daniel P. and Mark B. McClellan, "Is Hospital Competition Socially Wasteful?" *Quarterly Journal of Economics*, 115 (2000): 577–615.

[36]Town, Robert and Gregoy Vistnes, "Hospital Competition in HMO Networks," *Journal of Health Economics*, 20 (2001): 733–753.

[37]Krishan, Ranjani, "Market Restructuring and Pricing in the Hospital Industry," *Journal of Health Economics*, 20 (2001): 213–237.

[38]Vita, Michael G. and Seth Sacher, "The Competitive Effects of Not-for-Profit Hospital Mergers: A Case Study," *Journal of Industrial Economics,* 49 (March 2001): 63–84. E. B. Keeler, G. Melnick, and J. Zwanziger also found that the changing effects of mergers applied to non-profit as well as for-profit hospitals. See Keeler et al., "The Changing Effects of Competition on Non-Profit and For-Profit Hospital Pricing Behavior," *Journal of Health Economics,* 18 (January 1999): 69–86.

[39]Connor, Robert A., et al., "The Effects of Market Concentration and Horizontal Mergers on Hospital Costs and Prices," *International Journal of the Economics of Business,* 5 (July 1998): 159–181.The interaction effect of HMO penetration and market concentration was strong enough to swamp the effect of market concentration alone, measured by the HHI index.

[40]See, for instance, Brooks, John M., "Hospital-Insurer Bargaining: An Empirical Investigation of Appendectomy Pricing," *Journal of Health Economics,* 16 (August 1997): 417–434.

[41]See, for instance, Ho, V. and B. H. Hamilton, "Hospital Mergers and Acquisitions: Does Market Consolidation Hurt Patients?" *Journal of Health Economics,* 19 (2000): 767–791.

[42]Mannheim, L. M., et al., "Local Hospital Competition in Large Metropolitan Areas," *Journal of Economics and Management Strategy,* 3 (1994): 143–167.

[43]Braden, Bradley R., et al., "National Health Care Expenditures, 1997," *Health Care Financing Review,* 20 (1998): 83–110.

[44]An excellent comprehensive review of regulation of hospitals is provided in Salkever, D. S., "Regulation of Prices and Investment in Hospitals in the United States," in *Handbook of Health Economics,* Vol. 1B, Anthony J. Culyer and Joseph P. Newhouse, eds. (Amsterdam: Elsevier, 2000), Chap. 28, pp. 1489–1535. See particularly pp. 1493–1495.

[45]See, for instance, Gertler, P. J., "Subsidies, Quality, and the Regulation of Nursing Homes," *Journal for Public Economics,* 38 (1989): 33–52 and Nyman, John A., "The Effect of Market Concentration and Excess Demand on the Price of Nursing Home Care," *Journal of Industrial Economics,* XLII (1994): 193–204.

[46]Nyman (1994), op. cit., p. 193.

[47]Nyman (1994), op. cit., pp. 201–203.

[48]Gertler (1989), op. cit. and Nyman, J. A., "Prospective and 'Cost-plus' Medicaid Reimbusement, Excess Medicaid Demand, and the Quality of Nursing Home Care," *Journal of Health Economics,* 4 (1985): 237–259 and Grabowski, David C., et al., "The Effects of CON Repeal on Medicaid Nursing Home and Long-Term Care Expenditures," *Inquiry,* 40 (2003): 146–157.

[49]Hodgkin, D. and T. G. McGuire, "Payment Levels and Hospital Response to Prospective Payment," *Journal of Health Economics,* 13 (1994): 1–30.

[50]Newhouse, Joseph P. and D. J. Byrne, "Did Medicare's Prospective Payment System Cause Length of Stay to Fall?" *Journal of Health Economics,* 7 (1988): 413–416, found that the shorter length of stay is associated with less sick patients in PPS settings.

[51]Newhouse, Joseph P., "Do Unprofitable Patients Face Access Problems?" *Health Care Financing Review,* 11 (1989): 33–42.

[52]See, for instance, Ellis, Randall P. and Thomas G. McGuire, "Hospital Response to Prospective Payment: Moral Hazard, Selection, and Practice-Style Effects," *Journal of Health Economics,* 15 (1996): 257–277 and Dranove, David, "Rate-Setting by DRG and Hospital Specialization," *Rand Journal of Economics,* 18 (1987): 417–427.

[53]For an evaluation of effects on hospital admissions, length of stay, and expenditures, see Wickizer, Thomas M., et al., "Does Utilization Review Reduce Unnecessary Hospital Care and Contain Costs?" *Medical Care,* 27 (1989): 632–647.

[54]See Alpert, Geraldine and Thomas R. McCarty, "Beyond *Goldfarb*: Applying Traditional Antitrust Analysis to Changing Health Markets," *Antitrust Bulletin*, 29 (Summer 1984): 165–204.

[55]*United States v. Carilion Health System and Roanoke Valley Hospital*, 707, 840, 849 (W.D. Va.).

[56]Whitesell and Whitesell (1995), op. cit, and Noether, M., "Economic Issues in the Antitrust Assessment of Hospital Competition: Overview," *International Journal of the Economics of Business*, 5 (1998): 133–141.

[57]Morrisey, Michael A., "Movies and Myths: Hospital Cost Shifting," *Business Economics*, 30 (1995): 22–25. For a more lengthy and thorough treatment, see Morrisey, *Cost Shifting in Health Care: Separating Evidence from Rhetoric* (Washington, DC: AEI Press, 1994).

[58]Dranove, David, "Pricing by Nonprofit Institutions: The Case of Hospital Cost Shifting," *Journal of Health Economics*, 7 (1988): 47–57.

[59]Institute of Medicine, *Hidden Costs, Value Lost* (Washington, DC: The National Academies Press, 2003), p. 53.

[60]Sloan, F. A., et al., "The Demise of Hospital Philanthropy," *Economic Inquiry*, XXVIII (1990): 725, 737.

[61]Fraser, I. et al, *Direct Financing of Uncompensated Care: Critical Questions in the Use and Evaluation of Uncompensated Care Pools and Other Provider Focused Approaches. An Action Planning Guide Implementing Selected Recommendations of the Report of the Special Committee of Care for the Indigent* (Chicago: American Hospital Association, 1990).

[62]Frank, Richard G. and David S. Salkever, "The Supply of Charity Services for Nonprofit Hospitals: Motives and Market Structure," *RAND Journal of Economics*, 22 (Autumn 1991): 430–445.

[63]Frank and Salkever (1991), op. cit., pp. 434–435.

[64]Gruber, J., "The Effect of Price Shopping in Medical Markets: Hospital Responses to PPOs in California," *Journal of Health Economics*, 38 (1994): 183–212.

[65]Thorpe, K. E. and C. E. Phelps, "The Social Role of Not-for-Profit Organizations: Hospital Provision of Charity Care," *Economic Inquiry*, 29 (1991): 472–484.

[66]Abelson, Reed and Jonathan D. Glater, "Suits Challenge Hospital Bills of the Uninsured," *The New York Times*, June 17, 2004, p. C1.

[67]Gaskin, Darrell J., "Altruism or Moral Hazard: The Impact of Hospital Uncompensated Care Pools," *Journal of Health Economics*, 16 (1997): 397–416; Thorpe, K. E. and C. E. Phelps, "The Social Role of Not-for-Profit Organizations: Hospital Provision of Charity Care," *Economic Inquiry*, 21 (1992): 472–484; Thorpe K. E., and C. Spencer, "How Do Uncompensated Care Pools Affect the Level and Type of Care: Results from New York State," *Journal of Health Politics, Policy and Law*, 16 (1991): 363–380.

PART FOUR

Evaluation of Technology, Technological Change, and the Bio-Pharmaceutical Industry

CHAPTER NINE

Cost-Benefit and Cost-Effectiveness Analysis

Does the United States spend too much on medical care? Most policy makers believe that it does . . . . At the same time, we like what medical spending buys us. For example, we can now transplant livers, kidneys, hearts, and lungs, all of which we were unable to do a few decades ago; if this is what medical spending buys us, do we want to give it up?

The heart of this issue is perhaps the most fundamental question in health economics: how much is medical care worth, and how much should we be willing to pay for it? Or, to put the question in a more common vernacular, would you rather have more money or more life?*

1 Introduction

The authors of this quote conclude at the end of their study that improvement in medical technology over the past half-century has "almost certainly been worth its cost" when we compare the change in health capital that has been acquired with the increase in medical spending.† In doing so, they

---

*Cutler, David M. and Elizabeth Richardson, "Your Money and Your Life: The Value of Health and What Affects It," in *Frontiers in Health Policy Research*, Garber, Alan M. ed., (Cambridge, MA: MIT Press, 1999), p. 100.

†To reach their conclusion Cutler and Richardson estimate the value of a year of life at $100,000.

are engaging in cost-benefit analysis. To make this judgment requires assigning monetary values to both the costs and the benefits. It is particularly difficult to weigh benefits against costs in the context of health care because we have to place monetary values on life: additional years of life, or improvements in the quality of life. A number of estimates have been made of the present value of a remaining life, year of life, or quality adjusted year of life at different ages. A survey in 1994 found the range of values assigned to a life-year in the United States to be in the range of $70,000 to $ 175,000. The discounted present value of (remaining) life for a person of prime age in the United States was found to be worth $3 to $7 million.[1]

Although the present value of remaining life will decline with age, simply because there are fewer years left to enjoy, it has not been uncommon to also assume a declining value for each life-year as one ages, or at a least a "senior discount" for those over 60 years of age. Recent investigations on age-specific values that workers, in fact, assign to their lives and to life-years have found a more complex relationship between age and value of life-years. There appears to be an inverted U-shaped pattern over the adult life cycle, with the peak values occurring in one's late 30s.[2] Thus, using an average value of a life-year to make inferences about values of life-years for people of different ages is likely to lead to faulty results.

2   Cost-Benefit Analysis

Cost-benefit analysis can only be used when it is possible to determine a monetary value for benefits as well as costs. The rule employed to decide how many resources should be devoted to a project is:

> *Devote resources to an activity until the last unit has an extra (marginal) benefit just equal to the extra (marginal) cost.*

This is illustrated in Figure 9.1 which shows the relationship between total and marginal benefits and costs. The standard assumptions are made that marginal costs rise and marginal benefits decline as more resources are devoted to an activity.

This kind of reasoning is used by all of us, even if we do not call it cost-benefit analysis, whenever we evaluate whether an activity is worth undertaking or continuing. Any firm comparing revenues with costs is engaging in cost-benefit analysis. Let us begin with an apparently simple health-care question: "Is it worth getting a flu shot?" On reflection, even this question is not easy to answer, let alone frame correctly.* One has to begin by asking whose costs and whose benefits are going to be evaluated. The costs and benefits of the flu shot can be evaluated from the point of view of the individual, the society, the medical profession, or the insurance company.

---

*See Mullahy, John, "It'll Only Hurt a Second? Microeconomics of Who Gets Flu Shots," *Health Economics,* 8 (1999): 9–24.

Figure 9.1

Cost Benefit Analysis
Illustrated

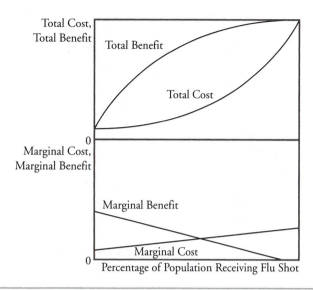

For an individual who is employed, the out-of-pocket cost of the physician visit plus any time off from work evaluated at the hourly wage would be the cost of the inoculation, if we assume that the "ouch factor," the unpleasantness of having the inoculation, is ignored and that any danger from side effects is not considered. But even this is not perfectly simple. If it is possible to have the inoculation in the evening, during one's lunch hour, or if one's pay is not docked when one takes time off from work to get the flu shot (or if it is a slack day at work so that one does not have to work longer to make up for the lost time), then the cost may be viewed as lower by the individual.

The benefit of the flu shot is the reduction in risk of catching the flu. The cost of having the flu is the value of the lost work and leisure time plus the costs of any medical treatment required (doctor visits, antibiotics) plus the loss to members of one's household if they catch it. These costs must be weighted by the probability of catching the flu. For instance, if the loss associated with having the flu is valued at $5,000 and the probability of catching the flu is .01, the expected loss is $50 and a risk-neutral person would be willing to get a flu shot if the cost of the inoculation were $50 or less.

Suppose that we now want to compute the societal costs and benefits of a flu shot for the same person. The cost to society is the cost of the resources used to provide the (additional) flu shot and the loss of productive time used in getting it. The benefit is the gain in production from having the worker not fall ill, plus the savings in costs of treating the illness weighted by the reduction in risk of illness, plus benefits that result from the reduction in risk of transmitting the flu to other members of society. Preventing the spread of a communicable disease therefore

has some of the aspects of a public good. At least there are major positive externalities or spill-over effects. The social benefit is thus more than the sum of the
private benefits accruing to those who have received the flu shots. In considering
the societal cost of inoculating a population, it may also be necessary to include
the cost of developing the year's flu vaccine as well as just the extra cost of providing it to an additional person. The question needs to be carefully defined. If
the question is the costs and effects of giving a flu shot to an additional person or
group of people when the vaccine is already developed, then only the marginal
cost of the additional shot will be relevant. As complicated as this cost-benefit
problem may seem, it is relatively simple. The society will decide to provide additional flu shots up to the point where the marginal social cost equals the marginal social benefit, if we assume that benefits will decline as more flu shots are
administered. For instance, it may be determined that the benefits only outweigh
the costs in the case of young children, the elderly, and people who come into
contact with a large number of others.

Let us consider another example. How would we evaluate the costs and benefits of providing a coronary artery bypass graft operation (CABG) to a retired person? We can no longer use the wage rate to value the opportunity cost of the patient's time. Another factor that complicates this example is the risk of an
unsuccessful outcome to the operation, which has to be factored into the determination of benefits. This was assumed to be negligible in the case of the flu
shot. Moreover, since CABG involves probable extension of years of life, cost-
benefit analysis involves a comparison of the present value of the streams of
costs and benefits that accrue over time. The operation will be worth undergoing
if

$$\Sigma\{C_i/(1 + r)^t\} \le \Sigma\{B_t/(1 + \lambda)^t\}$$

where r and λ are the discount rates of the cost and benefit streams. The discount
rate r is the interest rate. λ, the discount rate for the benefits stream, compares
the value of the benefits or utility received in different years. This discount rate is
a subjective value that varies across individuals. How does an individual decide
how to discount the future? Is pleasure (or health) a year from now worth 3 percent less, 10 percent less? How much one discounts the future is likely to be a
function of age or temperament and may vary with education level.[3] Evaluating
the benefits stream is a more difficult task than determining the costs.

Methods of Determining Values for Benefits

There are several methods that are usually employed in determining the value of
benefits.

Willingness to Pay

It has become common to use **willingness to pay** as a way to measure benefits.
If a person will get a flu shot when the total cost is $50 but will not do so if the
cost rises to $55, we can infer that the benefit to him or her is less than $55 but at

least $50. Willingness to pay can also be used to estimate the value of an additional life-year or a longer remaining life span.

Several techniques are used to determine willingness to pay. Survey research, in which people are directly questioned, is one technique. This approach involves contingent valuation. People are asked to state the hypothetical amount they would be willing to pay in return for a benefit. Market data may also be used to infer preferences. For instance, labor negotiations in which certain levels of pay increases are foregone in return for increased safety standards can be used to infer the monetary value of a given amount of reduction in risk of death or disablement to workers. Differences between combat pay and ordinary wages in the military or differences between pay for working at high elevations and on the ground in construction jobs can be used to estimate the value of the extra life-time associated with the reduction in risk. An objection to this method is that people who engage in high-risk activities are likely to have different tastes, that is, different rates at which they are willing to trade off wealth for life-years, than does the average individual.

Using Changes in Speed Limits to Estimate the Value of Life

Ashenfelter and Greenstone have used the 1987 change in federal law that allowed states to increase speed limits from 55 to 65 miles per hour in rural sections of interstate highways to estimate the value of a life. They have computed the value of the time saved by driving faster, using the average hourly wage in the state, and compared it with the increase in risk of fatal accident in order to come up with estimates of savings per fatality. The authors acknowledge that using decisions made by administrative agencies as proxies for individuals' preferences may involve distortions.

Ashenfelter and Greenstone found that the increase in the speed limit raised speeds by approximately 3.5 percent. Fatalities were increased by roughly 35 percent. This resulted in an estimate of 125,000 hours saved per fatality. The value of the time saved was estimated at an average of $1.54 million per fatality. A range of estimates for the present value of a life was found for the different states that raised their speed limits. Values ranging from $1 to $10 million were obtained.

Given this information, does it seem to have been a sensible social policy to raise the speed limit from 55 to 65 miles per hour?

Source: Ashenfelter, Orley and Michael Greenstone, *Using Mandated Speed Limits to Measure the Value of a Statistical Life*, NBER, Working Paper W9094 (Cambridge, MA: National Bureau of Economic Research, August 2002).

Human Capital Approach

Another method that is used to value incremental life-years is to value the stock of human capital, measured as the stream of expected future earnings. This approach is often used to compute the value of damages in accidental death or disability law cases. If used more broadly, this criterion tends to conflict with our society's ethical value that assigns equal worth to all individuals. If we apply the human capital approach to a retired heart disease patient, the monetary value of the remaining life-years will be zero if that individual is no longer engaged in any activity that earns money for him or her, or society. The willingness-to-pay approach may therefore give more reasonable results in this case. If the individual is willing to invest in the heart surgery, we assume that the value of remaining life is deemed to be equal to or greater than the cost of the operation.

3   Cost-Effectiveness and Cost-Utility Analysis

Cost-Effectiveness Analysis

In situations where there are measurement problems or ethical objections to establishing monetary equivalents for the value of human life, the strategy of cost-effectiveness analysis (CEA) may be used to compare the effectiveness of alternative medical interventions or alternative public investments in health. CEA is a technique used to compare mutually exclusive alternatives. It is a method that allows us to measure marginal costs in monetary terms and marginal benefits in natural units, such as reductions in cholesterol level. For instance, cost-effectiveness analysis is used to evaluate alternative treatments for early-stage breast cancer, mastectomy or lumpectomy plus radiation therapy, and alternative chemotherapy drugs for the treatment of late-stage breast cancer. The benefits are often measured in five-year survival rates or postoperative life expectancy. Many researchers are now using cost-effectiveness analysis to evaluate alternative treatments for AIDS. Cost-effectiveness analysis is also widely used in resource allocation decisions concerning the development of medical technologies.[4]

In performing cost-effectiveness analysis, *incremental* cost-effectiveness ratios (C/E) are used. Suppose we want to compare a new medical treatment T_1 with the one commonly in use T_0. Let μc_i represent the average cost of any treatment T_i and μE_i the average effect of treatment T_i. We can then define the C/E ratio as

$$C/E = (\mu_{C1} - \mu_{C0})/(\mu_{E1} - \mu_{E0})$$

When the ratios are computed using data from clinical trials, sample means, based on average outcomes for trial groups are used to approximate the population means, and it is necessary to compute the standard errors of the difference in the means in order to evaluate whether there are significant differences in outcomes.*

---

*Computing standard errors when working with C/E ratios can be quite complicated. The statistical technique of bootstrapping is often used. See Mennemeyer, S. T. and L. P. Cyr, "A Bootstrap Approach to Medical Decision Analysis," *Journal of Health Economics,* 16 (1997): 741–747.

Example of Incremental Cost Effectiveness

Use of the drug Tamoxifen for three years after surgery for the removal of a stage I breast cancer lesion is associated with an approximate 30 percent reduction in the probability of recurrence. Taking the drug for a full five-year period is associated with reducing the probability of recurrence by 45 percent. Thus, the incremental risk reduction of an extra two years on Tamoxifen is 15 percent. The extra cost of the drug should be figured in discounted present value terms. If the cost of the drug is $100 per month or $1,200 per year, we assume an interest rate of 5 percent, and, for purposes of simplification, that a full year's supply of Tamoxifen is purchased at the beginning of the year, then

$$C/E = \frac{\$1,200 + \$1,200/(1.05)}{15\% \text{ reduction in probability of recurrence}} = \frac{\$2,342}{.15}$$

with the result that the cost of a 1 percent reduction in probability of recurrence of the cancer is $156, in discounted present value terms.

Incremental cost-effectiveness analysis can never tell us whether some course of action "is worth it," but only whether it is better than the alternative(s). CEA gives us unambiguous results only when one alternative leads to at least as good an outcome with the use of fewer resources, or when it leads to a better outcome with no additional expenditure of resources.[5]

Cost-effectiveness analysis, in the form we have so far discussed, cannot be used to aggregate multidimensional effects. For instance, it can be used to evaluate the effectiveness of different treatments in terms of expected survival rates or life expectancy, but not in terms of differences in quality of life.

Cost-Utility Analysis

The technique of CEA has been expanded, since its original development, to include **cost-utility analysis (CUA)**. This technique is used to compare costs with benefits measured as utility increases. CUA may be regarded as a special case of CEA where utility enters explicitly into the evaluation. For instance, an incremental (C/E) ratio might be expressed as *incremental costs in monetary units / incremental utility of additional life-years*. It can be used to compare medical interventions that lead to multidimensional outcomes.

Let us assume a utility function of the form $U = U(L, Q)$, where U is utility, L is length of remaining life, and Q is quality of life during the remaining life-years. It is necessary to construct an index that embodies both L and Q. The values of the state(s) of health that a person experiences are weighted by the length of time spent in each state. The most commonly used index of this kind is the quality adjusted life-year (QALY). The World Health Organization (WHO) uses an alternative index, the disability adjusted life-year (DALY). The latter focuses on the extent of loss due to morbidity and mortality.[6]

Returning to the example of alternative treatments for breast cancer, we see that it is possible, using CUA, to consider whether a treatment method that allows breast preservation results in a higher QALY value, even if there is no significant difference in life expectancy or probability of recurrence of the disease.

Once the notion of utility is introduced into the analysis, it is also possible to compare a broader range of alternatives than different treatments for the same disease. CUA is useful for evaluating medical procedures that benefit patients with different diseases, or even for comparing investments in health with other investments, such as education. For example, CUA could be used to discern whether using a given budget in an Indian rural village yields better results when spent providing a source of potable drinking water, schooling, or a medical clinic. Since diminishing returns usually apply at some point when incremental investments in any project are made, the results of CUA will depend on the previous allocations of resources to the alternative projects.

Methods of Arriving at Individuals' QALY Values

Researchers use three main strategies to elicit an individual's preferences:

1. The individual may be asked to choose between a certain outcome (present state of health) and a risky treatment option that might lead to either a better or worse state. This is known as the **standard gamble method**.
2. The individual may be asked to specify how much time in perfect health he or she would trade for a year in the current state of health. This is the **time-trade-off method**.
3. The individual may be asked to rate his or her own health in terms of some prescribed scale before and after the treatment. Individuals can be asked to either rank states of health or rate them in categorical terms (excellent, good, fair, poor).

There are some theoretical difficulties with all three strategies, in terms of eliciting information that is a good approximation to an individual's utility function, but as this text is not a treatise on the theory of constructing utility functions, these difficulties will not be examined in detail here.[7] There are also some practical problems using these strategies: There may be problems of misjudgment in all three methods. The standard gamble method may be troublesome for people who cannot easily estimate values of hypothetical outcomes. If people have trouble assessing how to discount the future, the time-trade-off method may give faulty results. And there is the very real problem associated with making interpersonal comparisons of rankings or categorical terms. How do we compare rankings of different people? How good is "good"? To illustrate the difficulty, researchers have found that women tend to rate their health in more extreme ways than men, who much more often and across large samples rate their health in some continuum around a middle state.

Research Example Using QALY

Studies in several countries have investigated the cost-effectiveness of different treatment options in prolonging life and improving quality of life in patients with advanced (stage III) breast cancer. One British study by Brown and co-authors computed the incremental cost-effectiveness of three alternative chemotherapy drugs: docetaxel, paclitaxel, and vinorelbine. Data from randomized clinical trials were used to provide the estimates of incremental effects of the most effective drug, docetaxel, compared with the other two alternatives. Responses from oncology nurses in six countries were used to estimate patients' utilities. Cost variables were obtained from practicing oncologists. A discount rate of 6 percent was used for both costs and benefits.

Incremental Cost/Utility Ratios: Marginal Cost per Additional QALY

Docetaxel/paclitaxel	1,995£
Docetaxel/vinorelbine	14,055£

Information from the National Institute for Clinical Excellence in the United Kingdom determined 20,000 to 30,000 British £ per QALY to be an acceptable cost. Given this decision the substitution of docetaxel for both paclitaxel and vinorelbine was supported.

Source: Brown, Ruth E. et al., "Cost Effectiveness of Treatment Options in Advanced Breast Cancer in the U.K." *PharmacoEconomics,* 19 (2001), 1091–1102.

---

4 Can Cost-Effectiveness Analysis Be Converted into Cost-Benefit Analysis?

Use of Thresholds of Acceptability

When public policy makers in the health care arena are given a fixed budget constraint, they often use some **threshold of acceptability** when applying CEA or CUA analysis. Programs, ranked among a group of competing ones, will not be funded if they fall below the accepted threshold level. In the example just considered, the threshold level of acceptable cost per QALY was determined to be 20,000 to 30,000 British £. Using thresholds of acceptability implicitly converts cost-effectiveness analysis into cost-benefit analysis.

A method has been developed for converting cost-effectiveness analysis into cost-benefit analysis when one publicly funded project is replaced by another. Building on the work of Phelps and Mushlin (1991) and Garber and Phelps (1997), Robert Brent developed a strategy for equating CBA and CEA without directly using the controversial willingness-to-pay measure.[8] He reasons that price can be arrived at from either the demand side (marginal utility) or the supply side (marginal cost) since in a competitive market situation $MU = P = MC$. He sets up an incremental effectiveness-cost criterion for the introduction of a new program compared with an older one that has a cost of C_1 and an effectiveness level E_1. If the cost and effectiveness of the new program are C_2 and E_2 respectively, the marginal cost of public funds is MCF, and the price of the new program is P, then $(E_2 - E_1/C_2 - C_1) > MCF/P$ represents the cost-benefit criterion for acceptance of the new program. Brent argues that the MCF converts the cost-effectiveness formulation into cost-benefit terms. His reasoning is that the incremental effectiveness-cost ratio of the new program must be greater than the value of the marginal effectiveness-cost ratio of the activity that was eliminated to make way for the new program. Assuming that the foregone activity had a (social) value just equal to the marginal cost of the public funds used to fund it, we can infer the marginal benefit level of the new program. This, of course, assumes that the original allocation of funds to the last (marginal) project did, in fact, reflect society's marginal social value (i.e., collective marginal utility).

The strategy can only be used where there is a fixed public budget and competing projects are to be funded out of it, for then the MCF of the project just at the threshold of acceptability is, in essence, a measure of the public's willingness to pay. The methodology rests on the assumption that public expenditure decisions correctly reflect the community's preferences. Brent used this framework of analysis to look at decisions of state governments about funding alternative mental health projects.

5   Problems That Must Be Addressed in Implementing Cost-Effectiveness Analysis

Whose Utility Functions Should Be Used in Decision Making?

Assuming that interpersonal utility comparisons can be made, we are still left with the problem of deciding whose utility functions are to be used when collective decisions are made. Health economists have debated whether it should be the preferences of the actual patients or the general public that should inform policy makers.* It is argued that at least part of the general public may have had experience with the disease or treatment in question, which gives it a perspective

---

*As Dolan points out, the difference in practice is often blurred. Dolan, Paul, "The Measurement of Health-Related Quality of Life," *Health Economics* Vol. 1B, Culyer, Anthony J. and Joseph P. Newhouse, eds. (Amsterdam: Elsevier, 2000), p. 1738.

similar to that of the actual patients. Moreover, if patients' evaluations are to be used, there is the question of the optimal time to poll them, since different evaluations have been found to be given in the course of the treatment of a disease. Moreover, groups of patients with the same health condition may have widely differing preferences with respect to the changes in their health states that alternative treatments would involve. Research on men with benign prostate hyperplasia illustrates this. The operation that relieves the urinary symptoms of the disease involves a risk of permanent incontinence and impotence. Studies have shown great variability in preferences for the operation versus living with the known symptoms.[9]

A commonly accepted principle in public finance is that preferences of the general public should be the basis for resource allocations where health care is financed out of general tax revenues.[10] But how should the public's preferences be aggregated? Should the mean or the median value be used to reflect the value for the community? There is no easy answer to this, but as it may affect the outcome of CUA, this should be carefully considered.

Nonindependence of Value of Health and Wealth and Consumption Patterns

An underlying assumption of CUA is that the utility of various health states is independent of both consumption and wealth, each of which also provides utility. With respect to wealth, since wealth may enhance the value of time spent in a higher quality of health, it is frequently argued that a person's utility function is generally of the form

$$U = U(H, W)$$

where H is health, W is wealth, and the two are *not* independent.

Health states frequently cause major alterations in overall consumption patterns. The utility or disutility associated with a given health status will therefore also be a function of one's consumption patterns. Consider the following hypothetical example: John and Henry are two individuals who differ only in tastes about how to spend their leisure time. In other ways, they are identical: They have the same occupation, income, education, marital status, and number of children, are the same age, live in the same community, and have the same arthritic condition in one knee. Direct questioning reveals that curing John's arthritic knee has a higher QALY value than curing Henry's. This is because John is a skilled (avocational) mountain climber and Henry's passion is reading. A likely outcome, if having the knee surgery is entirely a matter of individual choice, will be that John will have the surgery at a higher cost-effectiveness level than will Henry. This implies that repairing a knee has a higher QALY value for John than for Henry.

If health care is provided out of public resources, do we as a society assign scarce resources to a knee replacement operation for John but require Henry to limp around in pain? Would the conclusion be different if John earned his income climbing mountains and Henry his teaching English literature? Many people will be made uneasy by a society's discriminating between the two men on the basis of their different consumption patterns and will be even less sanguine about an allocation of resources based on QALY rankings if these rankings are the result of income rather than taste differences.

How Is Inequality in Health to Be Treated?

Decisions about how to allocate scarce resources among competing health-care projects require a decision about how health inequality is to be treated. Are we to equalize health states of different individuals, which would involve devoting more resources to the sickest in society? Do we devote resources to helping those who will most benefit, which might well lead to the opposite result? A heart transplant to someone who is young and otherwise healthy will almost certainly lead to a higher QALY value than giving one to an elderly person with multiple health disabilities. Or, should we just equalize opportunity to receive health care irrespective of other characteristics of individuals? Equalizing opportunity might be achieved through having a lottery in which those who desire heart transplants would be assigned them on a random basis.[11]

Oregon's Method of Determining Medicaid Benefits Packages*

An original protocol was developed by the State of Oregon in administering its Medicaid funds. All people below a certain income level are eligible for Medicaid coverage in Oregon. Instead of choosing between people, choices are made about which treatments will be covered from Medicaid. funds. Oregon was one of the first examples of an attempt to use cost-effectiveness analysis in public policy in the United States. In 1990–1991, a ranking of treatments for Medicaid recipients was developed using a cost-effectiveness index:

$$\text{Priority Rank} = \frac{\text{cost of treatment}}{\text{net expected benefit} \times \text{duration of benefit}}$$

Beginning with the top (lowest) rankings, treatments were to be funded in descending rank order until the entire state Medicaid budget for a current time period was exhausted. For example, treatment for colds and flu in otherwise healthy children was not to be funded on the ground that it was less cost-effective than treatments for some other diseases. The cost was not very great compared with some other treatments, but the expected benefit and the benefit duration were both very low.

Benefits were originally calculated using a Quality of Well-Being Scale (QWB). The method of ranking was modified after Medicaid objected that there might be a conflict with the Americans with Disability Act. The argument was something like

this: If quality of life for a disabled person is considered to be lower, then even an equal improvement in the quality of life might lead to a lower priority ranking if it were weighted by the original quality of life level. In other words, a 20 percent improvement in the health of a person who had an 80 percent rating on the quality of well-being scale would be construed as a 16 percent improvement. A 20 percent improvement in the health of a person who had a 40 percent rating would be construed as only an 8 percent improvement. As a result of the concerns, the cost-effectiveness based rankings were never used.

At a later date, the Clinton administration ruled that (revised) rankings could not even take account of the probability that treatment would result in the patient returning to an asymptomatic state of health. Again, there was concern that this would violate the Americans with Disability Act.

The algorithms used by the State of Oregon to rank treatments that will be covered by Medicaid have been revised a number of times. By 1993, the criteria had been reduced to five-year survival rates and costs. Some hand adjustments are also made. No form of cost-effectiveness ranking has actually been used in Oregon to allocate resources to Medicaid clients. The cost-effectiveness measure was abandoned not only because of potential conflicts with the Americans with Disability Act, but also because the results were so counterintuitive that the board which administered Medicaid found itself unable to justify the outcomes obtained by using the QWB scale.

*For an analysis of the difficulties the State of Oregon encountered in trying to use the QWB, see Tengs, Tammy O., "An Evaluation of Oregon's Medicaid Rationing Algorithms," *Health Economics*, 5 (1996): 171–181.

Should Incremental Cost-Effectiveness Analysis Take Account of Fixed Costs?

Programs that have equal cost-effectiveness values may nonetheless have very different levels of fixed costs. For instance, a program costing $1,000 with an expected value of one additional life-year will be indistinguishable in its cost-effectiveness ratio from a program costing $10,000 with an expected value of 10 incremental life-years. However, the more expensive program may not be practical unless the full $10,000 is budgeted for the project. Initial fixed costs are frequently an important part of the cost of establishing new programs, and programs are not divisible. Thus, the fixed costs are marginal costs at the time the initiation of a new program is being considered. They only become fixed costs once the program has been launched.

Ignoring these costs can be a problem when a program requires such a large proportion of an annual budget that it is not *marginally* cost-effective because a range of other projects, all of which rank above the acceptability cut-off threshold and some of which may even rank above the program under consideration, will have to be sacrificed if the proposed program is undertaken. Sendi and Briggs propose that measures be used which combine the criteria of affordability and cost-effectiveness.[12]

Practical Problems in Establishing Values in Cost-Effectiveness Analysis

When the public has been polled to arrive at valuations of health-care alternatives, it may be possible to increase welfare by using what has come to be known as preference subgroup analysis.[13] This provides a way of addressing the criticism that community preferences are too often based on average values. Using average values results in programs being judged either cost-effective or not cost-effective for all individuals, ignoring the variance in preferences between identifiable groups. By contrast, in clinical studies there is a long tradition of patients being defined in terms of personal characteristics that appear to predict outcomes. The result is that the same treatments are not recommended for everyone. It has been argued that the same attention to interpersonal variations should be paid in applying cost-effectiveness analysis. If a formal subgroup can be identified that has significantly different preferences, this subgroup might be offered a different choice of treatments when doing so will increase utility (i.e., the sum of QALY values).

Recommendations of the Panel on Cost-Effectiveness Analysis in Health and Medicine

In the early 1990s, the U.S. Public Health System convened a group to study the problems and make some recommendations about the correct use of CEA.[14] A number of practical and theoretical concerns, some of which have already been addressed in this chapter, were discussed. The panel emphasized the importance of using incremental rather than average cost-effectiveness ratios, noting that many clinical studies have used the average. They pointed out the importance of using opportunity costs, including the cost of unpaid family caretaking and costs to the environment when considering health-care alternatives. They raised the issue of whether costs associated solely with lengthening life, but otherwise unrelated to a treatment, should be included as part of the cost of the medical intervention. For instance, if a coronary artery bypass operation causes a patient to live longer and that patient subsequently develops cancer, should the cost of the cancer treatment be included as part of the cost of the coronary artery bypass operation? They discussed the arbitrariness of any particular discount rate, but ended up recommending 3 percent in real terms as a moderate estimate that seemed to reflect reasonably well the long-term interest rate. They raised the issue of double counting and the problem of needing to decide whether certain items belong in the numerator or the denominator of the C/E ratio. For example, is the change in the amount of sick time (valued in terms of lost wages) to be included as a cost item (numerator) or an effects item? Here the only thing that matters is consistency.

Panel members emphasized the number of ethical assumptions that have to be solved. For instance, should the QALY value be equal if a few people are helped a lot versus a lot of people helped a little by the new intervention? They also raised the issue of whether all QALYs are equal no matter to whom they apply or at what point in an individual's life they occur. They also brought up the familiar problem of whether it is appropriate to use the wage rate to value patients' time. They rejected the idea that cost-effectiveness analysis can be converted into cost-benefit analysis.

Summary

Cost-benefit analysis flounders when we cannot find a basis for arriving at monetary values for benefits. If we look at the material used as examples in this chapter, we find that even where values are established for a year of life, the range is very wide. In the United States, values ranged from $70,000 to $175,000 (in 1994 U.S. $). We found British researchers using 20,000 to 30,000 British £ as an acceptable range for the value of a year spent in perfect health in 1998. If we assume an exchange rate of approximately 1 British £ = $1.65, the upper value for a year of life in perfect health in the United Kingdom was valued at $49,500, compared with $175,000 in the United States, and this does not factor in inflation. Does this reflect differences in the cost of living or average incomes between the countries? This is but one of the many questions that have to be answered if cost-benefit analysis is to be used. Although cost-benefit analysis is harder to use and involves more difficult assumptions, it is still favored by economists because it is the technique that allows the question "Is the project worth it?" to be answered.

Cost-effectiveness analysis, viewed broadly to include cost-utility analysis, is also widely used. But even cost-effectiveness analysis is very hard to use when values have to be established for heterogeneous groups of people. In such cases, it is extremely unlikely that a single cost-effectiveness cut-off level for public health programs will satisfy either the theoretical requirements of utility theory or the individual members of the community. The use of the analysis to evaluate public programs is least troublesome when outcomes of alternatives can be established in objective measures such as additional years of life. CUA analysis is least problematic when individuals, such as patients and their doctors, make treatment choices, since only individuals have preference functions that meet the consistency requirements for utility maximization.

The extension of cost-effectiveness analysis to cost-utility analysis is an important advance, but it needs to be used with care. Study groups such as the panel convened by the U.S. Public Health Service are helping to advance its use. It is now often necessary to use cost-utility analysis in setting priorities for public health budgets or establishing protocols for different medical treatments since variations in quality of life may be the main differences in outcomes of alternative medical interventions.

Appendix: Some Underlying Welfare Considerations

This section presents some of the current problems in welfare theory, that is the theoretical underpinning of cost-benefit and cost-utility analysis. The issues discussed in this appendix tend to be more frequently articulated concerns in societies that have health-care systems financed to a greater extent through social insurance and public funding than is the case in the United States. That is because individual willingness to pay is more often replaced by decisions about rationing goods that are provided through public monies.

Utilitarian versus Rawlsian Approach to Social Welfare Functions

A social welfare function is a formal way of representing society's collective preferences.* There are several different ways of approaching the construction of a social welfare function. The first approach makes use of a utilitarian-based social welfare function. Social welfare is assumed to be an aggregate of individual welfare. One common form of aggregate utility function treats each person equally by making the aggregate an additive function of individual utilities. For example, this approach has been generalized to deal with multidimensional utility functions, such as one in which utility is a function of both health and income:

$$U = U(H, I)$$

This necessitates making assumptions about the relationship between the two dimensions. Health and income may be assumed to be substitutes or complements, or they may be assumed to be unrelated. A formal argument has been made that using this approach, it is impossible to find any aggregate utility function that rejects all forms of income-based discrimination in access to health care.[15] Some forms of the function will lead to discriminating in favor of the poor, others to discriminating in favor of the rich; however, some discrimination will take place even when health is not conditional on income.[16]

An alternative that gets around this problem is a Rawlsian approach in which access to health-care resources is treated as a basic freedom. Rawls's ethical principle states that in any departure from distributing society's resources equally, we must always consider the welfare of the least well-off person. If we view the world through a "veil of ignorance" with respect to our own status, we would opt for either equality or a state that improves the lot of the least fortunate person, since we might turn out to be that person. Rawls viewed his principle as both ethical and rational for risk-averse people in a world with uncertainty.

---

*The concept of a social welfare function is usually associated with the early work of Paul Samuelson. It was developed originally to deal with the inequality of income. See Samuelson, Paul A., *Foundations of Economic Analysis* (Cambridge, MA: Harvard University Press, 1947).

An implication of the Rawlsian social welfare function is that two people with the same health endowments should have equal probabilities of attaining the same health level, regardless of their socioeconomic status. Their utilities do not have to be computed. In this approach, it is not necessary to assume that everyone in society has an equal endowment of health, so this is not equivalent to specifying that all individuals are entitled to the same level of health. All that is necessary to satisfy the criterion of equality in access to health care is that there should be no correlation between access to health care and income.[17]

Should Social Planners Be Risk-Averse?

Another important question is whether cost-effectiveness analysis should be undertaken with assumptions of risk neutrality or risk aversion on the part of social planners. An argument can be made that a society consisting of individuals who are themselves risk-averse should have social planners who are also risk-averse.[18] But many clinical studies are now set up on the assumption that risk neutrality is appropriate in deciding whether or not new medical interventions should be supported. The case has been made that risk neutrality is only appropriate in a world where (1) there is a random distribution such that the benefits and harms average out and where (2) if some are benefited and others are harmed, the winners must compensate the losers (the Pareto compensation principle). Since uncertainty with respect to the outcome of new experimental medical treatments is often *ex ante* uncertainty about outcomes, the results will either tend to be better than expected, with benefits to all or most who participate, or worse, in which case there will be a predominance of losers. Moreover, even if the experiment involves truly random processes, the Pareto compensation principle is not practical. For most people, there probably is no adequate compensation for loss of life or serious permanent disability. And even if there were, could a person who benefits from an artificial heart implant operation be expected to compensate an individual (or the family of the individual) who dies on the operating table?

Graff Zivin argues that the relationship between the appropriate levels of societal and individual risk aversion depends on the type of social welfare function that is assumed. A Rawlsian social welfare function, defined as one that maximizes the utility of the person in the society who is least well off, implies a societal level of risk aversion greater than that of the average individual. In contrast, a social welfare function that assumes all individual utility functions are given equal weight implies a societal level of risk aversion that is lower than the average individual risk aversion level *if the government can pool and spread risks*.[19]

Risk of death or serious harm to health is precisely the kind of risk that cannot be successfully pooled or fully compensated.[20] If you are old and poor, a social insurance program can compensate you for low income. If you are permanently disabled (or dead) because of an unsuccessful medical experiment, you cannot be made well again by any transfer payment!

Key Concepts

Willingness to pay

Incremental cost-effectiveness analysis

Cost-utility analysis (CUA)

Quality-adjusted life-year (QALY)

Standard gamble method

Time-trade-off method

Threshold of acceptability

Suggested Readings

1. Garber, Alan M., "Advances in CE Analysis," *Handbook of Health Economics,* Vol. 1A, Culyer, Anthony J. and Joseph P. Newhouse, eds.(Amsterdam: Elsevier, 2000), Chap. 4

2. Dolan, Paul, "The Measurement of Health-Related Quality of Life," *Handbook of Health Economics*, Vol. 1B., op. cit., Chap. 32.

3. Cutler, David, et al., "What Has Increased Medical Care Spending Bought?" *American Economic Review*, 88 (1998): 132–136.

Questions for Discussion and Review

1. What are some of the difficulties encountered in using cost-benefit analysis to decide whether to adopt a new technology?

2. Explain how you might use cost-effectiveness analysis in deciding whether to purchase an over-the-counter analgesic or obtain a prescription from a physician for a newer prescription drug to treat the same medical symptom.

3. Define the circumstances under which there is an unambiguous cost-effectiveness ranking, when alternative treatments for a given disease are considered.

4. When are fixed costs relevant in using incremental cost-effectiveness analysis in deciding between projects?

5. Why is income relevant to evaluations using cost-utility analysis?

6. In a publicly financed program for the treatment of a disease, what are the advantages and disadvantages of weighting patients' preferences more heavily than those of the general public?

7. Do you agree with Cutler and Richardson that the level of expenditure on health care in the United States is "probably worth it"? What criteria did you use in arriving at your answer?

Resources

[1] For a review of the literature on values for life-years, see Tolley, George, et al., *Valuing Health for Policy: An Economic Approach* (Chicago: University of Chicago Press, 1994) and Viscusi, W. Kip, "The Value of Risks to Life and Death," *Journal of Economic Literature*, 31 (1993): 1912–1946.

[2] Aldy, J. E. and W. K. Viscusi, *Age Variations in Workers' Value of Statistical Life,* NBER Working Paper No. 10199 (Cambridge, MA: National Bureau of Economic Research, 2003).

[3] See Fuchs, Victor R., "Time Preference and Health: An Exploratory Study," in *Economic Aspects of Health*, Fuchs, V. R., ed. (Chicago: University of Chicago Press, 1982), pp. 93–120 and the discussion in Chapter Two of this book.

[4] Meltzer, David, "Theoretical Foundations of Medical Cost-Effectiveness Analysis: Implications for the Measurement of Benefits and Costs of Medical Interventions," in *Medical Care Output and Productivity*, NBER Studies in Income and Wealth, Vol. 62, Cutler, David M. and Ernst R. Berndt, eds. (Chicago: University of Chicago Press, 2001), pp. 97–113.

[5] A number of studies using cost-effectiveness analyses in evaluating the treatments of particular diseases have been done. Some representative studies are Chirikos, T. N., "Appraising the Economic Efficiency of Cancer Treatment: An Exploratory Analysis of Lung Cancer," *Health Care Management Science*, 6 (2003): 87–95; Leshno, Moshe, et al., "Cost-Effectiveness of Colorectal Cancer Screening in the Average Risk Population," *Health Care Management Science,* 6 (2003): 165–174, Ramsdell, J. W., "Economic Models of First-Line Drug Strategies to Achieve Recommended Glycaemic Control of Newly Diagnosed Type 2 Diabetes Mellitus," *PharmacoEconomics*, 21 (2003): 819–837; and Trussell, James and Tara Shoshett, "Cost-Effectiveness of Emergency Contraceptive Pills in the Public Sector in the USA," *Expert Review of Pharmacoeconomics and Outcomes Research*, 3 (2003): 433–440.

[6] An excellent discussion of this concept is found in Dolan, Paul, "The Measurement of Health-Related Quality of Life," in *Handbook of Health Economics,* Vol. lB, Culyer, Anthony J. and Joseph Newhouse, eds. (Amsterdam: Elsevier, 2000), Chap. 32, pp. 1723–1755.

[7] See, for instance, Dolan (2000), op. cit.; Bennett, K., et al., "Methodologic Challenges in the Development of Utility Measures of Health Related Quality of Life in Rheumatoid Arthritis," *Controlled Clinical Trials*, 12 (1991); Bleichrodt, H. and M. Johannesson, "Standard Gamble, Time-Trade Off, and Rating Scale: Experimental Results on the Ranking Properties of QALYs," *Journal of Health Economics*, 16 (1997): 155–175; Read, J. L., et al., "Preferences for Health Outcomes: Comparison of Assessment Methods," *Medical Decision Making*, 4 (1984): 315–329; and Torrance, G. W., "Social Preferences for Health States: An Empirical Evaluation of Three Measurement Techniques," *Socio-economic Planning Sciences*, 10 (1976): 129–136.

[8] Brent, Robert J., "A Simple Method for Converting a Cost-Effectiveness Analysis into a Cost-Benefit Analysis with an Application to State Mental Health Expenditures," *Public Finance Review*, 30 (2002): 144–160. In this article references are made to Garber, A. M. and C. E. Phelps "Economic Foundations of Cost-Effectiveness Analysis," *Journal of Health Economics,* 16 (1997): 1–31 and Phelps, C. E. and A. I. Mushlin, "On the (Near) Equivalence of Cost-Effectiveness and Cost-Benefit Analyses," *International Journal of Technology Assessment in Health Care*, 7 (1991): 12–21.

[9] Garber, Alan, "Advances in CE Analysis," in *Handbook of Health Economics* (2000), op. cit., Vol. 1A, Chap. 4, p. 216, makes references to studies by Barry, M. J., "Watchful Watching vs. Immediate Transurethral Resection for Symptomatic Prostatism: The Importance of Patients' Preferences," *Journal of the American Medical Association*, 259

(1988): 3010–3017 and Fowler, F. J., et al., "Symptom Status and Quality of Life Following Prostatectomy," *Journal of the American Medical Association*, 259: 3018–3022.

[10] See Gold, M. R., et al. eds., *Cost Effectiveness in Health and Medicine* (New York: Oxford University Press, 1996).

[11] A good review of this literature is given in Wagstaff, A. and E. van Doorslaer, "Equity in Health Care Finance and Delivery," in *Handbook of Health Economics* (2000), op. cit., Vol. 1B, Chap. 34, 1803–1857. Also see Wagstaff, A.,"QALYs and the Equity-Efficiency Tradeoff," *Journal of Health Economics*, 10 (1991): pp. 21–41.

[12] Sendi, P. Pedram and Andrew H. Briggs, "Affordability and Cost-Effectiveness: Decision Making on the Cost-Effectiveness Plane," *Health Economics*, 10 (2001): 675–680.

[13] Sculpher, Mark and Amiram Gafni, "Recognizing Diversity in Public Preferences: The Use of Preference Sub-Groups in Cost-Effectiveness Analysis," *Health Economics*, 10 (2001): 317–324.

[14] Russell, Louise B., et al., "The Role of Cost-Effectiveness Analysis in Health and Medicine," *Journal of the American Medical Association*, 276, (1996): 1172–1177, Weinstein, Milton C. et al., "Recommendations on the Panel on Cost-Effectiveness Analysis in Health and Medicine," *Journal of the American Medical Association,* 276: 1253–1258, and Siegel, Joanne E., et al.,"Recommendations for Reporting Cost-Effectiveness Analysis," *Journal of the American Medical Association*, 276: 1339–1341.

[15] Bommier, Antoine and Guy Stecklov, "Defining Health Inequality: Why Rawls Succeeds Where Social Welfare Theory Fails," *Journal of Health Economics,* 21 (2002): 497–513.

[16] Ibid., pp. 501–503.

[17] Ibid., pp. 504–506.

[18] Graff Zivin, J., "Cost-Effectiveness Analysis with Risk Aversion," *Health Economics,* 10 (2001): 499–508.

[19] Ibid., p. 504.

[20] Arrow Kenneth J., "Uncertainty and the Welfare Economics of Medical Care" *American Economic Review*, 53 (1963): 941–973.

CHAPTER TEN

The Role of Technology in Health Care

The single most important medical innovation of the first half of the twentieth century, in terms of its effect on mortality rates, is generally believed to have been the discovery of antibiotics. This was followed in the second half of the century by the development of chemotherapy, innovations in diagnostic imaging devices, and a remarkable number of new pharmaceutical products. There were also major advances in surgical techniques and medical devices, such as laparoscopic equipment and stents for supporting arteries. As we move into the twenty-first century, the newest area of innovation is therapy based on information about genes, such as that provided by the Human Genome Project.*

1 Introduction

Health economists and policy makers are particularly interested in the role of technological change in medicine because of the need to assess both its benefits and its impact on the rising price of medical care. A related concern is that cost containment may impede the rate of technological change and its diffusion. In this chapter we will address the following questions: What promotes innovation and diffusion of technology? What are cost-increasing and

---

*The Human Genome Project is jointly sponsored by the National Institutes of Health, the Department of Energy, and private corporations (Celera Genomic Corporation and Incyte).

cost-saving technological changes? Can a technology be both cost-increasing and cost-effective? And finally, how accurate are indices of medical price inflation, given the rapid rate of technological change? In the course of dealing with these questions, several studies that attempt to measure the costs and cost-effectiveness of technology advances in the treatment of specific diseases will be reviewed.

Advances in medicine in the second half of the twentieth century raised expectations about attainable health levels and thus increased the demand for technologically sophisticated medical care. The demand for medical care was augmented by the characteristics of the U.S. health insurance system, which from the 1940s until the mid-1980s imposed little or no cost discipline. The increase in efficacy of medical treatments and the resulting increase in the cost of medical care further augmented the demand for health insurance. This interconnected process has been called the *health-care quadrilemma*.[1] Concern over potential medical malpractice law suits provides an additional incentive to use the highest technology available. Throughout much of the second half of the twentieth century, the combination of these factors provided a virtual guarantee of the demand for any new innovation that could be shown to provide any marginal improvement in treatment outcomes.

The consensus of those who have worked to identify the factors contributing to the increase in the cost of health care is that technological change has been the largest contributor to the upward trend in medical care prices. According to Joseph Newhouse, considerably less than half of the increase over time in the price of health care can be explained by the combination of increased insurance coverage, rising real income, supplier-induced demand, monopoly profits to suppliers, changing demographic characteristics of the population, or the labor-intensive character of health care.[2]

2   Process of Technological Change

What Is Innovation and What Promotes It?

Technological advances take place through the process of innovation. It is useful to distinguish between invention and innovation. Innovation, which may be integrated with the process of invention or discovery, includes the developing and marketing of new products. One can imagine a world in which scientists engage in a great deal of basic research leading to breakthroughs in knowledge in, for instance, molecular biology, but in which there is little or no product innovation resulting from the advances in knowledge. As Joseph Schumpeter pointed out when he made this distinction over 60 years ago, innovation in a market economy depends on the entrepreneurial spirit and the rewards associated with it. Schumpeter viewed innovation as the driving force in a market economy. He called the process by which one product or process is replaced by a better one *creative destruction*. He emphasized the role of profits in stimulating innovation and noted that innovation will be undertaken primarily by firms that have a good deal of market power, those that are monopolistically competitive or oligopolies.[3]

Such factors as professional prestige and the satisfaction derived from helping cure diseases may also be important stimuli in the process of innovation, as is government funding to support basic research. The latter was largely ignored by Schumpeter. Today it cannot be. For instance, in 1999, biotechnology firms in the United States doing research in molecular biology had the use of $20 billion in public funds, whereas private business research and development (R&D) budgets for research in biotechnology totaled only $9 billion.[4]

In the United States, medical research takes place within the government funded National Institutes of Health (NIH); in universities, where much research is also funded by the NIH, the National Science Foundation, and private industry; and within firms. Studies show that the rate of product development is greater in firms that have more contact with academic institutions; this seems to be particularly true with respect to the development of radically new products, as opposed to incremental improvements in existing ones.[5] We observe the clustering of biotech firms around university centers in not only the United States but also the United Kingdom and other countries that are leaders in innovations relevant to medicine.[6] It is not surprising that these countries all have large stocks of human capital, distinguished research universities, and active government support for research.

Demand for products and the expectation of profits are needed for innovations to occur. Although government support for research is very important in stimulating innovation, it may not lead to a direct pipeline to commercial products. For instance, a great deal of the fundamental biotechnology research originating at Oxford and Cambridge Universities has resulted in commercially valuable products being developed by companies outside of the United Kingdom. Price controls on pharmaceuticals imposed by the National Health Service may have contributed to this. There is a perennial concern in the United States that cost-containment policies may have a dampening effect on the rate of innovation in medical technology.[7] The inclusion of price controls on pharmaceutical products may have contributed to the failure of the Clinton health-care reform plan in the 1990s.

Role of Patents: Intellectual Property Rights

Another factor that is believed to promote innovation is patent protection for **intellectual property rights.** Patents are permits that grant exclusive ownership rights over processes or products for a specified length of time. In the United States, patents for drugs and medical devices are now granted for a 20-year period, including the testing period. The lengthy testing period often reduces the effective patent life to 10 years or less. It is also possible to receive patent protection for new information on individual genes. Patents on biomedical and pharmaceutical innovations may be renewed for up to 5 years if the Federal Drug

Administration (FDA) has delayed the introduction of the new drug onto the market by that long a period. However, the extension may not be granted for an effective patent life of more than 14 years.

Without patent protection, innovation would be greatly slowed unless governments were to fund product development as well as basic research into processes. The incentive to innovate would be reduced because copycat activity makes R&D activity less profitable. The problem of imitation is a particularly serious one in the pharmaceutical industry because product development costs loom so large in comparison with production costs. The cost of producing most pills is very minimal compared with the cost of discovering their underlying chemical characteristics and carrying out the extensive testing necessary to gain government approval to market them.

Since there is so much government subsidization of basic research relevant to the bio-medical field, there are externalities (spillover effects) that benefit those who develop products based on underlying publicly funded research. It is sometimes argued that patent protection, given these externalities, provides excess monopoly profits. We will look at rates of return on R&D in the biotechnology-pharmaceutical industries in Chapter Eleven in order to assess whether this is true. The subject of optimal patent breadth and length is beyond the scope of this book. Let us just note that patents that are too long or too broad lead to excess profits, stifling of competition, and higher prices to consumers, whereas patents that are too short or too limited in scope reduce the incentive to innovate. A balance must be found.

The relationship between degree of patent protection and rate of innovation is complex. This is illustrated by looking at differences across countries. Switzerland, which has long been the home of three of the world's largest and most lucrative pharmaceutical companies, introduced patent protection for drugs only in 1977. Canada had very lax patent law until 1987, but since strengthening its patent protection, it has experienced a significant increase in R&D activity by attracting foreign multinational firms' research activity. On the other hand, Italy, known for its pharmaceutical industry's successful imitation of drugs patented elsewhere, has not succeeded in developing an industry that engages in much innovation since it adopted patent protection.[8]

Reasons for the Success of U.S. Firms in Innovation

The United States has been the world's leading nation in the commercialization of biotechnological knowledge, although Germany, the United Kingdom and Canada appear to be beginning to close the gap.[9] The main reasons for its success appear to be:

1. Existence of a large stock of both human capital and research institutions
2. Government support for basic research

3. Well-enforced patent protection
4. Historically generous third-party payers
5. Extensive subsidized employment-based private insurance for the majority of U.S. citizens
6. Physicians and hospitals that are motivated to use the highest technology available

3   Diffusion of Technology

The United States ranks very high in the diffusion of most medical technologies. A study comparing the United States with two other countries known for their excellent health care, Canada and Germany, illustrates this.[10] The United States ranked highest in the diffusion of all technologies studied. The advantages were particularly large in the case of magnetic resonance imaging (MRI) and radiation therapy, both of which require very high levels of both physical and human capital investment. Studies of technology used in the treatment of heart attack found angioplasty to be used much more widely in the United States than in most other industrialized countries. Angioplasty is a technique of inserting a small balloon into an artery in order to open it. It is often an alternative to coronary artery bypass graft surgery. Angioplasty requires hospitals that have the medical expertise and equipment to handle cardiac catheterization, since only after catheterization has been used for diagnosis is it known whether angioplasty is the appropriate treatment. These examples illustrate the fact that use of advanced technologies requires complementary support in the form of well-equipped treatment centers and medical personnel with the specialized training to perform the procedures.

Factors Promoting the Diffusion of Technology

Economic incentives have been found to affect the rates of diffusion of new high-tech treatments. In a multicountry study of the rate with which advanced technology treatments for heart attack were adopted, higher rates of technology diffusion were found in countries that have fee-for-service reimbursement systems. Examples of this are Japan, Korea, Australia, and France. The United States, which currently has a blend of fee-for-service and prospective payment systems, was found to be experiencing an intermediate rate of growth in the utilization of high-tech treatments, although its stock of medical technology is still higher on a per capita basis than anywhere else in the world.[11]

A series of papers by Lawrence Baker, Ciaran Phibbs, Joanne Spetz, and others have found some evidence of a slowing in the rate of diffusion of technology, such as magnetic resonance imaging equipment, in hospital markets in the United States where managed care has a strong presence. The reader is referred to Chapter Four, Section 7, for a review of their findings.

4   Relating Technological Change to Costs of Medical Care

How Is the Contribution of Technological Change Measured?

In empirical studies of medical costs, technological change has often been treated as a residual, that which is left over as the unexplained variance after all known factors have been accounted for. There is a long history of treating technology this way, and a standard technique for measuring its effect in econometric studies of production functions is called, after economist Robert Solow, the *Solow residual.* Using the process of elimination to sort out the effects of other factors, technological change came to be widely regarded as the chief contributor to the increased expenditure on health care in the United States.[12] More recently, Newhouse, Cutler, McClellan, and others have developed an approach that measures the effects of technological advances more directly.[13] Their approach can only be used to study the relationship between cost and technology change in the treatment of specific diseases, such as heart attack.

Cost-Increasing Versus Cost-Saving Innovations

A **cost-increasing innovation** in medicine is an innovation that increases the cost of treatment for a particular disease. Where there is no incentive to contain costs, it may be more profitable for firms to develop more expensive (cost-increasing) technologies.[14] A number of economists have argued that at least until the mid-1980s, both Medicare and the prevalent indemnity form of private insurance encouraged a bias toward cost-increasing (as well as quality-increasing) innovation. The fact that health-care costs were so largely reimbursed on a fee-for-service basis by insurance companies contributed to the price insensitivity of demand for medical services. As Peter Zweifel points out, this helps to explain why technological innovation is considered a source of cost savings in the rest of the economy, but health insurers and policy makers are afraid of medical innovation.[15] "Would the price of computers (per amount of capacity) have declined to the extent that they have, if we all had insurance paying for our computers?" is a question that is often raised by those critical of the American health insurance system.

In this connection it may be useful to distinguish between *process* and *product* innovations. Process innovations are often, on balance, cost-saving. For example, the substitution of more expensive and more efficacious newer drugs has been shown to provide significant cost savings in nondrug expenditures that greatly outweigh the increase in the expenditure on drugs in the treatment of a number of diseases.[16] Using data for 1986 to 1998, the reduction in nondrug expenditure associated with the use of newer drugs was found to be, on average, 7.2 times the increase in the drug expenditure. For the Medicare population, the reduction in total expenditure on nondrug aspects of treatments, including both individual-out-of-pocket and Medicare's contribution, was 8.3 times the increase in the expenditure on drugs.[17] These are examples of unambiguous cost-saving improvements in technology.

An example of a cost-increasing innovation is laparoscopic cholecystectomy, surgery to remove the gallbladder using a small inserted camera to direct the surgeon's instruments. It is particularly notable because of the rapid diffusion of this technique after it became available in the United States in the 1980s. By 1992, 80 percent of the cholecystectomies performed in this country were laparoscopic. The technique is more frequently used in early stages of the disease among younger, non-Medicaid patients, but it has also come to be widely used among the elderly, including the very elderly (those over 80 years of age) for whom it is also appropriate and effective.[18] The new technique has been shown to cut mortality rates in half for all age groups. Among the elderly, it has also greatly reduced the need for stays in skilled nursing homes. It has shortened average recovery time. Patients are able to return to work in an average of 15, as opposed to 31, days; hospital stays have been reduced from 4.3 to 1.6 days.[19]

However, with all these advantages, this kind of new technique may be "cost-increasing" if it results in an expansion of medical intervention. In this case, before the new, less invasive technique was developed, surgery was performed less often in cases of a given severity. There was much more "watching and waiting." Both patients and surgeons will now choose surgery in cases where they formerly would have eschewed it. This means that the average cost, per case, of treating gall bladder disease has increased.[20] By definition this is a cost-increasing innovation.

Even if an increase in the use of gallbladder surgery had not accompanied the development of the laparoscopic technique, the innovation, defined narrowly, is more expensive. Operating room costs are much higher for laparoscopic than for open surgery. Moreover, equipment, supplies, and anesthesiology charges are all higher. Even though hospital stays are shorter, total surgeon and hospital charges are higher than for open surgery and they outbalance the savings in hospitalization costs.*

Certain stages in the development of medical treatments may tend to involve initially higher costs followed by lower costs. Therefore, it depends at what point in the life cycle of the innovation the costs are measured. Scientific discoveries often have life cycles that lead to first- and second-generation technological improvements. The two stages have been called halfway technology and high technology by Weisbrod.[21] Halfway technologies are usually more expensive than cures and are certainly cost-increasing when compared with no treatment or watching and waiting. Compare, for instance, the early treatments for polio myelitis, a disease that was life-threatening and crippling well into the 1950s in high-income countries. The iron lung was an expensive machine that kept paralyzed patients alive but required intensive care. Contrast this with the second

*For instance, Blue-Cross Blue-Shield of South Carolina reported hospital charges 14 percent higher and surgeon fees 55 percent higher than for open surgery, but this was for the first 22 cases using the new technology. See Jordan, Ashby M. and Robert J. Fitzgibbons, Jr., Letter to the editor, *Journal of the American Medical Association*, 266 (1991): 3426.

generation innovation, the Salk and Sabine vaccines, that prevented the disease and were inexpensive and noninvasive. Many people today are hopeful that research will lead to a treatment for HIV/AIDS that mirrors this life-cycle history, with the development of a vaccine replacing the expensive "cocktails" of maintenance drugs.

Treatments for heart attack (acute myocardial infarction or AMI) in the United States show an interesting cost trajectory. Using inflation-adjusted dollars, it has been noted that average treatment costs per case for AMI rose in the period 1964–1971 and then declined from 1971 to 1981.[22] From the mid-1980s to the mid-1990s, there were introductions of important new techniques, particularly cardiac catheterization, that proved particularly effective in diagnosis and treatments for 80- to 89-year-old patients. The period 1981 to 1989 showed large increases in the average cost of treating a heart attack, due primarily to expansion of treatments to more AMI patients. Intensive followup procedures occurred more frequently and also sooner after onset of AMI, usually within 7 days and often within 24 hours. This raised costs, but also brought about improved patient outcomes. Expenditures on elderly hospitalized AMI patients showed a rate of increase of approximately 4 percent per annum during the early 1990s, but mortality rates were lowered and the quality of life of survivors improved greatly.* During the period 1990 to 2000, the cost increase was gradually offset by the substitution of catheterization (angioplasty) for coronary artery bypass graft surgery.[23] The invention of the intracoronary stent, a wire rim that keeps open the blood vessels, promoted the use of angioplasty. The introduction of angioplasty accompanied by the use of the intracoronary stent is a cost-decreasing innovation compared with the previous stage in the treatment of AMI.

In comparing costs of different treatments, patients' time is usually not factored into the costs, since what is being measured is the cost of the medical resources used to treat the morbidity. For many purposes, it is more useful to take a broader view of the costs and include the value of savings in patients' time.

Use of Incremental Cost-Effectiveness Analysis and Cost-Utility Analysis

Cost-effectiveness is for many purposes a much more useful measure of the appropriate use of resources in the treatment of disease. If there is a difference in outcome that accompanies the use of a new technology, cost-effectiveness analysis should be employed. For example, Cutler, McClellan and Newhouse, when studying changes in heart attack treatment methods, adjust for such factors as changes in survival rates and speed of recovery.[24] They then assess the cost of the treatment per extra amount of life-time gained. It is after making this adjust-

---

*As we will see in Section 5 that follows, the CPI overestimates the cost of treatments, compared with measures that take account of the changes in morbidity and mortality that accompany the use of new technologies.

ment that they conclude that changes in the treatment for heart attack are more effective per unit cost.

We need to note here that the term "cost-effective" is commonly used in a very different way from its use in formal incremental cost-effectiveness analysis. People say that something is more cost-effective when the beneficial effects are greater per unit cost. In Chapter Nine, CEA ratios were defined in such a way that a higher ratio represented a higher cost per degree of effectiveness. For the balance of this chapter, the term "cost-effectiveness" will be used as it is in ordinary language. A more cost-effective alternative will be one that provides more benefit per unit of cost.

Let us return to the example of treatment for heart attack and evaluate its cost-effectiveness. Studies of the treatment of AMI provide a model for other studies of relative cost-effectiveness since AMI usually has a clearly defined onset, and mortality reduction is an important and clear-cut measure of patient outcome. AMI can be treated in a number of different ways: There can be low-tech treatments consisting largely of the administration of drugs and changes in lifestyle. A familiar regimen is the administration over time of low doses of aspirin. Higher-tech treatment alternatives include diagnostic catheterization (inserting a catheter accompanied by a small camera to diagnose blockages in arteries) followed by angioplasty (inserting a small balloon into clogged arteries to reopen them), with or without the use of a stent, and/or coronary artery bypass graft surgery (CABG), which is often accompanied by the ancillary use of drugs. In comparing different technologies for the treatment of heart attack, the extent of improvement in patient outcome is often measured both in life-years gained and in amount of quality-adjusted life-years (QALYs) gained. Even in the period during which treatment for heart attack was "cost-increasing," there were improvements in mortality and QALY values increased.[25] If we look at the cost-effectiveness of laparoscopic surgery compared with open surgery for gallbladder disease, taking into account the much better patient health outcomes and the faster recovery period, we find that it also appears to be cost-effective when compared with the older technique, open heart surgery.[26]

Where there are significant improvements in patient outcome, using cost-effectiveness shifts the focus to what many researchers think is the appropriate question in evaluating technological change.

Productive Efficiency

Studies of alternative technologies used in the treatment of specific diseases often compare treatment methods in terms of their **productive efficiency**. Productive efficiency compares the quantities of inputs used to produce a given output. If production functions are being compared over time or between regions or countries, differences in marginal product cannot be equated with differences in cost-effectiveness, because prices of the inputs may be very different from one environment to another. Comparing production functions without reference to prices of inputs is a fairly standard way of making intercountry comparisons of the use of various medical technologies. Several excellent studies provide us with this type of cross-country comparison: For example, Baily and Garber compared the United States, Germany, and the United Kingdom in the treatments of diabetes, gallstones, breast cancer, and lung cancer.[27] Except for the treatment of diabetes, which involves long-term case management rather than high technology, the United States was found to be more productively efficient than Germany in the treatment of each of the several diseases studied.

The lack of capacity in capital equipment imposed by the British National Health Service budget limited its use of laparoscopic surgery. In Germany as well, laparoscopic equipment and techniques were less widely available than in the United States, resulting in the use of more resources (including patient time in recovery) to achieve no better or worse patient outcomes. Productive efficiency is thus not independent of previous decisions made in the several countries about how much to allocate to developing capital capacity in technology.

In the treatment of breast cancer, the United States and United Kingdom were both found to be unambiguously more productive than Germany: The United States achieved a 9 percent better outcome using 38 percent fewer inputs and the United Kingdom achieved a 6 percent better outcome using 53 percent fewer inputs. Compared with the United Kingdom, the United States used 15 percent more inputs to achieve a 3 percent better outcome.[28] In this case, to decide which country had a better result requires assigning values to both the resources used and the outcomes. In other words, a judgment can only be made as to which country's technology is better if we are able to convert the relative productive efficiency ratios into a comparative cost-benefit analysis.

5   Use of Price Indices to Measure the Rate of Increase in Prices of Medical Care

Medical Care Components of the Producer and Consumer Price Indices[29]

So far we have looked at treatment costs for several diseases and discovered that treatments which are more cost-effective, measured in life-years or quality of life years, may nonetheless cost more than older treatments, particularly if we measure the average cost of treatment of a particular disease when newer techniques also involve more frequent intervention.

The **Consumer Price Index (CPI)** and **Producer Price Index (PPI)** measure costs (prices) of separate inputs into the production of health. Particularly in the case of medical diseases for which the treatments have undergone rapid technological change, using these measures is hazardous. As these indices are the basis for most statements that are made about the rising cost of medical care, it is important that the methodology be understood.

The Bureau of Labor Statistics has over time revised its techniques, but the medical component in the CPI and the PPI are still both very imperfect measures of the rate of price inflation in medical care.

The CPI

Since medical care is not, strictly speaking, a consumer good but rather a series of inputs into the production of health, one might ask whether it is even appropriate to include it in the CPI. However, other services that also might be considered investments, such as expenditure on education, are also included in the index. The index compares the prices at different times of goods that make up a typical consumer's market basket of goods. Since the original goods in the CPI basket are assumed not to change within a 10-year period, the index will overstate the extent of price increases (be biased upward) in so far as it fails to take account of the consumer's ability to substitute cheaper goods as relative prices shift. This problem is not trivial since the CPI is only updated every 10 to 12 years and assumes that the same composition of goods remains in the basket in between updates.

Let us construct a price index for two periods. It values the original basket of goods, those consumed at time T_1, by the prices of those goods in the second period T_2. If the consumer has three goods x, y, and z in his or her consumption basket in year 1,

$$\frac{p_2 x_1 + p_2 y_1 + p_2 z_1}{p_1 x_1 + p_1 y_1 + p_1 z_1}$$

represents the CPI's technique for measuring the price inflation from year 1 to year 2. This is known as a Laspeyres index.

The CPI not only does not take account of substitutions that the consumer may make, if relative prices change, it also does not fully take account of the introduction of new goods or measure quality changes in existing ones. A consumer price index should, ideally, adjust for quality changes and omit price changes that only reflect this.*

A difficulty in evaluating the rate of inflation in medical care using this index results from the definition of the "product" itself. The good that people purchase is the treatment for a medical condition, not the separate inputs into that treatment. The CPI will thus not pick up the cost savings that result from shifts in the production functions in the treatment of particular diseases. The CPI also does

*There are a number of other problems that are peculiar to the medical care component of the CPI. It omits both the nonhospital services paid for by Medicare and payments from private third-party payers, which results in an exclusion of about two-thirds of the total expenditure on medical care and causes the hospital component to be greatly overweighted.

Very thorough treatments of the problems in constructing price indices for medical care are given in Berndt, Ernst R., et al., *Price Indexes for Medical Care Goods and Services: An Overview of Medical Issues*, NBER Working Paper No. 6817 (Cambridge, MA: National Bureau of Economic Research, November 1998), and in Newhouse, Joseph P., *Medical Care Price Indices: Problems and Opportunites: The Chung-Hua Lectures*, NBER Working Paper No. 8168 (Cambridge, MA: March 2001).

not reflect any declines in the cost of producing health itself that result from improved efficacy of treatments and the resulting improvements in longevity and/or quality of life. Newhouse, Triplett, and others have argued that it is particularly important to take account of this in the case of health care.[30]

Problematic as it is, the CPI is still the most widely used indicator of the increase in the price of medical care. It is the source of much anxiety about rising costs of medical care in the United States. For instance, during the period 1985 to 1996, the medical care component of the CPI increased by 101 percent, whereas the overall CPI increased by only 46 percent.[31]

The PPI

The PPI is a measure of the average prices received by domestic producers for their products. PPIs are published for separate industries. A sample is taken for each industry approximately every seven years. Since 1996, for certain industries, including the electronics and pharmaceutical industries, samples have been supplemented every one or two years.[32] This represents an important improvement. Prior to 1995, this index oversampled older drugs. Within each industry, the same kind of price index is constructed as that which is used in the CPI. Indices are constructed for manufacturing industries such as hospital beds, medical books, pharmaceuticals, and surgical, medical, and dental instruments and supplies. An important measurement problem arises with respect to medical care when changes in medical technology result in the substitution of inputs from one industry to another. For instance, if there are changes in the mix of psychotherapy and psychotherapeutic drugs used to treat clinical depression, the PPI will fail to pick up any savings resulting from the shift.

The PPI has attempted to cover services (as well as tangible goods) since 1986, but it is still less than completely inclusive. Medical service PPIs have been aggregated for physician services and for hospital services since the mid-1990s. As with the medical component of the CPI, there are problems resulting from unmeasured quality changes. One other curiosity, which may lead to nontrivial overestimation of the rate of price increases in drugs, results from excluding drugs manufactured by U.S. pharmaceutical companies in Puerto Rico. The value of prescription pharmaceuticals manufactured in Puerto Rico for sale on the mainland is approximately 20 to 25 percent of the value of those manufactured on the mainland.[33] As the pharmaceutical and biotechnology industries become more global, this problem will be compounded.

Alternative Estimates of the Rate of Inflation in Medical Care

More conservative estimates of the rate of inflation in the cost of medical services have been obtained by using indices developed by researchers to study time trends in the costs of treating particular illnesses. Good examples of this are the work of Cutler and co-authors measuring the cost of treating heart attacks and the work of Berndt and co-authors measuring the cost of treating depression. Two types of indices have been developed: a Service Price Index and a Cost of Living

Index.[34] The Service Price Index measures the price of treatments, adjusting for changes in technology over time. The Cost of Living Index further weights the cost of treatment by its effect on morbidity and mortality.* With the Service Price Index, the rate of medical price inflation was reduced from approximately 3 percent above the overall CPI to only 1 to 2 percent above it. Using the Cost of Living Index resulted in a medical component that fell below the CPI by 1 to 2 percent.

Summary

The United States still leads the world in the introduction of medical technology in spite of cost-containment policies on the part of government and private managed care insurers. In the best-case scenario, cost-containment will tip the balance toward "cost-saving" technologies but not significantly reduce the rate of innovation.

If we ask the question, "Has the cost of health risen?" rather than "How much has the cost of medical care risen?" the answer in many cases is that it has not. This is certainly true in the case of restoring better states of health to heart attack patients, to those with gallbladder disease, and to those who suffer from depression. The counterargument is that the practice of medicine in the United States employs techniques that are too capital-intensive, driving up the price of health care in return for only marginal improvements in health outcomes.[35] We are left with the question, what is the value of the marginal improvement in health outcomes that this capital-intensive medical care provides?

Key Concepts

Intellectual property rights

Cost-increasing innovation

Productive efficiency

Consumer Price Index (CPI)

Producer Price Index (PPI)

Suggested Readings

1. Berndt, Ernst R., et al., "Medical Care Prices and Output," *Handbook of Health Economics*, Vol. 1A, Culyer, Anthony J. and Joseph P. Newhouse, eds. (Amsterdam: Elsevier, 2000), Chap. 3.

2. Cutler, David M., et al., "What Has Increased Medical Spending Care Bought?" *American Economic Review*, 88 (1998): 132–136.

---

*This requires making some assumptions about the value of an additional year of life for a heart attack patient. This was discussed further in Chapter Nine, in the section on cost-benefit analysis.

3. Griliches, Zvi, "What's Different About Health? Human Repair and Car Repair in National Accounts and in National Health Accounts: Comment," in *Medical Care Output and Productivity*, NBER Studies in Income and Wealth, 62 (2001): 94–95.

4. Newhouse, Joseph P., The Baxter Foundation Prize Address, "Measuring Medical Prices and Understanding their Effects," *Journal of Health Administration*, 7 (Winter 1989): 19–25.

5. Newhouse, Joseph P., "Medical Care Costs: How Much Welfare Loss?" *Journal of Economic Perspectives,* 6 (Summer 1992): 3–22.

Questions for Discussion and Review

1. How would you characterize the effect of the U.S. health insurance system on medical technology changes from 1960 to 1990?

2. Why do you think the United States has more MRI machines but fewer nurses than the United Kingdom?

3. Why may the cost-effectiveness of angioplasty (for the treatment of coronary artery disease) be different in different countries?

4. How may the way in which providers are reimbursed affect the diffusion of technology? In framing your answer, consider the evidence about systems that reimburse on a fee-for-service versus capitation basis.

5. What is the difference between the medical PPI and the medical CPI? What other measures of price changes in medical services have health economists developed?

6. Why is the CPI a more imperfect measure of price inflation for medical services than for many other consumer goods?

Resources

[1] Weisbrod, Burton A., "The Health Care Quadrilemma: An Essay on Technological Change, Insurance, Quality of Care, and Cost Containment," *Journal of Economic Literature*, 29 (1991): 523–552.

[2] Newhouse, Joseph P., "Medical Care Costs: How Much Welfare Loss?" *Journal of Economic Perspectives*, 6 (1992): 3–22; and Newhouse, Joseph P. and the Insurance Experiment Group, *Free for All? Lessons from the RAND Health Insurance Experiment* (Cambridge, MA: Harvard University Press, 1993).

[3] For a treatment of the effects of innovation on the economy and the effect of capitalism on the entrepreneurial spirit, see Schumpeter, Joseph A., *Capitalism, Socialism, and Democracy* (New York: Harper, 1942) and *Business Cycles: A Theoretical, Historical, Statistical Analysis of the Capitalist Process* (New York: McGraw Hill, 1939).

[4] Cooke, Philip, "Biotechnology Clusters in the U.K., Lessons from Localisation in the Commercialisation of Science," *Small Business Economics*, 17 (2001): 58.

[5] MacPherson, Alan, "The Contribution of Academic-Industry Interaction to Product Innovation: The Case of New York State's Medical Devices Sector," *Regional Science*, 81 (2002): 121–129 and Bobrowski, Paula E., "A Framework for Integrating External Information into New Product Development: Lessons from the Medical Technology Industry," *Journal of Technology Transfer*, 25 (2000): 181–192.

[6] In the United Kingdom, of 40 biotechnology firms identified in 1995, 75 percent were spun off from university or other public research bases. Cooke (2001), op. cit., p. 52, quoting Mihell, D. D., et al., *The Development of the Biotechnology Sector in Oxfordshire: Implications for Public Policy* (Oxford: Oxford Innovation Ltd., 1997).

[7] Baker, L.C. and J. Spetz, "Managed Care and Medical Technology Growth," NBER Working Paper No. 6894 (Cambridge, MA: National Bureau of Economic Research, 1999). See also Hill, Steven C. and Barbara L. Wolfe, "Testing the HMO Competitive Strategy: An Analysis of Its Impact on Medical Care Resources," *Journal of Health Economics,* 16 (1997): 261–286; Friedman, Bernard and Claudia Steiner, "Does Managed Care Affect the Supply and Use of ICU Services?" *Inquiry*, 36 (1999): 68–77.

[8] McRae, J. J. and F. Tapon, "Some Empirical Evidence on Post-Patent Barriers to Entry in the Canadian Pharmaceutical Industry," *Journal of Health Economics*, 4 (1985): 43–61.

[9] Cooke (2001), op. cit., pp. 43–59.

[10] Rublee, Dale A., "Medical Technology in Canada, Germany, and the United States: An Update," *Health Affairs*, 13 (1994): 113–117.

[11] McClellan, Mark B., et al., "Technological Change in Heart Attack Care in the United States," in *Technological Change in Heath Care: A Global Analysis of Heart Attack*, McClellan, M.B. and D. P. Kessler, eds. (Ann Arbor: University of Michigan Press, 2002), pp. 390–391.

[12] Newhouse, et al. (1993), op. cit.

[13] Cutler, David, Mark McClellan, and Joseph Newhouse, "The Costs and Benefits of Intensive Treatment for Cardiovascular Disease," in *Measuring the Price of Medical Treatments*, J. Triplett, ed. (Washington, DC: Brookings Institution Press, 1999).

[14] Goddeeris, John H., "Insurance and Incentives for Innovation in Medical Care," *Southern Economic Journal,* 51 (1984): 530–539 and Weisbrod (1991), op. cit.

[15] Zweifel, Peter, "Medical Innovation: A Challenge to Society and Insurance," *Geneva Papers on Risk and Insurance*, 28 (2003): 194–202.

[16] Lichtenberg, Frank, *Benefits and Costs of Newer Drugs: An Update*, NBER Working Paper No. 8996 (Cambridge, MA: National Bureau of Economic Research, June 2002) and *Pharmaceutical Innovation, Mortality Reduction, and Economic Growth*, NBER Working Paper No. 6569 (Cambridge, MA: National Bureau of Economic Research, May 1998).

[17] Ibid. (2002), pp. 5–7.

[18] Walling, Anne D., MD, et al., "Laparoscopic Cholecystectomy vs. Open Surgery in the Elderly," *American Family Physician*, 59 (1999): 2321 and Maxwell, J. G., et al., "Comparison of Laparoscopic and Open Cholecystectomy," *American Family Physician*, 51 (1995): 1736.

[19] Ibid.

[20] Meyer, Harris, "Procedure Cuts Stays But Still May Increase Costs," *American Medical News*, 35 (1995): 9.

[21] Weisbrod (1991), op. cit.

[22] Scitovsky, Anne A., "Changes in the Cost of Treatment of Selected Illnesses, 1971–1981," *Medical Care*, 23 (1985): 1345–1357; Scitovsky, Anne A. and Nelda McCall, "Changes

in the Cost of Treatment of Selected Illnesses, 1951–1964–1971," in *Health Policy Program, Palo Alto Medical Research Program* (Palo Alto, CA: Stanford, 1975).

[23] Cutler, David M. and Robert S. Huckman, "Technological Development and Medical Productivity: The Diffusion of Angioplasty in New York State," *Journal of Health Economics,* 22 (2003): 187–217.

[24] Cutler, et al.(1999), op. cit.

[25] See Cutler, David M., et al., "Are Medical Prices Declining? Evidence for Heart Attack Treatment," *Quarterly Journal of Economics,* 108 (1998): 991–1024.

[26] Meyer (1995), op. cit.

[27] Baily, Martin Neil and Alan M. Garber, "Health Care Productivity," *Brookings Papers on Economic Activity: Microeconomics 1997:* 143–202.

[28] Ibid., p. 166.

[29] Two particularly good short pieces on this subject are Griliches, Zvi, "Research on Price Index Measurement: Agendas for the Next Twenty Years: Comments," *Journal of Economic and Social Measurement,* 27 (2001): 100–101 and Griliches, Zvi, "What's Different About Health? Human Repair and Car Repair in National Accounts and in National Health Accounts: Comment," *Medical Care Output and Productivity,* NBER Studies in Income and Wealth, 62 (2001): 94–95. A thorough treatment is provided in Triplett, Jack E., ed., *Measuring the Prices of Medical Products* (Washington, DC: Brookings Institution Press, 1999).

[30] Newhouse (2001), op. cit., pp. 29–30.

[31] U.S. Department of Labor, Bureau of Labor Statistics, *Handbook of Labor Statistics,* 1989. Figures for the 1990s available online at http://stats.bls.gov.

[32] Berndt, Ernst R., et al. *Price Indexes for Medical Care Goods and Services: An Overview of Medical Issues,* NBER Working Paper No. 6817 (Cambridge, MA: National Bureau of Economic Research, November 1998), pp. 23–24.

[33] Ibid., p. 35.

[34] Cutler, et al. (1999), op. cit.

[35] For instance, this is the position taken by David Drake in *Reforming the Health Care Market: An Interpretive Economic History* (Washington, DC: Georgetown University Press, 1994).

CHAPTER ELEVEN

The Economics of Prescription Drugs

People frequently ask why a month's supply of a prescription drug costs hundreds of dollars when the production cost of the pills is only pennies. Reports of those who travel to Canada or Mexico and find cheaper drugs raise further questions about drug prices in the United States. It is commonly believed that the greed of pharmaceutical companies, or at least their monopoly level profits, account for the high prices of drugs. Stories of elderly Americans having to choose between filling their prescriptions and having enough food to eat and of people in Africa or Asia with AIDS not being able to afford any of the newer anti-retroviral drugs further anger the public.

1   Introduction

This chapter will help you to understand why drugs are priced as they are and to evaluate the pros and cons of government regulation of the pharmaceutical industry. An understanding of the bio-pharmaceutical industry requires us to study its market structure, pricing policies, the effects of government regulation, the effects of cost-containment strategies of third-party payers, and the role of international competition. The behavior of the industry can only be understood if we are careful to distinguish between the short-run costs of manufacturing a drug, after it has been developed and introduced into the market, and the long-run costs, which include R&D costs. In this chapter we will also consider the effects of new products, insurance coverage, and advertising on the demand for prescription drugs.

What Is the Bio-Pharmaceutical Industry?

Biotechnology, which involves research into the nature of fundamental genetic material, is the new cutting edge in the biomedical field. In contrast, products developed by the pharmaceutical industry have historically been based on chemistry rather than biology, and new pharmaceutical products are often called **new chemical entities (NCEs)**. The distinction is becoming blurred, and both industries are now producing therapeutic drugs.* Examples of important new biotech drugs are erythropoietin, for the treatment of anemia in AIDs, cancer, and patients undergoing kidney dialysis; and α- and β-interferons used for treating cancer and multiple sclerosis.[1] The large pharmaceutical companies have come to be mutually interdependent with many smaller biotechnology firms.[†] The former vary considerably in how much basic research is carried on in-house. Throughout this chapter we will use the word "pharmaceuticals" to refer to the whole class of bio-pharmaceutical products.

Importance of Pharmaceuticals in Health Care

Even though pharmaceuticals still make up only a small fraction of total health-care expenditure, the proportion devoted to these products has been increasing rapidly in recent years. Between 1990 and 2000, the proportion of health-care costs in the United States devoted to prescription drugs increased from approximately 5 to 10 percent.[2] If we use constant 1998 dollars, the average per capita prescription drug expenditure in the United States was about $550 in 2001 compared with $323 in 1998, $191 in 1990, and $86 in 1963.[3] Increases in expenditure are partly the result of price increases and partly the result of increases in quantity utilized. Although the average annual growth in expenditures on pharmaceuticals between 1987 and 2000 was about 11.9 percent over the whole period, price increases accounted for more than half the expenditure growth between 1987 and 1994, but only about one-fifth of it from 1994 to 2000.[4] The increase in quantity is a mixture of higher utilization of existing drugs and the purchase of new pharmaceuticals.

---

*This is often done in conjunction with pharmaceutical companies. For instance, Genzyme, a biotech company, is comarketing Aldurazyme, a drug used in the treatment of Hurler–Schele Syndrome, with BioMarin Pharmaceutica.

[†]A good example is Genentech, which was acquired by the Swiss Hoffman LaRoche in 1990. Although now listed as a separate company on the stock exchanges, it is still controlled by Hoffman LaRoche, its major stockholder.

2 Market Structure

How Concentrated Is the Industry?

It is often assumed that the firms in the pharmaceutical industry are oligopolies, since what comes to mind when we think of this industry are a few very large firms such as Glaxo, Pfizer, Merck, and Johnson & Johnson. However, the bio-pharmaceutical industry is far less concentrated than is commonly believed and is better described as monopolistically competitive in structure.* Pharmaceutical firms exhibit behavior typical of this market structure.[†] They engage in vigorous marketing; selling costs are an important component of costs. Ownership of brand names is important, and licensing to foreign distributors is a major source of revenue. Even among the subset of smaller, newer biomedical firms, those which survive over time in the world market tend to gain larger market shares through internal growth or through mergers and acquisitions, although they still tend to be located in one country, unlike the pharmaceutical giants that are typically multinational corporations.

Competition at the Product Level: Within- and Between-Patent Competition

Although patent protection confers monopoly power in the production of a drug over the life of the patent, most brand-name drugs experience some competition from other drugs used to treat the same symptoms during their period of patent protection, and most new brand-name drugs have at least one fairly close substitute at the time of their introduction into the market.[‡] It is therefore useful to distinguish between **within-** and **between-patent competition.** Within-patent competition from imitators occurs after patent expiration and also during on-patent time from firms in countries that do not enforce patent law. Between-patent competition from firms developing different products to treat the same diseases may be even more important. Lichtenberg and Philipson use the example of the class of drugs, antihistamines, for which 13 separate patents were granted in the United States between 1982 and 1996. In 1982 alone, nine separate patents

---

*The Herfindahl–Hirschman Index (HHI) value for this industry, computed for 1992, was found to be only 341. See, Santerre, R. E. and S. P. Neun, *Health Economics*, revised ed. (Orlando, FL: Dryden Press, 2000), p. 509. The HHI is explained in Chap. Eight of this text. The HHI value for a pure monopoly is 10,000. The HHI for a market consisting of 100 firms, each of which has 1 percent of the market share, would be 100.

[†]If you would like to review the model of monopolistic competition, please turn to Chapter Seven, pages 139–140.

[‡]Scherer, F. M., "The Pharmaceutical Industry," in *Handbook of Health Economics,* Vol 1B, Culyer and Newhouse eds. (Amsterdam: Elsevier, 2000), Chap. 25, pp. 1319–1320, notes that the formulary published in 1993 by the pharmacy benefit management company PAID shows number of drugs per symptom averaging 6.04, with a median number of 5 drugs per symptom.

were granted to firms producing antihistimines.[5] One of the implications of be-tween-patent competition and its effect on the returns from R&D is that it may make changes in patent policy, such as the increase in patent life from 17 to 20 years, less important.[6]

Effect of Firm Size on R&D Productivity

A number of studies have investigated the effect of pharmaceutical firm size on research productivity. It is widely believed that large firms have advantages in both economies of scale and scope, but there is evidence that the situation is somewhat more complicated.[7] Economies of scope occur when there are positive spillover effects within the firm from having a number of different R&D projects at the same time. A study covering all research projects in 10 major pharmaceuti-cal firms over 20 years used data at the level of individual research programs within firms. No evidence of increasing returns to scale or scope per se was found, but complicated sets of interdependencies between economies of scale and scope, and the greater ability of large firms to absorb both intrafirm economies and external spillover effects, appeared to give larger firms an advan-tage. The net result was that larger firms which had more research projects tended also to have more productive research programs.[8] Larger firms were also found to be more likely to undertake research that integrates process and product development.*

3   Government Regulation of the Pharmaceutical Industry in the United States

Pharmaceutical products, unlike medical and surgical devices, are heavily regu-lated by the U.S. government, particularly with respect to the extensive testing re-quired by the Food and Drug Administration before new products can be launched. A drug receives approval only if it meets the requirements with respect to both safety and efficacy. Another type of regulation is the legal requirement that certain drugs can be purchased only if prescribed by a licensed physician. An important question is how much regulation is optimal.

Regulation by the Food and Drug Administration

Federal regulation of the quality of drugs marketed in the United States began with the enactment of the Pure Food and Drug Act in 1906 that created the Food and Drug Administration (FDA). The passage of the Kefauver–Harris Act in 1962 greatly strengthened the FDA, which had just gained widespread applause for

---

*The history of the German company Bayer (now I.B. Farber) provides a model of a firm that developed a worldwide market in a product, aspirin, but also engaged in the more ba-sic chemical research underlying the development of that product.

banning the sedative thalidomide, the source of serious birth defects in Europe. The Kefauver-Harris Act required a more stringent regime of clinical testing to launch both new chemical entities (NCEs) and generic versions of drugs already on the market. The number of new drugs launched per year declined after 1962.

An unintended consequence of the more stringent regulatory climate appears to have been a differential impact on small firms. Smaller firms suffered a decline in both their research productivity and market share. Why this occurred is not clear, but it appears that firms need both breadth and depth of research capacity to be successful in launching drugs when there is a more arduous testing process required for drug approval. R&D costs per project have also been shown to decline with firm size.[9] There is evidence that the largest U.S. pharmaceutical firms actually benefitted from the harsher regulatory climate. Declines in their own research productivity were more than offset by the gains in sales resulting from less competition.[10]

In 1971, the government added a proof of efficacy to the requirements for the introduction of new drugs. Overall requirements became more stringent, and by the 1990s the average time from first application to FDA approval of a drug had risen to over nine years. The following schedule shows the average time required for the development of an NCE in the late 1980s[11]:

Stages in the R&D Process in the Introduction of a New Chemical Entity

I. Discovery of a New Chemical Entity.

II. Preclinical Animal Testing

III. File Application for Authorization for Human Testing

(estimated time, discovery, preclinical, and application approval: 3.5 years)

IV. Phase I Clinical Testing: Test Effects on a Limited Number of Healthy Volunteers: Test of Absorption Rate, Metabolic Effects, etc. (average time: 15 months)

V. Phase II Clinical Testing: Administer Drug to Larger Sample of Humans: Those with Conditions the NCE Is Intended to Treat (average time: 2 years)

VI. Long-Term Animal Studies (usually concurrent with human testing)

VII. Phase III Clinical Testing: Large-Scale Testing to Determine Efficacy and Side Effects (average time: 3 years)

VIII. New-Drug Approval Process (average time: 2.5 years)

Liberalization of the FDA Process

Generic Drugs

When patents expire on brand-name drugs, chemically equivalent copies of the drug can be produced. These copies are known as *generic* versions of the drug or *generic drugs*. In 1984, the Waxman–Hatch Act was passed; it allowed generic drugs to be introduced with much less burdensome testing requirements.* Between 1984 and 1998, the generic share of the drug market increased dramatically, from about 19 to 44 percent, in part because of this change.[12]

Orphan Drugs

The Orphan Drug Act, passed in 1983, defines **orphan drugs** as those used to treat rare diseases (those with fewer than 200,000 diagnosed cases). The purpose of the legislation was to encourage the production of drugs for which there was little market potential. Firms are given tax breaks, funding help, and exclusive rights to market orphan drugs for seven years, even when they are not on patent. As of May 2003, the FDA had approved orphan status for 240 drugs. However, in many cases the so-called orphan drugs are also used to treat multiple diseases, some of which are far from rare. Presenting separate evidence to the FDA on only one of a number of possible uses for a drug is called "salami slicing." If a firm is able to obtain orphan status for a drug that has good market potential in other uses, the firm receives a monopoly rent that serves no public purpose.

From 1998 to 2003, orphan drug prices rose by 40 percent per year compared with an increase of 15 percent per year in nonorphan drug prices. In 2003, the Centers for Medicare and Medicaid Services reduced rates of reimbursement to hospitals and doctors for most orphan drugs. In order to keep down costs, Medicare now classifies multiuse orphan drugs like all other drugs and reimburses accordingly. As a result of this change only four therapeutic drugs are currently reimbursed by Medicare on the basis of their orphan drug status.[†]

Compassionate Use of Experimental Drugs

Criticism of the FDA's conservatism led to the adoption of a new drug approval procedure in the 1980s, whereby experimental drugs awaiting approval may be made available to physicians for limited use in treatments for patients in advanced stages of diseases. This approval procedure releases drugs for use in the treatment of patients with such diseases as advanced AIDS and late-stage cancer.

The Prescription Drug User Fee Act of 1992

This legislation caused some speeding up of the drug approval process by granting the FDA authority to collect fees from firms when applications are filed and

---

*Manufacturers had only to show that the active ingredients in the generic version were the same as those in the patented drug and that the drug would be absorbed into the bloodstream within a plus or minus range of 20 percent. The same legislation also allowed generic drug producers to engage in testing and submission of results to the FDA before the expiration of the patent on the brand-name drug. To compensate the original patented drug manufacturers, patents on the original drug could be extended for up to five years.

†Genzyme's drug for Gaucher's disease, Cerezyme, is one of these. Only about 3,500 people take Cerezyme, but even so it generated $619 million in revenue for Genzyme in 2002. See Elias, Paul, "'Orphan' Drugs Save Lives, But Come at a Hefty Price," *The Seattle Times,* May 26, 2003, page C3.

when they are accepted. The fees increase the FDA's operating budget; this permits it to act more rapidly. The average time from the start of clinical testing to market approval has declined from 98.9 to 90.3 months This is largely because the approval phase has been shortened from, on average, 30.3 to 18.2 months.[13]

Requirement of Prescriptions (Rx)

A second type of regulation intended to promote the safety of the general public is the requirement that a wide range of drugs be available to consumers only when prescribed by a licensed physician. This regulation is also controversial. One study has found no statistically significant different outcomes in such indicators as rates of poisoning between the United States and other industrialized nations that do not require prescriptions for most nonnarcotic drugs.[14] Since lower dosages of prescription drugs are often available over the counter and anyone can take multiple pills, this does not seem to be a very fail-safe method of preventing toxicity.

The argument that the requirement of prescriptions from physicians is not in the public interest is made more plausible when one observes the many near-equivalents to newer prescription drugs that are available without prescription in the over-the-counter market. An argument can be made that requiring physician input to obtain drugs facilitates rent-seeking behavior on the part of physicians. Limited refills of prescriptions promote more patient return visits.

An unintended negative consequence of the Rx requirement is that consumers may choose higher-cost prescription drugs rather than over-the-counter drugs when their medical insurance covers the former. This may result in inflated drug expenditures and extra costs for physician visits.*

A counterargument can be made that self-medication may not lead to easily measurable harm but to long-run gradual damage to health. Requiring physician Rx prevents overmedication or misuse of medication, which may also have negative long-term effects on the community as a whole. The problem of new strains of antibiotic-resistant bacteria that have resulted from the wide use of antibiotics illustrates the danger of unrestricted use of medication. This also illustrates the "public goods aspect" of prescription drug usage. This will be discussed in Chapter Thirteen.

Liberalization of the Rx Requirement

Beginning in the 1970s, the FDA began to allow the conversion from prescription (Rx) status to over-the-counter (OTC) status for a limited number of drugs when

---

*In Germany, until reforms were instituted in the 1990s, patients typically asked for prescriptions for ordinary-strength aspirin since prescription drugs were 100 percent covered by their health insurance. See Winkelman, Rainer, *Health Care Reform and the Number of Doctor Visits: An Econometric Analysis,* Discussion Paper No. 3021 [Institute for the Study of Labor (IZA) Center for Economic Policy Research, October, 2001], available through Social Science Research Network.

pharmaceutical companies could prove that even misuse of the drug would not have harmful effects. It is in the interest of insurance companies to promote OTC status for drugs since they are not usually covered by insurance. The popular allergy medication, Claritin, became available over-the-counter in the United States at the instigation of an insurer, Wellpath, and against the will of both the manufacturer, Schering-Plough, and physician groups.[15] However, pharmaceutical companies may also benefit from their drugs being changed to OTC status. The Waxman–Hatch Act enables companies that have been granted OTC status for a drug to apply for a three-year exclusive period during which time no other company may market a similar OTC version of the drug. A second advantage to manufacturers of over-the-counter status for drugs is that the FDA regulates OTC versions of drugs much less heavily than drugs requiring an Rx.

Cost-Benefit Analysis of Regulation

Lively debate continues over the welfare effects of the FDA's strict policies with respect to the introduction of new drugs. The costs of safety regulation have to be evaluated in terms of the trade-off between the costs of approving a drug that is not safe or effective and the costs of regulatory authorities holding a safe and effective drug off the market. Stricter regulation has two kinds of costs: It raises the costs of innovation and the resulting prices of new drugs, and it imposes costs on patients who cannot obtain products.[16] The easing of regulations to allow compassionate use of experimental drugs in cases of last resort is meant to reduce the second type of cost.

We can discuss the costs and benefits of regulation, taking account of the two types of errors in judgment that can be made by the FDA in its evaluation of new drugs. A type I error occurs when a safe and effective drug is rejected. A type II error occurs when a drug that is unsafe or ineffective is approved. Table 11.1 shows the possible outcomes that can result from decisions made by the FDA. An argument can be made that there is a bias toward type I errors, since it is more costly to the career of an FDA commissioner to make a type II error, but costs of a type I error are borne by the firm that has developed the drug and by consumers. This can lead to a bias toward rejecting new drug applications

Table 11.1 Possible Outcomes of FDA Decisions

	SAFE DRUG	UNSAFE DRUG
Accept	Correct decision	Type II error
Reject	Type I error	Correct decision

Source: Grabowski, H. G. and J. M. Vernon, *The Regulation of Pharmaceuticals: Balancing the Benefits and Risks* (Washington, DC: American Enterprise Institute, 1983), Figure 1.

Effects of Regulation on Pharmaceutical Firms' Success in World Markets

A positive effect of stricter regulation of pharmaceutical products has been found: Firms whose home countries impose higher safety standards in the introduction of new drugs into the domestic market have been shown to benefit in their command over market share in foreign markets.[17] This seems to be true for European and Asian as well as North American firms.* Moreover, stringent regulations with respect to efficacy also seem to positively affect success in world markets. In countries where approval of drugs has an efficacy requirement, firms seem to direct more research toward producing products embodying significant improvements over existing drugs.[18]

4   Demand for Pharmaceuticals

The demand for pharmaceuticals is affected by the introduction of significant new products and by the substitution of pharmaceuticals for other more invasive treatments (see the discussion in Chapter Ten), by the aging of the population, by the expansion of insurance coverage for prescription drugs, and to some extent by the advent of direct marketing to consumers in 1997.

Effects of Increased Insurance Coverage for Prescription Drugs

Between 1965 and 1998, the proportion of U.S. prescription drug expenditure that was paid out-of-pocket by consumers decreased from 92.6 to 26.6 percent. In 1965, private insurance covered only about 3.5 percent of expenditures on prescription drugs, as opposed to 52.7 percent in 1998.[19] In addition, there was no Medicaid drug coverage in 1965. With the introduction of the Medicare prescription drug benefit, the share of out-of-pocket payment for prescription drugs will decline even more.

Third-party payers now routinely reimburse a higher proportion of the cost of generic than brand-name drugs in an attempt to make consumers and physicians more cost-conscious. Medicaid also reimburses only the price of the generic drug when substitutes for brand-name drugs are available. In this way, insurance com-

---

*An example of regulation that has inhibited success of its nation's pharmaceutical industry in world markets is given by Japan. Japan has higher levels of spending on R&D for therapeutic drugs than either the United States or Germany. Yet, safety regulations are far less stringent than in many other countries. Historically, Japanese pharmaceuticals have not been very successful in world markets, although their market shares have begun to increase. See Thomas, Lacy Glenn, "Pricing, Regulation and Competitiveness: Lessons for the US from the Japanese Pharmaceutical Industry," *PharmacoEconomics*, 6 (Supplement 1, 1994): pp 68–69.

panies can affect the balance of generic and brand-name drugs utilized by altering relative prices to consumers.

Effect of Direct Marketing to Consumers

Since 1997, direct marketing of prescription drugs to consumers has been legal in the United States. This makes it possible for drug companies to create a consumer demand for products that physicians might not otherwise recommend. Consumers are presented with an attractive sales pitch that often ends with, "Ask your doctor about drug X." Pharmaceutical companies are particularly likely to aggressively advertise drugs being introduced as substitutes for drugs that are going off-patent.

> AstraZeneca's marketing of its "new purple pill," Nexium, when its blockbuster drug for the treatment of heartburn, Prilosec, was going off-patent, is a good example of this phenomenon. Nexium was introduced not only as an acid-reducing pill, but also as a treatment for the damaging effects of chronic acid reflux syndrome on tissue. Prilosec had not been sold for this purpose.

Direct marketing to consumers also provides a greater incentive to develop lifestyle products such as treatments for hair loss or sexual dysfunction. This kind of advertising serves to both provide information and induce demand.

5   Pricing Issues

No aspect of the medical economy receives more attention today than the prices of prescription drugs, even though the substitution of pharmaceuticals for other medical treatments often involves significant savings to patients in both time and money.[20] Many countries now control the prices of drugs and there are a variety of fairly complicated ways in which this is done.[21] Public policy regarding the pricing of pharmaceuticals for its citizens is more complicated when a country is also the home of a major pharmaceutical industry, and in the case of the United States, the one that still leads the world in the introduction of new drugs. It is much easier for a country such as Canada, which does not have a major domestic pharmaceutical industry, to regulate the price of prescription drugs.* The United States has generally not imposed price controls on pharmaceuticals.†

Price Differentials Between Brand-Name and Generic Drugs

Once drugs are off-patent, generic versions that are chemically identical can be marketed. It is widely believed that generic drugs are sold for lower prices than

---

*Most R&D that takes place in Canada employs Canadians, but is conducted by foreign multinational firms.

†An exception was a brief period in the 1970s during the presidency of Richard M. Nixon.

Figure 11.1

Demand and price of
brand-name drug
before and after
patent expiration.

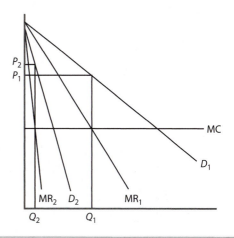

equivalent brand-name drugs, even when produced by the same company. What may appear to be a peculiar phenomenon exists: Brand-name drugs are frequently sold at higher prices after the introduction of generic substitutes than before. The reason for this is the decline in price elasticity of demand for the brand-name drug after it is off-patent. When the generic drug is introduced, the demand for the brand-name drug decreases. However, the segment of consumers who remain loyal to the brand-name drug have a demand that is less price-elastic than the total demand for the product during the time it was on-patent. The producers of the brand-name drug often decide not to compete with the generic version of the drug, but rather to raise prices in response to the decline in demand elasticity.[22] This strategy seems to be employed whether or not they also sell the generic version of the drug. Figure 11.1 illustrates this. The demand for the drug when it is still patent-protected is shown as D_1. The demand after expiration of the patent is shown as D_2. The profit-maximizing price, set where MR = MC, is P_1 when the drug is on-patent and P_2 when it is off-patent.*

Although the phenomenon illustrated in Figure 11.1 is believed to be common behavior, some researchers have found evidence that the introduction of generic substitutes may be associated with lower prices for the brand-name drug. This will happen if the producers of the brand-name drug decide to compete with the generics for market share.[23]

Discounting of Drugs to Third-Party Payers

Discounts to insurers below the retail price is another form of price discrimination and one that has become increasingly important in the United States in the age of managed care. HMOs and other large insurance companies are able to use

*For a review of the economics of price discrimination, see Chapter Seven, pages 140–141.

their buying power to negotiate price discounts with manufacturers and whole-salers in return for higher rates of insurance coverage for the product or for in-cluding the product on an approved list called a formulary list. When Medicare purchases drugs for its hospitalized patients, it also negotiates a discounted price with manufacturers. (Note that this does not apply to Medicare Part D reimburse-ment for out-patient drug purchases.) Medicaid reimburses only at the generic price level when substitutes are available for brand-name drugs. The Department of Veterans Affairs (VA) and the Department of Defense are known for negotiat-ing the lowest drug prices in the United States.[24]

Pharmacy Benefit Management Firms

Insurance companies also employ other firms to negotiate for them. **Pharmacy benefit management firms (PBMs)** have emerged as service institutions for large insurance companies. PBMs act as intermediaries in the retail market for prescription drugs for insured patients. They both manage the paperwork and negotiate prices with druggists. In addition, they make their own formulary lists and obtain discounts from drug manufacturers in return for having their products included on the lists. PBMs also exert pressure on physicians to prescribe lower-priced drugs. This has resulted in the widespread substitution of generic for brand-name drugs and substitution between brand-name drugs. The United States is known for its high drug prices, but it is not widely known that although its brand-name drug prices are usually the highest in the world, its generic drug prices are among the lowest.[25] Pressure from insurance companies is one of the reasons for the wider differential in price between brand-name and generic ver-sions of a drug in the United States than in many other parts of the world.

Price Differences Between Countries

The cost of pharmaceutical products varies widely between countries. This phe-nomenon is not just the result of firms' decisions to engage in price discrimination based on differences in elasticity of demand. It also reflects differences in cost of production. Some countries bear more of the cost of drug development. Moreover, governments engage in a wide variety of techniques for controlling drug prices, including direct price controls. A number of governments in countries that have extensive social insurance programs relate their rates of reimbursement for newer patented drugs to prices of the same drug in other nations. Two effects of this are to cause multinational companies to charge higher prices in some countries than they otherwise would and to withhold marketing new drugs in countries, such as India, that have both low incomes and regulation limiting prices.[26]

Effect of a Country's Pricing Policy on the Launching of New Drugs

Price regulation in domestic markets also affects both the timing and the number of drugs launched in a country.[27] Countries that regulate launch prices tend to have the lowest rate of launching of new drugs. Most countries now have as part of the process of new drug approval a requirement that third-party payers will reimburse this drug, if introduced. Germany, the United Kingdom, and the United States are exceptions in not having this requirement. A study by Danzen, Wang and Wang covering 25 countries, including 14 European Union (EU) member nations, found that between 1994 and 1998, the United States led in new drug launches (73), followed by Germany (66) and the United Kingdom (64).[28]

Effects of Parallel Importing on Price Differentials Between Countries

International price differentials tend to be undercut by commercial reimportation of pharmaceutical products manufactured abroad. A review of the economics of price discrimination reminds us that price discrimination can only be effective when resale can be prevented between markets. The difficulty in practicing price discrimination based on geographical market segmentation is likely to increase in the future with more trade agreements leading to legal reimporting of drugs manufactured in foreign countries. The commercial reimporting of drugs, called **parallel importing**, is now permitted within the EU. This has resulted in significant south-north drug trade as licensing agreements permit cheaper manufacture in southern Europe of drugs developed and patented in northern Europe. Price differentials between drugs sold in Canada and the United States could be reduced somewhat if commercial reimportation of drugs from Canada, currently being challenged, becomes legal.[29] However, one main source of the current difference in Canadian and United States drug prices is the much greater tort liability risk that drug manufacturers face in the United States. It is unclear how this would apply to drugs manufactured in Canada but sold in the United States.[30]

Opponents of reimportation usually invoke the rationale that quality might suffer since foreign manufacturers may not be subject to the same quality monitoring, particularly in the case of drugs that are produced specifically for export. If reimportation becomes a legal source of the commercial supply of prescription drugs in the United States, the FDA budget will probably have to be expanded to monitor the quality of imported drugs.* This will be an added cost that will tend to narrow the differential between domestically produced and reimported drugs.

6   Profitability of the U.S. Pharmaceutical Industry

Profits are often thought to be higher in the pharmaceutical than in most other industries in the United States. This was particularly true during the economic boom of the late 1990s. A frequently used measure of profits is the ratio of current earnings to the value of the company's capital stock. This is called the *return on equity*. The average rate of return on equity in 1998 for the five largest pharmaceutical companies was 42.4 percent, whereas the return on equity for Microsoft in the same year was only 27 percent. The only other company in the top

---

*This point was made by Mark McClellan, MD in testimony before the Senate Commerce Committee, at his confirmation hearing as Commissioner of the FDA, May 2004.

10 largest U.S. corporations with comparable profit levels was Coca-Cola, with a return of 42 percent.[31]

However, since the proportion of cost devoted to R&D and the rate of technological change are substantially higher in the pharmaceutical than in most other industries, the return on equity tends to exaggerate the profitability of pharmaceutical firms, given the way R&D expenditures are treated on corporate balance sheets. Measuring current return on equity largely ignores costs already incurred in previous time periods (sunk costs). Scherer maintains that a better measure of profitability is *quasi-rents*, which are the revenues in excess of the sum of current production costs and the amounts used to defray research and development costs that have already been incurred. This makes great sense when we think of the wide disparity between the marginal cost of producing another batch of pills and the R&D costs associated with developing and introducing a new drug. Using this approach, Scherer has found profit margins in the pharmaceutical industry to not be significantly higher than the average for other industries.[32]

It is important to take account of the high probability of research ending in products that never reach the market. The failure rate has to be factored in when considering the cost of introducing new chemical entities. Even in the case of drugs that receive FDA approval, only a small proportion provide enough revenue through sales to cover the R&D costs incurred in their development. Among 100 new drugs introduced into the domestic market in the United States in the 1970s, the top 10 products produced 55 percent of the quasi-rents from sales both at home and abroad. These drugs are often called *blockbuster drugs*. Only the top 20 most profitable drugs fully covered their producer's R&D.[33]

The return/risk ratio also appears to be falling over time. It was found to be lower for drugs introduced in the 1980s compared with those introduced in the 1970s.[34] It was lower still for those introduced in the 1990s. Studies show that the distribution of returns on expenditure on R&D for drugs introduced between 1990 and 1994 continued to be highly skewed.[35] Drugs with returns in the top decile accounted for more than 50 percent of returns on all drugs launched. The recent work of Dimasi, Hansen, and Grabowski (2003) carries this story forward. The remarkable difference between the 1990s and earlier periods is in the amount of R&D cost per new drug introduced. Estimates of the average capitalized cost per approved drug, factoring in expected success rates, were (in constant year 2000 $U.S.) $543 million in the early 1990s compared with $897 million by the end of the 1990s. The growth rate in R&D costs was much greater than the growth in gross profit margins during this same period.[36] Clinical testing costs appeared to be the major source of the higher cost of developing new drugs. The higher cost of clinical trials seems to be related to the cost-containment policies of insurers. Greater concern with cost-effectiveness increases R&D expenditure by requiring clinical tests comparing the effects of the new chemical entity with drugs already on the market rather than just placebos.[37]

7 International Trade and the Globalization of the Biotech and Pharmaceutical Industries

TRIPS Agreement

Intellectual property rights (patents) play a very important role in the process of development of new bio-pharmaceutical products. The 1994 Agreement on Trade-Related Aspects of Intellectual Property Rights (called the TRIPS agreement) makes enforcement of foreign product patents a requirement for membership in the World Trade Organization (WTO). This agreement, which is already in effect for industrialized nations, was originally to have been extended to developing nations by the end of 2004. Countries such as India, mainland China, and Taiwan, which have pharmaceutical industries known for producing less expensive generic copies of on-patent drugs through the process of copy-catting or *reverse engineering*, have opposed the TRIPS agreement. The application of the TRIPS agreement to the least developed nations has been postponed, due largely to public concern over the pricing of AIDS drugs.*

If and when the TRIPS agreement is enforced, it is likely to increase international competition in the development of biotechnology and pharmaceuticals by creating incentives for innovation on the part of firms whose country's previous laxity in enforcing patents discouraged this. It may also increase efficiency in research by facilitating contracting between firms, since under patent protection firms can reveal their innovations without losing control of them. (In India, patents have been granted in the bio-pharmaceutical field for *processes* but not for *products*.) It may also promote research in middle- and high-income nations by reducing downward pressure on prices from the copying of their patented drugs.[38]

In countries that have become adept at producing copies of on-patent drugs, there will be some costs to firms, at least in the short run.[39] India in particular has had a comparative advantage in marketing products abroad as they go off-patent. Time is of the essence in being competitive in the world of generic products, and agility in copying and producing drugs while they are still under patent protection has been a forte of the Indian drug industry.

Although patent protection may stimulate research on drugs for tropical diseases endemic to developing nations, it is likely that substantial gains to Third World pharmaceutical companies from patent enforcement will only occur if they can also acquire patents for drugs used in the treatment of such diseases as cancer and heart disease, for which there is a also a demand in high-income countries. It is argued

---

*Some advocates of the TRIPS agreement have proposed an alternative, that is, to have pharmaceutical firms simply donate products (such as AIDS drugs) to the poorer countries while maintaining patent protection where the drugs are sold. This approach has been opposed by AIDS activists who fear that firms would discontinue their donations after an initial demonstration period for the project. See Kremer, M., "Pharmaceuticals and the Developing World," *Journal of Economic Perspectives*, 16 (2002): 67–90.

that there is too thin a domestic market in the lower-income countries to support research into drugs that will be sold in primarily domestic markets. This argument seems plausible when we look at cross-country comparative figures on drug expenditures. In 1990, annual per capita expenditure on pharmaceuticals was $222 in Germany, $191 in the United States, $124 in Canada, $97 in the United Kingdom, and $3 in India. Updated figures are not available for India, but even if the per capita expenditure has quadrupled, it remains very small compared with the 2001 per capita expenditures of $606 in the United States, $452 in Canada, $401 in Germany, and $231 in the United Kingdom.[40] However, given the size of the populations in India and China (over a billion each) and the low marginal cost of manufacturing a pill after it has been developed, this argument may be overstated.

The net effect of patent protection on economies of countries such as India and Taiwan will depend on how much drug prices are raised to consumers within these countries and on who gets the balance of patents for new innovations. Simulation studies have projected significant drug price increases for Third World consumers with the enforcement of the TRIPS agreement.[41] If new patents are granted primarily to foreign companies, there will be a net welfare loss in developing nations, at least in the short run, since both consumers and the domestic pharmaceutical industry will suffer. Licensing agreements with companies holding foreign patents may somewhat offset this by making it possible for drugs to be more cheaply manufactured and distributed within a developing nation. If new patents are granted to domestic firms, it will be an open question whether price increases to consumers will be outweighed by benefits to the domestic pharmaceutical industry.* Long-run welfare gains are possible, regardless of who holds the patents, if patent protection leads to more research into products particularly useful for curing the diseases that most afflict developing nations.

The long-run effect of the TRIPS agreement on the pharmaceutical industries in the OECD nations will be a significant increase in the amount of between-patent competition, if India and China develop a large capacity to produce new patented drugs. The strengthening of pharmaceutical industries in countries with lower costs of production will also tend to reduce world prices of off-patent drugs.

Summary

At the end of the twentieth century, the United States still led the world in the development of new pharmaceuticals, although the costs of developing new drugs had risen dramatically at the same time that managed care had imposed down-

---

*Chaudhuri, Goldberg, and Jia find that there will be significant welfare losses to developing nations such as India if domestic producers have to withdraw their products from the domestic market as a result of enforcement of the TRIPS agreement. See Chaudhuri, Shubham, Pinelopi K. Goldberg, and Panle Jia, "Estimating the Effects of Global Patent Protection in Pharmaceuticals: A Case Study of Quinolones in India," Yale University Economics Department Working Paper, October 6, 2004.

ward pressure on the domestic prices of drugs. Between 1996 and 1999, the number of new drugs approved per year was, on average, 65 percent greater than for the period 1986 to 1995; there is little evidence that the rate of new drugs entering the market is declining.[42] The reduction in the average FDA approval time associated with the Prescription Drug User Fee Act of 1992 provides the possibility of increased economic returns from product development, since it speeds up the approval process, leaving more patent-protected years for NCEs. The orphan drug provision also supports research. These policies partly offset the downward pressure on prices and profits imposed by managed care and global competition.

The flow of new products continues to stimulate demand for pharmaceuticals, as does the increase in third-party prescription drug coverage. Growth in revenues of U.S. pharmaceutical companies since 1994 has resulted primarily from an increase in the volume of sales.[43] Berndt and Grabowski both predict that the ongoing rate of R&D should lead to a continuing flow of new products through the next decade.[44] The work of Dimasi, and co-authors (2003) implies a somewhat more pessimistic prediction. It focuses on the rising cost of introducing new drugs.

Balancing the goals of consumer welfare and the economic health of the pharmaceutical industry is a problem in countries that are homes to major bio-pharmaceutical industries. It is also a worldwide problem in that medical care can only advance if people are able to afford the newer drugs and if innovations in bio-pharmaceuticals continue. The possibilities for new products based on the revolution in information about genetic structure provide grounds for cautious optimism that a healthy rate of technological change will continue in the global pharmaceutical industry.

Key Concepts

New chemical entities (NCEs)

Within-patent competition

Between-patent competition

Orphan drugs

Pharmacy benefit management firms (PBM)

Parallel importing

Suggested Readings

1. Scherer, F. M., "The Pharmaceutical Industry," *Handbook of Health Economics,* Vol. 1B, Culyer, Anthony J. and Joseph P. Newhouse, eds. (Amsterdam: Elsevier, 2000), Chap. 25.

2. Berndt., Ernst R., "Pharmaceuticals in U.S. Health Care: Determinants of Quantity and Price," *Journal of Economic Perspectives,* 16 (2002): 45–66.

3. Kremer, Michael, "Pharmaceuticals and the Developing World," *Journal of Economic Perspectives,* 16 (2002): 67–90.

4. Dimasi, J. A., R. W. Hansen, and H. G. Grabowski, "The Price of Innovation: New Estimates of Drug Development Costs," *Journal of Health Economics,* 22 (2003): 151–185.

Questions for Discussion and Review

1. Would you expect a patent-protected drug to be a monopoly? Why or why not.

2. Is the bio-pharmaceutical industry becoming more or less highly concentrated? Explain your answer.

3. What are type I and type II errors in the context of FDA decisions about the acceptance of new drugs? Do you think there is a bias toward one type of error?

4. Why might a drug company raise the price of its brand-name drug when it comes off-patent?

5. Discuss the pro's and con's of the conservative stance of the FDA with respect to the introduction of new pharmaceutical products onto the market.

6. Given the following information, what is the cost of introducing and marketing an NCE?
   a. On average, 1 in 20 new drugs receive FDA approval.
   b. Average preclinical testing cost per drug is $2 million.
   c. Average clinical testing cost per drug is $6 million.
   d. The approval process costs, on average, $1 million.
   e. Marketing of an NCE costs, on average, $3 million.

7. You use a pharmaceutical product on a continuing basis for a year. Would you prefer the drug to be available only by prescription or over-the-counter, given the following information?
   a. If the drug is over-the-counter, it costs $30 for a month's supply and is not covered by insurance.
   b. If it is Rx, a month's supply retails for $100. You have a 20 percent drug co-pay. You must get a new prescription from your physician once every 6 months. An office visit costs $150. Your co-pay for physician visits is 30 percent.

8. How would your answer to question 7 change if you factor in your time cost given that a physician visit takes an hour, your physician is only available during working hours, and you earn $100 per hour?

9. Why may a pharmaceutical manufacturer prefer to have its product changed from Rx to over-the-counter status?

10. What factors have contributed to the increase in the cost of successfully launching a NCE?

11. A pharmaceutical company has a patent for a new allergy medicine, Drug X. There is another drug already on the market, Drug Y, which can be used to treat the same symptoms. Use the table below to answer the following:
   a. After some time on the market, the company producing Drug X is able to get it accepted on formulary lists of insurance companies so that consumers now typically pay only $10 out-of-pocket versus a $40 retail price for the drug. What is the cross-price elasticity of demand between Y and X in that price range?
   b. Would you describe Drug X as a product monopoly in this market?
   c. If you were an FDA commissioner, would this information enable you to judge whether Drug X had passed the "efficacy requirement" for introduction of new drugs onto the market? Explain your reasoning.

Price of X (30 tablets)	Quantity of Y Demanded
$10	300,000
$15	350,000
$25	480,000
$40	600,000

Resources

[1] Grabowski, Henry, et al., "Returns on Research and Development for 1990s: New Drug Introductions," *PharmacoEconomics*, 20 Supplement 3, (2002): 11–29.

[2] Phelps, Charles E., *Health Economics*, 3rd ed. (Boston: Addison Wesley, 2003), p. 522.

[3] For figures for 1963 to 1998, Glied, Sherry A., "Health Insurance and Market Failure Since Arrow," *Journal of Health Politics, Policy and Law*, 26 (2001): 962. The 2001 figures were computed from *OECD Health Data 2003* (Paris: Organization for Economic Co-operation and Development, July 2003).

[4] Berndt, Ernst R., "Pharmaceuticals in U.S. Health Care: Determinants of Quantity and Price," *Journal of Economic Perspectives*, 16 (2002): 45–66.

[5] See Lichtenberg, Frank R. and Tomas J. Philipson, *The Dual Effects of Intellectual Property Regulations: Within- and Between-Patent Competition in the U.S. Pharmaceutical Industry*, NBER Working Paper No. 9303 (Cambridge, MA: National Bureau of Economic Research, October, 2002).

[6] Ibid., pp. 8–10.

[7] Chandler, A., *Scale and Scope* (Cambridge, MA: MIT Press, 1990).

[8] Henderson, Rebecca and Iain Cockburn, "Scale, Scope and Spillovers: The Determinants of Research Productivity in the Pharmaceutical Industry," *RAND Journal of Economics*, 27 (1996): 32–59.

[9] Dimasi, J. A., et al., "R&D Costs, Innovative Output, and Firm Size in the Pharmaceutical Industry," *International Journal of the Economics of Business*, 2 (1995): 201–209.

[10] See Thomas, Lacy Glenn, "Regulation and Firm Size: FDA Impacts on Innovation," *RAND Journal of Economics*, 21 (1990): 497–517.

[11] Dimasi, Joseph A., et al., "Cost of Innovation in the Pharmaceutical Industry," *Journal of Health Economics,* 10 (1991): 107–142.

[12] *PhRMA Industry Profile 1998* (Washington, DC: Pharmaceutical Research and Manufacturers of America, 1998).

[13] Dimasi, J. A., et al. "The Price of Innovation: New Estimates of Drug Development Costs," *Journal of Health Economics,* 22 (2003): 151–185.

[14] Peltzman, S., "The Health Effects of Mandatory Prescriptions," *Journal of Law and Economics,* 30 (1987): 207–238.

[15] Peterson, Melody, "Claritin to Sell Over the Counter," *The New York Times,* November 28, 2002, page C1.

[16] Peltzman, S., "An Evaluation of Consumer Protection Legislation: The 1962 Drug Amendments," *Journal of Political Economy,* 81 (1973): 1049–1091.

[17] See Thomas, L. G., "Industrial Policy and International Competitiveness in the Pharmaceutical Industry," in *Competitive Strategies in the Pharmaceutical Industry,* Helms, R. B. ed. (Washington, DC: AEI Press, 1996), pp. 107–129.

[18] Tomas, (1996), op. cit.

[19] Department of Health and Human Services, *Report to the President: Prescription Drug Coverage, Spending, Utilization and Prices* (Washington, DC: DHHS, April 2000), Table 2-30.

[20] See the discussion in Chapter Ten, p. 208, and Lichtenberg, Frank, *Benefits and Costs of Newer Drugs: An Update,* NBER Working Paper No. 8996 (Cambridge, MA: National Bureau of Economic Research, June 2002) and *Pharmaceutical Innovation, Mortality Reduction, and Economic Growth,* NBER Working Paper No. 6569 (Cambridge, MA: National Bureau of Economic Research, May 1998).

[21] An excellent brief summary of ways in which governments regulate drug prices is provided in Scherer, F. M., "The Pharmaceutical Industry," in *Handbook of Health Economics,* Vol. 1B, Culyer, Anthony J. and Joseph P. Newhouse, eds. (Amsterdam: Elsevier, 2000), op. cit., pp. 1328–1331.

[22] See Frank, R. G. and D. S. Salkever, "Pricing, Patent Loss, and the Market for Pharmaceuticals," *Southern Economic Journal,* 59 (1992): 165–179; Frank R. G. and D. S. Salkever, "Generic Entry and the Pricing of Pharmaceuticals," *Journal of Economics and Management Strategy,* 6 (1997): 75–90; Grabowski, H. G. and J. M. Vernon, "Brand Loyalty, Entry, and Price Competition in Pharmaceuticals After the 1984 Drug Act," *Journal of Law and Economics,* 35 (1992): 331–350; and Marco, Alan "Size and Duration Effects of Post-Patent Pharmaceutical Pricing: Evidence from Patent Data," Working paper for Mellon Intercollegiate Economics Conference, Vassar College, Poughkeepsie, New York, May 2004.

[23] Caves, R. E., M. D. Whinston, and M. A. Hurwitz, "Patent Expiration, Entry and Competition in the U.S. Pharmaceutical Industry," *Brookings Papers on Economic Activity: Microeconomics* (1991): 1–48.

[24] Frank, R. G., "Prescription Drug Prices: Why Do Some Pay More than Others?" *Health Affairs,* 20 (2001): 115–128.

[25] Danzon, Patricia M., "Price Discrimination for Pharmaceuticals: Welfare Effects in the U.S. and the E.U.," *International Journal of the Economics of Business,* 4 (1997): 301–321.

[26] Scherer (2000), op. cit., p. 1330.

[27] Danzon, P. M., Y. R. Wang, and L. Wang, *The Impact of Price Regulation on the Launch Delay of New Drugs: Evidence from Twenty-Five Major Markets in the 1990s,* NBER Working Paper No. 9874 (Cambridge, MA: National Bureau of Economic Research, 2003).

[28] Ibid., p. 6.

[29] Pecorino, Paul, "Should the U.S. Allow Prescription Drug Reimports from Canada?" *Journal of Health Economics,* 21 (2002): 699–708.

[30] Manning, Richard L., "Product Liability and Prescription Drug Prices in Canada and the United States," *Journal of Law and Economics,* 49 (1997): 203–243.

[31] These figures are computed from information in Folland, Sherman, Allen C. Goodman, and Miron Stano, *The Economics of Health and Health Care,* 3rd ed. (Upper Saddle River, NJ: Prentice Hall, 2001), Table 26.1, p. 585. The source of information for Table 26.1 is *Fortune* (April 26, 1999).

[32] Scherer (2000), op. cit., p. 1328. He cites the U.S. Congress Office of Technology Assessment, *Pharmaceutial R&D: Costs, Risks and Rewards,* OTA-H-522 (Washington, DC: U.S. Government Printing Office, 1993).

[33] Grabowski, H. G. and J. M. Vernon, "A New Look at the Returns and Risks of Pharmaceutical R&D," *Management Science,* 36 (1990): 804–821; Grabowski H. G. and J. M. Vernon, "Returns on New Drug Introductions in the 1980s," *Journal of Health Economics,* 13 (1994): 383–406.

[34] Grabowski, et al. (1994), op. cit.

[35] Grabowski, H. G., J., Vernon, and J. A. Dimasi, "Returns on Research and Development for 1990s New Drug Introductions," *PharmacoEconomics,* 20, (Supplement 2002): 27–28.

[36] Dimasi, et. al. (2003), op. cit.

[37] Ibid., p.181

[38] Kremer (2002), op. cit., p. 78.

[39] See the discussion on pp. 268-269 in Lanjouw, Jean O. and Iain M. Cockburn, "New Pills for Poor People? Empirical Evidence After GATT," *World Development,* 29 (2001): 265–289.

[40] Ibid., for the 1991 figures. The 2001 figures have been computed from *OECD Health Data 2003* (Paris: Organization for Economic Cooperation and Development, 2003).

[41] Watal, Jayashree, "Pharmaceutical Patents, Prices and Welfare Losses: Policy Options for India Under the WTO TRIPS Agreement," *World Economy,* 23 (2000): 735–752.

[42] Lichtenberg and Philipson (2002), op. cit., p. 18.

[43] Berndt, Ernst R., "The U.S. Pharmaceutical Industry: Why Major Growth in Times of Cost Containment?" *Health Affairs,* 20 (2001): 100-111.

[44] Grabowski et al. (2002), op. cit.

PART FIVE

Comparative Systems and Public Policy

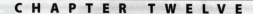
Comparative Health-Care Systems

From the standpoint of Social Security, a health service providing full preventive and curative treatment of every kind to every citizen without exceptions, without remuneration limits and without an economic barrier at any point to delay recourse to it, is the ideal plan.*

1 Introduction

All modern health-care systems, including that of the United States, share certain characteristics. All are subject to a good deal of government regulation. All are strained by rising costs. Although there are unique characteristics to every country's health-care system, they can be grouped into four main categories:

1. National health insurance, where the government assumes the role of a third-party payer (Canada)
2. National health-care system, where the government provides health-care services (United Kingdom)
3. Community sickness funds with government subsidies (France and Germany)

---

*Beveridge, Sir William, *Social Insurance and Allied Services: A Report by Sir William Beveridge* (New York: Macmillian, 1942), Part VI, Section 432, as quoted in Cutler, David M., "Equality, Efficiency and Market Fundamentals: The Dynamics of International Medical-Care Reform," *Journal of Economic Literature*, XL (2002): 883. The Beveridge Report led to the institution of the National Health Service in the United Kingdom in 1946.

4. A mixed public and private market system (Australia, Japan, and the United States)

In this chapter, we will explore the ways in which market incentives and government directives interact in the health-care systems of Canada, Germany, and the United Kingdom. These three countries have been chosen because their systems represent examples of 1, 2, and 3 above and because they are the systems most often used as references when reforms of the U.S. health-care system are contemplated. The chapter also provides an overview of the health-care system of a developing nation, India.

Health Care in Canada, Germany, and the United Kingdom

2   Canadian Health-Care System

History

Before 1947, the Canadian and U.S. health-care systems were very similar. Private insurance, including Blue-Cross, was available in Canada as well as the United States. Most Canadian hospitals were private, not-for-profit institutions, and physician practices were organized in much the same way in both countries. In 1947, Saskatchewan instituted a provincial universal hospital insurance plan. Other provinces followed suit; 10 years later the Hospital and Diagnostic Services Act created a national system in which the federal government paid half the hospital costs in return for provincial governments paying the other half and assuming responsibility for overseeing budgets and capital investments of hospitals and guaranteeing universal access to services. In 1961, Saskatchewan extended its universal insurance program to physician services. There was much more opposition to this than to universal hospital insurance; and the physicians of Saskatchewan went out on strike. Negotiations with physicians' lobbies in Saskatchewan and elsewhere led to a nationwide system in which physicians retained their private practices and were paid on a fee-for-service basis.[1]

Structure

In 1966, Canada established its current universal social insurance system, known as Medicare. In return for subsidies from the federal government, every province is required to make a comprehensive package of services available to all legal residents, to create a public authority to administer the system, and to make its coverage portable outside the province. Canadian Medicare covers all "medically necessary services." Private insurance for medical care and procedures covered by Medicare (known as parallel private insurance) is not allowed. Supplementary, as opposed to parallel, private insurance is subsidized by the federal government, since it is exempt from income tax if purchased through one's employer. The tax treatment is virtually identical to that of employer-provided health insurance in the United States.

Canadian Medicare is financed out of general income tax revenues. It is a **single-payer system** because the government does not subcontract out to any insurance intermediaries. Before 1977, the federal contribution to the provincial health plans was made on a cost-sharing basis. Since then block grants to the provinces have been made for a combined health-care and post-secondary-education budget, the amount depending on population size and rate of economic growth but not on historical health-care expenditure levels. Since the early 1990s, the percentage of the cost of provincial health plans covered by federal contributions has been greatly reduced from its original 50 percent. In fact, between 1990 and 1997 real per capita federal expenditure on health care in Canada did not increase at all.[2] Many provincial plans had to reduce their budgets, particularly during the 1992 and 1993 recession. At one point, Ontario even considered withdrawing from the Medicare system. Since 1998, the federal government has resumed some increases in its funding of the provincial systems.

Under Canadian Medicare, citizens are free to consult a physician of their choice, including a specialist. The Canadian system has no official gatekeepers. However, visits to specialists that are not referred by a general practitioner may not be fully reimbursed. This acts as an informal gatekeeping device, but the system does not provide incentives for general practitioners to ration referrals, as is the case in Germany, The United Kingdom and some managed care plans in the United States.

In September 2004, Prime Minister Paul Martin reached an agreement with provincial and territorial leaders to provide 14 billion Canadian dollars of additional federal funding for Medicare over the next 6 years and to guarantee 6 percent annual increases in the program's funding through 2015. It is estimated that this will barely keep up with rising costs of the program.[3]

The provincial Ministries of Health are the purchasers of hospital services. The provincial Medicare plans are the sole purchasers of physician services. Physician and hospital associations negotiate fees with these government authorities. The negotiations between provincial health ministries or Medicare plan administrators and the medical associations can be understood as bilateral monopoly situations in which the provincial health ministries are the monopoly buyers (monopsonists) and the regional physician and hospital associations are the monopoly sellers.* The difference between the price (fee schedule) desired by the physician associations and by the provincial health ministries provides a bargaining range analogous to that which exists in negotiations between unions and firms. Since physicians in Canada can and do go out on strike, this analogy is a realistic one.

---

*See Appendix 1, pp. 336–337, for a presentation of the bilateral monopoly model in the context of a profit-maximizing monopoly employer and a profit-maximizing union.

The provincial Medicare budgets, limited by the federal contribution and the province's ability to raise taxes, provide an upper limit to the level of fees that can be negotiated.

Since the physicians are not employees of the government, there will not be direct negotiations over the quantity of physician services "hired." However, the provincial governments employ various incentives to try to alter the geographical distribution of physicians, since rural areas tend to be underserved. Both regulatory restrictions on licenses and financial incentives are used. For instance, in Ontario the New Entrant Fee Discount pays reduced fees for three years to newly certified medical graduates who set up practices in areas designated by the government as "oversupplied." The Specialist Retention Initiative and the Underserviced Areas Program offer positive financial incentives to attract physicians to underserved areas. Quebec and most other provinces have similar legislation. In spite of this, the spatial distribution of physicians in Canada remains very uneven.

The government incentives do not appear to be sufficient to make up for the disutility to physicians of locating medical practices away from urban centers such as Montreal, which have major teaching institutions and research facilities.[4] The shortage of primary care physicians in small towns and rural communities appears to be increasing. A recent article quotes a resident of an upper middle class community as saying, "It's like winning a lottery to get in to see the doctor." An estimated 22,000 people in the community have no primary care physicians and use hospital emergency rooms for routine services like getting prescriptions refilled.[5]

Canadian physicians have payment arrangements with their Medicare system similar to those of physicians in the United States who "accept assignment" with Medicare. Since 1984, when the Canada Health Act made it illegal, Canadian physicians and hospitals cannot engage in balance billing, that is, charging patients a fee in excess of the government reimbursement rate.

Capacity and Performance

Physicians and Hospitals

Physician training is of similar quality to that in the United States. Each country recognizes the other's training in admitting medical school graduates to residency programs. The physician per capita ratio is about 80 percent of the U.S. ratio.* The main difference is that the ratio of general practitioners to specialists is much higher in Canada. Approximately two thirds of Canadian physicians are general practitioners, contrasted with roughly one-third in the United States.[6]

The capacity of hospital beds per capita is about 110 percent that of the United States.† On the other hand, the number of nurses per hospital bed is roughly half that in the United States. This suggests that intensity of care in hospitals is proba-

*See Table 12.1 on page 256.
†See Table 12.1 on page 256.

bly lower in Canada. Average length of stay for those hospitalized is somewhat longer in Canada than in the United States (7.2 days vs. 5.8 days), and the proportion of the total annual expenditure on health that is devoted to in-patient care is slightly higher than in the United States (29.8 % vs. 27.1 %).[7]

Diffusion and Use of Technology

The amount of medical technology per capita available in Canada is less than in the United States. For instance, in 1997 the number of CT scanners per 100,000 people was 8.2, as opposed to 13.7 in the United States, and the number of MRI units per 100,000 people was 1.8 versus 7.6 in the United States.[8]

Canadian patients have been found to receive 22 percent fewer diagnostic tests than United States patients.[9] For example, the rate of mammography for women in Canada, compared with U.S. women in the same age groups who have private or public health insurance, is about 50 percent lower. However, the incidence of breast cancer is also lower.[10] Canadians with coronary artery disease receive fewer coronary artery bypass graft operations (on an age-adjusted rate) and fewer coronary arteriograms.[11] The rate of cardiac catheterization is only about 40 percent of that in the United States.[12]

Role of the Insurance Systems: Public and Private

The contribution of the insurance system to the lower cost of medical care in Canada should not be ignored. Since Medicare is a single-payer system, there are lower administrative costs than in a multiple-payer system like that of the United States.

Whether parallel private insurance should be permitted for basic medical services has long been a subject of intense debate in Canada. An argument against it is that it creates a two-tiered system in which the private sector competes with the public, driving up costs and reducing quality of public care by luring providers away to the more lucrative private system. The counter economic arguments are that parallel private insurance will reduce the pressure on the public system, thus reducing costs and shortening waiting periods for nonemergency services, and that it will increase quality through competition. Research based on experience in Australia and the United Kingdom, which do permit parallel private insurance, has led to the conclusion that a parallel private insurance system would not significantly reduce waiting time in the public sector, would require the creation of a regulatory bureaucracy, and would probably require public subsidies in order to survive.[13]

Having supplementary private insurance has been found to have no effect on hospital utilization in Canada but to increase the utilization of doctors' services by about 4 percent. This may be related to a higher use of prescription drugs and the resulting visits to physicians to obtain prescriptions. This notion is supported by the finding that Canadians who have only supplementary dental insurance had no higher rate of physician visits.[14]

No discussion of the Canadian health-care system would be complete without noting that the large open border between Canada and the United States provides easy access to medical care in the United States for Canadians with the necessary financial means. The case is often made that Canadians have only been willing to accept a one-tiered system of social insurance because proximity to the United States and its abundant supply of health care is the de facto second tier of the Canadian single-payer system. This may, however, be a misperception since research has shown that very few Canadians actually cross the border for the purpose of utilizing medical care.[15] Most medical care provided to Canadians in the United States results from either unexpected medical needs arising while visiting the United States for other purposes or from the Canadian government's cross-border contracting for services to augment existing Canadian capacity.[16] The latter does support the position that the Canadian system benefits from access to the greater capacity of high-tech equipment and procedures available in the United States. We can think of the rate of innovation and diffusion of technology in the United States as providing a positive externality to Canada's health system.

Divergence Between Canada and the United States in Proportion of GDP Spent on Health Care

In 1960, before either country instituted its Medicare system, the percentage of gross domestic product (GDP) spent on health care in Canada was slightly greater than in the United States (5.5% vs. 5.2%). By 2001, health-care expenditure in Canada constituted 9.7 percent of GDP, compared with 13.9 percent in the United States.[17] Factors contributing to the difference are the lower rate of diffusion and use of advanced technology in Canada, the federal and provincial governments' caps on health-care spending, and possible differences in the underlying health status of the population. These factors appear to more than offset the longer average stays in hospital and the higher proportion of in-patient hospital care.

3   German Health-Care System

History

The German health-care system has evolved from institutions dating back to the Middle Ages when guilds created funds to help their members pay for disability, hospital, and funeral expenses.[18] Bismarck is attributed with starting the first modern system of social insurance in the 1880s when he required German workers in certain occupations to join sickness funds and their employers to contribute to the funds, and imposed regulations requiring funds to provide a standard set of benefits. The number of occupations covered was expanded to create the present universal system.

Structure

In Germany today all employees are required to join a sickness fund unless they have incomes above a certain threshold. The **sickness funds** are quasi-public non-profit institutions organized on the basis of workplace, occupation, or union. Although the government requires each fund to provide a standard benefit package, coverage varies among funds. The system is financed through employer and employee contributions in the form of payroll taxes. Employee contributions are scaled according to income up to a certain ceiling. Unlike the United States, all employers are required to contribute to employee health insurance. About 90 percent of the population is insured through the public system.

The sickness fund system is renowned for its generosity, including items that are not usually part of health insurance packages, such as sick pay and long-term care. The out-of-pocket proportions of costs for various services have been increased in the 1990s, but co-payments still tend to be a much lower percentage of costs than in the United States, averaging about 7.5 percent across services. Insurance premiums are, however, higher relative to wages than in most employment-based insurance plans in the United States.[19] Premiums for sickness funds represented 13.4 percent of wages in 1997.[20]

The National Association of Sickness Fund Physicians, the *Kassenarztliche Vereinigugn* (KV), negotiates with national representatives of the sickness funds to set fee schedules for different services. These negotiations cover only physician office visits, since in Germany hospital physicians are salaried employees. Regional associations of sickness fund physicians traditionally negotiate physician budgets with individual funds.

The German government has imposed fixed **global budgets** for payments to physician associations since 1977. There are separate caps for office consultations, laboratory tests, and so on. Since 1986, caps have also been imposed on the amount that can be distributed from each sickness fund. If doctors treating a particular sickness fund's members perform services whose aggregate fees exceed the cap, the fee per service declines and all physicians treating members of that fund will have their fees reduced. If the physicians association finds a particular physician excessive in his or her expenses per case, he or she may also be subject to deductions in future reimbursements. Compared to the Canadian system, the physicians association (KV) has structurally more power since it negotiates with multiple sickness funds. However, the institution of budget caps has tipped the balance of power somewhat more in favor of the sickness funds.

The German hospital system is a mixed private and public one. State governments oversee the state hospitals, but private hospitals are also subject to a good deal of regulation. Sickness fund associations negotiate fees with area hospital associations. Until reforms in the period 1981 to 1986, hospital budgets were set on the basis of past costs and utilization rates. Since the mid-1980s, hospital budgets have had caps imposed by the government. The caps limit the ability of both physician and hospital associations to bargain for higher fees.

Private Insurance

Professional civil servants (including teachers in public schools) are insured directly by the government for part of their expenses and may buy supplementary private insurance to cover the balance. The self-employed must also buy private insurance unless they have been previously covered by a sickness fund in former employment. Employees with incomes above the threshold level may buy private insurance or self-insure themselves.

The private insurance system shares an aspect of social insurance, in that experience rating is technically illegal. However, the privately insured who require no insurance payout for a certain period of time receive rebates from their insurance companies. This is an implicit form of experience rating. German private insurance charges level premiums over the lifetime of the insured. Younger privately insured persons pay premiums greater than the expected payout for people of their age, but continue to be billed at the same level throughout their tenure with the same insurance carrier. This provides intertemporal risk sharing. It also limits the degree of switching between insurance companies and thus reduces the amount of adverse selection that is always a potential problem in a nonmandatory insurance system. To further limit adverse selection, people are not allowed to switch between the private and public system unless their income or employment status changes.

Reforms of the 1990s

The Health Care Reform Act of 1993 introduced competition into the system by giving citizens the opportunity to choose among different sickness funds. To offset this and to preserve the social insurance aspects of the system, funds with low-risk populations are now required to subsidize funds with higher-risk populations.[21]

The reforms imposed tighter limits on budgets for physician payments and hospitals. A prospective payment system for German hospitals, not unlike the DRG system in the United States, was instituted. Since 1993, targets have been set for length of stay, with hospitals reimbursed at only a fraction of the daily rate for stays in excess of the target length, but with additional payments to hospitals of 75 percent of the daily rate for each day between discharge and the end of the target period when stays are shorter than the targeted length. Despite the reforms, length of stay in German acute-care hospitals still tends to be much longer than for comparable illnesses in the United States; the difference is even more striking when stays in convalescent facilities are included.[22]*

The reforms of the 1990s also imposed cost constraints on the regional budgets for pharmaceuticals; but unlike Canada, Germany has not imposed direct

*See Table 12.1 on page 256.

price controls. Rather, penalties are imposed on doctors collectively if they prescribe too many pharmaceuticals. Billings for prescriptions in excess of the target are paid out of the physicians' reimbursement fund. When this form of risk sharing with doctors was introduced, physicians responded by reducing billings for pharmaceuticals by 20 percent within six months of the reform.[23] However, pharmaceutical expenditures still exceeded budgets throughout much of the 1990s.[24]

Two additional reform measures, the Neuordnungsgesetz (NOG) 1 and 2, were put into effect in 1997. NOG 1 raises co-payments of subscribers when funds raise their premiums and allows people to switch between funds when their fund raises its premium. NOG 2 increases co-payments on prescription drugs, hospital stays, massage, physical therapy, dental care, stays in health spas, and medical transportation.[25] The system still includes free physician visits and extensive coverage for glasses, hearing aids, and prostheses. Although physician visits are still free, physician visits have declined by about 10 percent since the reforms of 1997.[26]

Capacity and Performance

Physicians and Hospitals

The proportion of expenditure on health that is devoted to in-patient hospital care is much higher than in either Canada or the United States, 36.1 percent compared with about 30 percent in Canada and 27 percent in the United States.[27] The ratio of physicians to population is also higher in Germany than in Britain, Canada or the United States. (See Table 12.1 on page 256.)

One reason for the greater degree of hospitalization and also the higher physician/population ratio is the strict separation between office- and hospital-based physicians. Nonhospital physicians may not treat patients in hospitals, and hospital physicians may not have office practices. This leads to some duplication of services in both pretesting and postoperative care. Critics argue that there is a chronic oversupply of both hospital beds and physicians in Germany.[28]

Medical Technology

A 1993 comparison of Canada, Germany, and the United States in the use of advanced technologies in the treatment of selected diseases showed Germany having a lower rate of cardiac catheterization, radiation therapy, extra-corporeal shock wave lithotripsy, and magnetic resonance imaging than the United States, but outranking Canada in the rates at which all these procedures are performed.[29]

Effects of Financing the Insurance System Through Payroll Taxation

A mandated payroll tax may have adverse labor market effects. The employer contribution to the sickness fund is a fixed cost per worker. Figure 12.1 depicts supply and demand in a labor market. The effect of the sickness fund contribution is shown as a shift in the demand for workers from DD to D_1D_1. If the supply of workers is highly elastic, the effect will be primarily on employment. (If

Figure 12.1

Quantity of Workers
Employed

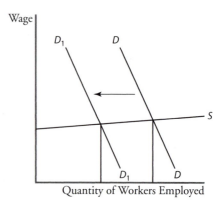

the supply of workers is more inelastic, the adjustment will affect wages more and employment less.) Because postunification Germany has had a chronically high unemployment rate and a ready supply of workers who can be imported from other European Union (EU) countries, it is reasonable to model the labor supply curve as quite wage-elastic.

Proportion of GDP Spent on Health Care

Germany ranks near the top among Organization for Economic Cooperation and Development (OECD) countries in the proportion of its GDP devoted to health care. For years, it has been virtually tied with Switzerland for second place behind the United States. The proportion of GDP devoted to health-care expenditure in 2001, the last year for which comparative OECD figures are available, was 10.7 percent, compared with 10.9 percent for Switzerland and 13.9 percent for the United States.

4   United Kingdom: The National Health Service (NHS)

Structure of the NHS

The National Health Service (NHS) was introduced in the United Kingdom at the end of World War II. It is not an insurance system, but a health service in which the providers are paid by the government. The NHS is financed out of general income tax revenues, is available to all British subjects and residents, and provides free physician visits and hospital procedures, with some co-payments for other services such as pharmaceuticals, dental care, and eyeglasses.

From its inception, office-based physicians have generally been paid by the NHS on a capitation basis. Hospital-based physicians receive salaries from the

NHS. Patients have a primary care physician (GP) who acts as a gatekeeper in much the same way as in HMOs in the United States. The GP makes all referrals to "consultants," the British term for specialists. Until reforms in the 1990s, all payments to consultants and hospitals were made by the district health authorities (DHAs). The DHAs also had the responsibility for overseeing the provision of care within the district.

The NHS is constrained by a fixed global budget. Rationing is done on a triage basis. This results in waits for nonemergency services. In fact, the British system is often characterized as one in which rationing is achieved primarily through the waiting process, sometimes called **rationing by queuing**. After several attempts at major reforms, queuing is still a prominent feature of the system.[30]

Unlike Canada, private parallel insurance is available to consumers. Use of private health-care services has risen over time as eligibility for certain publicly funded treatment has changed and waiting periods have lengthened. Within the public system, co-payments have risen for dental, optometry services, and pharmaceuticals. This lowers the *relative* price of the more convenient private services. Providers may remain within the NHS and also treat private clients on a fee-for-service basis. Accident and emergency services are not available in the private market.

In spite of the long queues for elective services provided by the NHS, it is still the case that approximately 85 percent of health-care expenditures in the United Kingdom are for services provided through the NHS. Most people still continue to use the public system for basic services. Although there are demographic, socioeconomic, and attitudinal variables that affect the use of private health-care services, there seems to be an identifiable separate group of users only for inpatient hospital services, for which private insurance is more likely to be purchased.[31]

Reforms of the 1990s

In 1991 a major reform took place under the NHS and Community Care Act. This reform followed the publication of a controversial white paper, *Working for Patients*, commissioned under Prime Minister Margaret Thatcher.* A main feature of this reform was the introduction of elements of market competition into the system. Provider groups were given greater autonomy from the district health authorities and hospitals were encouraged to become self-governing trusts, organizations similar to non-profit hospitals in the United States.

---

*Secretary of State and others, *Working for Patients* (London: HMSO, 1989). Criticism focused on two aspects of the reform: competition between health-care providers and a proposal that private health insurance be subsidized for people over 60 years of age. For good coverage of this reform see Ham, C., "Managed Markets in Health Care; the U.K. Experiment," *Health Policy,* 35 (1996): 279–292.

Introduction of the GP Fundholder System

This reform introduced an innovation that has been studied by many researchers. Larger physician practices (known as **fundholders**) were given the option of having their own budgets to pay for some secondary services that they ordered for their patients. The intent of this reform was to provide competition between the fundholders and the health authorities in the purchasing of specialist and hospital services.*

Several studies have found that fundholders paid lower prices for their patients' hospital services than did regional health authorities.[32] The reason appears to be that fundholders were more willing to shift between hospitals. Hospitals saw the fundholders as having more price-elastic demands for their services and behaved like rational price-discriminating firms. In cases where GP fundholders paid hospitals directly for patients' services, their patients waited less time than others.[33]

Fundholder physicians, as well as hospitals, appear to have responded to economic incentives in their role as agents for their patients. A study of referrals for cataract surgery illustrates this. Fundholders were found to be more willing to make referrals when the probability that their patients would receive the surgery under the NHS was lower. They were more likely to refer upper-income or educated patients, known to have higher rates of parallel private insurance. They were also more likely to refer patients for surgery when waiting lines were longer, since longer waits encourage patients to drop out of the queue and either have no surgery or "go private."[34] The behavior of a control group of physicians who did not pay for their patients' services out of their own budgets showed no difference in the rate of referral by socioeconomic status of patients or length of queues for surgery. This behavior of fundholder physicians is an example of imperfect agency in a system that provided a strong incentive for it.

Architects of the NHS reform hoped that there would be net efficiency improvements in hospitals when GP fundholders became competitive buyers of secondary services. They were influenced by the U.S. managed competition model and by the U.S. experience with competitive purchasing of hospital services by managed care plans. It appears that the national goal of reducing overall waiting time for hospital treatments was not accomplished by this scheme. There is some conflicting evidence, specifically a study showing a reduction in waiting time for hip fracture surgery after the NHS reform of 1991, but this appears not to be the case in general. On the whole, there was simply a redistribution of waiting time between patients, based on their referral process.[35] Moreover, just as managed competition has not developed in areas in the United States where there are no competing managed care plans, many localities in Great Britain did not develop effective competition because there was only one regional hospital.

---

*The original requirement was 11,000 patients, which was reduced to 7,000 in England and Wales and 6,000 in Scotland.

The GP fundholder system was abolished in 1999. All general practitioners were placed into one of approximately 500 primary care groups. Each group became the budget holder responsible for the medical services for the entire population in a geographically defined area. Primary care groups may keep any savings that they accumulate and use them to improve care for their patients.[36] Primary care groups have much the same function as the individual GP fundholders formerly had, but there is no longer competition between physicians and regional health authorities in the buying of services. The system provides less incentive for primary care groups to ration referrals, since risk is averaged over a much larger patient group.

The 1997 reform also imposed quality review (based on patient outcomes) and cost-effectiveness evaluations at the national level. A National Institute for Clinical Effectiveness was created. Thus, the 1997 reform moved the NHS in the direction of more centralized control over quality. Local self-governance of hospitals has also been limited by the continuance of the national Pay Review Boards and the national Whitley Councils that determine employment terms and conditions for all employees of the NHS.[37] Therefore, despite reforms, the NHS is still essentially a centralized system in which "the chain of accountability is entirely upwards," as only the Secretary of State for Health is accountable to the electorate with everyone below him or her an appointed official.[38]

Capacity and Performance

The United Kingdom lags behind Germany and the United States in its stock of technologically advanced equipment such as MRI machines and CT scanners, but has, on average, similar levels of equipment as Canada.[39] The physician/population ratio in the United Kingdom is also lower than in the United States, Canada, or Germany, although the capacity of hospital beds is greater than in either the United States or Canada.* A study of the comparative productive efficiency in the treatment of cholelithiesis, breast cancer, lung cancer, and diabetes found that, with the exception of skilled nursing services, fewer inputs per patient were used in the United Kingdom in the treatment of each of these diseases than in either the United States or Germany. The supply of hospital nurses is, however, relatively larger in the United Kingdom than in any of the other three countries. This seems to lead to relatively greater success in the treatment of chronic diseases that need on-going case management.[40]

There are significant regional disparities in available health-care resources. For instance, the northeast of England has significantly fewer health-care facilities than the rest of the country.[41] There is also evidence that members of the professional and managerial classes tend to receive more care from the NHS for the same illness than do people of lower occupational status.[42]

*See Table 12.1 on page 256.

5   Comparative Capacity of Health-Care Services, Expenditure on Health Care, and Health Outcomes

Tables 12.1 and 12.2 do not show any correspondence between capacity in physicians and hospitals or proportion of GDP spent on health care and health outcomes in the countries studied. This serves as a reminder that factors other than intensity of medical treatment influence health outcomes. Moreover, averages do not reveal disparities in health outcomes within countries.

Canada outranks Germany, the United Kingdom, and United States in all measures of health outcome even though it has less capacity and spends a smaller proportion of its GDP on health care than do Germany and the United States. The greater hospital capacity, extensive use of in-patient care, coverage for long-term care, and lack of price controls on prescription drugs contribute to the relatively greater proportion of GDP spent on health care in Germany. The United Kingdom allocates a considerably smaller proportion of its GDP to public health care but has greater hospital capacity than Canada or the United States.

When comparing countries that have global caps on health-care budgets, the simple answer as to why relatively more is spent on health care in one country than in another is that its government has chosen to allocate a higher proportion of the national budget to this use. One reason that such a high proportion of GDP is spent on health care in the United States is that the United States is at least partly a market-driven system, which imposes price rationing rather than rationing of capacity of services available.

Summary

The Canadian, German, and British systems embody three distinct types of universal health care systems. Canadian Medicare represents a classic case of the single-payer health insurance system. The British NHS is a national health system in which the government is the supplier of public health care. Germany provides universal social insurance through a decentralized system of quasi-public non-

Table 12.1   Capacity: Physicians and Hospital Beds per 1,000 Population, 2001

Country	Physicians per 1,000 Population	Hospital Beds per 1,000 Population	Average Length of Stay in Acute-Care Hospital (days)[a]
Canada	2.1	3.2	7.2
Germany	3.3	6.5	9.6
United Kingdom	2.0	3.9	6.9
United States	2.7	2.9	5.8

Source: *OECD Health Data 2003,* (2003) op. cit.

[a]These figures for 2000 are from *OECD Health Data 2003* (Paris: Organization for Economic Cooperation and Development, 2003).

Table 12.2   Expenditure on Health-Care and Comparative Health Outcomes

Country	Health Care as % GDP (2000)	Female Life Expectancy at Birth (2001)	Male Life Expectancy at Birth (2001)	Female Healthy Life Expectancy at Age 60 (1999)	Male Healthy Life Expectancy at Age 60 (1999)
Canada	9.2	81.7	76.3	17.9	15.3
Germany	10.6	80.7	74.7	17.3	15.0
United Kingdom	7.3	79.8	75.0	16.9	15.0
United States	13.1	79.4	73.9	16.6	14.9

Source: *OECD Health Data 2003*, (Paris: Organization for Economic Cooperation and Development, 2003)

profit sickness funds. In all three systems, the national governments impose limits on annual public health-care spending.

All three systems rely more heavily on risk sharing with providers than with consumers to control costs. In Germany, in spite of a fee-for-service system, fees are reduced if physician groups exceed budget caps. In Canada, global budgets provide caps on the fees that physician and hospital associations can negotiate. In the United Kingdom, risk sharing with NHS physicians is accomplished by paying office physicians on a capitation basis. Additional risk sharing results from physician practices having to pay for referral services for patients out of their fixed budgets. This is intended to provide an incentive for efficiency. Efficiency is hard to measure in this context, but the system does provide an incentive for limiting referrals.

Both the British and Canadian health-care systems are financed out of general income taxes, which are progressive in structure, with higher rates charged to higher-income earners. The German system is largely financed out of payroll taxes, paid jointly by employers and employees, and is capped at certain income levels. The German system is less progressive both because of its method of financing and because high-income individuals can opt out of the public system. The financing system also has risks of causing adverse labor market effects, since a mandatory employer contribution to workers' sick fund premium is an added fixed cost per worker. Another difficulty with a system based on a payroll tax is that the base of workers with regular full-time employment must support the health insurance of retired people.*

Reforms have been introduced into the health-care systems of all three countries studied. The main reform in the Canadian system has been the move from cost-based budgeting to global caps based on the rates of growth of the populations and economies of the provinces. Both Germany and the United Kingdom have experimented with versions of managed competition. In Germany, consumers now have a choice of sickness fund and can shift between them. The sickness funds therefore have to compete with each other to attract members. In

*However, unlike the Medicare system in the United States, taxes other than payroll taxes help support the sickness-fund contributions for retirees.

the United Kingdom, for five years during the 1990s, fundholder physician practices were allowed to compete with district health authorities in the purchasing of services for their enrolled patients. This was discontinued in 1997. Now large area physician groups control the budgets used for patient referrals. This gives more control to physicians rather than bureaucrats. Risk is shared over much larger groups of patients than was the case under the fundholder system.

A Case Study of Health Care in a Developing Nation

6 India

Overview

Chapter Eleven described India's thriving domestic pharmaceutical industry. India also has excellent government-funded universities, including medical colleges, and post-graduate training sponsored by the Indian Council of Medical Research. Although Indian members of the biomedical profession represent a significant part of the world's stock of human capital, India faces the problem of a brain-drain of its physicians and scientists.

India's main public health problems are those common to developing nations. A significant part of the population lacks the basic prerequisites for good health: adequate nutrition and clean drinking water. Communicable diseases account for a much higher proportion of illness and death than in Western industrialized nations, and HIV/AIDS has become an important health problem.(See Chapter Thirteen.) Even though the GDP per capita has been growing at 5 percent per annum in recent years, about a third of India's population lives below the Indian-defined poverty level. In 2000 it was estimated that 600 million of the billion people in India were living on less than $2 per day.*

India devotes a higher proportion, roughly 6 percent, of its GDP to health care than do many developing nations, but the average level of public care is still much lower than in most higher-income nations.† The uneven distribution of income and infrastructure between regions and between cities and rural areas results in very unequal access to health care. There are still many geographical areas in which only the most rudimentary health care, if any, is available.

The nature of medical care in India is highly pluralistic. Western medicine, known as **allopathy**, coexists with several schools of traditional healing such as **ayurveda**.‡ Medical colleges offer courses in various non-Western systems of

---

*The National Sample Survey, conducted in 1993 and 1994, found 37 percent of the population to be below the poverty level. A newer survey, conducted in 2000, provides preliminary figures showing the below-poverty proportion of Indians to have declined to 29 percent.

†According to the figures compiled by the World Bank in 1990, India spent 6 percent of its GNP on health compared with an average of 4.7 percent for all the developing nations.

‡Homeopathic medicine is an umbrella term used in India as a shorthand for all forms of non-Western medicine including homeopathy, *ayurveda, unani*, and Tibetan medicine.

medicine, but basic training in allopathy is the required course of study. However, a large number of Indians use primarily non-Western forms of healing that rely primarily on herbal remedies, yoga-based techniques, and meditation. Western medicine tends to be used to treat illnesses such as cancer and heart attacks, and invasive surgery or the use of Western-style drugs is often seen as the treatment of last resort. This contributes to the difficulty of making meaningful comparisons between India and the West with respect to expenditure per capita on health care.

It is also hard to define health care in India as a "health-care system." Public-health-related programs at the national level are organized under a large number of different government departments. Individual states have their own health-care budgets, supplemented by funds provided by the national government. Public health-care facilities coexist with private facilities financed from a wide variety of sources. Some private facilities are for-profit firms owned by physicians or businessmen. Others are funded by Indian and foreign nongovernmental organizations (NGOs), by international agencies such as the World Health Organization (WHO), and by government agencies from abroad such as the U.S. Agency for International Development (USAID).

Public Health Care in India

There is no public health insurance in India with the exception of that provided to people employed in the public sector who are covered by state employment insurance and treated in their own industry-based hospitals. The Indian public health-care system consists of health centers and hospitals financed through taxes and other government funds. These are open to all Indian citizens and treatment is heavily subsidized, but individuals are usually charged some fees for services. For example, a study of a very poor area in which 40 percent of the people were below the Indian poverty level found an average expenditure per visit to a public health center of 110 rupees, even for services that were supposed to be free.[43]

Health and Family Welfare Centers

Health and family welfare centers are mandated at the district, community and local levels throughout the country. Except in the most remote and scarcely populated rural areas, the plan is for each community health center to cover approximately 120,000 people. Each is allotted four medical specialists (in surgery, medicine, gynecology, and pediatrics) plus paramedical and other staff, a 30-bed facility, an operating room, an X-ray machine, labor and delivery room, and laboratory facilities.

Primary health centers are mandated by the Ministry of Health for each 30,000 population. These are authorized to have one medical officer, support staff, a four- to six-bed in-patient facility, and basic laboratory services in order to provide "curative and preventive health services" and family planning. Subcenters are also designated for each 5,000 population (and for each 3,000 in hilly or tribal areas).

Primary health centers and subcenters sometimes exist only on the books or, if they do exist, are frequently not open. A study of a group of villages near Udaipur (in Rajasthan) found an average weekly 45 percent absentee rate of medical personnel in local subcenters and a 36 percent absentee rate in large primary and community health centers. The former is particularly disheartening since the subcenters are often staffed by only one person and are therefore closed if that person does not show up. Rural villagers were found to spend about 1.5 times as much on treatment per illness episode as urban dwellers.[44] This was partly because of the need to travel to find available services. Low-income villagers and rural families were also more likely to use traditional healers or *bhopas* than government clinics. The traditional healers are unregulated and many have no medical training and not even a high-school degree. Sixty-five percent of the cost of medical care in rural villages was attributed to visits to *bhopas*.[45]

Designated low-income urban areas are entitled to have special health stations, established under the National Integrated Child Development Scheme. These consist of a one-room health station staffed by a woman with minimal health-care training (an *anganwadi*) whose job is to run a crèche, provide nutritional supplements, general health care, and health education, and maintain basic statistics about members of the community.[46] These are being used, not always successfully, to disseminate information about HIV/AIDS, a delicate subject in Indian culture.

Public Hospital System

Primary hospitals that provide only basic care treat the largest number of people. They are usually located in rural areas. Secondary hospitals, which are larger, better-equipped facilities with more staff, are located in bigger villages and towns. Tertiary hospitals are chiefly located in large urban areas and serve both city residents and critical cases transferred from primary and secondary hospitals. They often have research facilities and training for registrars (the Indian name for medical residents). The staff in all public hospitals and clinics are salaried government employees. Financing is shared between the federal government, the state government, and localities. Cities often bear a disproportionate share of the cost. For instance, the Municipal Corporation of Bombay is the major source of funding for the many government hospitals in that city.

Since hospitals represent a high proportion of the public expenditure on health, a good deal of research has been devoted to evaluating their efficiency. Several studies of utilization and productivity of secondary-level hospitals in the state of Andhra Pradesh are illustrative of the work that has been undertaken.[47] Regression analysis was used to examine productivity indicators including bed turnover rates, bed occupancy rates, and average length of stay. Bed occupancy rates often exceed 100 percent during peak seasons for disease or epidemics, since patients are placed on temporary floor mats or cots that are not counted as part of the hospital's bed capacity. For some time periods, bed occupancy rates exceeding 300 percent have been reported in community (secondary) hospitals.[48] The major determinant of hospital quality is the quantity of medically trained hospital staff. An additional doctor was associated with a 300 percent increase in hospital productivity. An additional nurse increased hospital productivity by about 20 percent. An overall deterioration in the quality of secondary hospitals was observed between the 1980s and 1998. This seems to be related to competition from a growing private sector.[49]

Private and Nongovernmental Health-Care Facilities

Private health insurance has been available in India only in the past few years.* As of 1997, less than 4 percent of the Indian population had any private medical insurance coverage (Mediclaim.)[50] Nonetheless, those who can afford health care in private hospitals generally do not use the government hospitals. Many private for-profit and non-profit hospitals and clinics available to paying clients also provide some charity care. This is true of hospitals specializing in ayurvedic medicine as well as those providing allopathic treatment.†

Private markets for medicines and birth control exist in villages as well as large cities. Some are part of large for-profit or non-profit networks; some receive funding from international agencies and foreign NGOs.‡ These programs often employ local people, particularly in health education. For example, one USAID program in Uttar Pradesh employs milkmaids from local dairy cooperatives as health and family planning educators. In some cases, Indian pharmaceutical companies have provided low-cost or even free drugs for the treatment of diseases such as HIV/AIDS.

---

*Life insurance and general insurance were nationalized in 1956 and 1972, respectively. A private insurance market has only begun to develop in India since the economic liberalization in 1991. Most Indian insurance companies sell only life insurance and business insurance. There is no well-developed private health insurance market, but recent changes in the law are allowing competition among insurance companies.

†For instance, a full-service ayurvedic hospital and research center opened in New Delhi in 2000 with India's president presiding at the opening ceremony. Many celebrities have made use of a similar facility in the state of Kerala, which has long waiting lists for admission. The demand for the new hospital in Delhi is expected to be even greater. This hospital has VIP suites, regular rooms, and free wards (*The Hindu*, October 28, 2000, p.2).

‡An example of this is a network called "Butterfly" that has branches throughout the northern state of Bihar. It receives funding from Janani, an Indian NGO affiliate of a Washington, DC, based non-profit group, DKT International. It employs local medicine men and women to sell birth control pills and condoms. It advertises on local radio, displays a colorful butterfly logo, and markets its products by word of mouth. Similar networks exist in northern states such as Uttar Pradesh.

Free or Cheap Drugs for Poor People: Cipla's AIDS Program

A project of Yusuf Hamied, head of Cipla Ltd, one of India's largest pharmaceutical companies, has received international attention. Cipla is viewed as the prototype of a "pirate company." It is known for copying the molecular formulas of new drugs and selling for pennies in India what would cost a hundred times as much in Europe or America. In 2000, Hamied started a campaign to get multinational companies and foreign countries to sell drugs to the poor at affordable prices. At a meeting of the European Commission in Brussels, he provided a list of drugs that his company would produce and the prices at which it would distribute them. Since then, Cipla has donated free supplies of nevirapine, a drug that prevents transmission of the HIV virus from mothers to infants.

Source: Specter, Michael, "India's Plague," *The New Yorker* (December 17, 2001), pp. 76–84.

Effect of Education on Indian Health

Health outcomes in India vary greatly by region, and factors other than availability of health-care facilities are extremely important. Education, particularly the education of women, appears to contribute at least as much to the healthiness of communities, as does the income level or availability of health-care facilities. For example, the state of Kerala has relatively good health outcomes. Compared to other Indian states, it has low per capita income but high female literacy rates.[51] The combination of higher literacy rates and basic health education has been shown to have significant positive effects on the infant mortality rates and health of children in even the poorest communities.[52] This has also been found to be true for many countries other than India.[53]

Summary

India spends more on public health care than does the average developing nation. However, the quality and quantity of public health facilities in India vary widely geographically. Facilities mandated by the Ministry of Health often exist "only on the books." Even patients with below-poverty-level incomes are frequently charged fees for services that are supposed to be free. A large number of private and governmental philanthropic institutions supplement the public health care available in India, but more extensive public provision of many services is necessary if there is to be wide access to quality health care. Health education is particularly important in combating the spread of HIV/AIDS. Nobel laureates Amartya Sen, Kenneth Arrow, and many other economists who have turned their attention to developing nations agree that improved health care and education require social investment on a much larger scale than is currently taking place.[54]

Key Concepts

Single-payer system

Sickness funds

Global budgets

Rationing by queuing

GP Fundholder

Allopathy

Ayurveda

Suggested Readings

1. Gerdtham, Ulf-G, and Bengt Jonsson, "International Comparisons of Health Expenditure," *Handbook of Health Economics,* Vol. 1A., Culyer, Anthony J. and Joseph P. Newhouse eds. (Amsterdam: Elsevier, 2000), Chap. 2.

2. White, Joseph, *Competing Solutions: American Health Care Proposals for Reform and International Experience* (Washington, DC: Brookings Institution, 1995).

Questions for Discussion and Review

1. What are the advantages and disadvantages of a single-payer insurance system?

2. What are the chief areas of efficiency and inefficiency in the German health-care system?

3. How has the American model of managed competition influenced reforms in other nations?

4. What were the aims of the reforms to the NHS instituted under the Thatcher government? Do you think they provided improvements? If so, what kinds of improvements?

5. If you became the minister of health in India and could make recommendations for improving the country's current system, what would they be?

6. What examples of imperfect physician agency have you found in this chapter?

Resources

[1] An excellent overview of the Canadian health-care system is provided in White, Joseph, *Competing Solutions: American Health Care Proposals for Reform and International Experience* (Washington, DC: Brookings Institution, 1995).

[2] Tuohy, Carolyn Hughes, "The Politics of Medicare North and South," *Journal of Health Politics, Policy and Law,* 26 (2001): 161–167.

[3] Kraus, Clifford, the *New York Times,* September 17, 2004, http://www.nytimes.com/2004/09/17/international/americas/17canada.html.

[4] See, for instance, Kralj, Boris, "Physician Distribution and Physician Shortage Intensity in Ontario," *Canadian Public Policy,* XXVII (2001): 167–178.

[5] Kraus, Clifford, "Canada Looks for Ways to Fix Its Health Care System" the *New York Times,* Setember 12, 2004, http://www.nytimes.com/2004/09/12/international/americas/12canada/html.

[6] Ibid.

[7] *OECD Health Data 2003,* (Paris: Organization for Economic Cooperation and Development, 2003).

[8] Rublee, Dale A., "Medical Technology in Canada, Germany, and the United States: An Update," *Health Affairs,* 13 (1994): 113–117.

[9] Katz, Steven J., et al., "Comparing the Use of Diagnostic Tests in Canadian and U.S. Hospitals," *Medical Care,* 34 (1996): 117–125.

[10] Tudifer, F. and E. Fuller-Thomson, "Who Has Screening Mammography: Results from the 1994–1995 National Population Health Survey," *Canadian Family Physicians,* 45 (1999): 1901–1907.

[11] Anderson, Geoffrey M. et al., "Use of Coronary By-Pass Surgery in the United States and Canada," *Journal of the American Medical Association,* 269 (1993): 1661–1666; Rouleau, Jean L., et al., "A Comparison of Management Patterns After Acute Myocardial Infarction in Canada and the United States," *New England Journal of Medicine,* 328 (1993): 779–784, and Slaughter, P. M., "Differences in Access to Care," *Canadian Journal of Cardiology,* 79 Suppl. D: (2001) 63D–67D.

[12] Rublee, (1994) op. cit., p. 114.

[13] Hurley, Jeremiah, et al., "Parallel Private Health Insurance in Australia: A Cautionary Tale and Lessons for Canada," IZA Discussion Paper No. 515, Social Science Research Network, Institute For the Study of Labor, (June 2002).

[14] Stabile, Mark, "Private Insurance Subsidies and Public Health Care Markets: Evidence from Canada," *Canadian Journal of Economics,* 34 (2001): 921–942.

[15] Katz, Steven J., et al., "Phantoms in the Snow: Canadians' Use of Health Care Services in the United States," *Health Affairs,* 21 (2002): 19–31.

[16] Ibid., p. 27.

[17] *OECD Health Data, 2003,* op. cit.

[18] White (1995) op. cit., pp. 72–73.

[19] Two excellent sources of information about the German health-care system are Arnold, Michael, *Health Care in the Federal Republic of Germany* (Cologne: Deutscher-Artzte-Verlag, 1991) and Eliot K. Wicks, *German Health Care: Financing, Administration, and Coverage* (Washington, DC: Health Insurance Association of America, 1992).

[20] Jost, Timothy, "German Health Care Reform: The Next Steps," *Journal of Health Politics, Policy and Law,* 23 (1998): 697–711.

[21] For a description and appraisal of the Health Care Reform Act, see Henke, Klaus-Dirk, et al., "Global Budgeting in Germany: Lessons for the United States," *Health Affairs,* 13 (1994): 7–21.

[22] Baily, Martin Neil and Alan M. Garber, "Health Care Productivity," *Brookings Papers on Economic Activity: Microeconomics, 1997* (1997): 143–202. See especially p. 163.

[23] Henke, (1994), et al., op. cit.

[24] Ibid., p. 10.

[25] Jost, (1998) op. cit., 705–706.

[26] Winkelman, Rainer, "Health Care Reform and the Number of Doctor Visits: An Econometric Analysis," Social Science Research Network, Institute for the Study of Labor, IZA Discussion Paper No. 3021 (October, 2001.)

[27] *OECD Health Data 2003* (2003), op. cit.

[28] Winkelman (2001), op. cit.

[29] Rublee, (1994) op. cit., pp. 113–117.

[30] Gravelle, Hugh, et al., "The Demand for Elective Surgery in a Public System: Time and Money Prices in the UK National Health Service," *Journal of Health Economics,* 21 (2002): p. 424.

[31] Propper, Carol, "The Demand for Private Health Care in the U.K," *Journal of Health Economics,* 19 (2000): 855–876.

[32] Cutler, David M., "Equality, Efficiency, and Market Fundamentals: The Dynamics of International Medical-Care Reform," *Journal of Economic Literature,* XL (2002): 904.

[33] Propper, Carol, et. al., "Waiting Times of Hospital Admissions: The Impact of GP Fundholding," *Journal of Health Economics,* 21 (2002): 227–252 and Dowling, B., "Effect of Fundholding on Waiting Times: Database Study," *British Medical Journal,* 314 (1997): 290–292.

[34] Gravelle, Hugh, et al., "The Demand for Elective Surgery in a Public System: Time and Money Prices in the UK National Health Service," *Journal of Health Economics,* 21 (2002): 424.

[35] Hamilton, B. H. and R. E. Bramley-Harker, "The Impact of the NHS Reforms on Queues and Surgery in England: Evidence from Hip Fracture Patients," *Economic Journal,* 109 (1999): 437–462.

[36] Gravelle et al. (2002), op. cit., pp. 424–425.

[37] A good discussion of this is given in Arrowsmith, James and Philippe Mosse, "Health Care Reform and the Working Time of Hospital Nurses in England and France," *European Journal of Industrial Relations,* 6 (2000): 287–289.

[38] Ross, Wendy and John Tomaney, "Devolution and Health Policy in England," *Regional Science,* 35 (2001): 266.

[39] OECD *Health Data, 2000* (Paris: Organization for Economic Cooperation and Development, 2000).

[40] Baily and Garber (1997), op. cit.

[41] Ross and Tomaney (2001), op. cit., pp. 265–270.

[42] Maynard, Alan, "The United Kingdom" in *Health Economics and Health Services Research, Supplement I: Comparative Health Systems,* J. J. Rosa ed. (Greenwich, CT: JAI Press, 1990), pp. 1–26.

[43] Banerjee, Abhijit, Angus Deaton, and Esther Duflo, "Wealth, Health and Health Services in Rural Rajasthan," *American Economic Review,* 94 (2004): 326–330.

[44] Sodani, P. R. and S. D. Gupta, "Health Care Expenditure: Results from a Study in Tribal Areas of Rajasthan," *Margin,* 31 (1998): 66–78.

[45] Banerjee, et al. (2004), op. cit., p. 330.

[46] Awasthi, Shally, et al., "Developing an Interactive STD-Prevention Program for Youth:

Lessons from a North Indian Slum," *Studies in Family Planning*, 31 (2000): 138–150.

[47] Dash, Purna Chandra and K. N. Murty, "Evaluation of Hospital Performance in Andhra Pradesh Using Combined Utilisation and Productivity Analysis," *Margin,* 33 (2001): 92–119. See also, Mahapatra, P. and P. Berman,"Evaluating Public Hospital Performance: Combined Utilization and Productivity Analysis of Secondary-Level Hospitals in Andhra Pradesh, India," unpublished manuscript, Institute of Health Systems, Hyderabad, 1990; and Mahapatra P. and P. Berman, "Using Hospital Activity Indicators to Evaluate Performance in Andhra Pradesh," *International Journal of Health Planning and Management*, 9 (1994): 199–211.

[48] Mahapatra and Berman (1994), op. cit.

[49] Dash and Murty (2001), op. cit.

[50] Lanjouw, J. O., *The Introduction of Pharmaceutical Product Patents in India: Heartless Exploitation of the Poor and Suffering?* NBER Working Paper No. 6366 (Cambridge, MA: National Bureau of Economic Research, 1998), p. 10.

[51] Jean Dreze and Amartya Sen, *India: Economic Development and Social Opportunity* (Oxford: Oxford University Press, 1995).

[52] Dreze and Sen (1995) op. cit.; Gopal, K. Rani, "Health Status and Female Literacy," *Indian Economic Journal*, 38 (1991): 117–119; and Pal, Sharmistha, "An Analysis of Childhood Malnutrition in Rural India: Role of Gender, Income, and Other Household Characteristics," *World Development,* 27 (1999): 1151-1171.

[53] See, for instance, Gregson, Simon, et al. "School Education and HIV Control in Sub-Saharan Africa," *Journal of International Development*, 13 (2001): 487–511 and Lin, Shin-Jong and Mei Lin, "Estimating the Infant Health Production Function in Taiwan," *Taiwan Economic Review*, 30, (2002): 77–111.

[54] Arrow, Kenneth J., Amartya Sen, and Kotoro Suzumara, eds., *Handbook of Social Choice and Welfare* (Amsterdam: North Holland/Elsevier, 2002).

CHAPTER THIRTEEN

Health Care: A Global Perspective

*Some academic leaders see a silver lining in the recent spate of emerging infectious outbreaks and the public health response they engendered: the events put public health into the forefront of people's minds. Until SARS erupted, most people took public health for granted, believing that the public faced little, if any, risk from infectious diseases.**

1 Introduction

The first section of this chapter focuses on issues of global public health. It considers the public goods aspects of the treatment of communicable diseases, introduces the new field of economic epidemiology and provides analyses of programs to combat malaria, tuberculosis, and HIV/AIDS. The second section provides a review of the empirical literature on elasticities of demand for medical care in a variety of countries in order to ascertain whether income and price effects are similar in other parts of the world to those found in the industrialized West.

---

*Lovinger, S. P., "Emerging Infections and Bioterrorism Raise Profile of Schools of Public Health," *Journal of the American Medical Association*, 290 (2003): 1306–1307, as quoted in Nash, David, MD, "From the Editor," *Health Policy Newsletter, Jefferson Medical College*, 17 (June 2004): 1–2.

Global Public Health Issues

Modern medicine has the potential to drastically reduce mortality and morbidity from diseases such as malaria, small pox, polio, diarrhea, and HIV/AIDS in developing nations as well as highly industrialized ones. However, communicable diseases continue to be a major cause of morbidity and death and a major strain on the economies of developing nations. The transmission of communicable diseases is a global problem heightened by extensive movements of people and goods and services across national boundaries. The concern with bioterrorism further increases the public's demand for comprehensive public health programs. The control of communicable diseases has aspects that make it "an **international public good**." For example, the emergence of drug-resistant strains of a disease in one region may be the result of the use of particular drugs to combat the disease in another part of the world.

It is popular to decry the atrophying of public health budgets in the United States, which took place in the 1980s when it was believed that comprehensive public programs of immunization had virtually eradicated many communicable diseases. However, there is a growing body of literature in the field of economic epidemiology that investigates the interaction between private incentives for disease prevention and public programs and provides models that indicate conditions under which a public program may be ineffective. Before considering this literature, let us look at some facts about the incidence of diseases in different parts of the world.

Global Causes of Disability and Death

Table 13.1 illustrates the sources of losses due to disability and death in different regions of the world. The losses are measured in disability-adjusted life-years (DALYs). This is the measure most commonly used by the World Health Organization (WHO).* WHO uses the DALY instead of the quality-adjusted life-year (QALY) because it focuses more directly on the impact of disease and malnutrition.

As this table shows comparative figures for 1990, we can safely assume that the DALY losses from HIV shown here underestimate the current losses due to this disease, particularly in sub-Saharan Africa and South Asia. However, the continuing prevalence of malaria and diarrhea as major causes of loss are well illustrated in this table.[†] (See Table 13.4, p. 279 of this chapter.)

---

*The DALY is a measure of morbidity and mortality due to disease and injury that is constructed using six classes of varying degrees of disability.

[†]The United Nations (UN) has undertaken a major initiative to reduce the incidence of malaria in the world by 2010. It has been estimated that reaching this goal will require an annual expenditure of $2 billion.

Table 13.1   Percentage of DALY Losses in a Region Associated with Given Causes, 1990

Category	Sub-Saharan Africa	India	China	Latin America and Caribbean	EME[a]
Injuries	9.3	9.1	16.7	15.0	11.9
Cerebro-vascular	1.5	2.1	6.3	2.6	5.3
Neuro-psychological	3.3	6.1	8.0	8.0	15.0
Nutritional deficiency	2.8	6.2	3.3	4.6	1.7
Cancer	1.5	4.1	9.2	5.2	19.1
Malaria	10.8	0.3		0.4	
Vaccine-preventable childhood infection	9.6	6.7	0.9	1.6	0.1
Diarrhea	10.4	9.6	2.1	5.7	0.3
STDs and HIV	8.8	2.7	1.7	6.6	3.4

Source: Jack, William, *Principles of Health Economics for Developing Countries*, WBI Development Studies (Washington, DC: World Bank, 1999), Table 9.2, pp. 266–267; *World Bank, 1993* (Washington, DC: World Bank, 1993), Table 1.3, p. 27.

[a]The term *established market economies* (EME) is roughly equivalent to the OECD member countries, particularly the 20 nations who were historic members of the OECD.

It is also useful to look at the prevalence of different diseases in high- and low-income countries. The relative burden of malaria, TB, HIV/AIDS, cancer, and heart disease in different regions is shown in Table 13.2. The "burden" is computed using DALYs.

Table 13.2   Percentage of Disease Burden by Region, 2001

Cause	World (%)	Low-Income Countries (%)	High-Income Countries (%)
Tuberculosis	2.4	2.9	0.3
HIV/AIDS	6.1	9.7	0.7
Malaria	2.7	4.5	0.0
Cancers	5.3	2.9	14.4
Cardiovascular diseases	10.3	7.7	16.4

Source: Kremer, Michael, "Pharmaceuticals and the Developing World," *Journal of Economic Perspectives*, 16 (2002): 67–90, Table 2, p. 71. This table is based on data from the World Health Report 2001 and World Bank, *World Development Indicators* (Washington, DC: Oxford University Press, 2001).

Importance of Communicable Diseases

The geographical distribution of DALY losses from the broad category of "communicable diseases" shown in Table 13.3 further highlights the differences in health problems in different regions of the world. We should note, however, that

Table 13.3   Percentage of DALY Losses due to Communicable Diseases, 1990

Established market economies	9.7
Sub-Saharan Africa	71.3
Asia (excluding China and India)	48.0
China	25.3
India	50.5
Latin America	42.2
Middle Eastern Crescent	51.0

Source: Jack, William, *Principles of Health Economics for Developing Countries,* WBI Development Studies (Washington, DC: World Bank, 1999), Table 9.2, pp. 266–267.

even though the incidence of communicable diseases is dramatically different in different parts of the world, the growth in international travel and trade has increased the likelihood of worldwide infection, regardless of where a disease originates or is most prevalent. The global concern over the outbreak of Sudden Acute Respiratory Syndrome (SARS) in 2003 and several outbreaks of Mad Cow disease in the past decade illustrate this.

Within the category of communicable diseases, the three diseases HIV/AIDS, tuberculosis, and malaria currently account for more than 6 million deaths in the world annually.[1] Tuberculosis has resurfaced as a serious health problem in the United States and European countries as well. The study of the epidemiology of communicable diseases throughout the world is a major task of the U.S. Centers for Disease Control and Prevention (CDC).*

2   Economics of Immunization and Prevention of Communicable Diseases

The control of communicable diseases through vaccinations and other preventive measures has public goods aspects, since preventing or curing a disease in one person or one community provides positive externalities to other people, communities, countries, and in many cases, the whole world.

Prevention Versus Treatment of Disease

Establishing relative values for prevention versus treatment of those already infected requires taking into account much more than the direct medical costs of the alternatives. It involves both biology and economics. It depends on whether infection is transmitted person to person or by other carriers, and also depends on the effects of the disease. Does the disease, if contracted, lead to death, im-

*A very good source of up-to-date information about communicable diseases, not only in the United States but throughout the world, is the CDC's website at http://www.cdc.gov.

munity, or recovery and further susceptibility?[2] What constitutes effective prevention also has to be considered in the context of particular countries at particular times. Research on the cost-effectiveness of alternative ways of managing communicable diseases has become a very important input into the health policy decisions of all nations.

Economists have been able to provide unique insights into many areas of health economics using the concepts of utility maximization and market equilibrium. The newly emerging field of **economic epidemiology** has applied these concepts to the evaluation of prevention versus treatment of disease.[3]

Economics of Vaccinations

Wherever there are significant externalities, the private market is not likely to result in efficient levels of either the production or utilization of goods.[†] The private decision to be vaccinated has been found to be a complicated interaction between prevalence of a contagious disease in one's community and price of the vaccination. Individuals are likely to be reactive rather than pro-active, waiting until there is a critical level of the contagious disease in their localities, defined by level of risk to their own family's health, before choosing to purchase vaccinations. They also have little incentive to take account of dynamic effects, for example, effects on future generations.

Tomas Philipson, studying private vaccinations for measles, makes the point that price is often only a secondary factor in the likelihood of choosing to vaccinate oneself or one's children. More important is the prevalence of the disease, which affects the risk of contracting it. Public interventions in such cases often need to include both price subsidies and mandatory vaccination programs if the prevalence of a communicable disease is to be reduced.[4]

This can be illustrated by the outbreak of measles in the United States late in the twentieth century, which disproved the 1978 prediction of the U.S. Surgeon General that measles would be completely eradicated from the country by 1982. Between 1989 and 1991, certain urban areas in the United States experienced serious outbreaks of measles. What became apparent was that the 99 percent measles vaccination rate of young children, which had been achieved in the United States by the early 1980s, had broken down in low-income neighborhoods of major cities such as New York, Chicago, Houston, and Los Angeles. More than 27,000 children contracted measles and 100 died from the disease during this period.[5] The children hardest hit were those who had never received primary vaccinations, but some who had received their primary shots but no booster shots

---

[†]This statement has been qualified since at least one study has shown that a theoretical case can be constructed in which there are no positive externalities to individuals being vaccinated. See Francis, Peter J., "Dynamic Epidemiology and the Market for Vaccinations," *Journal of Public Economics*, 63 (1997): 383–406.

(which are part of the protocol) also became ill. The infected children mostly lived in areas where the public health oversight in schools was largely missing. In parts of inner-city New York, only 50 percent of the children had been vaccinated.[6]

Universal coverage of young children by public programs of inoculation against common childhood diseases is even more unlikely in low-income countries. Even in the case of communicable diseases for which highly effective low-cost vaccines have been developed, governments often fail to purchase or to widely distribute the vaccines. The lack of an effective program of vaccination may be a result of lack of understanding of the positive value of the vaccines, or it may be because there are simply not enough public funds to allocate money even to projects that are recognized to have high value. In some cases where vaccines are available, there is inadequate infrastructure to distribute them throughout various regions, or corruption may cause the distribution system to fail. For instance, low-paid health workers may appropriate the vaccines and sell them on the black market.

Contribution of Economic Epidemiology: Prevalence Elasticity

Economic epidemiology does not automatically assume that more extensive public programs of vaccinations are necessarily optimal. It focuses on the interaction between private behavior and public policy. Although it may be difficult for private markets to achieve total eradication of diseases, public programs to reduce the prevalence of communicable diseases also reduce private incentives to undergo vaccination. Philipson developed the concept of **prevalence elasticity**.* He argues that the private demand for vaccinations may decline or even disappear when the prevalence of a disease has been reduced to some critical level. The hazard rate, which is the "propensity to be infected conditional on not yet being infected," is a function of prevalence. Because people alter their behavior, based on prevalence of a disease, the hazard rate is likely to be a decreasing function of the prevalence of the disease.[7] There will be some equilibrium level of voluntary vaccinations, conditional on the prevalence of the disease.

An implication of the model is that the public policy of subsidizing vaccinations will become ineffective when prevalence falls below the critical level. Since mandatory vaccination programs are generally limited to certain age groups or certain high-risk individuals, the analysis can still be employed where there are targeted mandatory policies. In that case, prevalence elasticity will determine the demand for vaccinations in groups not covered by the mandatory programs.

---

*Prevalence elasticity is the percentage change in demand for vaccinations divided by the percentage change in the prevalence rate of the disease. See Philipson, Tomas, "Economic Epidemiology and Infectious Diseases," in *Handbook of Health Economics*, Vol. 1B, Culyer, Anthony J. and Joseph P. Newhouse, eds. (Amsterdam: Elsevier, 2000), Chap. 33.

A full consideration of the optimal equilibrium level of disease control and eradication must also consider the dynamic welfare effects that involve loss to future generations from the failure to eradicate the disease. The intergenerational effects of communicable diseases are a public good and another source of individual market failure. A rational utility-maximizing model of private behavior may also fail in situations where there is a high degree of imperfect information about the transmission of a communicable disease or the health effects of contracting it.[8] The field of economic epidemiology provides important insights into the limits of the effectiveness of public policy with respect to not only vaccinations but also other forms of prevention of communicable diseases, for instance, campaigns to alter risky behavior such as promoting the use of condoms to prevent the spread of HIV/AIDS.

Emergence of Multiple-Drug-Resistant Diseases (MDRs)

A public goods problem may exist if the treatment of a disease results in mutations that make the original treatment no longer effective. Even proper use of a medication may result in mutations to organisms. However, overuse, underuse, and misuse of antibiotics are major causes of the development of drug-resistant strains of disease. Poor people everywhere in the world are likely to use only part of the prescribed dose of an antibiotic, use outdated leftovers of drugs prescribed for other family members, buy or sell drugs on the black market, or self-medicate in cases of illness. But overuse of antibiotics is also a problem in high-income countries where physicians prescribe antibiotics liberally to people who want the short-run benefits of a rapid recovery. Moreover, the use of high-tech equipment in hospitals can also facilitate the spread of antibiotic-resistant bacteria. For instance in the early 1990s, it was discovered that a new form of bacteria resistant to the only drug known to be effective in the treatment of staph and strep infections was being spread from patient to patient in acute-care hospitals by the use of electronic thermometers, intravenous lines, mechanical ventilators, catheters, and surgical instruments. This resulted in serious outbreaks of these diseases in New York area hospitals and similar outbreaks in London, Sheffield, England, and Italy.[9]

Other examples of diseases in which drug-resistant strains have evolved are leprosy, gonorrhea, malaria, tuberculosis, and diarrhea. These require more expensive new treatments and sometimes none are available at any price. For example, an untreatable form of leprosy has surfaced in Ethiopia.

The monitoring of drug usage has therefore become an international public health concern. The WHO develops protocols, but monitoring drug use is extremely difficult and expensive, Governments of countries that still have strains of a disease which are amenable to conventional treatments are unlikely to legislate that more expensive treatments must be used unless international sanctions are imposed.

Emergence of MDR Tuberculosis (TB) in the United States

Tuberculosis is still a major killer. For many years it was an infectious disease responsible for one of the highest worldwide mortality rates. It is carried airborne and spread through person-to-person contact. TB is one of the chief opportunistic infections associated with HIV, that is, it occurs because HIV-positive individuals have virtually no resistance to it. The HIV-positive population is thus at very high risk of TB-caused death. WHO has referred to TB and HIV as "parallel pandemics."[10]

MDR forms of TB have emerged throughout the world, including the United States and Europe.[11] The U.S. Public Health Service was caught largely unaware of this new problem in the late 1980s. The rate of TB had declined due to the introduction of antibiotics into its treatment. Even though a TB epidemic was raging in Africa, the CDC issued a statement in 1989 proclaiming that the goal of completely eliminating TB from the United States by 2010 was still tenable and that the program was on track.[12] But during the 1990s there were major outbreaks of TB, including multiple-drug-resistant strains, throughout high-population-density areas of the United States.

The reemergence of TB in the United States was related to not only HIV but also rising poverty, homelessness, and an increase in the number of prison inmates. This was a case in which a model of individual utility maximization did not lead to results that were acceptable to the community. Demand for public intervention increased when the disease began to spread to physicians and other health workers and to others outside the homeless and prison inmate population. The federal government increased its TB funding from $17 million in 1991 to $55 million in 1992.[13] Between 1989 and 1994, it spent more than $1 billion attempting to deal with the new strains of TB. National Institutes of Health research budgets for TB increased from $3.5 million in 1991 to $46 million in 1994.[14] Although this expenditure began to make inroads into conquering the epidemic by 1994, as late as 1993, the treatment success rate in the United States was considerably worse than in many very poor Third World countries.

This was largely because the compliance rate of those being treated was so low in the United States. Mozambique, Nicaragua, China, Tanzania, Zululand, and South Africa were all doing a better job of isolating cases of TB and monitoring compliance with respect to medication. In 1991, Christopher Murray, a medical economist at Harvard University, joined with several epidemiologists to perform a cost-effectiveness analysis of TB programs around the world.[15] When the study was completed and submitted to the World Bank, Murray issued the following statement:

There is no country in the developing world that has a treatment compliance as bad as New York City. New York City has around a 10 percent compliance. While India, which is very bad, has 25 percent compliance. China has 80 to 90 percent. Mozambique in a civil war attained 80 percent.[16]

Problems in the Treatment of Tuberculosis in Urban America: A Case Study

The low compliance rate is exemplified by a case history from Dr. Karen Brudney's clinic practice in Lincoln Hospital in the Bronx, New York. A typical client, a 33-year-old male with MDR TB, was hospitalized in 1989 with what was initially diagnosed as pneumonia. After three weeks, the hospital's lab tests revealed that he had an ordinary form of TB. Released from the hospital, he went through more than a year of sporadic, improper use of the two drugs that had been prescribed for daily use. He was no longer monitored by the City Health Department. He simply disappeared. At the end of 1991 he was back in Lincoln Hospital, near death, with a severe case of MDR TB. Discharged in 1992, after three months' hospitalization, he again disappeared. He occasionally showed up for appointments at the clinic, but missed about 75 percent of them. Although he claimed to be living with his mother and siblings, it was discovered that he was moving in and out of several of the city's crowded homeless shelters, still with an active case of MDR TB, in late 1992. He was using a false name so that the New York City Health Department would not be able to track him. This material was gathered in an interview conducted by Dr. Brudney and a social worker when the client showed up at the hospital on a day when he had no appointment. There was little coordination between the city's public health department and the hospital program, and the hospital had no authority to detain and isolate this patient.

Source: Garrett, Laurie, *The Coming Plague: Newly Emerging Diseases in a World Out of Balance* (New York: Farrar, Straus and Giroux, 1994), pp. 516–519.

This example illustrates the negative externalities imposed on a community by infected individuals who have a low level of incentive to be cured. Other countries, such as China, have had better success rates in treating TB because they have been able to impose mandatory isolation on infected individuals and have imposed additional punitive measures on those who do not follow the mandated protocol. The United States has not been particularly aggressive in "taxing" individual behavior that provides negative externalities to communities.

The Case of Malaria

Malaria is another disease that has developed drug-resistant strains. In some regions of Africa, over 90 percent of the population is infected more than once a year. People who survive infancy and early childhood in this environment develop antibodies that protect them later in life. This provides a natural limit to the prevalence of the disease. For others, who encounter malaria mosquitos only intermittently, a very cheap and effective synthetic version of quinine, chloroquinine, has been used throughout the world since 1950. However, the malaria parasite has become resistant to this drug in Southeast Asia and East Africa, and drug-resistant strains of malaria are spreading elsewhere.[17] Slightly more expensive alternative drugs, such as sulfadoxine-pyremethamine, were subsequently developed, but strains of malaria that are resistant to these drugs soon evolved. Subsequently, the Chinese developed an alternative, based on an ancient herbal treatment for malaria, sweet wormwood (*artemisia annua*), artemisinin.

The difficulty for low-income African nations is that artemisinin costs about $2 a treatment, as opposed to $.10 for chloroquinine. They therefore have a tendency to continue to use chloroquinine, although artemisinin is now being used effectively in India, Vietnam, Thailand, and elsewhere. The CDC and WHO are concerned that a mutant strain of malaria will develop which is resistant to this drug as well. This has prompted them to promote the use of a more expensive combination of drugs, ACT, since the disease is not likely to become resistant to all the drugs in the combination. However, both the production and distribution of ACT will probably have to be subsidized if it is to become widely used, since low-income countries cannot provide a market for this drug at current prices. Moreover, research leading to the creation of a malaria vaccine is not likely to take place without subsidies, given the geographic distribution of malarial infection.[18]

Economics of Drug Development for the Treatment of Communicable Diseases

Multinational pharmaceutical firms look to world markets in order to estimate whether they can recoup the R&D costs of new product development. Vaccines, which are one-time-use products, are generally less profitable than drugs for treating on-going disease.[19] There is therefore particularly little incentive to develop vaccines for diseases such as malaria that have been virtually eliminated in high-income countries.

The tendency of private markets to develop drugs only for treatment of diseases that occur in high-income countries is the result of a number of factors: Poor countries have small markets, since the poor cannot afford the new drugs even at greatly discounted prices. If low-income countries' governments are the purchasers, they are also likely to purchase drugs only if low prices can be negotiated. Protection of intellectual property rights (enforceable patent law) makes it possible to price discriminate and charge higher prices in high-income countries. Moreover, poor protection of intellectual property rights in many low-income countries leads to local production of cheaper copies of the on-patent drug.*

---

*Part of the motivation behind the TRIPS agreement of the World Trade Organization was the hope that more stringent enforcement of patent laws in developing nations would stimulate the production of drugs useful to diseases endemic in low-income countries. (See Chapter Eleven for a fuller discussion of patterns of innovation in pharmaceuticals.)

There is likely to be public, as well as private, underinvestment in pharmaceutical R&D projects whose major use is in the low-income countries because governments face free-rider problems in supplying what Michael Kremer calls the global public good of R&D. He makes the case that high-income countries should provide aid to stimulate public R&D in poor countries on the grounds that their welfare will be improved if foreign aid is redirected from goods such as food and roads to health-care-related R&D.[20]

3   Combating the HIV/AIDS Pandemic

Background

The emergence of the human immune deficiency virus (HIV) in the late 1970s, for which there is to date no cure, continues to be a major source of death among prime-age men and women throughout the developing world. The disease has a number of unique characteristics. Unlike many epidemics, it appears not to burn out on its own. In the epidemiology of most diseases, a number of people become partially or totally immune to the disease without any intervention. This appears not to be true with HIV. Moreover, the long asymptomatic period when HIV is dormant in the lymph system heightens the problem of person-to-person infection. In addition, the social stigma attached to the disease has made many governments reluctant to admit that HIV was a problem in their cultures and has made it difficult for public health authorities to engage in active health education programs and to locate infected individuals, even when programs for combating HIV/AIDS are in place. The initial reaction in the 1980s throughout much of the developing world was to insist that HIV/AIDS was a disease of Westerners. Foreign visitors, particularly foreign students, were often subjected to mandatory AIDS testing. This was true in both India and China. A survey conducted in Nigeria in 1987 revealed that 85 percent of the respondents believed that AIDS could only be contracted through having sex with a white man.[21]

As Table 13.3 shows, the incidence of HIV/AIDS is highest in Africa. At the beginning of the twenty-first century, South Africa had the most rapid rate of increase in HIV/AIDS of any country in the world and also the largest number of HIV-positive people.[22] One projection of the effects on overall life expectancy in South Africa forecasted a drop from 65 years (the preepidemic national peak) to 40 years. Life expectancy in Botswana is now 39 years. It has been estimated that it would be 72 years in the absence of AIDS.[23]

The economic, as well as the human, consequences of HIV/AIDS for areas of the world that have a high incidence of the disease are devastating, as productivity and earnings decline due to workers becoming ill, public schools and health centers close for lack of teachers and nurses, and at the same time the costs of treating the sick and caring for orphaned children surge upward.[24] A major problem throughout developing nations is the increasing number of AIDS orphans.

The sheer enormity of the problem is often more than the traditional extended family systems can cope with. One USAID projection forecasts that there will be 7.2 million AIDS orphans generated annually in Africa by 2015.[25]

Attempts have been made to estimate the value of productive lives lost through AIDS. The loss from an AIDS death in Zaire was estimated to equal 19 years of average per capita income and a typical Tanzanian AIDS death involved a loss of 18.3 years of average per capita income.[26] This analysis, carried out in the 1980s, underestimates the current cost, since there have subsequently been increases in macroeconomic costs resulting from the expanding dimensions of the epidemic. These include costs associated with the closing of factories and schools and the lack of family members to provide in-home care for the infected.

Although HIV/AIDS emerged somewhat later in Asia, it is now an increasingly serious problem there as well. The incidence is lower, but the sheer size of the population and the low per capita income in a country such as India make the problem a formidable one. In 2004, India and South Africa were virtually tied in the total number of HIV-positive individuals, which in both countries was only slightly under 5 million. Although the high-income nations have made great advances in treating HIV/AIDS, there is also evidence that infection rates are again rising in North America, Europe, and Australia.[27]

Since combating HIV/AIDS requires allocating resources to reduce the future rate of infection in populations and to provide health care for those already infected, countries are faced with difficult choices between spending money on prevention and treatment. Moreover, they always face the broader choice between allocating health-care budgets to combat other major killers, such as diarrhea and malaria, and allocating it to combat HIV/AIDS. The long-term costs associated with allowing HIV/AIDS to continue to infect ever larger proportions of the population must be compared with the costs of treatment and prevention programs. Most countries with a high incidence of HIV/AIDS have by now concluded that they must devote a major effort to combating HIV/AIDS, although many have been slow to recognize this. The Global Fund, the CDC, UN AIDS, and many other foundations are actively working alongside governments in African nations. Table 13.4 summarizes WHO data on the incidence of HIV/AIDS worldwide and by region in 2001.

A vast amount of statistics on HIV/AIDS is available and a large body of scholarly research is devoted to it. Three excellent sources of current data on HIV/AIDS are available electronically through the UN, the WHO, and the Global Fund to Fight AIDS, Tuberculosis and Malaria.[28] A number of studies have attempted to assess the cost of HIV/AIDS by studying both the macroeconomic effects and the effects of AIDS on local communities.*

---

*A bibliography of scholarly studies focusing on Africa, and in particular on Botswana and South Africa, is provided as an appendix to this chapter.

Table 13.4 Global Incidence of HIV/AIDS in 2001

Total people living with HIV/AIDS:	40	million
Adults	37.2	million
Women	17.6	million
Children under 15	2.7	million
People newly infected in 2001	5	million
Adults	4.3	million
Women	1.8	million
Children under 15	800,000	
AIDS deaths in 2001	3	million
Adults	2.4	million
Children under 15	580,000	
Total number of reported adults and children living with HIV/AIDS by region		
Sub-Saharan Africa	28.1	million
South and Southeast Asia	6.1	million[a]
Latin America	1.4	million
East Europe and Central Asia	1	million
Western Europe	560,000	
North America	940,000	

[a]In India alone there were 4.8 million acknowledged cases of AIDS in 2004.

Source: *AIDS Epidemic Update 2001* (Geneva: UN AIDS/WHO, December 2001).

Botswana's HIV/AIDS Program

Botswana's program is considered a model for other nations with a high incidence of HIV/AIDS. Public health programs directed at HIV/AIDS have been in place since 1987, when screening blood to prevent HIV transmission through transfusions was undertaken. Botswana was the first African nation to adopt a national policy of providing anti-retroviral drugs to all its citizens. Since 2000, a National AIDS Coordinating Agency has coordinated the various programs within the country, including the partnership between the government and the Bill and Melinda Gates Foundation and the Merck Company Foundation. These two foundations are committed to each providing $50 million over a five-year period.[29] In addition, Merck & Co. is donating free anti-retroviral drugs. Botswana also receives help from the U.S. President's Emergency Fund, which funds a collaboration between the CDC and the government of Botswana (the Botusa Project.)[30] The Botswana-Harvard AIDS

(continued)

Institute Partnership runs a training program for health professionals in the country and the Peace Corps has returned to the country.

The multifaceted government program focuses on both prevention and treatment and includes public education programs on radio, TV, and billboards, social marketing of condoms, targeting of high-risk highly mobile populations, prevention of mother-to-child transmission, voluntary testing and counseling, and the national anti-retroviral therapy program (MASA) whose aim is to ultimately reach all infected citizens.

As of May 2004, more than 24,000, of the 110,000 who were deemed capable of being helped, were enrolled in the program. Although this may seem a modest step toward the goal of providing treatment to all of Botswana's HIV-positive citizens, compared with many other African nations, this is a relative success story. The adherence rate to the drug regimen of those enrolled in the programs is 90 to 100 percent. The HIV prevalence rate of pregnant women was reduced from 38.5 percent in 2001 to 35.4 percent in 2002.[31]

Source: Grunwald, M., "A Small Nation's Big Effort Against AIDS," *The Washington Post Foreign Service*, December 2, 2002.

Case Studies of the Cost-Effectiveness of Anti-Retroviral Drugs

Cost-effectiveness analysis has been employed in a number of studies to evaluate alternative anti-retroviral drug programs. These studies help governments make decisions about programs and also help clinicians make treatment decisions in cases where HIV treatments are provided through private markets.

Cost-Effectiveness of Anti-Retroviral Drug Treatment for Pregnant Women in South Africa

Background Although by 2002, approximately 1/9 of the population and 1/4 of the adults in South Africa were HIV-positive, education and treatment programs were delayed, in part because President Thabo Mbeki doubted that HIV caused AIDS. South African public health officials also had reservations about supplying anti-retroviral drugs to AIDS patients. Finally, in December 2003, South Africa announced that the public health sector would begin to provide anti-retroviral drugs to its HIV/AIDS population.[32] The goal is to have 1.2 million South Africans in treatment by 2008. A government task force has estimated that at least 1.7 million lives will be saved between 2003 and 2010. Like Botswana, South Africa has a good deal of international help with its AIDS program. However, South Africa, unlike most other African countries, has a pharmaceutical industry and complex intellectual property laws that some AIDS activists believe impedes the supply of cheaper drugs.*

Pilot Projects Using AZT and Nevirapine In 1998, one provincial government began a pilot project testing pregnant women for HIV and providing the anti-retroviral drug, AZT, and free infant formula (since transmission from mother to child occurs through breast feeding). The national government subsequently introduced pilot projects in selected hospitals using an alternative anti-retroviral drug, Nevirapine. These projects provided experimental data enabling researchers to undertake cost-effectiveness analyses to compare no treatment with drug intervention and to compare the effects of the two alternative retroviral therapies, AZT and Nevirapine.

Results of the research strongly suggested that the South African government could ill afford to do nothing to combat mother-to-child transmission of HIV, on the assumption that it is unacceptable for the government to deny HIV-positive children access to any health care.[33] The study reached this conclusion even when the estimated cost of treating an HIV-positive child excluded costs of medicines used to treat opportunistic infections, transportation of child to health-care centers, and adult time home from work to care for the sick child. The direct costs of treating the infected children are also biased downward since hospitals treating HIV-positive children are already rationing care due to lack of facilities. With respect to alternative drug interventions, AZT was found to be more effective, but Nevirapine has a lower cost per life saved and is easier to administer, since it can be taken in pill form by women before they give birth.[34]

Public health officials decided to begin using Nevirapine. The agency that regulates the use of medicines in South Africa, the Medicines Control Council, temporarily held up the use of Nevirapine until it was forced, by court order, to allow the drug to be administered in 2002.[35] After several years of use, during which time the transmission rate of HIV from mother to infant fell from 20 to 9 percent, the Medicines Control Council has, as of July 2004, rejected the use of Nevirapine, recommending instead a more expensive and complicated treatment regime that is likely to reach fewer people.[36] This decision is widely believed to be counterproductive to achieving the goals of the government's initiative set forth in 2003. It appears to be the result of interaction between politicians and the domestic drug industry.

Canadian Research Study: Relative Cost-Effectiveness of Three Anti-Retroviral Drug Regimes

A large-scale Canadian study of the cost-effectiveness of treatments for HIV/AIDS has investigated the incremental cost-effectiveness of three different composite drug regimens, using a longitudinal cohort of HIV-positive Canadian men.[37] An

---

*Aspen Pharmacare, a South African Company, has made licensing agreements with multinational firms, GlaxoSmith Kline, BristolMyers Squibb, and Boehringer Ingelheim, which allow it to supply a cocktail of anti-retroviral drugs to the South African government.

avowed purpose of the study is to test the incremental effects of newer treatment regimens in order to discover whether it is sensible for developing nations to skip over therapies that are older, less expensive but also less effective, and use the newest combinations of drugs.

Many participants in the study were followed for 13 years. Since there are ethical objections to using less than state-of-the-art treatments or withholding treatment altogether from a control group, this study takes advantage of the advances in drug therapy over the course of the study. Three drug regimes, called ERA I, ERA II, and ERA III, were considered. The treatment drugs include combination of nucleosides with protease inhibitors and nonnucleoside analogues. Using five different estimating models, the study provides robust support for moving directly to the most up-to-date therapy, even though it is more expensive.

The study also compares the cost-effectiveness of the HIV/AIDS regime with funded therapies for the treatment of other diseases in Canada. The incremental cost of the drug combination, ERA III, per life-year gained was estimated to be Canadian $46,971, compared with Canadian $303,201 per life-year gained by the treatment of anaemia in dialysis patients, $46,862 per life-year gained by drug therapy for osteoporosis, or $39,637 per life-year gained by home dialysis. Therefore, using ERA III in the treatment of HIV/AIDS was judged to be well within the acceptable range of public health expenditures in Canada for treatments of individual diseases.

These costs are likely to be regarded as unreasonable in South Africa or Botswana. However, it is also likely that the same drugs can be acquired by African nations at much lower cost.

Summary

Although it was believed in the 1970s that public health programs had nearly eliminated communicable diseases such as measles, chicken pox, mumps, and tuberculosis, a number of diseases, including some that are multiple-drug-resistant, have reemerged in the United States. This fact plus the greater risk of international transmission of diseases has awakened the need to increase funding for vaccination programs that had been greatly cut. However, economic epidemiologists caution against automatically assuming that greater public expenditure on prevention is always optimal. They provide analytical models for evaluating the optimal amounts and types of public health programs. The general conclusion is that public programs continue to be very important when there are significant public goods aspects to the prevention of disease and to the R&D expenditure on drugs to treat them.

In low-income countries struggling to combat an increasing incidence of HIV, public health programs are even more important. International support from high-income countries and from nongovernmental organizations (NGOs) and multinational pharmaceutical companies are also crucial to the success of developing nations' programs to combat HIV/AIDS and other major killers such as malaria and tuberculosis. However, there are still many unanswered questions about which particular treatments for these diseases should receive public funding and support.

4 Demand for Medical Care in Developing Nations: Income and Price Effects

Is Medical Care a Superior Good in Developing Nations?

Medical care is widely believed to be a superior good, that is, one that comprises a higher proportion of higher-income consumers' budgets. A number of studies using cross-country data have found income elasticities greater than +1 for medical care, which lends support to the notion that medical care is a superior good.[38]

Studies have also been conducted using individual household data, and the results are quite different. Income elasticities for medical care on the part of workers in urban China were found to be in the range of +0.65 to +0.82, when location was not taken into account. When province was included as an explanatory variable, the income elasticities fell to within the range of +0.28 to +0.32. Both sets of estimates lie within the range of income elasticity estimates found by researchers who have studied the behavior of households in the United States.[39] The effect of some additional explanatory variables used in the regression analysis indicates a positive wealth effect in the use of medical services in China.

Wealth is often indirectly estimated for households in developing nations by using indicators of the consumption standard. Wealth elasticity coefficients for medical care with respect to household central heating, number of rooms per capita, and availability of indoor toilet and bath facilities were all found to be positive and significant.[40] In summary, the differences between the studies based on macro- and micro-data mirror the results found for the United States. (See Chapter Two.)

Estimates of Price Elasticity of Demand for Medical Care

The relationship between price of medical services and quantity of health care consumed has been investigated for a number of countries.

Experimental Studies

As in studies of the United States and OECD countries, selection bias is always a potential problem. To combat this, experimental strategies were employed that provide approximations to randomized samples.

RAND China Study

The demand for medical care in a number of local districts in rural China was studied.[41] Medical care was provided by doctors on a fee-for-service basis, and coinsurance rates varied by district. Since people were required to use medical facilities within their district, there should be no selection bias unless people choose location of residence on the basis of cost of medical care. This was deemed to be unlikely in this setting. Price elasticity of demand for ambulatory care, estimated using coinsurance rates that varied between 100 and 20 percent, was found to be approximately −0.6. This estimate lies within the range of estimates found in the United States, although it is higher than the estimates based on the RAND Health Insurance Experiment.*

Study of Indonesia

Experimental data were provided when the Indonesian government raised fees in some public clinics but not in others that were similar and frequented by patients of similar socioeconomic backgrounds. Gertler and Molyneaux found price elasticities for services provided by public health clinics for both children and adults to be slightly greater than −1. This study did not provide any estimates for medical care purchased through the private sector.[42]

Price-Elasticity Estimates for Low- and High-Income Households

Studies estimating separate price elasticities of demand for medical care for low- and high-income households have been conducted in urban China, Peru, the Ivory Coast, and Pakistan.

The ranges of price-elasticity estimates obtained from a study by Mocan and colleagues of 6,000 households in 10 provinces in urban China are shown in Table 13.5 below.

Gertler and van der Gaag estimated price elasticities for hospital out-patient services and health clinics in the Ivory Coast. Coefficients were obtained in the range of −0.29 to −0.38 for high-income households and in the range −0.47 to −0.61 for low-income households.

The same researchers estimated price elasticities for the services of private doctors, public clinics, pharmacists, and traditional healers in Peru. The demand

Table 13.5 Price Elasticities for Medical Care in Urban China: Selected Income Deciles

Lowest-income decile	−0.74 to −0.97
Median-income decile	−0.66 to −0.87
Highest-income decile (90th percentile)	−0.55 to −0.80

Source: Derived from regression results presented in Mocan, H. Naci, E. Tekin, and J. S. Zax, *The Demand for Medical Care in Urban China*, NBER Working Paper No. 7673 (Cambridge; MA: National Bureau of Economic Research, 2000).

*The latter yielded price elasticities of approximately −0.2. See Chapter Two.

for all these services was found to be price-inelastic, with estimates ranging from −0.12 (for low-income households' demand for services of private doctors) to −0.76 (for low-income households' demand for health clinic services).[43] Price elasticities of demand for traditional healers were in the middle of this range.

Alderman and Gertler examined the demand for various health-care services for male and female children in high- and low-income families in Pakistan.[44] Estimates of price elasticity of demand were generally higher for low-income families, as was found to be true in studies of urban China and the Ivory Coast. In addition, across income levels, elasticities were lower for private physicians' services than for public clinics or traditional healers. For high-income families there was not much difference between elasticities of demand for medical care for male and female children. But for low-income families, demand elasticity estimates were significantly higher for male than for female children.

Summary and Interpretation of Findings

Throughout the studies, the price-elasticity coefficients were generally found to be lower for private medical services than for public clinics or traditional healers. If private medical services are more likely to be used only for very serious and intractable illnesses, it would make sense that these services would have a lower price elasticity. In other words, medical spending on less serious illnesses might be regarded as discretionary. For less serious illnesses, there are substitutes such as home remedies.

The differences in price elasticities of demand for medical services purchased for male and female children are probably a reflection of lower levels of expenditure on medical care for female children. In that case, medical care for girls is likely to be limited to the more serious illnesses for which home remedies or just waiting and watching are not good substitutes. This interpretation is supported by the fact that significantly lower price-elasticity estimates for medical care for female children were only found for lower-income families.

The studies reviewed provide evidence that the demand for medical care has some similar characteristics worldwide. Income elasticities estimated from individual household data are generally found to be lower than those computed from aggregate country or regional data. The range of price-elasticity coefficients were also similar to those found in studies using U.S. data. Standard assumptions of economic theory seem to hold when the behavior of people in a variety of nations is studied.

Appendix: Bibliography

Economic Consequences of HIV/AIDS in Africa

Ambert, Cecile, "The Economics Impact of HIV/AIDS on the Construction Sector: Supply Side Implications for Housing Policy," *South African Journal of Economics*, 70 (2002): 1235–1261.

Arndt, Channing and J. D. Lewis, "The HIV/AIDS Pandemic in South Africa: Sectoral Impacts and Unemployment," *Journal of International Development*, 13 (2001): 427–449.

————"The Macro Implications of HIV/AIDS in South Africa: A Preliminary Assessment," *South African Journal of Economics*, 68 (2000): 856–887.

Barnett, Tony and Alan Whiteside, "The World Development Report 2000/01: HIV/AIDS Still Not Properly Considered," *Journal of International Development*, 13 (2001): 369–376.

————,"HIV/AIDS and Development: Case Studies and a Conceptual Framework," *European Journal of Development Research*, 11 (1999): 200–234.

Barnett, Tony, et al., "The Social and Economic Impact of HIV/AIDS on Farming Systems and Livelihoods in Rural Africa: Some Experience and Lessons from Uganda, Tanzania, and Zambia," *Journal of International Development*, 7 (1995): 163–176.

Baylies, Carolyn, "The Impact of AIDS on Rural Households in Africa: A Shock Like Any Other?" *Development and Change*, 33 (2002): 611–632.

Bonnel, R., "HIV/AIDS and Economic Growth: A Global Perspective," *South African Journal of Economics*, 68 (2000): 820–855.

Booysen, F. le R., "Financial Responses of Households in the Free State Province to HIV/AIDS-Related Morbidity and Mortality," *South African Journal of Economics*, 70 (2002): 1193–1215.

————, "The Benefits of HIV/AIDS Intervention in the Workplace: A Case Study," *South African Journal of Economic and Management Sciences*, 5 (2002): 180–202.

————, "HIV/AIDS and Poverty: Evidence from the Free State Province," *South African Journal of Economic and Management Sciences*, 6 (2003): 419–438.

————, "Poverty and Health in Southern Africa: Evidence from the Demographic and Health Survey (DHS)," *South African Journal of Economics*, 70 (2002): 391–415.

Bos, Eduard and Rodolfo A. Bulatao, "The Demographic Impact of AIDS in Sub-Saharan Africa: Short and Long-Term Projections," *International Journal of Forecasting*, 8 (1992): 367–384.

Craven, B. M., et al., "Time Consistency and the Development of Vaccines to Treat HIV/AIDS in Africa," *Economics Issues*, 8 (2003): 15–31.

Deininger, Klaus, et al., "AIDS-Induced Orphanhood as a Systematic Shock: Magnitude, Impact, and Program Intervention in Africa," *World Development*, 31 (2003): 1201–1220.

Dickinsen, David, "Managing HIV/AIDS in the South African Workplace: Just Another Duty," *South African Journal of Economic and Management Sciences*, 6 (2003): 25–49.

Dike, Stephen, "Research on the Economic Impact of HIV/AIDS in South Africa," *South African Journal of Economics*, 70 (2002): 1283–1291.

Dixon, Scott, et al., "AIDS and Economic Growth in Africa: A Panel Data Analysis," *Journal of Economic Development*, 13 (2001): 411–426.

———, "HIV/AIDS and Development in Africa," *Journal of International Development*, 13 (2001): 381–389.

Drimie, Scott, "HIV/AIDS and Land: Case Studies from Kenya, Lesotho and South Africa," *Development Southern Africa*, 20 (2003): 647–658.

Ellis, L. L., et al., "The Macro-Economic Impact of HIV/AIDS in South Africa," *Journal of Studies in Economics and Econometrics*, 27 (2003): 1–28.

Fraser, F. K., et al., "The Impact of HIV/AIDS on Small and Medium Enterprises in South Africa," *South African Journal of Economics*, 70 (2002): 1216–1234.

Garnett, Geoff P., et al., "AIDS: The Making of a Development Disaster?" *Journal of International Development*, 13 (2001): 391–409.

Greener, R, et al., "The Impact of HIV/AIDS on Poverty and Inequality in Botswana," *South African Journal of Economics*, 68 (2000): 888–915.

Haacker, Marcus, "The Economic Consequences of HIV/AIDS in Southern Africa," International Monetary Fund Working Paper (Washington, DC: February 2002).

———, "Providing Health Care to HIV Patients in Southern Africa," International Monetary Fund Policy Discussion Paper (Washington, DC: October 2001).

Haddad, Lawrence, and Stuart Gillespie, "Effective Food and Nutrition Policy Responses to HIV/AIDS: What We Know and What We Need to Know," *Journal of International Development*, 13 (2001): 487–511.

Jenkins, Carol and David A. Robalino, *HIV/AIDS in the Middle East and North Africa: The Costs of Inaction*, Orientations in Development Series (Washington, DC: World Bank, 2003).

Kumaranayake, Lilani and Charlotte Watts, "Resource Allocation and Priority Setting of HIV/AIDS Interventions: Addressing the Generalized Epidemic in Sub-Saharan Africa," *Journal of International Development*, 13 (2001): 451–466.

———, "HIV/AIDS Prevention and Care Interventions in Sub-Saharan Africa: An Econometric Analysis of the Costs of Scaling Up," *South African Journal of Economics*, 68 (2000): 1012–1032.

MacFarlan, Maitland and Silvia Sgherri, "The Macroeconomic Impact of HIV/AIDS in Botswana," International Monetary Fund Working Paper WP/01/80 (Washington, DC: June 2001).

Mahadea, D., "Employment and Growth in South Africa: Hope or Despair?" *South African Journal of Economics*, 71 (2003): 21–48.

Morris, C. N. et al., "Economic Impact of HIV Infection in a Cohort of Male Sugar Mill Workers in South Africa," *South African Journal of Economics*, 68 (2000): 933–946.

Nattrass, Nicoll, "Unemployment and AIDS: The Social-Democratic Challenge for South Africa," *Development Southern Africa*, 21 (Special Issue, March 2004): 87–108.

Oni, S. A., et al., "The Economic Impact of HIV/AIDS on Rural Households in Limpopo Province," *South African Journal of Economics*, 70 (2002): 1173–1192.

Samson, Michael J., "HIV/AIDS and Poverty in Households with Children Suffering from Malnutrition: The Role of Social Security in Mount Frere," *South African Journal of Economics*, 70 (2002): 1148–1172.

Schoepf, Brooke G., "Uganda: Lessons for AIDS Control in Africa," *Review of African Political Economy*, 30 (2003): 553–572.

Skordis, Jolene and Nicoll Nattrass, "HIV in South Africa," *Journal of Health Economics*, 21 (2002): 405–421.

———, "Paying to Waste Lives: The Affordability of Reducing Mother-to-Child Transmission of HIV in South Africa," *Journal of Health Economics*, 21 (2002): 405–421.

Stillwaggon, Eileen, "HIV/AIDS in Africa: Fertile Terrain," *Journal of Development Studies*, 38 (2002): 1–22.

World Bank, *Education and HIV/AIDS: A Sourcebook of HIV/AIDS Prevention Programs* (Washington, DC: World Bank, 2004).

Key Concepts

International public good

Economic epidemiology

Prevalence elasticity

Suggested Readings

1. Philipson, Tomas, "Economic Epidemiology and Infectious Diseases," *Handbook of Health Economics*, Vol. 1B, Culyer, Anthony J. and Joseph P. Newhouse, eds. (Amsterdam: Elsevier, 2000), Chap. 33.

2. Kenkel, Donald S., "Prevention," *Handbook of Health Economics*, Vol. 1B, op. cit., Chap. 31.

3. Arrow, Kenneth J., "New Antimalarial Drugs: Biology and Economics Meet," *Finance and Development*, 41 (2004): 20–21.

4. Particularly for students interested in the interaction between public health programs and epidemiology, see Chap. 13 and 14 in Garrett, Laurie, *The Coming Plague: Newly Emerging Diseases in a World Out of Balance* (New York: Farrar, Straus and Giroux, 1994).

Questions for Discussion and Review

1. How does the time horizon affect the cost-benefit analysis of the use of antibiotics in the treatment of communicable diseases?

2. In what sense are vaccinations a public good?

3. What are some of the economic costs of allowing public health department budgets to be slashed?

4. What different calculations may low- versus high-income nations make in looking at the appropriateness of budgeting money for anti-retroviral treatments for HIV/AIDS?

5. Why might a country target pregnant women for HIV/AIDS prevention and treatment programs over other high-risk people? Does this not involve gender discrimination?

6. Is medical care a superior good in most developing nations? Explain, referring to the empirical evidence.

7. Why do you think the price elasticity of demand for private physicians is lower than for public clinics and traditional healers in developing nations?

Resources

[1] The Global Fund, *Fight AIDS, Tuberculosis and Malaria,* http://www.theglobalfund.org/en.

[2] Gersovitz M., "The Economic Control of Infectious Diseases," *Economic Journal,* 114 (2004): 1–27.

[3] Kenkel, D. S., "Prevention," in *Handbook of Health Economics*, Vol. 1B, Culyer, Anthony J. and Joseph P. Newhouse, eds. (Amsterdam: Elsevier, 2000), Chap. 31, pp. 1712–1713.

[4] Philipson, Tomas, "Private Vaccination and Public Health: An Empirical Examination for U.S. Measles," *Journal of Human Resources*, 31 (1996): 611–630.

[5] Garrett, Laurie, *The Coming Plague, Newly Emerging Diseases in a World Out of Balance* (New York: Farrar, Straus and Giroux, 1994), pp. 440–446, 510–512.

[6] Ibid, pp. 510–512.

[7] Philipson, Tomas, *Handbook of Health Economics*, Vol. 1B, Culyer, Anthony J. and Joseph P. Newhouse, eds. (Amsterdam; Elsevier, 2000), pp. 1770–1771.

[8] A very useful discussion is provided in Kenkel, op. cit., pp. 1696 ff.

[9] Garrett (1994), op. cit., pp. 422–424.

[10] Joint Statement of the World Health Organization Tuberculosis and AIDS Programs, 1989.

[11] For a good summary of the economic cost of the disease, see Holger, Sawert, "The Re-Emergence of Tuberculosis and Its Economic Implications," *PharmacoEconomics*, 9 (1996): 379–381.

[12] Rieder, H. L., et al., "Epidemiology of Tuberculosis in the United States," *Epidemiological Review*, 11 (1989): 79–96.

[13] National MDR-TB Task Force, "National Action Plan to Combat Multidrug-Resistant Tuberculosis," U.S. Department of Health and Human Services, Washington, DC, April 1992.

[14] An excellent and very graphic description of problems of identifying and treating TB patients in the United States is provided in Chap. 14, "Thirdworldization," in Garrett (1994), op. cit.

[15] Murray, C., K. Styglo, and A. Rouillon, "Tuberculosis" in *Disease Control Priorities in Developing Countries*, Jamison, D. T. and W. H. Mosley, eds., (New York: Oxford University Press, 1991).

[16] Quoted in Garrett (1994), op. cit., p.527.

[17] Arrow, Kenneth J., "New Antimalarial Drugs: Biology and Economics Meet," *Finance and Development,* 41 (2004): 20–21.

[18] Ibid.

[19] See Kremer, Michael, *Creating Markets for New Vaccines Part I: Rationale* and *Creating Markets for New Vaccines Part II: Design Issues*, NBER Working Papers No. 2216 and 2217 (Cambridge, MA: National Bureau of Economic Research, 2000).

[20] Kremer, Michael, "Pharmaceuticals and the Developing World," *Journal of Economic Perspectives*, 16 (2002), pp. 73–77.

[21] Reported in Soyinka, Wole, "Culture, Memory, and Development" in *Proceedings of an International Conference Held at the World Bank, Washington D.C., April 2 and 3, 1992* (Washington, DC: World Bank, 1994), pp. 201–218.

[22] Skordis, Jolene and Nicoli Nattrass, "Paying to Waste Lives: The Affordability of Reducing Mother-to-Child Transmission of HIV in South Africa," *Journal of Health Economics*, 21 (2002): 405–421.

[23] Arndt, C. and J. D. Lewis, "The Macro Implication of HIV/AIDS in South Africa: A Preliminary Assessment," *South African Journal of Economics*, 68 (2000): 856–885.

[24] Online news report, *New York Daily News*, April 26, 2004.

[25] Center for International Research, *World Population Profile: 1994* (Washington, DC: U.S. Census Bureau, Department of Commerce, 1994).

[26] Over, Mead, et al., "The Direct and Indirect Cost of HIV Infection in Developing Countries: The Cases of Zaire and Tanzania," paper presented at the 4th International Conference on AIDS, Stockholm, June 12–16, 1988.

[27] *AIDS Epidemic Update 2001* (Geneva: UNAIDS/WHO, December 2001).

[28] http://www.UNAIDS.org, http://www.WHO.org, and http://www.theglobalfund.org.

[29] African Comprehensive HIV/AIDS Partnerships, http://www.achap.org/Gates/htm.

[30] National Center for HIV, STD and TB Prevention Global AIDS Program, http://www.cdc.gov/nchstp/od/gap/countries/botswana.htm.

[31] Grunwald, M., "A Small Nation's Big Effort Against AIDS," *The Washington Post Foreign Service*, December 2, 2002.

[32] Marseille, E. and Kahn, J., "Manual for Use of a Cost-Effectiveness Tool for Evaluating Antiretroviral Drug and Substitute Feeding Interventions to Prevent Mother-to-Child Transmission of HIV" (December 1999), available at http://www.unaids.org; and Marseille, E., et al., *Cost Effectiveness of Antiviral Drug Therapy to Reduce Mother-to-Child HIV Transmission in Sub-Saharan Africa* (Amsterdam: Elsevier, BIOBASE, 1998).

[33] Skordis and Nattrass (2002), op. cit., pp. 417–418.

[34] Marseille and Kahn (1999), op. cit.

[35] *British Medical Journal*, 325 (2002): 923.

[36] Lafraniere, Sharon, "South Africa Rejects Use of AIDS Drug for Women," *The New York Times*, July 14, 2004, Section A, p. 11.

[37] Anis, Aslam H. et al., "The Cost-Effectiveness of Antiretroviral Regimens for the Treatment of HIV/AIDS," *PharmacoEconomics*, 18 (2000): 393–404.

[38] For instance, Newhouse, Joseph, "Medical Care Expenditure: A Cross-National Survey," *Journal of Human Resources*, 126 (1977): 115–125; Parkin, D., et al., "Aggregate Health Care Expenditures and National Income: Is Health a Luxury Good?" *Journal of Health Economics*, 6 (1987): 109–127; and Blomquist, A. G. and R. A. L. Carter, "Is Health Care Really a Luxury?" *Journal of Health Economics*, 16 (1997): 207–229.

[39] Mocan, H. Naci, E. Tekin, and J. S. Zax, *The Demand for Medical Care in Urban China*, NBER Working Paper No. 7673 (Cambridge, MA: National Bureau of Economics Research, 2000).

[40] Ibid., p. 21.

[41] Cretin, S., et al., *Modelling the Effect of Insurance in Health Expenditures in the People's Republic of China* (Santa Monica, CA: RAND Corporation, 1988).

[42] Gertler, Paul and Jack Molyneaux, *Experimental Evidence on the Effect of Raising User Fees for Publicly Delivered Health Care Services: Utilization, Health Outcomes and Private Provider Response* (Santa Monica, CA: RAND Corporation, 1997).

[43] Gertler, Paul and Jacques van der Gaag, *The Willingness to Pay for Medical Care: Evidence from Two Developing Countries* (Baltimore, MD: Johns Hopkins University Press, 1990).

[44] Alderman, Harold and Paul Gertler, "Family Resources and Gender Differences in Human Capital Investments: The Demand for Children's Medical Care in Pakistan," In *Intrahousehold Resource Allocation in Developing Countries: Models, Methods, and Policy* (Baltimore MD, and London: Johns Hopkins University Press for the International Food Policy Research Institute, 1997).

CHAPTER FOURTEEN

The Health-Care System of the United States: Where Do We Go Next?

[The] "tiering" of health care is exactly opposite the pattern in the United States, where most people have fairly decent coverage but a large segment has less. In other countries, everybody is guaranteed decent standard coverage, and a few have more. One approach creates a (weak) "safety net" for the poor; the other creates an "escape valve" for the well-to-do.*

1 Introduction

In this chapter we will consider problems of efficiency and access to the health-care system in the United States in the context of rising prices of medical care and health insurance and an increasing number of uninsured Americans. We will consider the virtues and drawbacks of the main proposals for reform of the system.

The fundamental difference between the approach to the provision of health care in the United States and most other industrialized nations is succinctly expressed in the quote by Joseph White given above. The U.S. system is more market-oriented, and insurance coverage is less inclusive. When health insurance is offered to workers as part of their compensation package, it is a trade-off for

---

*White, Joseph, *Competing Solutions: American Health Care Proposals and International Experience* (Washington, DC: Brooking Institution, 1995) p. 6. When White wrote this, the group of leading industrial nations was the G-7. Russia had not yet joined the group that is now known as the G-8. The G-7 nations were the United States, Canada, France, Germany, Great Britain, Italy, and Japan.

higher cash wages or salary, not a "right." In most states, employers are not required to offer health insurance to employees.* Whether they do so depends on
the labor negotiations between workers and employers. As Chapter Twelve has
shown, in other industrialized nations people generally contribute to a system of
social insurance, either through general income taxes or payroll taxes. This is true
in the United States only of the Medicare contribution, although personal income
taxes also support Medicaid, SCHIPS, the National Institutes of Health, and the
health-care infrastructure, including subsidies to hospitals and medical schools.

All societies ration scarce goods. The issue is therefore not rationing versus no
rationing, but what basis should be used to ration access to medical care. A market system relies more heavily on the price mechanism as a rationing device. The
U.S. health-care system is a mixture of a market system and a system in which
services are allocated on other bases. For instance, Medicaid and SCHIP do not
use the price mechanism to allocate health-care services. Medicare relies less on
it, since services are so heavily subsidized.

Demand Versus Need

The greater reliance in the United States on the market and on rationing by price
rather than by government fiat is paralleled by an approach in health-care economics that focuses on supply and demand. The appropriateness of this approach has not gone unquestioned. For example, Robert Evans argues that willingness to pay satisfies neither equity nor efficiency criteria in a market
environment that does not even approximate perfect competition. He also suggests that there is a hidden agenda behind the preference for a market-based allocation of health care that is related to attitudes about income distribution. In
other words, those who do not wish to redistribute income through a system of
social insurance prefer a market-based system. Evans argues for an evidence-
based health-care system that will classify medical treatments in terms of their efficacy and in which treatments that "do no good" will not be provided by anyone
to anybody, even if someone is willing to pay for them.[1] He also argues for a separation between clinical decisions and financial consequences to health-care
providers, pointing to the self-interested behavior of American physicians and
British fundholder physicians during the early 1990s.

Thomas Rice is equally critical of a demand-driven system.[2] He questions the
concept of consumer sovereignty in a situation where demand determines the direction of technology development in medical care. "If tastes are based on past
consumption, then perhaps in demanding things like more medical technology,
patients and their physicians are, in part, wanting what they *got* rather than getting what they *want*."[3]

Rice's and Evans's criticisms rely on assumptions that non-market-based methods can and should be used to prioritize the resources that a society decides to

---

*Hawaii is an example of an exception to this generalization.

devote to health care and to determine the way in which they are distributed among the population. Their approach requires faith that there is a way of determining an objective standard of health "needs" and an appropriate distribution of care. Their points of view are much more representative of European and Canadian political-economic philosophy than of views that still prevail in the United States, although their approach resonates with the views of political reformers who maintain that health care should be a right and not a market good. Their approach to defining the appropriate capacity of the system also resembles those of the health planners and medical professionals that were presented in Chapter Six. Reflecting on this critical point of view provides a good segue into considering reforms of the health-care system that might be undertaken in the United States.

Evaluating "Efficiency Versus Equity"

Critiques of a health-care system usually subject it to two criteria: One concerns its efficiency. Is health care being produced and delivered at as low a cost as possible? The other has to do with fairness or equity. In most economic decisions, there is some degree of trade-off between the two.[4] To use a familiar example, pricing insurance using experience rating is more efficient than broad-based community rating because it relates the marginal cost of insuring an individual to the price of the insurance policy. However, risk sharing through community rating is thought to be more equitable.

In the case of health care, equity and efficiency may also be complementary. It is widely believed that the social costs of health care for the uninsured are higher than if they were insured, given that our society does not generally refuse to provide some medical care to the sick, even if they cannot pay. It is argued that the uninsured do not receive medical care until illnesses are more advanced and that this results in higher treatment costs than if they had access to preventive care or earlier treatment (in spite of the fact that evidence on the cost-effectiveness of preventive care in mixed). Moreover, people without health insurance tend to overuse hospital emergency rooms, which are more expensive than physician office visits for nonemergency services.

This is not a question that need be left to idle speculation. A good deal of research has provided estimates of the incremental costs associated with insuring the uninsured. A 1993 study by Long and Marquis provides an estimate of $28.6 billion (adjusted to 2001 dollars).[5] Adjusting for increases in the number of uninsured between 1993 and 2001 raised the estimate to $35 billion.[6] A more recent study by Miller, Banthin, and Moeller provides 2002 estimates ranging from $44.9 to $57.4 billion, if the spending of the currently uninsured mirrors that of the privately insured. If we assume that health-care utilization and spending are comparable to those of the Medicaid population, the range is from $35.1 to $38.1 billion.[7] Both sets of estimates deduct the value of in-kind uncompensated care that this group would receive if uninsured.[8] A third set of estimates was developed by

Hadley and Holahan using the same data but a different model and set of assumptions. The model estimates spending separately for children and assumes insuring the uninsured raises their spending level to that of the segment of the privately insured population who have incomes no greater than 400 percent of the poverty level. One set of estimates is based on the assumption that the formerly uninsured are provided with the same private insurance coverage as the reference group in the insured population, and another set of estimates is based on the assumption that the uninsured are provided with public insurance (Medicaid or SCHIP). The increase in costs for 2001 was estimated at $33.9 billion for the public option and $68.7 billion for the private insurance option.[9]

The health status of the Community also has public goods aspects since poor health is associated with low labor-force productivity, poverty, and homelessness. Low health status is also associated with increased risks of spreading communicable diseases to other members of the community. The reduction in these indirect social costs that would be accomplished by insuring the uninsured should be subtracted from the increase in direct medical care costs. A full cost analysis of the lack of access to medical care also needs to take account of losses due to shorter lives or a lower quality of remaining life-years (QALYs).

2   The Rising Cost of Medical Care

Increases in Health-Care Costs are an International Problem

David Cutler points out that social insurance systems were originally more concerned with equity and provided most of what people wanted without a great deal of concern with efficiency. Today this is no longer possible.[10] Global budget caps on health-care expenditure put a temporary damper on costs in Canada, Germany, and the United Kingdom in the 1990s, but the international upward trend in costs has resumed. The common problem facing all industrialized nations is how to pay for the level of medical care that their citizens want. Everywhere, given the dramatic improvements in medical technology, people have rising expectations about what can be done to improve their health. The public health care systems are finding it necessary to cut back on coverage by limiting access to technologies, ration services through long waiting periods for nonemergency care, and/or require higher co-payments for services. Given this trend, it is not surprising that surveys reveal satisfaction with health-care systems is much lower in most countries than it was a decade ago.[11]

Technology Change and the Cost of Medical Care

Joseph Newhouse, along with a number of other health economists, has demonstrated that the largest contributor to rising medical costs is the advance in technology. Newhouse also notes that no one wants to buy an insurance policy that only provides 1950s or 1960s health care, even at a heavily discounted price.* In the course of this text, we have seen compelling arguments from David Cutler and his colleagues that the cost of modern medical care is, on the whole, worth it.[12] They do point out that it is nonetheless important to develop strategies to identify particular components of medical care expenditures that have low *marginal* benefits.[13]

Lawrence Baker has estimated the contribution of a number of different medical technologies to the upward trend in the cost of medical care. Free-standing diagnostic imaging appears to be a major contributor. In contrast, greater availability of neonatal intensive care units and technologies associated with cancer treatment do not appear to have been associated with significant increases in health-care costs.[14]

Technological change shifts the "production function for health" in favor of more medical care versus other inputs. This has been the story of health care in America during much of the second half of the twentieth century. Thus, there is no mystery about why the total amount of medical spending is rising. A projection made in 2002 estimated that medical care would absorb 16.8 percent of the U.S. GDP by the year 2010.[15]

If we shift our focus from looking at costs to considering the cost-effectiveness of medical care, abundant evidence has been provided in the previous chapters that treatments for many diseases, most notably heart disease, now cost less per unit of additional healthy life gained than formerly. William Baumol has argued for decades that the allocation of an increasing proportion of the national income to human-capital-intensive services such as education and medical care is an inevitable consequence of cost-saving innovations in agriculture and manufactured goods. He believes that this trend will not lead to a decline in the real standard of living, and argues that it is rational for nations and individuals to spend higher proportions of their budgets on health care, when food, automobiles and the like are, in real terms, cheaper.[16]

The Efficiency Issue: The Role of Market Imperfections

The contribution of market imperfections to the cost of health care has been a perennial concern in economics. Critics have often associated a combination of fee-for-service payment and lack of price competition with monopoly rents to providers. This view was reflected in the 1950s in the work of Milton Friedman and Reuben Kessel and in the 1970s and 1980s in the work of Uwe Reinhardt:

> The allocation of resources in health care is seen to emerge from bargaining over the distribution of economic privilege among members of society. . . .

---

*Offering out-of-date health care would also leave providers and insurers open to malpractice suits: See Newhouse, Joseph P., "Medical Care Costs: How Much Welfare Loss?" *Journal of Economic Perspectives*, 6 (1992): 3–21.

> In return for the much higher allocation of financial resources from American society to American providers of health care collectively, do American patients receive a commensurately superior flow of real health care services [compared with Canadians]?[17]

The health-care market does not consist of small, perfectly competitive firms, subject to long-run zero profit competitive equilibrium. By their very nature, the markets for the goods and services provided by physicians, hospitals, and pharmaceutical companies are at best monopolistically competitive. (See Chapters Six through Eight and Eleven.) Nonetheless, the degree of price competition has increased greatly since Reinhardt's 1987 statement quoted above. Price competition has been introduced largely because of the active role of third-party payers, both private and public. Managed care has provided a mechanism for negotiating fees with hospitals, physicians, and pharmaceutical manufacturers.

Countervailing Power   Here it is useful to employ a concept introduced by John Kenneth Galbraith in the 1950s, **countervailing power.**[18] Galbraith demonstrated that when large buyers and large sellers, each of whom has considerable market power, face off, the result can be similar to the equilibrium that would be achieved in a classically competitive market consisting of many small buyers and sellers. The price competition that emerged in the 1990s in markets for hospital services illustrates this. Negotiations between independent practice associations of physicians (IPAs) and managed care insurers provides another example. The market for health-care services has almost certainly become, on average, more competitive.

To be sure, there are still many examples of monopolies or cartels in the health-care market. In some areas integrated delivery systems owned by one HMO have effective monopoly control, over an area's health services.[19] Antitrust can be used to reduce this kind of monopoly power. However, if antitrust is applied unwisely, it may upset the countervailing power balance and lead to results that are farther away from those that would pertain in conditions of competitive equilibrium.

Imperfect Information

As we have learned, problems associated with imperfect information permeate not only insurance markets but also the provision of health care. Integrated delivery systems may contribute to this since HMO subscribers often have little knowledge of the costs of different services they consume. One way to improve efficiency is for health plans to provide information about the costs of particular services. This is likely to be more helpful in decisions about nonacute care.[20]

Another area of imperfect information that affects both costs and quality of care is the lack of systemization of medical records of patients. Another form of imperfect information is lack of formally articulated instructions from patients about their desires for end-of-life treatment. A not insignificant proportion of the total expenditure on health care in the United States is devoted to keeping very sick terminally ill people alive by artificial means that are frequently counter to their wishes, which can no longer be expressed.[21] In many cases, the treatment is not regarded by the medical profession, members of the family, or most members of our society as humane.

Other Types of Inefficiency

Inefficiency in Insurance Markets

Processing of Claims Advocates of a Canadian-type single-payer system often point to the costs of administering an insurance system that consists of insurance contracts with such a confusing array of technicalities about coverage. A system of multiple insurers is administratively more expensive than a single-payer system. However, it provides more choice to consumers (as well as more problems of adverse selection). There is no simple answer to whether streamlining and standardizing insurance coverage, which would require additional regulatory costs and limit consumers' options, would bring about a net improvement in welfare.

Inefficiency Associated with Low Deductibles A lower deductible on an insurance policy is inefficient when its marginal cost is greater than the marginal benefit of additional coverage. The load or loading fee is a much higher proportion of the insurance premium in low deductible policies. This is one of the reasons why some economists have advocated a combination of high-deductible insurance policies (usually called catastrophic insurance coverage) and personal medical savings accounts.[22] Individual medical savings accounts will be discussed later in this chapter.

Experience Versus Community Rating Revisited Experience rating is a well-known form of achieving greater efficiency in insurance markets. Price discrimination based on differences in the costs of insuring different individuals promotes efficiency in that it relates marginal cost and price. It is common practice in the automobile insurance market. Experience rating also removes the incentive for "cherry picking" or "cream skimming," the practice whereby insurance companies select out the healthier clients.*

The argument for community rating is that risk sharing among members of the community is more equitable. It is thought to be unfair to charge people more for insurance because they experience unavoidable bouts of illness or deterioration

---

*Allowing exclusion of coverage for preexisting conditions is another possible way of achieving efficiency. People may have no insurance coverage rather than partial coverage because of the inability of insurance companies to exclude certain preexisting conditions. However, public policy is strongly opposed to allowing exclusion of preexisting conditions.

of health. Since the purpose of insurance is to pool risks, experience rating, if carried to an extreme, undermines the goal of insurance.

Inefficiency Resulting from Medical Malpractice Law

As noted in Chapter Seven, there is considerable evidence that medical malpractice law in many states does not promote higher-quality medical care, but contributes substantially to the costs of medical practice and encourages the practice of defensive medicine.

Short Menu of Recommendations for Improving the Efficiency of the U.S. Health-Care System

The following list of recommendations, some of which are already taking place, do not require a major overhaul of the U.S. health-care system. They are possible ways of improving its efficiency. As you read through this section, see if you can add to this short list!

■ **Reduce Medical Errors through System Reform** Critics maintain that there are few financial incentives for hospitals and integrated health-care delivery systems to reorganize so as to reduce medical (iatrogenic) errors by monitoring overuse or misuse of medical treatments.[23] Drawing on the familiar analogy with the American auto industry, critics have suggested that the absence of competition of the kind Toyota provided for Detroit auto makers has resulted in lack of quality improvements in medicine.[24] Physician groups within leading schools of public health have, however, been devoting considerable effort to designing ways of reorganizing clinical settings so as to provide more fail-safe checks on potential medical errors. Their point of view is that human error is inevitable. Failure to disclose it is promoted by fears of individual tort liability. If the system could provide more checks so that errors could be detected before damage is done to patients, and if the institutions, not the individuals, were the focus of responsibility for medical errors, the organization of operating rooms, intensive care units, and so on could be improved so as to greatly reduce medical errors.[25]

■ **Make Better Use of Information Technology** Information technology can be used in a variety of ways to improve health-care systems. These include compilation of patients' medical records, monitoring of safety procedures in clinical settings, and dissemination of information to doctors about new technologies and bio-pharmaceutical products.

It is technically possible to have computerized records of patients' medical histories available on line to patients, with password protection of the kind that is used for computerized financial information. Concerns about privacy and reluctance of the medical profession to "tool up" to provide this kind of record-keeping have so far prevented this system from being employed.[26] However, this would both reduce unnecessary duplication in testing and reduce medical errors that result from providers undertaking treatment with lack of information about a patient's medication and general health history.

■ **Employ Health-Care Provider Report Cards** In both the private and public sectors, there are strong advocates of reporting systems that provide consumers with statistics on treatment outcomes. Some medical delivery systems, health associations, and government agencies have been established to perform this kind of monitoring. The Centers for Medicare and Medicaid Services are working on developing more programs in this area.

Such programs may appear to have no downside, but critics of this innovation argue that it can lead to providers attempting to avoid treating the most difficult cases or even to the falsifying of records. Any system of reporting health outcomes of treatments must be carefully designed to adjust for severity of illness of the patient pool treated.

A program that has served as a model is the Cardiac Surgery Reporting System of New York. It has collected and published hospital and surgeon data on adjusted death rates following coronary artery bypass graft surgery since 1989. It is operated by the New York State Health Department and is guided by a multidisciplinary advisory committee. It has been effective in causing cardiac units to restrict operating privileges of surgeons whose patients have high mortality rates. Since this reporting system was instituted, New York has been found to have the lowest risk-adjusted mortality rates following CABG surgery and the most rapid rate of decline in mortality rates following cardiac surgery.[27]

■ **Continue Medical Malpractice Tort Reform** As noted in Chapter Seven, many states have already engaged in legal reforms affecting medical malpractice law. Reforms that appear to have reduced the extent of the practice of defensive medicine include limiting the proportion of damage awards that attorneys can claim as fees, paying damages over the life time of the injured rather than in one lump sum, and establishing state wide pools to pay for serious iatrogenic injuries even when they are not the result of negligence or incompetence.

■ **Implement Strategies for Promoting Healthier Lifestyles** One reason why the aggregate cost of health care is higher in the United States than in many other countries is that Americans are, on average, less healthy. The proportion of low-birth-weight babies is much higher than in many comparable societies. The rate of obesity is higher. For the elderly, most of the medical expenditure is on circulatory disorders and cancers. This country has relatively high rates of heart disease and cerebrovascular disease. On an optimistic note, death rates from these diseases have fallen by 50 to 60 percent since the 1960s.* Campaigns to improve health through better diet and more exercise could further reduce the incidence of disease and therefore reduce medical expenditures.

Healthier lifestyles might also be encouraged by giving insurance discounts for healthy behavior. However, this kind of price discrimination is very difficult to

---

*This is not true of cancer treatment for the elderly where the mortality rates have not improved significantly.

implement in a system that is dominated by group insurance, where community rating is applied over the group.*

■ **Encourage Written Instructions for End-of-Life Treatment** If it became routine practice for adults to establish health-care powers of attorney combined with written instructions for end-of-life treatment, this could reduce the per capita cost of medical care as well as provide utility to patients and their families.†

■ **Revive and Expand the Role of Public Health** Chapter Thirteen provided dramatic examples of the inadequacy of the U.S. public health system. For example, the United States has failed to maintain vaccination programs for children at the level once achieved in this country. The private market has failed to provide enough flu vaccine in 2004, and the public sector has not been able to obtain an adequate supply. Moreover, the emergence of multiple-disease-resistant strains of communicable diseases such as tuberculosis requires a major public health effort. Prevention programs need to be in place, infected individuals need to be located, treated, and monitored. The research at the CDC needs to be maintained or expanded. The possibility of international crises such as the SARS scare in 2002 and 2003 and threats of bioterrorism provide additional reasons for enhancing public health in the United States.

Greater use of public health nurses and paramedical workers could raise the level of health in underserved communities and provide savings, by reducing the use of hospital emergency rooms. This is one lesson to be learned from the developing nations, where health workers are widely used to promote community health.

3   Access to Health Care: Alternative Plans for Universal Health-Care Coverage

Background

In January 2004, the prestigious Institute of Medicine announced its goal of universal health insurance coverage for all Americans by 2010.[28] For the majority of Americans, the fact that approximately 16 percent of their fellow citizens lack health insurance coverage is seen as a significant social problem. Some view it as

---

*Just as drivers with good records and those who take defensive driving courses receive discounts on automobile insurance, so individuals who can be shown to be non-smokers, non-substance abusers, and participants in activities such as cardiovascular fitness programs could be given discounts on health insurance premiums. Programs would need to be designed carefully so as not to be discriminatory against individuals whose health status is not the result of voluntary behavior. Would this lead us into experience rating on the part of insurers? This would be a danger unless the plan were carefully constructed to give points for healthy lifestyle rather than health status. This type of program would be difficult to monitor.

†However, given technological changes in medical science, it becomes increasingly difficult to specify what constitutes irreversible medical states.

a problem because they believe that cost shifting results in their paying higher prices for their own medical services. Others focus more on the indirect social costs of the uninsured. Still others are primarily concerned with equity in itself, viewing access to a standard level of health care as a right to which all members of the community are entitled, regardless of their ability to pay. There appears to be more public concern with the problem now that the proportion of American workers who do not have health insurance coverage has increased. Lack of access to health insurance is no longer seen as just a problem of the indigent. If it becomes the public will to provide health insurance coverage to all citizens and/or residents, there are three main types of plans that are viable options for accomplishing this at the national level. There is also the possibility of expanding state initiatives.

State Initiatives

Canadian Medicare evolved from provincial-level initiatives. At the present time, some states have gone a long way toward achieving universal health insurance coverage. Given that states already are the administrators of programs which receive federal funding, such as Medicaid and SCHIP, the expansion of social programs to universal coverage may be achieved more easily at the state level. However, a barrier to this goal is the **Employment Retirement Income Security Act of 1974 (ERISA)**. It constrains the states' ability to require employment-based health insurance coverage by removing their jurisdiction over employers' health plans. Nonetheless, a number of states have significantly extended coverage.

Hawaii: An Example of a State-Level Employer-Mandated Health Insurance Program

A functioning system using **mandated employer contributions** to health insurance exists in Hawaii. Close to 90 percent of the residents of Hawaii are covered by health insurance. In 2002 its uninsured rate was 11.4 percent.[29] The move toward universal health insurance coverage began with the Hawaii Prepaid Health Care Act (PHCA). Under this plan, all employers were required to provide insurance to their workers. Although it has been hampered somewhat in its plans for expansion, the plan received an exemption from ERISA when it was enacted in 1975. PHCA evolved into the State Health Insurance Program of Hawaii, SHIP, that mandated a standard minimum universal benefit insurance package. The public plan covered all who were not covered by Medicaid or Medicare at their place of employment. In 1989, Hawaii QUEST absorbed SHIP. QUEST originally enrolled all whose income did not exceed 300 percent of the national poverty level. The means test for eligibility has since been scaled back to 200 percent of the poverty level. Participants contribute to QUEST on an income-based sliding scale. HMOs and other insurance companies compete for QUEST contracts. The Hawaiian insurance market is dominated by Blue-Cross Blue-Shield and Kaiser

Permanente, which makes the plan easier to administer than if there were a more fragmented insurance market.

Would this type of plan work in other states? There are unique aspects of Hawaii that may contribute to the plan's success. Under the plantation system, the foundation of the state's economy, employers provided health care for their workers. The Hawaiian climate and lifestyle are quite healthy, and therefore this system may be more affordable than it would be in certain industrial states on the mainland. Another factor that makes the employer-mandated coverage more viable in Hawaii is its geographical isolation. This reduces the probability of an employer-mandated insurance plan leading to the out migration of jobs.

Massachusetts

A referendum for universal health insurance coverage was defeated by a narrow margin in 2000 in Massachusetts.[30] However, in 1997, Massachusetts had created a program called MassHealth. MassHealth offers eligibility to the disabled, it extends coverage beyond the Medicaid guidelines to more pregnant women and infants, to children and parents who would be ineligible for SCHIP, and it provides emergency services for low-income persons who are not eligible for other social programs. The program receives funds from both Medicaid and SCHIP.

Massachusetts has achieved an uninsured rate approximately equal to Hawaii's, approximately 11.5 percent, although the program is less extensive than Hawaii's. The low uninsured rate is attributable, in part, to the high rate of Massachusetts citizens who have private employee-based group insurance.

Minnesota

Minnesota has achieved an impressive uninsured rate of 8.8 percent.[31] Minnesota has a lower-income population than Massachusetts, with over 20 percent of its citizens having household incomes that are less than 200 percent of the poverty level. It has supplemented its Medicaid funds with a plan called MinnesotaCare. The goal of the plan is to gradually cover all low- and moderate-income families. To maximize the benefit of its Medicaid budget, it has created insurance purchasing pools for county, town, and school district employees and families and extended membership in the pools to groups of pregnant women and children with incomes up to 300 percent of the poverty level. MinnesotaCare is financed from a mix of federal, state, county, and private dollars. The latter are contributions in the form of means-adjusted co-payments charged to participants in the program. The high rate of coverage in Minnesota is also aided by the high rate of employment-based private insurance coverage.

Oregon

Although Oregon's Medicaid program has received a lot of attention over the years because of its innovative experiments using cost-effectiveness analysis and its goal of providing health insurance to all low-income households, Oregon has not been very successful in achieving a low rate of uninsured. Its rate of uninsured is approximately equal to the national average. The state failed to receive an exemption from ERISA to implement its plan for mandated employer provision of health insurance for all workers. The uninsured rate was 16.4 percent in 2002.[32]

Tennessee

About 40 percent of Tennessee's households have incomes that are less than 200 percent of the poverty level. As discussed in Chapter Four, the state broadened its insurance coverage significantly by reforming its Medicaid program in 1994, creating TennCare. When TennCare was first adopted, the uninsured rate of 13.2 dropped by almost 50 percent. Tennessee's program is well designed and ambitious. It requires those who are covered by public insurance to enroll in HMOs. However, its low average household income and limited Medicaid funds constrict its ability to cover all the eligible households in the state. Its uninsured rate was 12.0 percent in 2002 and has risen substantially since then.

The states that have been the most successful in achieving low rates of uninsured are those that have high levels of employment, high levels of employment-based insurance coverage, and relatively lower proportions of poverty- and near-poverty-level households.

National Option 1: National Health Insurance: Expanding Medicare

Proponents of a national health insurance system have usually looked to Canadian Medicare as a model. This type of social health insurance system avoids the administrative complexity of having many separate insurance companies. It also removes the potential advantages of competition among insurers. We have a model in the United States in the original Medicare program for the elderly.*

Proposals have been made that involve gradually expanding Medicare by including more people at both ends of the age distribution. The expansion could begin by covering all young children and by reducing the age of eligibility for older people, for instance, by instituting a program in which they would be allowed to buy into this social insurance program. The Institute of Medicine's version of this option eliminates Medicaid and SCHIP and absorbs current Medicare recipients into the new program.[33]

The financing of Medicare through a payroll tax is already strained and will become more problematic with the aging of the population. A transition could be made to financing the program by means of income taxes rather than payroll taxes. This would not be easy to implement but would be preferable on both equity and efficiency grounds. Payroll taxes tend to be regressive since they exclude nonlabor income. They also involve questionable intergenerational income

---

*However, Medicare has evolved from a single-payer system into one that uses private insurance companies. This will be true for the new Medicare Prescription drug option as well.

transfers. In addition, without raising payroll taxes to levels that would be politically unviable and damaging to labor markets, the future base of workers will not be able to support the large pool of retired. Using very conservative assumptions about increases in utilization of medical care, Martin Feldstein has predicted a Medicare payroll tax of 14 percent of total wages by 2070 if the current system is maintained.[34]

Feldstein is a well-known advocate of using individual retirement **medical savings accounts** as a way of preserving the solvency of the Medicare program.[35] A combination of catastrophic health insurance coverage and individual medical savings accounts could be incorporated into a national social insurance system. Each individual could be covered from birth by a publicly funded catastrophic insurance plan, and families could be given direct subsidies or tax advantages to establish medical savings accounts. The system could be financed out of general income tax revenues or payroll taxes.* The medical savings accounts could be investment accounts similar to 401-K or 403-B type pension plans. These savings accounts could be used either to pay out-of-pocket for medical expenses below the catastrophic level or to buy more comprehensive health insurance. The balance in the account would be invested and would accumulate throughout life until used.

The substitution of individual medical savings accounts for comprehensive insurance coverage loses the advantage of risk sharing among people but retains inter-temporal smoothing of risk. Eichner, McClellan and Wise, who have analyzed the pattern of spending and saving within medical savings accounts over the life cycle, estimate that 80 percent of workers will have retained over 50 percent of their accumulated medical savings account balances when they reach retirement age and that only 5 percent will have retained less than 20 percent at this time.[36] They conclude that medical savings accounts typically involve enough inter-temporal risk smoothing to be viable.

Some of the problems that are associated with third-party payment tend to be addressed by a system in which people elect to pay more of their medical care expenses out of their own savings accounts.[37] Consumers of medical care will tend to be more sensitive to what they are getting per dollar of expenditure. The option of individual medical savings accounts may, however, result in higher premiums for those who choose to buy comprehensive policies, if adverse selection has a significant impact. The probable unintended consequence will be that an ever higher proportion of those who choose comprehensive insurance policies will be high-risk individuals. In extremis, this will create a "death spiral" and comprehensive health insurance will become a rarity. The coupling of individual medical savings accounts with public catastrophic insurance would tend to offset this.

*Feldstein has estimated that a combination of catastrophic coverage and individual health savings accounts, invested over the life of the individual, could cover the cost of Medicare through the year 2070 by imposing only a 1.4 percent payroll tax. Feldstein (1999) op. cit.

Singapore has established a social insurance program which employs individual medical savings accounts. Its experience is instructive.[38]

Singapore's Medisave Program

Singapore's use of medical savings accounts in its Medisave program provides a cautionary tale. The government sponsored health insurance program involves high deductibles and exclusion of most out-of-hospital expenses. The plan, which was intended to force consumers to be efficient in their use of health care, has resulted in extremely unequal access to health care, with poor, low-wage workers and people with serious chronic illness having little access. Moreover, the scheme has apparently not reduced the rate of inflation in health care expenditure since providers compete on the basis of quality (best physicians, most advanced technology, etc.) Market power seems to be heavily loaded onto the supply side rather than the consumer side.

National Option 2: Mandated Employer-Provided Health Insurance

A second way of instituting universal health-care coverage would be to have it centered on required contributions from employers. In this type of plan, employers are required either to provide health insurance for their employees or contribute to a fund that does. This has been called the "pay or play" model. Those who are unemployed, not in the labor force, or self-employed could be required to contribute to the system. Low-income individuals and families could receive refundable tax credits to pay for their contributions to the system. A refundable tax credit is one in which the government provides a cash payment if the credit is greater than the individual's tax bill. Federal subsidies to employers of low-wage workers have been suggested to help enable this type of plan. Contributions from the retired could also be based on means if the current Medicare system were phased out.

The mandated employer contribution could take many forms, including the provision of individual medical savings accounts. One study has concluded that medical savings accounts could be an important way for small businesses, who find it hard to purchase group insurance, to provide health-care coverage to their workers.[39]

Mandated employer contributions might be the easiest form of universal health insurance to implement since most private health insurance currently is provided through the workplace. However, programs that are employment-based bring with them a unique set of problems. As the labor market evolves from the old model of long-term full-time employment at the same firm to more nontraditional employment and part-time and short-term contractual work, employment-based plans are less likely to be successful. Furthermore, changes in family structure and in the labor-force participation of spouses make employment-based insurance less appropriate. Negative employment effects of mandated employer contributions must also be considered.[40]

National Option 3: Mandated Individual Insurance

Requiring individuals to have insurance coverage is not an unknown phenomenon. In most states, those who drive cars are required to have automobile liability insurance. A universal health insurance system built on **mandated individual coverage** was proposed by Pauly, Danzon, Feldstein, and Hoff in 1991.[41] In their proposal, everyone would be required to have a basic level of health insurance. Low-income individuals and families would receive refundable tax credits that would be progressively reduced as income rises. An individual mandate avoids the negative effects on the labor market of a mandated employment-based program. Like the employer mandate, this type of plan usually retains the private insurance market and managed care options. Given the difficulties associated with the individual and small group insurance market, this third option is likely to be the hardest to implement unless it differs little in practice from the current system, where most people tend to be insured through their place of employment or through social programs such as Medicare, Medicaid and/or SCHIP.

How Does Managed Competition Fit into the Picture?

Managed competition is not a type of health insurance plan. It is a way of organizing health-care markets.[42] Managed competition employs large buying alliances that can consist of firms, unions, or other conglomerates of citizens brought together for the purpose of buying health insurance efficiently. The alliances could be incorporated into both the employment-based and mandated individual coverage social insurance options. This model makes use of the idea of countervailing power. Competing buying groups face off against competing insurance companies.

An equitable system of mandated individual insurance coverage would probably require the development of some form of broad-based consumer buying groups, since the small group and individual insurance market often provides few options and higher prices than those available in the group insurance market. Buying alliances would also be useful for small businesses and the self-employed if universal health-care coverage were to be achieved through mandated employment-related insurance.

Summary

The proportion of GDP devoted to health care in the United States and other high-income countries is likely to continue to rise with improving medical technology, the shifting age distribution of the population, increases in longevity, and the fact that health care tends to be a "superior good." The rhetoric that treats health-care price inflation as a cause for alarm is familiar. However, if cost-effectiveness is taken into consideration, the trend in health-care costs is much less alarming.

Although there are many types of market imperfections in the production and distribution of health care, the rising cost of medical care does not at present appear to be primarily the result of market failure. Market imperfections in the production and delivery of health care have been somewhat offset by the countervailing power of large third-party buyers.

Technology, rather than market failure, appears to be the main cause of the increase in the cost of medical care. Countries that have succeeded in controlling medical-care costs to a greater extent than the United State have done so largely through direct price controls and/or limiting the diffusion of technology. Both of these cost-containment measures have negative dynamic effects on the quality of health care in that they tend to slow the rate of innovation. The negative effects of these cost-containment measures would be greater in the United States than in many other countries because U.S. companies lead in the innovation of new medical technology. However, there are a number of inefficiencies in the system that we should be able to overcome, with the help of the high level of information technology available. Programs to improve the overall health status of Americans could also reduce the proportion of GDP devoted to medical care.

Most people believe that universal access to a basic level of health insurance coverage, regardless of income or employment status, is an important goal. The United States has not succeeded in reaching this goal, although some states have succeeded in attaining uninsured rates of under 10 percent. There are three main types of programs that could be implemented to provide universal health insurance coverage at the national level: a single-payer system, an employer-mandate plus public programs to cover the nonemployed and the retired, and a system mandating that individuals have health insurance coverage. No one of the three options is completely trouble-free. As Mark Pauly has noted, there are only choices between imperfect market solutions and imperfect governmental programs.[43] Extending insurance coverage to the approximately 44 million uninsured Americans will involve additional costs. Estimates range from about $34 to $69 billion, measured in 2002 dollars.

Key Concepts

Countervailing power

Employment Retirement Income Security Act of 1974 (ERISA)

Mandated employer contributions

Medical savings accounts

Mandated individual coverage

Suggested Readings

1. Wagstaff, Adam, and Eddy Van Doorslaer, "Equity in Health Care Finance and Delivery," in *Handbook of Health Economics*, Vol. 1B, Culyer, Anthony J., and Joseph P. Newhouse, eds. (Amsterdam: Elsevier, 2000) Chap. 34.

2. Williams, Alan, and Richard Cookson, "Equity in Health," *Handbook of Health Economics*, Vol. 1B, op. cit., Chap. 35.

3. Cutler, David M., "Equality, Efficiency, and Market Fundamentals: The Dynamics of International Medical Care Reform," *Journal of Economic Literature*, XL (2002): 881–906.

4. Drake, David F., *Reforming the Health Care Market: An Interpretive Economic History* (Washington, DC: Georgetown University Press, 1994). This provides a nice counterbalance in the form of a negative criticism of high-tech medicine in the United States.

5. Newhouse, Joseph P., *Pricing the Priceless: A Health Care Conundrum* (Cambridge, MA: MIT Press, 2002).

6. Peterson, Mark A., ed. *Healthy Markets? The New Competition in Health Care* (Durham, NC: Duke University Press, 1998).

7. Institute of Medicine, *Hidden Costs, Value Lost: Uninsurance in America* (Washington, DC: The National Academies Press, 2003).

8. ———, *Insuring America's Health: Principles and Recommendations* (Washington, DC: The National Academies Press, 2004).

Questions for Discussion and Review

1. Approximately how much would it cost to insure the currently uninsured? (Give a range of estimates.) Explain what costs you are including in and excluding from these estimates.

2. What are some of the obstacles to state initiatives to provide universal health insurance coverage?

3. What are the main options available for establishing a universal health-care coverage system?

4. What are the pros and cons of individual medical savings accounts?

5. What are the problems associated with retaining a payroll-tax-based Medicare system?

6. It has been said that employment-based health insurance is obsolete. Do you agree? Give an argument on each side of this question.

Resources

[1] A very succinct presentation of Evan's point of view is found in Evans, Robert G., "Going for the Gold: The Redistributive Agenda Behind Market-Based Health Care Reform," in *Healthy Markets: The New Competition in Health Care*, Peterson, Mark A. ed. (Durham, NC: Duke University Press, 1998), pp. 61–103.

[2] Rice, Thomas, "Can Markets Give Us the Health System We Want?" in *Heathy Markets, The New Competition in Health Care*, Peterson, Mark A. ed. (Durham, NC: Duke University Press, 1998), pp. 27–65.

[3] Ibid., p. 43.

[4] The classic statement of this position was provided by Arthur Okun in *Equality and Efficiency: The Big Tradeoff* (Washington, DC: Brookings Institution, 1975).

[5] Long, Stephen H. and M. Susan Marquis, "The Uninsured 'Access Gap' and the Cost of Universal Coverage," *Health Affairs*, 13 (1994): 211–220.

[6] Adjustments made by Institute of Medicine (IOM), Committee on the Consequences of Uninsurance. *Hidden Costs, Value Lost* (Washington, DC: National Academies Press, 2003), p. 96.

[7] Miller, G. Edward, Jessica S. Banthin, and John F. Moeller, *Covering the Uninsured: Estimates of the Impact on Total Health Expenditures 2002* (Rockville, MD: Agency for Healthcare Research and Quality, 2003).

[8] Ibid, p. 99.

[9] Hadley, Jack and John Holahan, "Covering the Uninsured: How Much Would It Cost?" *Health Affairs* (Forthcoming).

[10] An excellent review article is Cutler, David M., "Equality, Efficiency, and Market Fundamentals: The Dynamics of International Medical Care Reform," *Journal of Economic Literature*, XL (2002): 881–906.

[11] See Blendon, Robert J., et al., "Inequities in Health Care: A Five-Country Survey," *Health Affairs*, 21 (2002): 182–191 and Donelan, Karen, et al., "The Cost of Health System Change: Public Discontent in Five Nations," *Health Affairs*, 18 (1999): 206–216.

[12] Cutler, David M. and Elizabeth Richardson, "Your Money and Your Life: The Value of Health and What Affects It," in *Frontiers in Health Policy Research*, Garber, Alan M. ed. (Cambridge, MA: MIT Press, 1999).

[13] Ibid., p. 100.

[14] On the other hand, the price of an MRI treatment was found to be, on average, lower where there is greater availability of equipment. See Baker, Lawrence, et al., "The Relationship Between Technology Availability and Health Care Spending," *Health Affairs* (Web exclusive, Project HOPE—The People-to-People Health Foundation, Inc., 2003), p. 5.

[15] Heffler, Stephen, et al., "Health Spending Projections for 2001–2011: The Latest Outlook," *Health Affairs*, 21 (2002): 207–218.

[16] Baumol, William, J., "Social Wants and the Dismal Science: The Curious Case of the Climbing Costs of Health and Teaching," Working Paper, C.V. Starr Center for Applied Economics, New York University (May 1993).

[17] Reinhardt, Uwe E., "Resource Allocation in Health Care: The Allocation of Lifestyles to Providers," *Millbank Quarterly*, 65 (1987): 153–176.

[18] Galbraith, J. K., *American Capitalism: The Concept of Countervailing Power* (Boston: Houghton Mifflin, 1956).

[19] See for example, Greenberg, Warren, "Marshfield Clinic, Physician Networks, and the Exercise of Monopoly Power," *Health Services Research*, 33 Part 2 (1998): 1461–1476.

[20] Baker, et al., (2003) op. cit.

[21] See discussions in Cutler, David M. and Ellen Meara, "The Medical Costs of the Young and Old: A Forty Year Perspective," in *Frontiers in the Economics of Aging: NBER Project Report* (Chicago: University of Chicago Press, 1998) 215–242 and Jones, Charles I., *Why Have Health Care Expenditures as a Share of GDP Risen So Much?* NBER Working Paper No. 9325 (Cambridge, MA: National Bureau of Economic Research, 2002).

[22] Eichner, M. J., M. McClellan, and D. A. Wise, "Insurance or Self-Insurance?: Variation, Persistance, and Individual Health Accounts," in National Bureau of Economics Research Project Report Series, Wise, David A., ed. *Advances in the Economics of Aging* (Chicago: University of Chicago Press, 1996); Feldstein, Martin, *Prefunding Medicare*, NBER Working Paper No. 6917 (Cambridge, MA: National Bureau of Economic Research, 1999); and Jensen, Gail A., "Making Room for Medical Savings Accounts in the U.S. Health Care System," in *American Health Care: Government, Market Processes and the Public Interest* (New Brunswick, NJ: Transaction Press, 2000), 119–143.

[23] A good overview is presented in Becher, Elise, C. and Mark R. Chassin, "Improving the Quality of Health Care: Who Will Lead?" *Health Affairs*, 20 (2001): 164–179.

[24] Coye, Molly Joel, "No Toyotas in Health Care: Why Medical Care has Not Evolved to Meet Patients' Needs," *Health Affairs*, 20 (2001): 44–56.

[25] See, for instance, Weiner, Bryan J., et al., "Promoting Clinical Involvement in Hospital Quality Improvement Efforts: The Effects of Top Management, Board, and Physician Leadership," *Health Services Research*, 32 (1997): 491–510.

[26] A persuasive argument for the benefits of this is provided in Clinton, Hillary Rodham, "Now Can We Talk About Medical Care?" *New York Times Sunday Magazine*, April 18, 2004, pp. 26–31, 56.

[27] Becher and Chassin, op. cit., p. 175.

[28] UPA Press release, January 14, 2004, referring to the publication of *Insuring America's Health: Principles and Recommendations* by the Institute of Medicine (IOM) Committee on the Consequences of Uninsurance (Washington, DC: National Academies Press, 2004).

[29] Committee on the Consequences of Uninsurance (2004) op. cit., p. 98.

[30] Ibid., see description of this program, pp. 98–99.

[31] Ibid., p. 90.

[32] Ibid., p. 91.

[33] See Committee on the Consequences of Uninsurance (2004) Chap. 5.

[34] Feldstein (1999), op. cit.

[35] Feldstein, Martin, "A New Approach to National Health Insurance," *The Public Interest*, 23 (1971): 93–105. He suggests a social catastrophic or "major risk" insurance that would have a deductible set at 10 percent of family income.

[36] Eichner, et al., (1996), op. cit.

[37] Pauly, Mark V., et al., "What Would Happen If Large Firms Offered MSAs?" *Health Affairs*, 19 (2000): 165–172.

[38] Hsaio, William C., "Medical Savings Accounts: Lessons from Singapore," *Health Affairs*, 14 (1995): 260–266 and Hsaio, "Behind the Ideology and Theory: What Is the Empirical Evidence for Medical Savings Accounts? Commentary," *Journal of Health Politics, Policy, and Law*, 26 (2001): 733–737.

[39] Goldman, D., P. J. L. Buchanan, and E. B. Keeler, "Simulating the Impact of Medical Savings Accounts on Small Business," *Health Services Research*, 35 (2000): 53–75.

[40] See discussion of the German health care system in Chapter Twelve and Amelung, Volker, Sherry Glied, and Angelina Topan, "Health Care and the Labor Market: Learning from the German Experience," *Journal of Health Politics, Policy, and Law*, 28 (2003): 693–714.

[41] Pauly, M., et al., "How Can We Get Responsible National Health Insurance?" *American Enterprise*, 3 (1992): 60–69.

[42] A summary of this model is provided in Enthoven, A. C., "The History and Principles of Managed Competition," *Health Affairs*, 10 (1993): 24–48.

[43] Pauly, M., "What Does Economics Have to Say About Health Policy Anyway?" in *Healthy Markets? The New Competition in Health Care*, Peterson, M. A. ed. (Durham, NC: Duke University Press, 1998), p. 73.

Brief Review of Economic Concepts and Tools of Analysis

1 Model of an Economy

Closed Economy

A closed economy is one that does not engage in trade with other countries in the world. There are therefore no exports or imports. In the simplified economy depicted in Figure A1.1, firms receive flows of workers from households. Workers, in turn, receive payments (income) that flow to the household sector. The household uses its income to purchase goods and services. This leads to a flow of payments to firms in return for a flow of goods. Households provide savings that can be used to purchase goods in a future time period. Firms can borrow this money and use it for investment. Taxes paid to the government can be thought of as *involuntary saving*. In return, the government provides some goods and services. Figure A1.1 embodies a number of simplifying assumptions. For instance, households are treated as engaging only in consumption and saving.

Open Economy

An open economy is one that engages in international trade. There are flows of goods and services and flows of inputs into production, labor and capital, between countries. The health-care sector of the economy cannot be adequately

Figure A1.1

A Simplified Closed
Economy

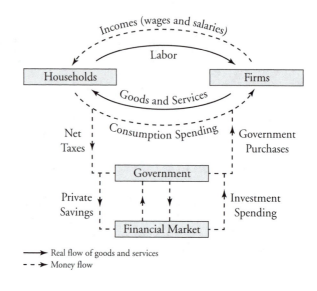

> Real flow of goods and services
> - - ➤ Money flow

described without considering imports and exports. For example, the United States exports technology, pharmaceuticals, and medical devices. Imports include physicians, nurses, and other medical personnel as well as pharmaceuticals and technology.

2   Opportunity Cost

When a society's resources are fully employed, it can only produce more of one good if it sacrifices some of another. In the short run, the endowment of resources is fixed. Any economic choice involves an opportunity cost. Opportunity cost is defined as the *cost of the foregone opportunity*. Individuals as well as societies constantly face opportunity costs. If you spend an evening going to a movie, you sacrifice time that could have been used for something else (studying economics) plus the money used to purchase the ticket. If we look at opportunity cost in the context of health care, triage decisions in an emergency room are revealed to be economic decisions.

Economics considers both the opportunity cost and the direct cost when measuring the total cost of any undertaking. The total cost of attending medical school includes both the tuition and fees (the direct costs) and the loss of income resulting from the inability to work at a full-time job during the years of study (the opportunity cost). A full consideration of costs should also include nonpecuniary as well as monetary costs. Whenever possible, we try to find monetary equivalents for nonpecuniary costs. An example of a nonpecuniary cost is the disutility of working at a job that is boring, stressful, or dangerous. For someone who will only work under stressful conditions if she receives a pay differential of $20,000 per year, $20,000 is the monetary value of the stress factor in her job. Extra combat pay in the military is another example of compensation for a nonpecuniary cost, the danger of being on the battlefield.

3 Who Are the Main Actors in the Economy?

Households or *families* are the units that make decisions about private consumption. Governments also purchase goods and services. Households and governments also make decisions about saving and investing. One form of investment made by both households and governments is investment in human capital, which includes investment in education and health.

Firms, and in the case of public goods, *governments*, make decisions about what to produce, how much to produce, how to produce it, and what prices to charge for the goods and services produced. In the context of health care, firms are hospitals, laboratories, physician and therapist practices, and suppliers of medical devices and pharmaceuticals. In the case of health care, the government plays an important role as a regulator as well as a producer and purchaser of services.

The Consumer

Utility Maximization

Individual consumers are considered to be rational if they make choices so as to obtain the most utility (satisfaction) from a given set of resources. Satisfaction or utility depends on tastes or preferences.

Given a fixed income, or budget constraint, a consumer will only be able to have more of one good if less is purchased of some other good(s). A consumer will continue to substitute between available goods until the extra satisfaction or utility *per dollar spent* on the last unit is equal for all goods purchased. Economic models assume that, in general, the utility of an additional unit of a good or service tends to decline as more of that good, relative to other goods, is added to the "consumption basket." This tendency is known as *diminishing marginal utility.* It can also be thought of as the *diminishing marginal rate of substitution.* If X and Y are the two goods in the economic system, as more X is acquired relative to Y, a person will be willing to exchange more X for a unit of Y.

Curve U in Figure A1.2 shows all the combinations of goods X and Y that will provide equal satisfaction or utility to a person. U is called an *indifference curve* since it traces out all the combinations between which an individual is indifferent. (Note that indifference in this context does not mean lack of interest.) The assumption of diminishing marginal utility or diminishing marginal rate of substitution explains why U in Figure A1.2 is a curve that is drawn convex to the origin rather than as a straight line.

BB is a *budget line* showing the various combinations of goods X and Y that can be purchased from a given income (the budget constraint), when prices of X

Figure A1.2

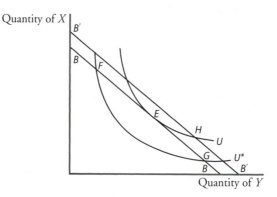

and Y have been specified. A consumer is maximizing the utility at point E because E shows the only combination of goods X and Y providing a utility level equal to U that can be purchased with income level, BB. F is an attainable combination of goods, but it represents a lower level of satisfaction or utility U*. Every point on U* is less desirable to the consumer than any point on U. The combination of goods attainable at point H provides the same level of satisfaction as those at E, but costs more. This is shown by its location on the higher budget line, B'B'. Test your understanding of this diagram by describing point G in Figure A1.2.

If the price of one of the goods increases, this will change the slope of the budget line. This is depicted in Figure A1.3. as a shift in the budget line from BB to B'B. In this case, the consumer will purchase relatively more of good Y (shown as a move from E_1 to E_2) when X becomes more expensive.

Figure A1.3

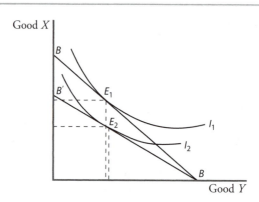

Demand

Demand refers to the amount of a good or service that an individual consumer or group of consumers will be willing to purchase at a given price. The relationship between price and quantity can only be isolated if the other factors influencing demand are held constant. These other factors include income, tastes or preferences, prices of related goods (both substitutes and complements), and expectations about the future. The phrase "other things being equal" or its Latin equivalent, *ceteris paribus*, is used as shorthand for this list of other variables.

The inverse relationship between price and quantity is depicted in the familiar downward-sloping demand curve, an example of which is shown in Figure A1.4. This diagram graphically represents the law of demand, according to which "*ceteris paribus*, more is demanded at a lower price." An individual's demand curve is made up of points, each of which is derived from one of the points E_1 or E_2 in Figure A1.3. A consumer with a given set of tastes and a given income who knows the prices of all allergy medications will have the following demand curve for the allergy medicine, NeverSneeze. The demand curve shows the *maximum amounts of a good or service that individual(s) are willing to purchase at given prices.*

Figure A1.4

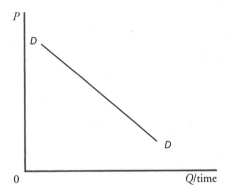

By historical convention, price is represented on the vertical axis and the flow of quantity (per day, week, month, etc.) is represented on the horizontal axis. The tendency for demand curves to be downward-sloping is explained by the concept of diminishing marginal utility. For instance, Jim takes an antiinflammatory pill only once a day, even though more frequent use is safe and provides a higher comfort level. If the price of the pill decreases, he will take it more than once a day.

Market demand curves are constructed by adding individual demand curves horizontally. Although we cannot add up indifference curves for different people, we can add individual demand curves since the latter represent a relationship between measurable prices and quantities rather than a relationship between quantities and a subjective measure, utility.

The Firm

Firms are the legal and economic units that make decisions about production. Standard economic models assume that the goal of a firm is to maximize profit. Total profit is the difference between total revenue and total cost. Therefore, firms also want to minimize cost by being as efficient as possible.

Production Functions

The formal relationship between inputs used to produce output and the resulting quantity of output is called a *production function*. If there are two inputs, capital k and labor ℓ, then the functional relationship can be expressed as follows:

$$\text{Output} = f(k, \ell)$$

The production function is conditional on technology. An improvement in technology occurs when more output can be produced with the same or fewer inputs.

The Short Versus the Long Run The extent to which inputs into a firm's production function can be varied depends on the time period under consideration. The longer the time period is, the more inputs that can be varied. For instance, hours of labor, amount of raw materials, and amount of energy (coal, gas, or electricity) are usually considered to be variable inputs in the short run, whereas plant size and technology are usually considered fixed in the short run, but variable in the long run. Time in this context is "logical time" rather than real time, measured as a particular number of days, weeks, or years. In the short run, the *extra* output resulting from adding an *extra* unit of a variable input (the *marginal product*) will tend to decline as the firm expands production, since it cannot increase the amounts of fixed inputs used. This tendency is called *diminishing returns*. In the long run, all inputs are considered to be variable and production is no longer subject to diminishing returns.

Decreasing, Increasing, and Constant Returns to Scale In the long run, firms may still find that when they change their scale of operation, the relationship between inputs and outputs is not constant:

1. If when all inputs are doubled, holding factor proportions constant, the resulting output is less than doubled, we have *decreasing returns to scale*, also called *dis-economies of scale*.
2. If when all inputs are doubled, the output more than doubles, we have *increasing returns to scale*, also known as *economies of scale*.
3. If when all inputs are doubled, the output exactly doubles, we have *constant returns to scale*.

Figure A1.5

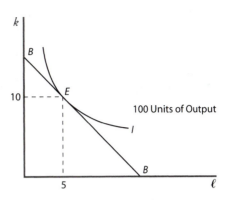

Curve *I* in Figure A1.5 is called an *isoquant.* It shows the different combinations of inputs *k* and *ℓ* that will produce a given level of output, in this case 100 units. Once the production function has been specified, if the prices of the inputs are known, the cost of any level of output can be determined. The *isocost* or budget line, *BB*, shows the combinations of inputs that the firm can purchase for a given cost. The point of tangency between the highest isoquant and the lowest budget line shows the cheapest combination of inputs that will yield a given level of output. Point *E* in Figure A1.5 is a point of *productive efficiency.*

Note the analogy between the point of tangency between an isoquant and an isocost curve and the point of tangency between an indifference curve and a budget line. Both are points of maximization. The consumer is maximizing utility relative to income and the firm is maximizing output relative to expenditure. The shape of a consumer's indifference curve depends on his or her tastes or preferences. The shape of a firm's isoquant curve depends on technology.

Costs

Firms need to know the total cost of production, the *average cost* or cost per unit (AC) and the *marginal cost* (MC), which is the extra cost of producing an extra unit.

Supply Curve Supply refers to the quantity of a good that a firm or group of firms (the industry) will be willing to produce and sell (bring to the market) at given prices. Supply conditions can only be observed if variations in price and quantity can be isolated. Other factors that must be held constant in order to isolate the relationship between price and quantity are the prices of inputs and the technology, in other words, the factors that affect the cost of production.

Supply curves show the maximum amounts of a good that a firm (or all the firms in the market) is willing to sell at given prices. The supply curve can be

Figure A1.6

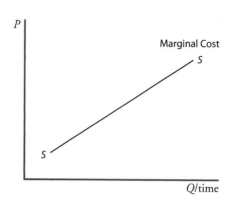

thought of as a *marginal cost curve*, since no firm will be willing to produce and sell an additional unit for less than the cost of producing that unit.

Short-run supply curves, such as the one shown in Figure A1.6, are typically upward-sloping because of diminishing returns. In the longer run, a firm may also have an upward-sloping supply curve if the production function is characterized by decreasing returns to scale. Firms must consider their marginal costs when they are making decisions about how much to produce and sell. For instance, a physician in private practice will consider marginal cost (compared with the marginal return) in the decision of whether or not to hold more office hours. What will be the extra cost of employing more hours of nurses and receptionists? What is the extra cost of the physician's own time?

Average Cost Curves A firm looks at average cost (cost per unit) when deciding whether to stay in business. In the short run, firms can continue to operate only if they are able to sell their goods at a price that covers their *average variable cost* (AVC). Variable costs include day-to-day operating costs such as employee wages, utility bills, costs of raw materials, and interest on any financial capital used.

From a longer-run point of view, a firm must be able sell its product at a price that at least covers its *average total cost* (ATC), which includes the short-run variable costs plus depreciation or replacement value of capital (plant and equipment and any financial capital used) and any costs of research and development. The latter are a major component of cost in companies developing pharmaceutical products. Since all costs are variable in the long run, the long-run average total cost curve (LATC) is often referred to as the long-run average cost curve (LAC).

Small competitive firms tend to have average costs that first fall and then rise, in other words, the cost curves tend to be U-shaped. For all firms the longer the time period under consideration is, the flatter the average cost

Figure A1.7

Long- and Short-Run
Average Costs

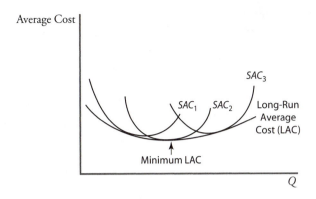

curves become, since in the long run the firm can substitute away from inputs that cause costs to rise. The relationship between long- and short-run average cost curves is shown in Figure A1.7.

4   Equilibrium

In economics, the most common use of the term "equilibrium" is with respect to demand and supply in competitive markets.* When the maximum quantity that consumers are willing to purchase at a given price just equals the maximum quantity that the producers are willing to sell at that price, the market clears. This is called equilibrium. It is shown as point E in Figure A1.8. It is the point where supply and demand intersect. The equilibrium price is P_E. The equilibrium quantity is Q_E. All the product brought to market sells; thus, producers are not building up inventory, and there are no consumers left queuing up to buy goods that are not available at the prices they are willing to pay. If there were either an excess supply or an excess demand, the price would adjust until equilibrium was reached. If there were an excess demand, some consumers would offer to pay more than the going price. If there were an excess supply, firms would offer their product at less than the going price.

Equilibrium is a concept that entered economics from the world of physics. It can be thought of as a condition when demand and supply are in balance. This balance will be tipped if one or more of the factors that is being held constant changes. There will be a shift in the demand if tastes (or incomes) of consumers change. For example, this might happen if the dissemination of information

---

*A competitive market consists of large numbers of sellers and large numbers of buyers, no one of whom has enough market power to alter the price.

Figure A1.8

Market Equilibrium

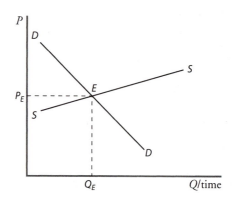

about the health hazards of smoking caused the taste for cigarettes to decline. Figure A1.9 shows a shift in demand, to a new equilibrium at E_1. The shift in demand results in a *change in the quantity supplied*, but not a shift in the supply curve.

The supply curve will shift if there is a change in technology or in the price of one or more inputs. If there is a failure of the tobacco crop, this will shift the supply curve to the left in Figure A1.9. This will result in a new equilibrium E_2, and a *change in quantity demanded.*

One of the problems that researchers face is the possibility that both demand and supply may shift during the course of their study. Since all that is observable in most situations is the equilibrium price at specific points in time, it is not known whether demand shifted, supply shifted, or both shifted. This uncertainty is known as the *identification problem.* It requires painstaking econometric analysis to sort out what has, in fact, happened.

Figure A1.9

Demand and Supply of Cigarettes

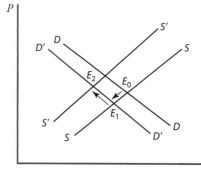

Before leaving this brief discussion of equilibrium, we should note that the equilibria shown in Figures A1.8 and A1.9 will only be reached in competitive markets. In Section 6 that follows, models of perfect competition, monopoly, monopolistic competition, and oligopoly will be distinguished.

5   Elasticity Concepts

Price Elasticity of Demand (or Supply)

These are measures of the degree of responsiveness of the consumer (or producer) to price changes. Price elasticity of demand (or supply) measures changes along the demand (or supply) curve. It is defined as the

$$\frac{\% \text{ change in quantity of } X \text{ demanded (or supplied)}}{\% \text{ change in price of } X}$$

that is,

$$\frac{\% \; \Delta Q_x}{\% \; \Delta P_x}$$

The elasticity coefficient is a ratio between two percentage changes. The coefficient is therefore independent of the units of measurement. Elasticity coefficients range in value from 0 to plus or minus infinity. If the coefficient of price elasticity of demand or supply equals 0, demand (supply) is described as *completely inelastic*. The resulting demand or supply curve will be a vertical line because a change in price results in *no* change in the quantity demanded (supplied).

An example of a price-inelastic demand is that of a person with acute appendicitis deciding to have an appendectomy. If the individual decides to have the operation and does not even consider the price, and will never have more than one operation even if the price of appendectomies falls, the coefficient of price elasticity of demand is equal to 0.

If the coefficient of price elasticity of demand (or supply) is infinite, that is, perfectly elastic, the curve will be a horizontal line. A demand curve will be infinitely price-elastic if there are perfect substitutes for the good or service. A supply curve will be infinitely elastic if the cost of each extra unit of output is constant. In that case, the marginal cost and average cost curves will be equal to each other.

When defining the degree of price elasticity of demand and supply, we use absolute values. The absolute value of a number is its value ignoring the positive or negative sign. If the absolute value of the coefficient is <1, the demand (or supply) is said to be price-inelastic. If the absolute value of the elasticity coefficient is equal to 1, this is called *unitary elasticity.*

In the case of unitary price elasticity, the percentage change in quantity just equals the percentage change in the price. When a demand curve has unitary price elasticity, total expenditure by consumers is constant along the demand curve and total revenue received by the seller is also constant along the demand curve. This is because of the inverse relationship between price and quantity.*

Other elasticity concepts that are frequently used are:

Cross-Price Elasticity of Demand

This measures the degree to which the quantity demanded of a good X is related to the price of another good Y. It is defined as the

$$\frac{\% \text{ change in quantity of } X \text{ demanded}}{\% \text{ change in price of } Y}$$

If the coefficient of cross-price elasticity of demand is negative, this provides indirect evidence that the goods are complements. If the sign of the coefficient is positive, this is evidence consistent with the notion that the goods are substitutes.

Income Elasticity

This measures the response in quantity of a good consumed to a change in income. It is defined as the

$$\frac{\% \text{ change in quantity of } X \text{ demanded}}{\% \text{ change in income}}$$

A good that has a positive income elasticity coefficient, with a value >0 and <1, is called a *normal good*. Goods with negative income elasticity coefficients are called *inferior goods*, since less is consumed when income rises. Goods with income elasticity coefficients that are both positive and >1 are called *superior goods*. The latter are goods that comprise higher proportions of the consumer budget as income rises. Superior goods are sometimes equated with luxuries, but this may be misleading. If bone marrow transplants for people in advanced stages of cancer have income elasticities >1, we would not tend to characterize these operations as luxuries.

Income and Substitution Effects

Much of economic analysis is concerned with isolating income and substitution effects. Some examples may make the distinction between these two effects clearer. We are dealing with the *substitution effect* if we study the effect of a price change on the amount of physician visits that someone will make *when his or her income does not change*. If insurance covers 80 percent of the physician's fee, someone may have an annual physical checkup, whereas that same individual will not do so if he or she has to pay the full price. The price elasticity of demand for annual physical exams is much higher than the price elasticity for in-hospital service. The price elasticity of well-baby visits to pediatricians is also found to be much higher than for many other types of physician services.

---

*This case illustrates that elasticity and slope are not the same thing. A demand curve with unitary elasticity is one in which ($p_i \times q_i$) is constant. It is represented graphically by a rectangular hyperbola. A demand curve with a constant slope would be a straight line.

Figure A1.10

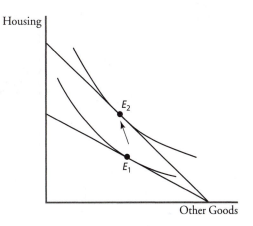

If instead we ask how the quantity of a medication taken will be altered if the patient has an increase in income and the price of the drug is held constant, we are isolating the income effect. For example, someone may be more likely to fill a perscription if he or she gets a salary increase, or the amount of that person's Social Security check increases, even when the price of the prescription drug does not change.

A price change in a good that represents a significant part of a family's budget may involve an important income effect as well as a substitution effect, if the income considered is "real income." Real income is often defined in relationship to a cost-of-living index. If you can purchase the same basket of goods, you are equally well off. In more theoretical terms, real income is constant when the level of utility provided is constant.

Consider the following example. Rent represents about a quarter of a certain family's budget. The family moves to a new community in which the cost of housing is 40 percent lower. If other prices are roughly constant and the family income does not change, the family is now better off and can have better housing and/or more other goods. In Figure A1.10, this is shown as a move to a higher indifference curve. The reduction in rent entails both a substitution and an income effect, shown as a move from E_1 to E_2 in Figure A1.10.

6   Market Structure

Perfect Competition

Perfect competition exists when no one buyer or seller is large enough, that is, has enough market power, to affect price by his or her own actions. A perfectly competitive firm is one that produces a good or service for which there are perfect substitutes (in the eyes of the consumers). This means that no consumer will

Figure A1.11

A Perfectly
Competitive Firm

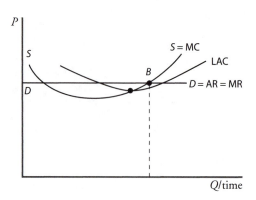

pay more than the going market price to buy the firm's product. It also means that a firm has no incentive to lower its price below the going market price, because it can sell as much as it chooses to produce at the existing market price. That is why it is said that perfectly competitive firms are "price takers." The demand curve for a perfectly competitive firm's product is a horizontal line, and the coefficient of price elasticity of demand has a value of infinity. This demand curve is *completely price elastic*.

The typical average cost curve for a perfectly competitive firm is U-shaped, with average cost first falling and then rising. This means that the firm is limited in size since the technology it uses entails marginal and average costs that rise as more is produced. For a perfectly competitive firm, costs begin to rise when the firm is relatively small compared with the capacity of the market to absorb the product it is producing. A large number of firms will compete in this type of market, and no one firm will dominate the market.

A perfectly competitive firm will produce a quantity shown at point B in Figure A1.11. It will not produce and sell more than this amount because if it did so, the marginal cost would exceed the price. At B, $P = MC$ with $MC > P$, if the firm expands production and sells more than the amount shown at B.

When the firm considers whether it should start up or remain in business, it needs to consider its average costs. In the short run, the price it can get for its product must at least cover its average variable costs. In the long run, it must at least cover its average total costs; otherwise, it will be losing money.

Long-Run Competitive Equilibrium

Since firms in perfectly competitive markets are small relative to market size, it is relatively easy for new firms to enter the market. As long as profits are being made by the typical firm in the market, new firms will have an incentive to enter the market. As groups of new firms enter the market, the price of the good or

Figure A1.12

A Firm in Long-run
Competitive
Equilibrium

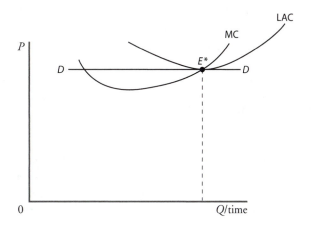

service falls, since supply increases relative to demand. This can be thought of as each small firm being faced with its own demand curve shifting downward.

Eventually, price will fall to the point where it just equals long-run average cost for the typical firm. This is shown as point E^* in Figure A1.12. Here, the price equals the long-run average cost (LAC). This is the point where, on balance, new firms will no longer choose to enter this market since the firms that are already in the market are now just breaking even, that is, earning no profits. This situation is called *long-run perfectly competitive equilibrium.* In long-run perfectly competitive equilibrium, the typical firm is producing at a capacity where average cost is at its minimum. The firm is therefore operating at its most efficient capacity level.

What Does Break-Even, or the Zero Profit Point, Mean to the Firm?

Why would a firm which is making no profit stay in business?. To answer this, we have to return to the concept of economic cost. If a firm is covering its long-run total costs, it is not only covering its operating expenses, but also is putting aside some money for the replacement of its plant and equipment and covering the opportunity cost of the capital it is using and the opportunity cost of the time its owners devote to running the business. This means that it would not be more profitable for the owners to liquidate the firm and become employees of some other firm or to take their capital and invest it elsewhere.

Monopoly

When considering alternative market structures, monopoly is at the opposite end of the spectrum from perfect competition. A monopoly exists when one firm is the whole industry. The monopoly firm produces and sells a product for which there is no close substitute. The demand curve facing the monopolist is the market demand for the good. This is not quite as cut-and-dried a definition as might appear at first glance, for the question remains, what is an industry? The simple answer is that it is all of the firms producing the same product. However, two or more commodities that do not appear to be the same good may nonetheless be close substitutes in the eyes of the consumers. For instance, the services of a chiropractor may be substitutes for those of an orthopedist, a masseuse, or a pain-relieving drug.

A firm may be a monopoly in one geographical area, but not in a wider region. When we study the hospital market, we learn that it is necessary to define both the relevant geographic and product markets. How far will people travel to use a particular hospital? It depends on the range of services offered and whether there are close substitutes for specialized services closer at hand.

Economists, and also the courts dealing with antitrust cases, often use the concept of cross-price elasticity of demand to measure whether a firm has monopoly power in supplying a goal or service in a given market. (See the definition on p. 326.) Microsoft used this concept in antitrust proceedings to argue that Netscape's browser is a close substitute for its Internet Explorer. If the coefficient of cross-price elasticity of demand for a good is positive and of large enough magnitude to be of some consequence, the firm probably does not have effective monopoly power.

Monopolists are faced with downward-sloping demand curves. Unlike perfectly competitive firms, the monopolist has control over both the quantity it produces and the price at which it sells its product. The monopolist will set the amount it produces and the price it charges so as to maximize profit. This occurs at (P_m, Q_m) in Figure A1.13.

Figure A1.13 includes a marginal revenue (MR) curve as well as a demand curve. Total revenue (TR) from selling any given quantity is the price charged times the quantity sold, that is, $P \times Q = TR$. Therefore, $TR/Q = P$. Total revenue divided by quantity is by definition average revenue (AR). Therefore, price is by definition average revenue. The demand curve is the schedule showing the amounts of average revenue that the firm will receive from selling different quantities of its product. There is a general arithmetic rule that when an average curve is declining, the marginal curve falls below it. Therefore, when a demand curve is downward-sloping, the marginal revenue curve falls below it and has a steeper slope. A profit-maximizing monopoly firm will not produce a quantity determined by the intersection of its demand and supply curves, but will instead produce where marginal revenue is equal to marginal cost.

To illustrate, consider this example. A firm produces 10 units of a good and can sell them at a price of $10 each. Total revenue will be $100. Now the firm considers selling 11 units. Demand information indicates that the firm can sell 11 units only if it lowers its price to $9.50. How much will the firm make if it sells 11 units? Its revenue will be $104.50 The *marginal revenue* from selling the 11th unit is therefore only $4.50 even though the price or average revenue is $9.50. Marginal revenue is less than price because the

Figure A1.13

A Monopoly

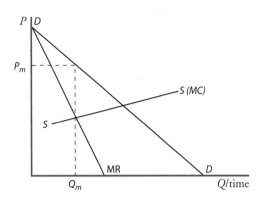

firm has had to reduce the price by $.50 on each of the first 10 units in order to sell the 11th unit. Since the profit-maximizing firm wants to produce only up to the point where the net incremental revenue from the last unit sold is greater than or equal to the cost of that unit, the firm will produce the 11th unit only if marginal cost is less than or equal to $4.50.

Since demand curves provide the firm with information about the highest price that consumers are willing to pay for any given quantity of its product, a firm will always set its price by referring to the demand curve, once it has determined the best quantity to produce. In Figure A1.13 the profit-maximizing monopoly firm produces a quantity Q_m determined by the intersection of the MR and MC curves and charges a price of P_m.

The monopolist is not using a different rule of behavior from the perfectly competitive firm. Perfect competition is the special case in which average revenue, that is, price, equals marginal revenue (AR = MR), since the competitive firm is able to sell as much as it wishes at the going market price and therefore has a horizontal line for a demand curve. In that special case, price is equal to MR. When price does not change with quantity sold, the extra revenue received (MR) is just equal to the price of each additional unit sold. The general rule for any firm that wants to maximize profits is *produce up to the quantity where MC = MR on the last unit produced, assuming that MC > MR at larger quantities of output.*

Price-Discriminating Monopolies

Theoretically, a firm could make even more profit if it could charge different prices to different consumers. Monopolies are able to do so under some circumstances. In order to price-discriminate, it is necessary for the firm to identify segments of the market for its product, differentiated by price elasticities of demand, and to prevent consumers from reselling the good. When these conditions hold, the firm maximizes profits by equating MC with MR in each of the submarkets, segmented by elasticity of demand. The relationship between price (average revenue) and MR is

$$MR = P(1 - 1/\eta)$$

where MR = marginal revenue, P = price, and η = price elasticity of demand. Profit maximization is achieved by setting

$$MC = MR_a = MR_b$$

which is equivalent to

$$MC = P_a(1 - 1/\eta_a) = P_b(1 - 1/\eta_b)$$

Higher prices will therefore be charged in that segment of the market characterized by the lower price elasticity of demand.

Price discrimination is not uncommon in markets for health care and insurance, since characteristics of patients are often known by their insurance companies and their physicians, and neither health insurance nor medical care can be resold to others. To use a dramatic example, one could not negotiate a good price on a liver transplant and then sell the operation to someone else. The subject of price discrimination by health-care providers is addressed in Chapters Seven, Eight, and Eleven.

Natural Monopolies

Monopolies are known as *natural monopolies* if average costs fall as output is increased or, in other words, if the production process is characterized by increasing returns to scale (also known as economies of scale). It is therefore inefficient to break up natural monopolies into smaller companies. Historically, the technology of most public utilities such as natural gas or electricity made them natural monopolies. Public utilities in the United States have usually had their prices (rates) regulated by the government, but have been allowed to maintain their monopoly position. Some community hospitals are also thought to be natural monopolies, although this is an empirical question that has to be decided in the context of a particular market. (See Chapter Eight.)

Monopolistic Competition

As we move along the spectrum away from perfect competition in the direction of markets comprised of fewer and larger firms, we enter the realm of monopolistic competition. Here individual firms are no longer seen by consumers as producing identical products, although they may be producing products that are fairly close substitutes for each other. The monopolistically competitive firm's demand curve is therefore at least slightly downward-sloping, and the firm makes choices about both price and quantity of output. As in the case of monopoly, the marginal revenue curve falls below the demand curve, and the quantity that the firm will produce and sell is determined by the intersection between its marginal cost and marginal revenue curves. In monopolistic competition, firms often vie

Figure A1.14

A Monopolistically
Competitive Firm in
Long-run
Equilibrium

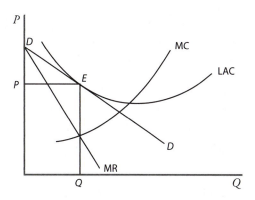

for customers by offering a distinctive product or at least one that consumers perceive as different from those of rival firms. Competition through *product differentiation* tends to replace pure price competition. A firm will expend effort persuading consumers that its product is, in fact, different from and superior to those of its competitors. However, if competition is just a little bit imperfect, as in situations where there are many firms selling similar products, the demand curve of the firm will have a much greater degree of price elasticity than the industry (market) demand curve. An example of a monopolistically competitive market in the health-care field is that of a physician office practice in a community that is large enough to support many such practices.

Long-Run Monopolistically Competitive Equilibrium

In monopolistically competitive markets consisting of many small firms, there is relative ease of entry into the marketplace by new firms. As long as profits are being made, there will be a tendency for new firms to enter the market and drive down the price. The logic is exactly the same as in a perfectly competitive market. However, firms will reach the break-even or zero profit point, where $P = $ LAC, before they are large enough to be producing at the minimum point on their long-run average cost curves. For this reason, long-run monopolistically competitive equilibrium is less efficient than equilibrium in a perfectly competitive market.

Figure A1.14 shows the condition of long-run monopolistically competitive equilibrium. Although $P = $ LAC and MR $= $ MC, price is greater than marginal revenue and, therefore, price is greater than marginal cost.

Oligopoly

Oligopoly is a market structure in which there are only a few firms competing. It is farther away from perfect competition and closer to monopoly than is monopolistic competition. Like monopolistic competitors, oligopolists will often try to differentiate their products from those of their competitors. They are likely to devote an even higher proportion of their budgets to advertising and selling costs. This behavior helps to erect barriers to new firms attempting to enter the market, since it develops brand loyalty to the firm's product. Oligopoly is associated with relatively high expenditures on research and development and product innovation, compared with firms in other types of market situations.

The pharmaceutical industry in the United States has often been characterized as an oligopoly. The firms in the industry are better described as monopolistically competitive in a world with more international competition and competition from smaller biotechnology firms. Pharmaceutical firms are generally multiproduct firms, so they may have monopoly or oligopoly power with respect to one particular product. Regardless of how we characterize the industry, pharmaceutical firms are characterized by high proportions of total cost devoted to research and development and high proportions of their returns associated with introducing new products.

Models of oligopoly incorporate assumptions about decision making under uncertainty. This requires some modification of the simple profit-maximizing model. Since there is usually uncertainty about what rival firms will do, management is likely to employ models such as those using game theory.* There is an example of the game theoretic approach in Chapter Eight. It is used to illustrate the strategies of the managers of two hospitals competing in the same regional market.

7   Demand and Supply in Factor Markets

The same tools of analysis developed to analyze product markets can be used to examine markets for the inputs into production, such as labor and capital. Inputs into production are called *factors of input*, hence the term *factor markets*. Demand curves for inputs are determined by the contribution of the inputs to the firm's revenue. Thus, the demand curve for a factor is its *marginal revenue product curve*, where the marginal revenue product is defined as the revenue from the extra quantity of output (marginal product) that is produced by an additional unit of input.

Labor Markets

The labor market is an interesting factor market. Workers decide to supply a certain number of hours to the labor market based on the cost of doing so and the returns (wages) from doing so. The costs may include direct costs: training to acquire skills, moving from one location to another, and also costs of commuting to the job. In addition, the opportunity cost of a worker's time determines whether

*The application of game theory to economics was introduced by Jon von Neumann and Oscar Morgenstern in *Theory of Games and Economic Behavior,* (Princeton, NJ: Princeton University, 1947).

the worker will take a particular job and how many hours he or she will be willing to work. The opportunity cost of a worker's time is the amount he or she can earn in some other employment, or the value of his or her nonmarket activities. A mother of small children may decide that she will only seek employment if she can earn at least $25 per hour. We would then regard her *reservation wage* as equal to $25. The reservation wage is the threshold wage that would just cause someone to take a job.

The demand for workers, or more precisely an hour of a worker's time, depends on the productivity of that hour of work. The demand schedule for any input is determined by its marginal revenue product. In a competitive labor market, equilibrium is achieved when the marginal revenue product of the last hour worked equals the wage paid for that hour of work. This is another example of MR = MC.

Monopoly in Labor Markets

When workers unionize, they do so in order to take advantage of collective bargaining. Collective bargaining gives them monopoly power when they have the ability to strike. We can use the monopoly model, developed in the context of the business firm, to examine union behavior. Individual workers who have unique talents or skills may also have monopoly power without joining a union. A surgeon who has a unique skill using a new technique of micro-surgery has monopoly power, as does a major league baseball player with an unparalleled batting average. The monopoly diagram (Figure A1.13 on p. 331) can be used to show the amount of work that will be supplied at a given wage by the workers in a unionized plant or by an individual worker who has monopoly power embodied in a unique skill or talent.

Monopsony

One aspect of markets, not yet considered, is particularly applicable to labor markets. This is monopoly power on the part of the buyer (employer.) This is called *monopsony.* The monopsony model is shown in Figure A1.15. It is often thought to be particularly applicable to the market for hospital nurses, although recent research has questioned this assumption.

Suppose that a certain hospital is the only source of employment for operating room nurses in a regional market. The hospital is therefore a "price setter." If the hospital is faced with an upward-sloping supply of labor curve, which means that it can only attract more nurses if it pays them more, it will have to raise wages (for all nurses) as it expands its nursing staff. (The model assumes that the hospital cannot pay each nurse a different wage, based on individual bargaining. This is probably realistic. Morale would deteriorate if workers found out that new hires were being paid more than they for doing the same work.) The hospital therefore drives up the wage rate by hiring more nurses. The nurses supply curve is an *average factor cost curve,* but the extra cost of hiring an additional nurse is the *marginal factor cost.* The marginal factor cost takes into account the addition

Figure A1.15

Monopsony

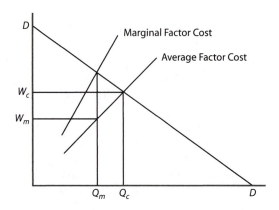

to cost resulting from having to raise the wages of all the nurses, not just the new hires. Figure A1.15 shows the monopsonist employing fewer nurses and paying them a lower wage than would be the case in a competitive market. The monopsony wage is W_m and the number of nurses hired is Q_m. Contrast this with the number of nurses that would be hired and the wage rate that would prevail in a perfectly competitive market (Q_c, W_c).

Bilateral Monopoly

The only way that nurses could offset the monopsony power of a hospital would be to gain monopoly power themselves, that is, to form a union.* We can use the model of bilateral monopoly to understand the bargaining between a monopoly buyer and a monopoly seller. The analysis requires superimposing the monopoly and monopsony models in the same diagram. Note that there are two optimal solutions, one from the point of view of the workers (suppliers) and one from the point of view of the employer (the demand side). The solution is formally indeterminate. The wage rate and quantity of workers hired will be determined through bargaining.

In Figure A1.16, the wage bargaining area is the difference between W_U and W_M, where W_U is the wage that the unionized workers want and W_M is the wage offered by the monopsonist. The bargaining area will vary, depending on the relative elasticities of demand and supply. Workers will want higher wages than those offered by the monopsonist, as shown in Figure A1.16. Whether the solu-

---

*The largest percentage of nurses ever unionized in the United States is about 20 percent, so this has not, in fact, been a dominant strategy in the nursing profession.

Figure A1.16

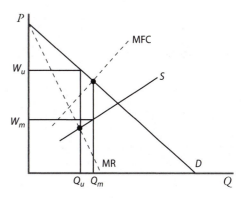

tion is more nearly that which satisfies the monopolist (the union) or that which satisfies the monopsonist depends on their relative bargaining strength. This is determined by the relative elasticities of demand and supply.

Capital Markets

Another important factor market is the market for capital. Capital includes physical capital such as plant and equipment, financial capital, and human capital that is embodied in skilled workers. It is probably easiest to think of the model as applying to a capital good such as a machine. Consider a piece of equipment, such as an MRI machine. The profit-maximizing firm will want to invest in additional MRI machines up to the point where the marginal revenue from the last unit of investment is equal to its cost. Suppose an additional MRI machine costs $2 million. If it lasts for five years and yields $500,000 per year in revenue, is the investment worth it? To answer that question, it is necessary to know the interest rate.

Capital yields a stream of returns over time. In deciding whether to acquire a capital good, its cost must be compared with the stream of returns it yields. The usual method of making this comparison is to find an equivalent value today for the stream of returns and compare it with the cost. This requires computing the *discounted present value* of the return on the investment.

Computing Discounted Present Value

To compare costs incurred at one time with returns that accrue at a different time, it is necessary to know the interest rate, since money that is received in the future is worth less than that received today by the amount of interest lost due to the delay in receiving it. The discounted present value (PV) is

$$PV = \frac{R_t}{(1 + r)} + \frac{R_{t+1}}{(1 + r)^2} + \cdots + \frac{R_{t+n}}{(1 + r)^n}$$

where R is the return received at the end of a given year, t the initial time period, r the interest rate, and n the number of time periods. In this case, we assume that interest is compounded once a year and paid at the end of each year.

The Investment Decision

In the above example, the firm will invest in the MRI machine if the PV of the stream of returns is equal to or greater than its cost. If costs are incurred over time, the discounted present value of the cost stream must also be computed.

In the example given above, should the firm invest in the MRI machine if the interest rate is 5 percent? In that case, PV of return = $500,000/(1.05) + $500,000/(1.05)^2 + $500,000/(1.05)^3 + $500,000/(1.05)^4 + $500,000/(1.05)^5 = $2,164,738 > $2,000,000. Therefore, it is worth investing in the machine.
  Would your answer change if the interest rate were to rise to 10 percent?

The demand for capital, like the demand for any input into production, is related to its productivity. We have used the term marginal revenue product in referring to the productivity of labor. When dealing with capital, the marginal revenue product schedule is usually called the *marginal efficiency of capital* (MEC).

8   Demand and Supply of Public Goods

Public goods have the characteristics of nonexcludability and nonrivalry. Nonexcludability means that if the goods are produced and distributed to some members of the community, none can be excluded. Common examples are pollution control and national defense. Nonrivalry means that one person's utility or enjoyment received from the public good is not diminished by someone else having access to it. Mosquito control in a community is a good example of this. Although roads and bridges and police and fire departments are often financed out of tax money, they are not, properly speaking, public goods, since nonexcludability does not apply. One can build toll roads and bridges and exclude those who do not pay. There can be private police and fire services available only to subscribers. Nonrivalry also does not apply. Utility from using a bridge or road declines if it becomes congested with traffic. In the field of health care, hospitals may be financed out of tax revenues but they also are not, strictly speaking, public goods. Society thus often decides to use public monies to produce goods and services that do not have all the characteristics of public goods.

  An intermediate category of goods are those that are not public goods per se but that involve spill-over effects or *externalities*. A spill-over effect may be external to those who actually consume the good (second-hand smoking effects) or may be external to the firm or industry that produces a good (various kinds of pollution). Externalities may be either positive (benefits) or negative (costs). Positive externalities are called *external economies*. Negative externalities are called *external dis-economies*. Many public expenditures are for services that generate externalities, for instance, fire departments and immunizations against contagious diseases.

The existence of externalities in any market will tend to lead to inefficiency in the form of under or overinvestment by the private market, since the social benefits (or costs) exceed the private benefits (or costs) and thus are not captured (or borne) by the individuals who produce and consume the goods and services. Externalities are very important in health-care markets.

Introduction to Statistical Techniques

Empirical economics tests hypotheses by subjecting sample data to statistical analysis. The usual procedure is to articulate a plausible hypothesis and then to specify a mutually exclusive *null hypothesis*. The research strategy attempts to disprove the null hypothesis by providing evidence that does not support it or is inconsistent with it. Data used to provide evidence consist of variables, each of which is a series of observations on some phenomenon. For instance, we might have observations on age, education, income, and health status for a number of individuals. Variables may be *continuous* (annual family income, number of years of education, etc.) or *categorical* (observations on characteristics such as gender and race, whether or not an individual is a college graduate, whether or not someone has a flu shot in a given year). Economists try to employ large sample sizes in their research. This enables them to use techniques based on the law of large numbers.

1 Descriptive Statistics: Central Tendency and Dispersion

One convenient way to describe an array of data is to use a frequency distribution that shows the pattern of observations within the upper and lower limits (the range). Arrays of data are also usually described by measures of central tendency and dispersion. The most commonly used measure of central tendency is the *mean* (arithmetic average), but we may also be interested in the *mode* (most frequently occurring value) or the *median* (the value of the variable for which there are an equal number of larger and smaller values). The most commonly used measure of dispersion is the *variance* or its square root, the *standard deviation.* The variance is the mean of the sum of the squares of the deviations of the individual observations from the mean. The variance is found by calculating the deviations, squaring each deviation, summing the squared deviations, and then finding their mean.

Example

X	x (deviations from the mean)	x^2	
10	-2	4	$\Sigma x^2 = 8$
12	0	0	$\Sigma x^2/n = 8/3 = 2.67*$
14	2	4	

2   Inferences from Sample to Population

The purpose of analyzing samples is to infer characteristics about the underlying population. Hypotheses are about the underlying population, not the sample. Measures of central tendency and dispersion in samples are computed in order to estimate the (unknown) population parameters. The larger the sample is, the more likely it is that the sample characteristics are good representations of the population.

According to the central limit theorem, sample means of a distribution are themselves grouped around their mean in an approximately normal or bell-shaped curve when the samples are of reasonable size ($n = 30$ observations or more). If we have a group of unbiased random samples, the mean of the sample means is the population mean. If we have only one sample, the sample mean is the best point estimate of the population mean.

To make inferences about the mean of the population from which a sample is drawn, it is necessary to compute the *standard error of the mean.* The probability distribution of the means of all possible samples of a given size that can be drawn from a population has a standard deviation that is the standard deviation of the population, σ, divided by the square root of the sample size, n. This is known as the standard error. Since it is usually not possible to know the actual population variance, the sample statistic is used to approximate it. The standard error formula that is used in practice is therefore $s/\sqrt{n}$, where s is the standard deviation computed from the (sample) data.

Think of the mean of any one of a number of samples of a given size that could be drawn as itself a random variable. Then the distribution of the sample means (means of all possible random samples of a given size) is itself approxi-

---

*This is the correct formula for variance if we have data about the whole population we are studying. If we must make inferences about the population from a sample, $(n - 1)$ rather than n is used to compute the sample variance.

mately normal. We know, from the characteristics of the normal (bell-shaped) distribution, that approximately 68 percent of the time, the sample mean will lie within plus or minus one standard error of the population mean and 95 percent of the time the sample mean will lie within plus or minus two standard errors of the population mean.

3   Test for Difference in Means

We often want to test whether there are differences between two populations. For instance, do patients suffering from the same disease but receiving different medical treatments have different survival rates. Once the means (average survival rates) and the standard errors have been computed for each of the two samples of patients, we can test to see whether the difference between the means of the samples is significant. The *variance of the difference in means* is the sum of the squares of the standard errors of each of the samples. If there are two samples, it is measured by $(s_1^2/n_1 + s_2^2/n_2)$. The square root of this statistic is called the *standard error of the difference*. We can compare the *difference between the means* of two samples with their standard error of the difference. Because the distribution of the sample mean is assumed to be normal, if the samples come from the same population we would expect the means of the samples to lie within two standard errors of each other 95 percent of the time. It is a convention in statistics to consider the difference between means to be significant if the probability that two samples come from the same population is 5 percent or less. This is equivalent to saying that the difference between means is equal to or greater than two standard errors of the difference.

Suppose we want to test whether women are less educated than men. The null hypothesis is that there is no difference in average years of education between men and women, that is, $d = 0$. This can also be stated as follows: Women and men are assumed to come from the same population with respect to the amount of education attained.

We have a sample of 40 women with a mean number of years of education of 12.5 and a sample of 40 men with a mean number of years of education of 13.0. The difference in means $d = 0.5$ years. The standard error of the mean is found to be 1 for women and 3 for men. The variance of the difference in means is therefore $1^2 + 3^2 = 10$, and the standard error of the difference (the square root of the variance) is 3.33 years. The difference in means, 0.5 years, lies well within two standard errors of the difference. Therefore, we *cannot* reject the null hypothesis and *cannot* conclude that the population of women differs from the population of men with respect to years of education, since the probability that the samples of women and men come from populations with different average education levels is less than .05. In other words, the difference in the average level of education of men and women is not great enough to be considered statistically significant.

4   Correlation Analysis

Correlation measures the proportion of the variance in two or more variables that is coordinated. The part of the variance of a variable X that is associated with variance in another variable Y is called the *covariance*.

Simple correlation is the correlation between two variables. Let x_i be a deviation from the mean of X and y_i be a deviation from the mean of Y.

The correlation coefficient estimated from the sample r is

$$\frac{\Sigma x_i y_i}{\sqrt{(\Sigma x_i^2)\,(\Sigma y_i^2)}}$$

The square of the correlation coefficient r^2, called the *coefficient of determination*, measures the proportion of the variance in x and in y that is covariance.

5   Linear Regression

When a hypothesis about systematic changes in two or more variables (the covariance) can be formulated in such a way that one variable Y is identified as the dependent variable and the others (X_i's) as independent or explanatory variables, we can express the hypothetical relationship as a function. This enables us to test whether changes in Y are, in fact, associated with changes in X in some systematic way. The statistical technique most commonly used by economists to examine functional relationships is regression. Linear regression is appropriate when the functional relationship between two variables is hypothesized to be a straight line, or when we can transform it into a straight line by appropriate transformations of the variables, such as expressing them in logarithmic form.

Let us start with a hypothesis that Y is a linear function of X:

$$Y = a + bX$$

If corresponding values of X and Y are plotted on a graph, as Figure A2.1 shows, many of the observations in the array of data will not lie exactly on the line defined by the equation, even if the hypothesis is correct. Linear regression is the statistical process used to fit a straight line to a set of observed coordinate points. The resulting estimating line is called a regression equation.

Whereas the equation for a straight line is $Y = a + bX$, since a linear regression equation is an estimating or statistical equation, it has the form

$$Y = a + bX + \varepsilon$$

where a is the value of the intercept, b the slope (the regression coefficient), and ε the error term. The problem is to find the line that best fits the scatter of points formed when corresponding values of X and Y are plotted. To find the best fit, we use the criterion of least squares. The aim is to find the line that minimizes the sum of the squared vertical deviations from the estimating line.

Figure A2.1

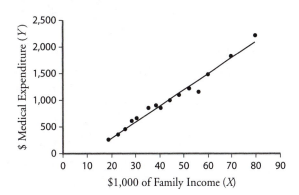

An example may make this clearer. Suppose that we want to estimate how family expenditure on medical care varies with income. Y, the dependent variable, is annual expenditure on medical care and X, the explanatory variable, is family income. Assume a data set has been found that consists of families who are homogeneous with respect to such characteristics as family composition, education level, place of residence, insurance coverage, and health status. In this ideal situation, the confounding effects of these other variables have been eliminated. It is therefore possible to test a simple, two-variable regression equation. An example is shown in Table A2.1.

If x_i stands for the deviation of a given value of X from its mean and y_i stands for the deviation of a given value of Y from its mean, then the slope of the line $Y = a + bX$, and b is equal to $\Sigma xy / \Sigma x^2$. Using the data in Table A2.1, We perform a regression using the least-squares method and find that $b = 30.25$. This can be interpreted as follows: For every \$1,000 increase in family income, the predicted increase in family expenditure on medical care will be approximately \$30.

Figure A2.1 showed the scatter of observations based on the sample data displayed in Table A2.1. Since repeated sampling is likely to give us different values for b even if all the samples are drawn from the same population, we will evaluate the reliability of the b coefficient obtained for our given sample by computing

Table A2.1

$1,000 of Family Income (X)	$ Medical Expenditure (Y)
18	250
22	350
25	450
28	600
30	650
35	850
38	900
40	950
44	1,000
48	1,100
52	1,225
56	1,175
60	1,500
70	1,850
80	2,250

the *standard error of the regression coefficient.* The standard error is meaningful when the distribution of b's can be assumed to be normally or approximately normally distributed around β, the regression coefficient in the underlying population. The standard error of the regression coefficient enables one to determine whether b, the estimated slope, is significant, that is, if it is significantly different from what could be expected if β in the underlying population were equal to 0. In other words, the null hypothesis underlying this test is that $\beta = 0$. In research results that are reported for regression analysis, values for the regression coefficients and their standard errors are usually given as well as the probability that the value of $\beta = 0$. *Significance* is conventionally defined as a 95 percent level of confidence that the β coefficient in the underlying population is *not* equal to 0. Results are called *highly significant* if the probability that $\beta = 0$ is 1 percent or less, that is, if the level of confidence is 99 percent or greater. Here are the results from the sample regression run:

Independent Variable	b Coefficient	Standard Error	p > z
X	30.25347	1.24375	0.000

The regression coefficient b has been found to be highly significant.

6   Multivariate Analysis

Economic models, from which regression equations are derived, often consist of a system of simultaneous equations. The terms *exogenous* variable and *endogenous* variable are used in referring to factors (variables) whose effects are of interest to the researcher. An exogenous variable is one whose values are determined by factors outside the model. An endogenous variable has values determined by the behavior of other variables in the model and is therefore not independent of them. One of the problems in research is attempting to discover whether variables that we want to include in the list of explanatory factors are really independent of other variables within the model. When some of the explanatory variables are endogenous, it is necessary to restructure the model, for instance, making it into a multistage model in which successive stages are conditional on outcomes of earlier stages.

7   Multiple Linear Regression Analysis

Complex hypotheses (models) are often capable of being reduced to a single equation, but one that has more than one explanatory variable. Multiple linear regression is a technique that is used to estimate the *net* effect of each explanatory variable X_i on the dependent variable Y when the regression equation includes more than one explanatory variable. Often, even when the functional relationship between the original variables is not well specified by a linear equation, linear regression can be used after variables are transformed into logarithmic form.

Referring back to the data shown in Table A2.1, We would need to use multiple regression whenever we do not have an ideal data set consisting of families in which income is the only variable that affects medical expenditures. In a more realistic situation, one would need to include such variables as number of family members, health status of each, age of family members, education level of adult family members, extent and type of health insurance, and place of residence. If the price of medical care varies between families, a price variable would also need to be included since the purpose of the empirical analysis is to find the net effect of income on family expenditure on medical care. The resulting equation would be of the form*

$$Y = a + b_1 X_1 + b_2 X_2 + b_3 X_3 + \ldots + b_n X_n + \varepsilon$$

The most common form of multiple linear regression used by researchers is ordinary least squares (OLS). The number of explanatory (independent) variables that can be included in a regression equation is limited by the size of the sample. There must be fewer variables than observations. Otherwise, the equation would

*When performing multiple regression analysis, it is convenient to use one of the available statistical programs, such as RATS, SAS, SPSS, or STATA, to solve for the regression coefficients b_i's and the standard error of each of the regression coefficients s_i.

have "zero degrees of freedom" and no valid results could be obtained. A proper treatment of degrees of freedom is beyond the scope of this brief appendix, but can be found in any college-level statistics text.

Economists typically work with large sample sizes, since tests usually require many factors to be taken into account, that is, many explanatory variables. In the biological sciences, laboratory conditions can be used to standardize for many variables that social scientists can only "hold constant" by using multivariate statistical techniques. Also, given the cost of double-blind experiments, acquiring large samples may be too costly in many biomedical studies.* However, in biomedical research and in particular in epidemiology, large sample sizes are also desirable and used whenever possible. Many of the well-known studies in epidemiology, such as studies of alternative breast cancer treatments, involve studying many thousands of participants over a number of years.

When performing regression analysis, it is usual to also compute the multiple correlation coefficient or its square, the coefficient of determination R^2. This statistic gives the proportion of the variance in the dependent variable Y, which is explained by the whole set of explanatory variables in the regression model.

8   Discrete Choice Analysis

When the dependent variable is a categorical instead of a continuous variable, it is necessary to use a different form of regression model, one appropriate to discrete choice analysis. The following is an example of a research problem in which the dependent variable is a categorical variable:

Imagine that we want to predict the likelihood of individuals in a community having a flu shot in a given year. Data from a sample of adults are gathered in order to examine the degree to which each of a set of explanatory variables helps to explain the probability of having the flu shot. Explanatory variables X's would typically include family income, the wage rate of the individual (if employed), insurance coverage, cost of the inoculation, time involved in getting the shot (waiting time, travel time), age, personal health history, and beliefs about the likelihood of catching the flu.

Having a flu shot will give the dependent variable Y a value of 1 (as opposed to 0). Even though Y can only assume values of 1 or 0, in understanding the logic of this approach, we need to consider that the underlying choice variable is some (unobserved) threshold at which Y shifts from a value of 0 to a value of 1. The threshold for an individual will be related to the other variables (the X's) in our equation and also the error term in the

---

*A double blind experiment is one in which patients are randomly assigned to groups receiving the treatment and groups receiving a placebo. Neither the patients nor the physicians evaluating the results know to which group a patient belongs.

Figure A2.2

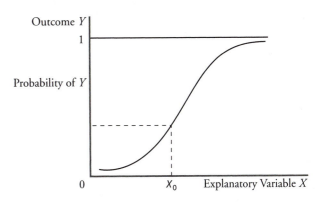

equation (which represents other factors not included in the equation). For instance, a college-educated woman in good health under 50 years of age may decide not to have the flu shot if the out-of-pocket cost to her is more than $50, if it takes more than an hour to get the shot, and if she deems herself to have a risk of catching the flu less than 10 percent. However, if a subsidized flu shot is offered at her place of employment or if it is a particularly bad year for flu when she thinks the probability of catching it is greater, she may be pushed over the threshold and decide to have the shot. The researchers will find estimates for the effects of the cost of the inoculation, the time consumed getting the shot, and the perceived risk of catching the flu. Each coefficient b_i will indicate the effect of one of the variables on the probability that the individual decides to get a flu shot.

Regression equations used when the dependent variable is a categorical variable will typically be either probit, tobit, or logit in form. For an understanding of these forms of regression equations, the reader is referred to a good undergraduate text in basic econometrics.* The underlying distributions will be in the form of an S-shaped curve such as that shown in Figure A2.2.

In the case of categorical variables and other nonlinear functions, least squares will no longer be an appropriate estimating technique. Least squares is a particular example of the more general principle of *maximum likelihood*. The principle of maximum likelihood states that the regression provides the maximum likelihood that the estimating equation is the one yielding the lowest variance.

*For instance, Gujarati, Damodar N., *Basic Econometrics*, 4th ed. (New York: McGraw-Hill, 2002).

Index

Note: Page numbers followed by b indicate boxes; f indicate figures; n indicate footnotes; t indicate tables.